NATIONHOOD AN

NATIONHOOD AND IDENTITY

The British State since 1800

David Powell

I.B.Tauris *Publishers*
LONDON • NEW YORK

Published in 2002 by I.B.Tauris & Co. Ltd
6 Salem Road, London W2 4BU
175 Fifth Avenue, New York, NY 10010
www.ibtauris.com

In the United States of America and Canada distributed by Palgrave Macmillan, a
division of St Martin's Press, 175 Fifth Avenue, New York, NY 10010

ISBN 1-86064-516-X (hardback); 1-86064-517-8 (paperback)

A full CIP record for this book is available from the British Library
A full CIP record for this book is available from the Library of Congress

Library of Congress catalog card: available

Typeset in Garamond by A. & D. Worthington, Newmarket
Printed and bound in Malaysia by SRM Production Services Sdn. Bhd.

CONTENTS

PREFACE

The concepts of nationhood and identity are at the heart of our modern history. Since the time of the French Revolution the nation has been seen increasingly as a basic social, political and cultural entity, the nation-state its logical goal and end product. Alternative badges of identification and social organization – most notably those of religion and social class – have been contenders for primacy, the latter especially in the late nineteenth century in Europe when the struggle between nationalism and internationalism (usually socialist or Marxist in character) became a common feature of the political landscape, a rivalry perpetuated by the triumph of an apparently class-based revolutionary movement in Russia in 1917 and subsequently over large parts of the twentieth-century world. But Communist regimes were often merely nationalist regimes in disguise, while the collapse of European Communism in the wake of the revolutions of 1989 re-opened the Pandora's box of national and ethnic conflicts which had been to some degree submerged or contained by the dead hand of the Soviet Empire since the 1920s or 1945. Nationalism again flourished as it had in the 'springtime of the peoples' of 1848, the wars of unification in Italy and Germany, and the internal politics of the Austro-Hungarian Empire before its demise during the First World War. As in the aftermath of that earlier upheaval, nationhood was once more the objective as well as the guarantee of identity, albeit with often tragic consequences for those who did not fit the appropriate national or racial stereotype, from the Jewish victims of Hitler's Holocaust to those who perished in the ethnic wars of the Balkans in the 1990s.

British history is often written, or used to be written, as if Britain was remote from questions and conflicts of this kind. Yet a moment's reflection will show that this was not the case. The history of Britain's relationship with Ireland offers the clearest refutation of such complacency, but the extent to which Britain shares in the general experience of Europe and the European-influenced world is even greater than this possibly exceptional example suggests. Britain in modern times has evolved as a multi-national state, admittedly within a unitary framework but with a much greater degree of internal diversity than nation-states such as Germany, Italy or France. Loyalty to a British state has had to co-exist or compete with alternative national identities in the constituent parts of the supposedly 'United' Kingdom, and nationalism – whether of the imperial, British, variety or in its Irish, Scots, Welsh or English forms – has played a major part in the development of politics and the political system, from the first stirrings of peripheral nationalism in the 1790s to the post-devolution landscape of the early twenty-first century. At the same time, the rise and fall of the British Empire, and the legacy of that empire in the United States and the Commonwealth, has made the qualities of 'Britishness' of world significance, just as the imperial adventure has indelibly stamped the character of the British people.

An examination of the themes of nationhood and national identity in the British context is thus an important strand in the history of modern Britain. What follows is an attempt to provide a synthesis of recent work on the topic which also reflects my own experiences and ideas. The extent of my obligations to previous writers will be apparent from the chapter notes and bibliography, but there are some more specific debts that I am happy to acknowledge from the outset. I was first introduced to the complexities of the subject by my tutors in the Departments of History and Welsh History at Aberystwyth, and I will always be grateful for their early stimulation and encouragement. Dr Lester Crook at I.B. Tauris was responsible for commissioning the book and has been extremely supportive throughout the project. My thanks are due to Dr Crook, as well as to Professors Denis Judd, Chris Wrigley, Fred Leventhal and David Cannadine, for reading the typescript and for their comments on it. In York, present and former colleagues and students have provided valuable and much appreciated moral support, and I owe special thanks to Dr Alan Young for giving me a medievalist's perspective on modern concerns. To my wife, Pyrrha, as always, I owe the greatest debt of all, for which mere words are inadequate.

INTRODUCTION

The passage in 1800 of the Act of Union, which in 1801 inaugurated the United Kingdom of Great Britain and Ireland, brought an unprecedented constitutional clarity to the government of the British Isles and can be seen as the culmination of a thousand-year process of political evolution that led to the creation of a unified 'British' state. The staging points in this evolutionary process can be variously described: the emergence of an 'English' polity under the Saxons, consolidated by the Normans and transformed into an English state by the Tudors; the conquest by the armies of successive kings of the autonomous principalities of Wales and their incorporation, together with the Marcher Lordships, into an expanded English state by the Acts of Union of 1536 and 1543; the long conflict between England and Scotland, terminating in the union of the crowns in 1603, the union of parliaments in 1707 and the defeat of Jacobitism in 1715 and 1745; the even more complex political interactions between England and Ireland, beginning with the first piecemeal conquests of the twelfth century, advancing through the traumatic sequence of plantation and rebellion of the seventeenth century and the establishment of a Protestant Ascendancy over a Catholic people which was modified but not entirely removed by the Act of Union in the wake of the unsuccessful risings of 1798. In the course of this evolution, an earlier multiplicity of governing mechanisms was from 1800 replaced by the deceptively simple unity of a single government, a single parliament and a single crown.

Simplification of governing structures – the creation of a more unified, unitary state – was accompanied in the nineteenth century by an apparently closer union of the societies of the different parts of the British Isles, as regional/national differences were rendered less prominent by the economic interdependence consequent on industrialization and the development of an integrationist infrastructure exemplified by the building of a national railway network in the 1830s and 1840s, the adoption of 'standard time' and the expansion of a 'British' state that steadily encroached on the preserves of local government and traditional local elites. Yet the integrationist movement was not without its counter-tendencies. Strong differences remained between the different parts of the United Kingdom: differences of language, religion and culture as well as those of a legal and institutional nature. Nineteenth-century Ireland was part of the United Kingdom, but was governed by a separate devolved administration at Dublin Castle; a majority of its population were Catholic, whereas the United Kingdom as a whole was publicly a Protestant state; its politics never integrated as fully into the British parliamentary and party system as did those of Scotland and Wales. The latter two areas also remained different from England in key respects: institutionally in the case of Scotland, with its separate legal, ecclesiastical and educational structures, and culturally and linguistically in the case of Wales. From the mid-nineteenth century these differences produced centrifugal tendencies reflected in the rise of political nationalism, most dramatically in Ireland, but in Scotland and Wales as well. Even England itself – the 'dominant partner' in the British state – remained a country of regions, the unifying bonds of 'Englishness' cross-cut with other loyalties of community, denomination and class. The external experience of Britain in the modern world – the rise and fall of the British Empire, the impact of two (or arguably three) world wars, the changing relationship with 'Europe' (especially after 1945) – further interacted with the domestic picture in a multiplicity of ways, some of which encouraged a transcending 'British' loyalty but which nevertheless added to the complexities of overlapping, even contradictory, identities and self-images.

It is this complex interaction of nationhood and identity that the present volume seeks to unravel. Its aims are threefold. Firstly, it seeks to provide an institutional and political analysis of the evolution of the 'British state' from the passage of the Act of Union in 1800 to the present day. In so doing it will trace the political history of Britain and Ireland, examining the interplay of central and devolved government in relation to the parallel trends of the expansion of the state and the democratization of the political system. In this context the term 'British state' is both a descriptive and an interpretative one: descriptive in the sense that what is being considered are the forms of government and politics of the British Isles (or at least the United

Kingdom); interpretative in that it needs to be determined to what extent the British state was genuinely 'British' in character and how far it succeeded in accommodating the diversity of the political communities over which its authority extended in the nineteenth and twentieth centuries.

The second aim of the book is to explore the social and cultural dimensions of nationhood and identity within the territorial community governed by the British state. In other words, how far did the creation of a British state reflect or encourage a sense of 'Britishness' which replaced or complemented 'Englishness', 'Irishness', 'Scottishness' or 'Welshness'? Indeed, how relevant are these notions of national identity in the history of modern Britain and what part have they played in the development of the British polity? There will be a need here to examine the multi-national and multi-cultural character of modern Britain, not only in terms of 'historic', indigenous, communities (English, Irish, Scots, Welsh), but also in relation to successive waves of immigration and their impact on British society (for example, Jewish immigration in the late nineteenth and early twentieth centuries, and Asian and Afro-Caribbean immigration since 1945). How have the competing internal nationalisms and multiple identities affected British society? Are they the antithesis of a true 'British' identity or one of its most crucial defining features?

Thirdly, the book will examine the external relations of Britain's nationhood and their repercussions on the identity and development of Britain itself. The creation of a British state in the eighteenth and nineteenth centuries coincided with the expansion of British influence over the rest of the world through the rise of the British Empire and the consequences of the Industrial Revolution. The empire in particular was crucial to the idea of a British identity and to the self-image of Britishness that was formed in these years. The wars in which the empire was involved rallied support for the imperial British government (except perhaps in Ireland), strengthening the sense of Britishness by opposing it to foreign threats – the Jacobinism and Bonapartism of the French, and the militarism and Nazism of Germany. But, more than that, in the twentieth century the gradual decline of the empire, the effects of two world wars and the emergence of a dominant United States and of the movement for European integration, together forced a reappraisal of Britain's place in the world and of the future purpose and boundaries of the British state. Coupled with the destabilizing effects of internal nationalisms, and the tendencies towards multi-culturalism in society, the transformation of Britain's external relations inevitably led to debate and controversy over the nature and future of 'Britain', and questioned whether Britain and the British had any longer a meaningful place to inhabit, either politically or psychologically.

Even from such a brief summary, it will be apparent that the book will touch on a number of areas of general interest and concern. Historiographically, it will make a contribution towards bringing together a genuinely 'British' perspective on recent British history. In the last 30 years the nature of historical scholarship has advanced dramatically on a variety of fronts. The national histories of Ireland, Scotland and Wales have been more thoroughly investigated and opened up to specialist research. New and highly acclaimed histories of the 'Celtic' nations have appeared.[1] In the same period, in the general textbooks on British history, the non-English aspects of the topic have gradually been accorded greater weight, as exemplified by the substitution of 'Britain' for 'England' in the new Oxford history. Historians have also discussed the specific problems and different conceptual approaches that the writing of the 'new' British history can generate. Put crudely, is it best tackled through a 'four nations' approach in which the history of Britain is simply the sum of its component national histories, or does it need to be conceived from a more overarching British perspective, in which the similarities and interdependency of the geographical components is given as much attention as their rivalries and distinctiveness? Then again, what is 'British' history? Does it include or exclude Ireland? Does it embrace the history of the British Empire ('Greater Britain')? Should it be approached on the assumption that it will consist of the history of nationalities, or from other social, economic and cultural perspectives that emphasize alternative ways of defining communities and constructing individual and group identities? These are some of the questions that the present study will address and attempt to answer.

Inevitably, though, while it would be possible to write a history of Britain with nationalism left out, it would also be perverse. As was indicated earlier, concepts of nationhood and identity have been crucial to the building of modern state structures in Britain as they have in other countries. An understanding of their contribution is therefore vital to an understanding of British history. It may equally have a wider application, since the study of these phenomena in Britain may have much to say about their importance in other parts of the world. The issues discussed here will thus feed into a more general debate about the character of nationalism and national identity, the role of ethnicity in politics and cultural formation, and the ways in which competing or overlapping perceptions of identity can be accommodated or cause tensions in a given geographical and historical space.

Finally, if general lessons can be drawn from the British experience, the study of that experience is important from the perspective of contemporary Britain as well. Since the end of the Second World War, perhaps since the end of the Victorian era, Britons have adjusted themselves to a version of national history based on the notion of decline. True, the decline has not been without its highs as well as lows. Some would challenge the idea of decline itself, since relative economic decline was accompanied, paradoxically, by rising living standards and improved social welfare.[2] The loss of empire gave rise to a certain pride in the smoothness of the transition of former colonies to independence and the legacy of the Commonwealth that the empire left behind. That said, by the late twentieth century 'Britishness' and the British state were under threat from various directions, internally and externally. Internally there were renewed calls for devolution and separation – a substantial remodelling if not the complete break up of the British state. In the multicultural, transatlanticized age the distinguishing features of a British identity were in any case more difficult to discern. Simultaneously, the United Kingdom faced a dilemma in its relations with the European Union – to be or not to be 'European' by accepting further political integration and the full implications of economic and monetary union. Europeanism and Britishness might not be incompatible, but tensions between them were evident. In any event, the Europeanization of politics meant that the role and nature of the British state were bound to alter. As this book will show, nationhood and identity might be preserved, but they could not exist irrespective of circumstances, and they were subject to change over time. The ways in which they had evolved over the nineteenth and twentieth centuries may contain some clues as to how they will develop in the new millennium.

CHAPTER 1

BRITONS AND BRITISHNESS: THE GEORGIAN LEGACY

In her widely read and justly praised book, *Britons: Forging the Nation*, Linda Colley outlined the factors that, in her view, superimposed the identity of an 'invented' British nation 'on to older alignments and loyalties' in England, Scotland and Wales between the Anglo-Scottish Union of 1707 and the accession of Queen Victoria 130 years later.[1] The new British identity was 'an invention forged above all by war',[2] as the external threat of prolonged conflict with the French encouraged a common British patriotism based on resistance to a foreign enemy. But there were other formative, bonding influences as well. The Protestant religion was an underlying unifying factor, especially when Britain was at war with Catholic Continental powers. The emergence of a common commercial culture ensured a more outward-looking British orientation on the part of the burgeoning bourgeoisie, while, particularly after 1760, a genuinely British aristocratic ruling class developed with a territorial basis that spanned not only Britain but Ireland too. In the years of the French wars of 1793–1815 British patriotism reached new heights, drawing on spontaneous popular enthusiasm for 'Church and King' in addition to more visceral anti-French tendencies. Stimulated by government propaganda and the activities of patriotic societies, artists and writers, the growing self-confidence of the British 'nation' was boosted by the heady wine of victory, from Trafalgar to Waterloo. This self-confidence was maintained after 1815, so that 'Britain' was handed on from the Georgians to the Victorians not just as a going but a growing concern.

Colley admits that her account is partial. It excludes coverage of Ireland as an area territorially and spiritually separate from 'Great Britain', though subject to the rule of the British state. In Britain itself, the pro-British elements are, she acknowledges, deliberately

1

given precedence over the dissident and marginal groups that attracted previous writers. The picture that emerges may therefore be of a more coherent and culturally integrated British nation than in fact existed in the eighteenth century. Yet, for that very reason, it raises questions that are central to the concerns of the present study. How far did the emerging British state rest on a genuine foundation of 'Britishness', how far was it an artificial creation imposed from above? What was the relationship between the British 'nation' and the 'older alignments and loyalties' to which Colley refers, and how far were those alignments themselves 'national' in character? This in turn links the study of the British experience to the wider debate about nationhood and identity in early-modern and modern Europe, in particular over the extent to which the 'Age of Revolution' of the late eighteenth and early nineteenth centuries was the crucial period in the emergence of the nation in its modern form and of nationalism as an ideology and a political movement that was to become one of the dominant forces in the modern world.[3] To begin to answer some of these questions, and to assess the achievement of the Georgian regime and the nature of its legacy, it is necessary to examine in more detail the origins of the British state in the eighteenth century, the cultures and identities within the British Isles that gave the British state its 'multi-national' character, and the external and internal impact on Britain and Ireland of the wars and revolutions of the later Hanoverian period.

The origins of the British state

Constitutionally a British state came into existence with the union between England and Scotland in 1707; historically its origins are more complex. Attempts had been made to bring Britain under a single government by the Romans. Their failure had led to the formation of competing kingdoms whose fortunes had been shaped by successive incursions and invasions: of Saxons, Vikings and Normans. English kings subdued the principalities of north Wales in the thirteenth century, and partly occupied Ireland; but even Edward I was unable wholly to conquer the independent Scottish kingdom which had been founded in the early Middle Ages. The Scots confirmed their national independence (and sowed the seeds of a considerable national myth) during the wars of 1297–1314 under the leadership of Wallace and Bruce, and enshrined it in the patriotic Declaration of Arbroath of 1320. Thereafter British history was marked internally by intermittent warfare between Scots and English, influenced by the broader alignments of European diplomacy (notably Scotland's 'Auld Alliance' with France, England's principal Continental foe). The affairs of the two nations became more closely – though still not entirely peacefully – intertwined following the union of crowns in 1603, and the century between 1603 and 1707 was in a sense the long pre-history of the eventual union. Yet even then it was one thing to enact a union, quite another to make it a reality. If a truly British state were to exist in more than name it needed to develop a workable constitutional structure supported by a common political system and a broad measure of popular consent. In 1707 its institutions were untried, its politics uncertain, and the degree of popular support that it could command was not yet known.

Politically and institutionally the eighteenth century did see the creation of a more cohesive British state, although the process was not without its conflicts and tensions. Central to the evolution of the state was the institution of monarchy. In the medieval period the English and Scottish states had developed as an extension of the power of the crown, and the kings of England had attempted to assert their overlordship in relation to other parts of the British Isles. The Tudor dynasty established by Henry VII laid the foundations of a closer union. The Tudors could claim descent from the former ruling houses of England and Wales, thus providing a focus of loyalty for their English and Welsh subjects. Henry VIII built on this by formalizing the 'union' of England and Wales through the legislation of 1536–43, which abolished the Marcher lordships and completed the work of assimilating Wales into the English shire system begun after the Edwardian conquest by the Statute of Rhuddlan of 1284.[4] At the same time Henry declared himself 'King of Ireland' and he and Elizabeth I attempted, though with limited success, to make a reality of their regal claim. The Tudors also brought Scotland into closer relations with England than at any point since the military conquests of Edward I. The marriage of James IV of Scotland and Margaret Tudor in 1503 forged a link between the houses of Tudor and Stuart. Elizabeth's childless reign led to her naming James VI (James IV's and Margaret's great-grandson) as her heir and to the union of the crowns of England and Scotland on her death in 1603.

James VI and I described himself at the start of his reign as 'King of Great Britain', and between 1603 and 1607 he did his best to complete a full constitutional union between his English and Scottish realms. His efforts were unavailing, however, and the Stuart sovereigns consequently found themselves governing three kingdoms without the benefit of a unified state apparatus. The problems that arose from this delicate balancing act were instrumental in creating the political crisis that led to the outbreak of the Civil Wars in the 1640s and the execution of Charles I in 1649.[5] During the Cromwellian Interregnum there were renewed attempts to unite the governments of England and Scotland and to subjugate a rebellious Ireland, but Cromwell's statutes were swept away at the Restoration and the later Stuarts faced the same problems of multiple kingship that had thwarted their predecessors. The accession of a Catholic sovereign, James II, in 1685 further complicated the task of unifying the realm. In the 'Glorious Revolution' of 1688–89 England overthrew the Catholic James and replaced him with the Protestant William and Mary, while in Ireland and Scotland 'Jacobite' armies loyal to James fought to prevent the Williamite succession. In Ireland the Jacobite challenge was not decisively beaten until after the Battles of the Boyne (July 1690) and Aughrim (July 1691). In Scotland Jacobitism had a longer life. Although the movement went into temporary decline after an early victory at the Battle of Killiecrankie in 1689, it revived after the Hanoverian succession replaced the last Stuart on the British throne in 1714. The Jacobite rebellions of 1715 and 1745 posed a major threat to the internal peace of the British state, not finally defeated until the rout of the Jacobite forces by the Duke of Cumberland at Culloden in April 1746.

By the time of Culloden, of course, James I's vision of closer integration had been at least partially realized by the Act of Union between England and Scotland in 1707. Nevertheless, for a full 40 years, the monarchy remained as much a divisive as a unifying force, just as it had been in the seventeenth century. Jacobite objections to William of Orange were based only in part on grounds of religion and theories of a divinely ordained succession; they also derived from the fact that William was a foreign prince, despite being married to a Stuart wife. Similarly, the accession of the German George of Hanover on the death of the childless Anne, although pre-sanctioned by the Act of Settlement, aroused hostility because of the idea of a foreign prince per se, irrespective of his personal merits. Neither George I (1714–27) nor George II (1727–60) was able totally to overcome this mistrust, even if after the events of 1745–46 it was clear that the Hanoverians were securely established on the throne. Not until the reign of George III, the first ruler of the House of Hanover to 'glory in the name of Briton' and to place the interests of his British dominions above those of his German ones, was this sense of suspicion of an exploitative 'incomer' at last set aside. Even then the actions of the monarch were not always uncontroversial. But George III achieved a general popularity denied his predecessors and was the first undisputed king of Britain in the real meaning of the term. In this way the monarchy became a focal point around which the other institutions of the emerging British state could be built.

Foremost among these was parliament. Initially events rather than institutions, parliaments had been summoned by English monarchs since the Middle Ages, usually to approve expenditure for war.[6] In the sixteenth and seventeenth centuries the role of parliament steadily expanded. Henry VIII used parliament as the legislative engine of the Protestant Reformation. Elizabeth and the Stuarts increasingly found themselves in conflict with parliament over issues of policy. The Civil War of the 1640s arose out of a clash between Charles I and parliament. Yet, while the 1640s proved that the king could not govern without parliament, the 1650s demonstrated that parliament could not govern without the king. Following the Restoration, and especially the revolution of 1688–89, parliament became a permanent part of the 'balanced constitution' of the eighteenth century, in which the sovereign could check a presumptuous parliament by the application of the royal veto and through the prerogatives of choosing ministers and dissolving parliament, but the Lords and Commons together acted as a safeguard against the unfettered exercise of arbitrary power as well as an outlet for the opinions of the aristocratic and propertied elites which they represented. As the eighteenth century progressed, ministers were chosen as much for their ability to manage parliament as for their closeness to the king, and government, though still more than nominally the king's, became more parliamentary in character.

In the process of expanding its power, parliament also extended the area of its territorial authority. The Acts of Union of 1536 and 1543 incorporated Welsh representatives into what had hitherto been an exclusively English parliament.[7] Ireland at this time had its own parliament, but one which under the terms of 'Poyning's Law' of 1494 could only pass laws subject to the approval of the English Privy Council and which, by the Declaratory Act of 1720, was explicitly subordinated to the parliament at Westminster. Scotland was a different case. As an independent country it retained its separate parliamentary bodies even after the regnal union of 1603. The Scottish and English parliaments were briefly united under the Cromwellian regime of the 1650s, but were then separated again at the Restoration. Only with the Union of 1707 was this situation altered, this time by negotiation rather than conquest. The Scottish parliament, which like its English counterpart had increased its independence from the crown at the time of the Glorious Revolution, and which had flexed its constitutional muscles again by withholding approval of the Hanoverian succession when the English parliament passed the Act of Settlement in 1701, was merged with that of its larger southern neighbour. From 1707, 45 Scottish MPs were elected to a British House of Commons (of 558 members) and 16 Scottish peers (out of a total of 154) were 'elected' as members of the House of Lords. A similar arrangement operated in 1800 when the Irish parliament ceased to exist as a separate body and in its place 100 Irish MPs (and 28 'representative' peers) were introduced into the new 'United Kingdom' parliament in London.

By 1801, therefore, the British state had acquired a common constitutional structure of parliamentary monarchy. Yet common did not necessarily mean uniform. The rules for electing MPs in Scotland and Ireland varied from those that applied in England and Wales. The fact that Scottish and Irish peers were denied the automatic right to sit in the House of Lords was another anomaly, only partly assuaged by the creation of a 'peerage of Great Britain' in 1707 and of the United Kingdom in 1801. More significantly, the Unions of 1707 and 1800 left Scotland and Ireland respectively with many distinctive institutional features. The union between England and Scotland explicitly preserved Scottish law and the Scottish legal system, as well as recognizing the existence of a separate established Presbyterian Church. Ireland, despite the union and the loss of its parliament, was administered by a lord lieutenant and a chief secretary appointed in London, and although the Dublin Castle regime could be seen as a form of devolution to which other parts of the Union might have aspired, it was more likely to be perceived as enforcing a semi-colonial status on Ireland which distinguished it from the British component of the United Kingdom. Given that Ireland in the eighteenth century and previously had evolved its own political and parliamentary system under the crown, this continuing distinctiveness was perhaps inevitable. Wales, on the other hand, having been united with England at an earlier date, and before it had achieved any institutional unity in its own right, was more fully assimilated into the British state. Yet here too, a separate Council of Wales (based at Ludlow) had met to discuss questions of Welsh administration until its abolition in 1689. The eldest son of the sovereign was still designated 'Prince of Wales' and the Welsh Courts of Great Sessions (established in 1543, admittedly to administer English law) retained their status until 1830.

Diversity of this sort was arguably a strength rather than a weakness. The creation or preservation of local institutional structures undoubtedly helped to reconcile critics of the unionist experiment, while the opening of a wider stage for political activity appealed to those with ambitions for personal advancement. Wales had no parliamentary tradition before the 1530s (Owain Glyn Dwr's parliament of the early 1400s had not lasted long enough to produce one). Nevertheless the Welsh gentry enthusiastically embraced their dual role as justices of the peace in the localities and as members of a parliamentary class after the union, forming a Welsh parliamentary presence at Westminster and sending their sons to be educated at the English universities and the inns of court. The Welsh experience of integration (assisted by the Welsh/British aspect of the Tudor dynasty) was a foretaste of the much larger Scottish incursions in the Stuart period and after 1707. To that extent, it is realistic to see the eighteenth century as witnessing the consolidation of a 'British' ruling elite within a British state, with Irishmen like Edmund Burke joining the ranks of the English, Welsh and Scots. Not that this was without its problems. An English 'backlash' against Welsh influence can be detected in the sixteenth century, for example in Shakespeare's disobliging portrayals of Welsh characters as well as in doggerel rhymes of the 'Taffy was a Welshman' variety. As Colley has demonstrated, the 'Scottophobia' of the eighteenth century was politically more serious. It stemmed partly from the identification of Scots with disloyalty, because of Scottish support for the Jacobite cause. There was also English resentment at the success of Scotsmen in securing jobs that might otherwise have been occupied by deserving Englishmen. In the 1760s Lord Bute suffered as much from anti-Scottish feeling as from being identified as the king's favourite when he was appointed prime minister by George III. John Wilkes's scurrilous campaign against the government was run initially through the newspaper *The North Briton*, the title of which was a deliberate play on fears of 'Scottification'.[8] Thus even when individual Scotsmen were availing themselves of the benefits of union, historical racial animosities bubbled under the surface of the politics of the British state.

That said, the significance of eighteenth-century developments in politics is broadly as Colley describes it. A united monarchy came to rule over a more unified, unitary state, with an increasingly centralized political structure. As government and decision-making became more concentrated at the centre, it was inevitable that politics would take on a more 'British' character. This did not mean the elimination of political differences between England, Ireland, Scotland and Wales, nor of conflicts within those nations. What did happen was that London and the Westminster parliament became more and more the centre of the political world, and that electoral politics and party alignments became more clearly determined by the metropolitan agenda. The emergence of a national (i.e. British) political culture was assisted by two further factors. One was that the main functions of the eighteenth-century state, apart from the maintenance of law and order, were externally focused – on diplomacy, war and the regulation of trade – so that they emphasized the all-British dimension of government. The other was that after the Glorious Revolution the constitutional arrangements of the eighteenth century (the 'balanced constitution') were being worked out from the first in a British context, and their operation was underpinned by a growing corpus of political theory from the pens of writers in all three kingdoms. Parliament may have been seen by some as originally an English creation, but in its eighteenth-century manifestation it was a genuinely British body, and increasingly was celebrated as such. Its role as the guardian of the liberties of the 'free-born Englishman' transmuted easily into a similar function for all Britain's citizens. Even those radicals who challenged aspects of the prevailing system wanted to reform parliament rather than to replace it. In short, there was plenty of evidence by the late eighteenth century that something like a common British political culture was beginning to be formed around the central institutions of monarchy, parliament and the British state. Whether the inhabitants of the British Isles had, in the course of this process, come to see themselves as 'British', and how far Britishness had superseded, or gained precedence over, 'older alignments and loyalties' were other matters. The possibility remained, to adapt a sentiment from the period of Italian unification a century later, that making a British state might be easier than making Britons.

Cultures and identities

Eighteenth-century Britain presents a complex intermixture of cultures and identities to the historian's eye. 'Britishness' co-existed with other national or regional identities, and was sometimes in conflict with them. Individual communities were divided by differences of religion, class, social or economic occupation. Elite cultures and popular cultures were also different in character. In these circumstances it is difficult to identify a single, common 'British' culture; it is much easier to emphasize the differences between competing cultures within the British state. The problem for the historian is in striking the right balance, and matching this with the perceptions of the eighteenth century itself. How much do we really know about how people – particularly the less literate mass of the population – saw themselves in relation to questions of nationality and cultural identity? By what yardsticks did they measure their judgements? Were these questions they seriously considered at all?

The consideration of national identities is in any case fraught with difficulties. What are nations? Are they cultural entities, enjoying an organic existence founded on ties of common race, language, religion and history, or are they political or geographical constructs dependent on territorial associations and on subordination to a particular jurisdictional or governmental structure? Is national identity inherent, inherited and instinctive, or can it be manufactured and imposed by artificial means? Do nations make states, or vice versa? And when? These questions are all part of an extensive historiographical debate about the character of nationalism and its place in the history of the modern world. They are especially apposite in the context of the 'invented' nation of eighteenth-century Britain. As has been shown, Britain had attained a measure of political nationhood, in which national identity was coming to be defined in relation to the governing institutions of the British state. But to what extent was political nationhood preceded, or accompanied by, the emergence of a common cultural identity? And if such an identity were beginning to develop, what was the relationship between this more organic sense of Britishness and the other cultural identities – national or otherwise – that existed in the communities of the British Isles in this period?

At first sight the limitations of Britishness are more obvious than its strengths. This was most obviously the case in religion.[9] Colley emphasizes the importance of Protestantism as a cultural cement for a sense of British nationality, a badge of identity forged in the Reformation of the sixteenth century (thus predating the political union) and gaining strength from the long experience of war with Catholic Continental powers. There is some force in this argument. The idea of Britain as a Protestant nation became deeply embedded in governing circles and popular culture alike. But the argument has weaknesses too. There were many varieties of Protestantism in

eighteenth-century Britain, and conflicts between their adherents
could be deep-seated, whether for social, political or theological
reasons. England and Scotland retained their separate Church
establishments, the Scottish Presbyterian, the English Anglican and
Episcopalian. But there were Episcopalians in Scotland, and divergent
tendencies within the Kirk itself – a legacy of the bitter conflicts of
the Covenanting period of the seventeenth century. The Kirk was to
suffer further disruption and division in the early nineteenth century.
In England and Wales, meanwhile, there was a strong dissenting
tradition, augmented by the growth of Methodism from the early
eighteenth century onwards. Dissenters (or Nonconformists) were,
moreover, subject to legal disabilities which affected their rights as
citizens. Although allowed freedom of worship, they were denied by
the Test and Corporation Acts of the late seventeenth century the
right to hold public office or to enter the English universities.[10]
Dissenting marriages were not recognized for legal purposes, and in
numerous other ways the legal position of those who did not belong
to the established Church was hedged around with discriminating
restrictions. The consequence was the growth of a lively 'counter
culture' in which those outside the Establishment – including many
prominent businessmen and scholars – built up their own educational, intellectual and political networks, reinforced by ties of
community and kinship, which operated separately from, and
sometimes in opposition to, those of the Anglican mainstream.

If there were divisions among Protestants, the Reformation had
driven an even deeper wedge between Protestants and Catholics
which was a source of correspondingly acute social and political
divisions within the eighteenth-century British state. The effects of
this were most evident in Ireland, where the triumph of William of
Orange at the Battle of the Boyne had been the prelude to the
imposition of a thoroughgoing 'Protestant Ascendancy' encompass-
ing all areas of religious and secular activity. The established Church
in Ireland was an Anglican Church, ministering to the needs of only a
minority of the population. The Catholic majority were subject to the
Penal Laws which limited their right to own land and property,
prevented them from voting in elections or holding public office, and
severely restricted the activities of the Catholic Church in worship
and education. For a century, Catholicism became, officially at least, a
furtive, semi-underground religion enjoying no protection or encouragement. In practice, the Penal Laws were not rigorously applied.
Catholicism flourished, and by the second half of the eighteenth

century a substantial Catholic middle class was emerging to give leadership to its co-religionists through organizations such as the Catholic Committee. However, despite the passing of a series of Catholic Relief Acts in the 1770s, 1780s and 1790s, the struggle for full Catholic emancipation was not successful until 1829. In the meantime Catholic–Protestant tensions ran high and sectarian violence was an endemic feature of Irish society. Nor was it in Ireland alone that Catholics found themselves cast as victims. The other side of building up Britain as a 'Protestant' nation was the identification of non-Protestants as an 'internal enemy'. Catholics in particular were seen as a potential fifth column in time of war, and popular anti-Catholicism was a powerful force, as the Gordon Riots of 1780 – a destructive spasm of protests against the enactment of Catholic relief which laid waste extensive areas of London – amply demonstrated.[11] Anti-Catholicism received sanction and even encouragement from the British Establishment. November the fifth was widely celebrated as the anniversary of the foiling of a Catholic plot against the state, and the Pope often joined Guy Fawkes in being burned in effigy. The Hanoverian monarchs, especially George III, took very seriously their role as head of the Church and defender of the Protestant faith, as witnessed by George III's veto of Pitt's proposal to emancipate Catholics at the time of the Anglo-Irish Union. It may even be that Catholicism provided both the external and internal threat that Protestant Britain needed to maintain its otherwise more tenuous unity.[12]

Religion was not the only area of cultural difference. The linguistic map of Britain and Ireland, for example, remained more complicated in the eighteenth century than has sometimes been realized. While English was the language of government and administration of the united state, and of its educated elite, other linguistic cultures contin-ued to thrive, suggesting the preservation of older cultural identities, especially in the non-English parts of the British Isles. Even in England, the differences in popular dialect between, say, Yorkshire and Cornwall were so great as to render the two almost mutually incomprehensible (although Cornish as a separate language was dying out by the eighteenth century). In Scotland, Scots English (or 'Scots') was a distinct language in its own right, spoken by the majority of the population of the Scottish Lowlands, preserved administratively in Scottish legal terminology and given new status in the printed works of the Romantic period and the writings of Burns and Scott. Beyond the Highland line and in the Scottish islands the older Gaelic (and often Catholic) culture continued to flourish, though it was subjected to increasing pressures of Anglicization (or Scottification?) after the suppression of Jacobitism following the rebellion of 1745. Ireland and Wales retained their national languages too. Welsh was the first (if not the only) language of a majority of the people in Wales in the mid-eighteenth century, sustained by the Welsh translation of the Bible and the use of Welsh as a language of worship and preaching as well as by its employment in everyday commerce. In Ireland, Irish was still widely spoken (less often written), though the language of the Ascendancy was English, and English, albeit with distinctive Irish patterns of syntax and phraseology, was the main language of most of the educated and propertied classes.

Different religious and linguistic patterns in turn reflected a more widespread variety of national cultures within the confines of the British state. Prior to the eighteenth century distinct national identities had evolved in England, Scotland, Ireland and Wales, based on a range of social, geographical, environmental and historical factors. These identities had not as yet given rise to nationalism in its modern political or ideological sense, but they provided an essential precondition for its later growth. Moreover, far from the creation of a British state eroding the sense of internal national differences, in many ways, particularly in the cases of Scotland, Wales and Ireland, it encouraged a greater interest in them, as part of an attempt to influence the character of the new united state by emphasizing its 'British' (i.e. multi-national) as opposed to its 'greater English' aspects. Perhaps understandably, the English were less receptive than the other nations to this view of Britishness, and the Irish had greater difficulties in engaging in the debate over Britishness than did the Welsh and the Scots – partly because the Irish union was enacted at later date, partly because the Irish did not necessarily conceive of themselves as 'Britons' in the first place. But for the Scots and Welsh a sense of dual identity was more congenial: a political identity as members of a British state, and a cultural identity that could be Welsh or Scots as well as (or instead of) being British. Thus in the eighteenth century a diversity of national cultures was being cultivated even while politically and economically the different parts of the United Kingdom were being drawn more closely together. For example, the Welsh scholar Edward Lhuyd, whose *Archaeologia Britannica* was published in 1707, explicitly intended his study of the development of Celtic languages to contribute to a sense of Welsh cultural nationhood within a British state.[13] The Georgian period as a whole was a great age of antiquarian and historical inquiry that helped to establish on a scholarly basis the traditions, customs and folklore, as well as the literary and linguistic identities, of the four nations that co-existed within the British polity.

At the same time, to see the British state as the product of the coming together of four separate and discreetly defined historic nations is misleading. Even in political terms it does not accord with reality. Culturally the 'four nations' approach is still more problematic. This is because first of all the four nations themselves were not culturally homogeneous entities. In Ireland, where religion was an especially important cultural factor, there were profound differences between Catholics, Anglicans and Presbyterians. In Scotland, the Highland–Lowland divide was the most obvious line of divergence, as much cultural as geographical in character. In Wales too, differences of religion, geography and language produced a spread of cultures or varieties of Welshness that may have had common features but were far from being completely uniform. Nor do we really know the extent to which the mass of the peoples in those countries, as opposed to their elites (or sections of those elites), perceived themselves in any meaningful sense in 'national terms'. Cultural identifiers such as class, gender, kinship or local community may well have been of far greater importance than the abstractions or 'imagined communities' (to use Benedict Anderson's phrase) associated with concepts of national identity.

A second complication of the four-nations approach is that even where national cultures can be traced or detected, they did not necessarily exist in self-contained national territories. In the eighteenth century, as before and subsequently, the distribution of nationalities within the British Isles was being modified by substantial internal migration and by inter-marriage and intermixture over the generations. This would make it extremely unprofitable (even if it were historically, anthropologically or politically correct) to attempt to trace the ancestry of eighteenth-century Britons back to the 'original' races or ethnic groups that occupied the islands, or to any later incomers – Saxons, Norsemen, Normans or others – whose blood lines had intermingled over the centuries to produce a 'British' people. It makes it equally difficult to write about an England, Scotland or Wales, much less an Ireland, that was monocultural or ethnically unified. Not only that, but there were significant inter-regional cultural links, many of them founded on historic ties predating the later nations, that united areas across four-nations boundaries.

The close bond between south-west Scotland and north-east Ireland is perhaps the best example, but there were other ties founded on trade or historic connection in which national differences could easily be obscured.

Thirdly, the four-nations approach risks obscuring the degree to which the evolution of cultures in what Hugh Kearney has described as 'the Britannic melting pot'[14] was a dynamic process, not a series of static relationships. Eighteenth-century Britain presents a kaleido-scopic picture of cultures and identities, both in their diversity (national/regional, religious, linguistic, social) and in the sense that these identities were themselves in the process of formation and change, so that the picture shifts over time or depending on the perspective from which it is viewed. The diversity can be made to seem so great that the outlines of any common 'British' culture become difficult to discern. But if the picture is shaken, a different view appears. The lineaments of a common culture are certainly there. The eighteenth century saw growing linguistic conformity, the consolidation of a common elite culture of literature and ideas, and convergence based on shared historical experience. Yet, as in the political sphere, convergence did not mean uniformity. Indeed, one of the defining features of British (as opposed to, say, purely English) culture was the way in which it made room for, and even seemed predicated upon, a range of dual or multiple identities alongside an identification with a British dimension. 'Britishness' was not mono-lithic or all-embracing; it was more of a cultural umbrella that facilitated the co-existence of a variety of cultures and sub-cultures within a single polity. In that sense, it was a cultural recognition of political realities, a consequence rather than a cause of the foundation of a British state that had been created from above to fulfil a gov-erning need rather than in response to popular demand. However, once formed, the existence of the state undoubtedly began to influence cultural forms, and also encouraged a reappraisal and redefinition of the identities of the constituent nations of the British state, just as it sparked a debate about the significance and meaning of the idea of 'Britain' itself.

External factors played an important part in stimulating a com-mon sense of British identity. This tendency had long been apparent in the internal relations of peoples within the British Isles, as the Scots, Welsh and Irish had been encouraged to an awareness of their national identities through contact and conflict with the English. The same process now operated to blur domestic distinctions in the face of threats and opportunities on the wider world stage. Central to this process, as Colley has argued, was the experience of war. The wars of the eighteenth century were integral to the growth of a British nation in a number of respects. From an institutional point of view, the exigencies of war led to the expansion of the activities of the central government of the British state, since armies and navies needed to be raised, financed and manned if wars were to be fought and the defence of the realm provided for. Because the resulting measures of recruitment and taxation were not always popular, there was a political imperative too for the state and its agents to rally public opinion behind the war efforts and to engage in active propaganda for the British cause. At the same time, however, as the eighteenth century progressed, the experience of war and fears of invasion began to generate a more spontaneous British patriotism that did not depend wholly on official prompting. Involvement in war, usually with the French, also helped to emphasize the common interests and characteristics of 'Britons' compared with their foreign enemies and was therefore a factor in creating a collective self-image for the British people. The appearance of patriotic songs like 'Rule Britannia' (performed for the first time in 1740 as part of the masque *Alfred*) symbolized the growing sense of Britishness. Popular identification with the fortunes of British arms was strengthened by the fact that the army and navy were now truly British in their composition, with Scottish regiments earning their laurels in the service of the Hanoverian monarchy and a number of Scottish officers achieving prominence in the previously supremely English navy.

In the eighteenth century, warfare went hand-in-hand with another major development that was crucial in shaping the contours of the British state and the notion of Britishness: the expansion of Britain's overseas empire. The British character of the empire was apparent from its inception. It was a Welshman, the celebrated Dr John Dee, who coined the term 'British Empire' in the sixteenth century, drawing on the semi-mythical Celtic associations of the idea of Britain as the community that had pre-dated the English state and on the legend that it was a Welsh prince, Madog, who had been the first Briton to travel to America, to underline the fact that the colonial initiatives of the Tudor regime were not simply an English enterprise.[15] This view of the empire as a multi-national undertaking was amply borne out by the subsequent history of British settlement in North America. At the start of the eighteenth century the population of the American colonies was only about 250,000. By the 1770s it had risen to over two million. Settlers came from other parts of Europe as well, but the highest proportion was from the British Isles, and these were a truly British mix, with Scots, Welsh and Irish (including as many as 250,000 'Scots-Irish' Ulster Presbyterians) alongside those of English origin.[16] The American colonies were part of a larger British Atlantic empire, including Canada and some of the West Indian islands as well as the British Isles themselves, and of an extended global-imperial trading network that stretched to Africa, India and beyond. The settlement colonies, though, had a special affinity – cultural, linguistic and religious – with the British heart of the empire, strengthened by commercial and family ties, so that, until the 1760s at least (and notwithstanding the fact that many colonists had left Britain originally because of religious persecution), they were a virtual overseas extension of the British state.

Not only did the colonies retain the stamp of their early British-ness, but Britain itself was shaped and moulded by the colonial experience. Throughout the eighteenth, nineteenth and early twenti-eth centuries Britain was by definition an imperial nation. The Scots, Welsh and English (and to a lesser extent the Irish, because of their ambiguous semi-colonial status) were able to sink their differences in the knowledge that together they were joint partners in the direction of the most ambitious imperial project the world had ever seen. The Scots in particular were quick to embrace their imperial British destiny, through trade, exploration, missionary work, and military and colonial administration. In the 1700s much of this was still in the future, but already the impact of expanding imperial commerce could be seen as the growth of an Atlantic economy based on slaves, sugar and tobacco led to the rapid development of ports like Bristol, Liverpool and Glasgow. After the failure of the Darien scheme in the 1690s and other attempts to establish Scottish colonies overseas, Scottish interests welcomed a union that gave them full access to the opportunities of an enlarged British Empire and were more than willing to place themselves under the protection of a British state.

This is not to say that foreign and imperial influences could not be disruptive as well as unifying in their effects. In time of war foreign powers tried to exploit internal divisions. After 1688 France sup-ported the Jacobite claimants to the British throne and gave assistance to the Jacobite cause. In the 1790s the governments of revolutionary France provided military backing for rebellion in Ireland. The wars of the American Revolution, arising out of a more general 'crisis of empire' in the 1770s, created even more problems for the cohesion of the British state. Although parliament and public opinion were initially united behind the king's government in the conflict that broke out with the American colonies in 1775–76, this unity was not unbroken.[17] Radicals and dissenters, alienated from the Establishment in Britain, supported their co-religionists in the colonies in their struggle for liberty against arbitrary power. The expense of the war, its disruption of trade and the defeats of British forces led to a campaign for parliamentary reform and eventually, following the surrender of Cornwallis at Yorktown in 1781, to the downfall of Lord North's government in 1782.[18] Most seriously of all, the example of the American colonists stimulated constitutional debate in Britain and Ireland, with Ireland's political leaders being encouraged to emulate the Americans in demanding greater autonomy for the Irish parliament and freedom to control Ireland's trade. In the late 1770s and early 1780s the Protestant Ascendancy championed (ironically in view of later, nineteenth-century developments in the campaign for Home Rule) the cause of legislative and commercial autonomy under the leadership of Henry Grattan. A Volunteer movement, recruited originally to protect Ireland from possible French attack, provided mass support for the parliamentary leaders through a series of rallies and conventions, culminating at Dungannon in February 1782. This combination of popular and parliamentary pressure persuaded the British government (led by North's successor, the Marquis of Rockingham) to grant more power to the Irish parliament.[19] As an experiment, 'Grattan's parliament' was to be short-lived, disappearing with the union of 1800. But coinciding with the granting of independence to the American colonies, it was the first devolutionary move to offset the otherwise centralizing tendencies of the British imperial state, and the events of 1778–82 as a whole were a reminder of the conditional nature of Britain's political arrangements as a mechanism for reconciling tensions between different cultural and national interests.

Ireland, it is true, may have been a special case. In Scotland and Wales in this period, political opinion remained for the most part loyal to the government (although in Wales there was some support for the American cause), and there were no real stirrings of nationalist or devolutionary enthusiasm, despite the growing cultural awareness of nationhood referred to earlier. Scotland, indeed, has been described as the most strongly loyalist part of Britain throughout the American crisis, evidence perhaps of links between Scotland and Scottish loyalist settlers in the New World, but also, on a more general level, of the extent to which Scotland was embracing the imperial culture. Thus the signs were that under the pressure of external forces and internal influences, a more widespread sense of Britishness was taking shape, and that a British nation was being formed in the minds of its people as well as in the institutions and structures of government. As the eighteenth century drew to a close, the question was how far Ireland could be drawn into a more harmonious relationship with the other parts of the British state, and how far that state itself would be affected by the storms of war and revolution that were about to assail the continent of Europe.

Wars and revolutions

From the outbreak of the French Revolution in 1789 Europe was in a state of turmoil. In France itself the revolution established first a moderate constitutional monarchy and then, in the second revolution of 1792, a republic. War engulfed the Continent as the revolutionaries strove to protect themselves against internal royalist enemies and their foreign allies, Austria and Prussia. In early 1793 Britain was drawn into the conflict and was almost continually at war with the French, under either their revolutionary or Napoleonic regimes, until 1814–15. The French Revolution and the Revolutionary and Napoleonic Wars played a major part in the evolution of the British state, not just in the formal sense that they provided the occasion for the enactment of political union between Britain and Ireland but also because of the way in which they shaped the internal politics of the state and stimulated the development of ideas of nationhood and national identity.

The British experience in these years is part of a bigger debate about the importance of the 'Age of Revolution' in the rise of nationalism and the growth of the nation-state in Europe as a whole. In one sense the political evolution of nations can be seen as a slow process, beginning in the earliest times, with countries like England and Scotland, or France and Spain, attaining nationhood (or national-statehood) by the late medieval or early modern period. ('Britain', in this interpretation, was an 'invented' nation, superimposed on existing national structures.) However, some historians, notably Eric Hobsbawm, emphasize the incomplete nature of pre-1789 national consciousness. They accept that a species of 'proto-nationalism' – involving a sense of patriotism, perhaps an inherent, culturally defined, sense of national community – might have existed before the late eighteenth century, but stress that in most instances these feelings were linked to loyalty to a traditional, dynastic power structure, and were not therefore representative of nationalism in the full meaning of the term.[20] According to this interpretation, the French Revolution marked a decisive break with the past. In overthrowing their sovereign and founding a republic, the French people created a new idea of nationhood as the embodiment of the popular will and a new form of state structure based (theoretically) on democratic principles. The upheavals of the revolutionary and Napoleonic period similarly redefined the relationship between rulers and ruled in other parts of Europe in a way that emphasized the importance of nationality as a connecting link. In some cases the example of the French Revolution inspired peoples elsewhere in Europe to revolt against dynastic rulers in the search for national independence. In others, such as Spain and Russia, French invasion had the opposite effect, strengthening the appeal of traditional institutions like Church or monarchy which could be identified as national in character. In Italy and Germany, the French, by disturbing dynastic structures, spreading new ideas and arousing the hostility of local populations, were instrumental in creating a more active sense of Italian and German national identity, which drew on previous underlying unifying factors but blended them with a heightened cultural and political national sentiment, providing a basis for the growth of Italian and German nationalism in the nineteenth century.

Britain exhibited the contrasting impacts of the revolutionary period in a manner that reflected the diversity of forces at work. One consequence of the threat posed by revolution and the renewal of war was the strengthening of that negative form of nationalism that provided definitions of Britishness based on reaction to external threat. Anti-French sentiment became more pervasive. Although there was some welcome for the French Revolution in its early stages, even this was more than tinged with a patriotic sense of superiority. The revolution was applauded either because France was seen as belatedly 'catching up' with the distinctively British form of mixed constitution or because it would sow confusion among the French and so give Britain fresh advantages in competition with her foremost rival. As the revolution took on a more extreme form, and particularly after the outbreak of war and the execution of King Louis XVI in 1793, anti-revolutionary feeling became a more powerful factor, and one that almost by definition rallied popular opinion around the government of the day and the institutions of the country. Edmund

Burke's *Reflections on the Revolution in France*, published in 1790, was influential in providing a reasoned basis for conservative reaction, emphasizing the superior virtues of the English–British constitution. In parliament and country the political elites placed themselves firmly behind Pitt's administration and the national war effort, a convergence symbolized by the decision of the opposition Portland Whigs to join a coalition government in 1794. Even before the outbreak of war the strength of popular, patriotic conservatism was demonstrated by the support given to organizations such as John Reeves's Association for the Preservation of Liberty and Property Against Republicans and Levellers, and to the various 'Church and King' groups that mushroomed on a local basis. The activities of the latter occasioned numerous public disturbances, most notoriously the 'Priestley Riots' in Birmingham in July 1791, when a patriotic mob attacked the home of the radical Joseph Priestley to punish him for his sympathetic attitude towards the French revolutionaries. Loyal addresses to the monarch multiplied as local authorities competed to give public assurances of their patriotic soundness, and there was a general closing of ranks against those who did not wholeheartedly subscribe to the emerging conservative consensus.

The spontaneity of this patriotic popular conservatism has attracted growing attention from historians interested in the process of nation-building and the interaction of elite and popular politics. Although the government used various means of propaganda to guide and influence public opinion, it seems inadequate to explain the strength of the patriotic reaction solely in terms of the manipulation of the masses 'from above'.[21] At the same time, there were those – admittedly a minority – who did not share the Establishment view. British radicals and parliamentary reformers defended the French Revolution despite the overwhelming hostility of the governing and propertied classes. A small group of aristocratic 'Friends of the People', including Charles Grey and Charles James Fox, set themselves up in opposition to Pitt's government and the war with France. The explosive writings of Tom Paine, whose *Rights of Man* was published in two parts in 1791 and 1792, opened up a more extreme alternative. Paine not only defended the French Revolution against Burke, but advocated a democratic, republican reform of the British constitution, the abolition of hereditary elites and the creation of a form of welfare state. *Rights of Man* was the most widely read political tract of its time, selling over 200,000 copies by 1793, and Paine's ideas were hotly debated in the many radical societies that sprang up in the

early 1790s – groups such as the Sheffield Constitutional Society
(founded December 1791) and the London Corresponding Society
(which issued its first public address in April 1792).[22] Not all radicals
necessarily shared the full Painite programme. The LCS, for example,
was publicly committed only to a reform of parliament, not to the
overthrow of the entire British state. But, especially after the outbreak
of war in January 1793, a more polarized political situation developed.
The government seized on the existence of links between French
revolutionaries and the Corresponding Societies to tar all British
radicals with the Jacobin brush. Paine was outlawed and forced to
flee to France. In 1794 the leaders of the London Corresponding
Society were arrested and tried for treason. They were acquitted.
However, following attacks on the king and the prime minister at the
opening of parliament in 1795, the government responded with
further repressive measures that restricted freedom of speech and
prohibited meetings of more than 50 people without the prior
consent of magistrates.

In some ways the gulf between the government and its opponents
was not as wide as it appeared, or as the government chose to make it
appear. There were deep divisions of opinion between conservatives
and radicals, but they were united by more common assumptions
than might at first be thought. Nevertheless, the events of the 1790s
introduced an increasingly sharp note of conflict, as government and
'Loyalist' forces identified radicals as the new 'internal enemy' and
sought to brand their activities as treasonable and 'un-British'. The
stakes were raised in the middle of the decade by the growing signs of
the unpopularity of the French war. In 1794–95 there were riots
against the activities of the press gangs and the recruitment policies
embodied in the Militia Act. The LCS organized well-supported
demonstrations against the war. There were serious outbreaks of food
rioting in 1795 and 1796 in protest against high prices and food
shortages produced partly by bad harvests but also by the economic
dislocation caused by the war. In 1797 there was a general mutiny of
sailors of the Channel and North Sea fleets. While these various
outbreaks probably did not betoken any concerted revolutionary
upsurge, they created a worrying situation for a government fighting
an expensive and, at that stage, far from victorious war.[23] When set
alongside the Irish rebellion of 1798 and evidence of revolutionary
conspiracies in other parts of the British Isles they help to explain the
further clampdown initiated by the government in 1799 and 1800
with the Combination Acts, which banned trade unions and other

economic combinations as well as the still extant radical political groups.

As a battle for control of the state, this was a very one-sided affair. In the 1790s the political advantages were all with the ruling authorities who were in a powerfully entrenched position, bolstered by strong popular loyalism and a heightened British patriotism. The patriotic tide was so strong that even those who wanted reform could not – or did not want to – cut themselves entirely adrift from the prevailing mood. The sailors who mutinied in 1797 made it clear that they would return to duty if the French threatened an invasion. A few months after the mutinies, the fleet scored a major victory at the Battle of Camperdown, in which there was no shortage of fighting spirit. On land, the war had its critics, but while there were advocates of a negotiated peace, few actively sought a British defeat. The 1790s, in other words, saw a consolidation of nationalism and national identity based on loyalty to established rulers and institutions, and on a resurgence of anti-French feelings. They were thus important in the making of Britons, as well as in the making of Britain. On the other hand, however, their influence was not entirely one way. The experience of the revolutionary period altered the relationship between the British state and its people in certain key respects. The role of the state became more evident in all kinds of ways. The enactment of repressive legislation, for example, introduced a more coercive aspect into a social and political system that had hitherto prided itself on the upholding of the 'liberties of the subject'. The demands of war extended the role of the state in other ways too: the army, navy and their accompanying machines of recruitment and supply expanded to unprecedented levels; the government levied income tax for the first time in 1799; the first national census of population was held in 1801. The government was coming to bear more directly on the lives of the people, even if the majority of those people were denied any say in its composition.

The consequence of this was that although from early in the 1790s radicalism was on the defensive, it did not entirely die away. The changes that were taking place reinforced rather than undercut the arguments in favour of reform. Over the long period of the French wars a steady increase of support for the ideas of the reformers can be seen, blossoming into the more general campaign for parliamentary reform after 1815. This campaign was concerned with a remodelling of the eighteenth-century British state. It also, in its earlier manifestations at least, offered an alternative model of

Britishness to that provided by the Pittite regime of the 1790s – a model that had more in common with the radical, democratic ideas of the French Revolution than the conservatism of the ruling elite. There was also a link between this more democratic radicalism and the national diversity of the British state, in that radical ideas took on different manifestations in different parts of the British Isles. It is too simplistic to see the resulting confrontation as one between 'nationalism from above' and 'nationalism from below', since, as has been shown, there was a popular dimension to the loyalist, pan-British nationalism of the 1790s, and in any case those who sought to express their radicalism in Scottish or Welsh terms were not necessarily nationalists in an ideological sense (Ireland was a different matter). But the interaction of radicalism and nationalism, or at least quasi-nationalism, was one of the main features of the political development of Britain and Ireland in the revolutionary period, and one that was to exercise a long-term influence on British politics in the nineteenth and twentieth centuries. If these were, as Colley asserts, the years in which Britain was invented under the pressure of war, they may equally have been the point at which the component nations of the British polity began to assume their modern form. It was from the resulting duality that the distinctive character of the British state was forged.

The first signs of an alternative pattern of politics were becoming apparent in Scotland in the 1780s. Scotland's ruling elite had integrated well into that of Britain as a whole in the period after the union. By the late eighteenth century even the Highlands were losing some of their rebellious distinctiveness as steps were taken to abolish the 'heritable jurisdictions' of Highland chiefs and to integrate the economies and cultures of Highlands and Lowlands. Scotland was effectively managed on behalf of the British government by a series of 'British' Scots – Islay in the 1750s, Bute in the 1760s, Dundas in the 1780s and 1790s. There were widespread demonstrations of loyalism in Scotland during the period of the French wars. Yet alongside the emergence of a pro-government, conservative Scotland, newer forces were taking shape. The late eighteenth century was marked by that intellectual flowering in the arts and sciences known as the Scottish Enlightenment, and through the works and writings of its leading exponents Scotland contributed to the ferment of ideas throughout the kingdom. By the same token, Scotland developed its own variant of the radical reform movements that were coming into existence elsewhere under the influence of the American and French

Revolutions. A Scottish parliamentary reform movement emerged in the 1780s. In the early 1790s a number of Scottish radical societies sprang up, including the Society of the Friends of the People in Edinburgh, and in 1792 the reformers organized a Scottish convention to debate the case for political change. The response of the authorities was swift and harsh. One of the convention's leaders, Thomas Muir, was found guilty of sedition and sentenced to 14 years' transportation by Lord Justice Braxfield. Thomas Palmer received seven years' transportation for allegedly having written a seditious pamphlet distributed by the 'Friends of Liberty' in Dundee. But although the reform movement was temporarily thwarted by repression, it had sown the seeds of a distinctively Scottish brand of radical politics, linked to developments elsewhere in Britain yet with a character of its own. The suppression of the radical movement by a government directed from London also highlighted the potential for a convergence between radicalism and nationalism, built upon the outrage felt by many Scots at the severity of the treatment meted out to Muir and Palmer. Burns's *Scots Wha Hae*, written in the wake of the treason trials, made the nationalist message explicit, even though the fact that Burns himself had testified his willingness to rally to the British state by joining his local Volunteers emphasized the divergent forces that were at work.[24]

The conjunction of radicalism and nationalism was perhaps closer in the case of Wales. A Welsh radical tradition was already establishing itself prior to the French Revolution, associated mainly with the rise of religious dissent. One of its leading figures was the Unitarian Dr Richard Price, a supporter of the American Revolution, campaigner for the repeal of the Test and Corporation Acts and the author of the *Discourse on the Love of Our Country* which, with its praise of the French Revolution, provoked Burke's celebrated *Reflections*. Price's radicalism was universal rather than nationalist; his country was the world. But he was operating in the context of a Welsh cultural revival that gradually developed a more political dynamic. Throughout the eighteenth century there was a steadily rising interest in Welsh history, language and culture, reflected in the work of antiquarian societies like the Cymmrodorian (founded in 1751) and the London–Welsh Gwyneddigion (1770), by the popularity of published works such as Theophilus Evans's *Drych y Prif Oesedd* (*Mirror of Past Ages*, a history of Wales) and the research of scholars of the eminence of Edward Lhuyd or the indefatigability of Iolo Morganwg. The latter – part poet, part fantasist – was a leading figure in the cultural festivals, or *eisteddfodau*, which flourished from the 1780s and which helped to create a growing sense of Welshness among Wales's intellectual and educated elite. Into this burgeoning culture of Welshness a Welsh variant of French revolutionary radicalism fitted easily, though this is not to say – contrary to later myth – that the Welsh in the 1790s were overwhelmingly a radical nation. Nor did the sense of national cultural identity necessarily take a political form. Many of those who espoused the cause of Welsh culture were happy within a British state, and some were undoubtedly conservative in their political outlook. Nevertheless, in the early 1790s, radicals like the young Baptist minister Morgan John Rhys did briefly gain an audience for their particular brand of Welsh Jacobinism.[25] Through publications like the short-lived *Cylchgrawn Cymraeg* (*Welsh Review*) they pioneered radical political journalism through the medium of the Welsh language. In the short term this had only a limited impact. By the mid-1790s economic hardship and political repression had driven many Welsh radicals – Rhys included – to leave Wales in search of a radical-religious 'Beulah land' in the Americas.[26] But in the longer run the cultural and political events of the late eighteenth century were important in shaping a more distinctively Welsh political culture within the British state, keeping alive (or perhaps creating) an idea of nationhood on which later generations of Welshmen could draw.

A similar process, but on a much larger scale, was at work in Ireland. Ireland in the eighteenth century was politically as well as geographically separate from Britain. The establishment of Grattan's parliament in 1783 gave her a greater degree of legislative autonomy. Yet this had only exacerbated the domestic conflict between ruling elite and disfranchised majority which was a mirror of those conflicts taking place in Britain. In Ireland's case the situation was complicated by the religious divide between the Anglican members of the Protestant Ascendancy and the Catholics and Presbyterians who comprised 90 per cent of the population. The French Revolution injected new life into the domestic political struggle. Wolfe Tone, the Protestant lawyer who emerged as one of the main leaders of the radical and revolutionary movement, recorded in his journal how the events in France and the political debate they engendered 'changed in an instant the politics of Ireland. The nation was fairly divided into two great parties, the Aristocrats and the Democrats',[27] between which the main issues were the reform of the Irish parliament and the extension of Catholic (and Presbyterian) rights. Tone himself in 1791 published a pamphlet, *An Argument on Behalf of the Catholics of Ireland*, putting the case for Catholic emancipation. In 1792 he became secretary to the revitalized Catholic Committee. Already he was coming to believe that the only real solution to Ireland's internal divisions was to build up a sense of common Irishness in place of the divisive designation of Catholic and Protestant. To this end he took a leading part in forming the democratic and nationalist Society of United Irishmen in 1791, the objective of which was to secure the foundation of an independent, non-sectarian Irish state free from British control. The UI's methods were initially constitutional, but as the situation in Ireland moved to a crisis in the mid-1790s the organization became increasingly revolutionary in character. Ironically, despite the UI's avowedly non-sectarian outlook, it became caught in the downward spiral of Protestant–Catholic tension. The British government's attempts to reduce tensions only served to make matters worse. Further measures of Catholic relief forced through by Pitt's government in the early 1790s (including giving some Catholics the right to vote in elections to the Irish parliament) alarmed the Protestant Establishment. Their fears were heightened by the suggestion of the newly appointed lord lieutenant, Lord Fitzwilliam, in 1795, that full emancipation was imminent, a suggestion leant force by his dismissal of some known anti-emancipationists from the Dublin Castle administration. The resulting Ascendancy backlash forced Fitzwilliam's resignation, dashing Catholic hopes of peaceful change and throwing into doubt the good intentions of the government. A simultaneous clampdown by the authorities on the activities of the United Irishmen, involving the arrest of prominent leaders, completed the work of turning what had been a constitutional reforming movement into a fully fledged revolutionary underground. Final disillusionment with British politicians also focused the nationalist agenda more squarely on the demand for independence. Tone, who fled first to America and then to France to avoid arrest, began, with the other UI leaders, to plan an armed rising with French support. A rebellion in 1796 was aborted when a French fleet was prevented by the weather (a 'Protestant wind') from landing troops in Bantry Bay. Planning continued, however, and a second rising was prepared for 1798.[28]

The Irish rebellion of 1798 was the largest insurrection in the British Isles since the Jacobite rising of 1745–46. Had it coincided, as planned, with simultaneous risings in England and Scotland it would have presented an even greater threat to the stability of the state. As it was, the other risings did not occur and the Irish rebellion itself was beset by lack of coordination and inadequate leadership.[29] By the time French troops landed at Killala in County Mayo in August 1798 the main southern rising in County Wexford had already been defeated at Vinegar Hill. The French and their Irish allies were forced to surrender at Ballinamuck, and a further attempt to land French troops in Donegal in October was foiled by the Royal Navy. One of the victims of this final act of the tragedy was Wolfe Tone. Captured in French uniform and sentenced to death as a traitor, he cheated the executioner by taking his own life in prison.

Although the rebellion of 1798 failed, it cast a long shadow over the subsequent history both of Irish nationalism – particularly in its insurrectionary, revolutionary form – and of the British state of which Ireland became such an uneasy part. In the aftermath of the rising the main problem in Ireland itself was enhanced sectarian bitterness, fuelled by rebel violence and Ascendancy reprisals. From the British perspective there were fears of a further incursion by the French to take advantage of Irish discontent at a crucial stage in the revolutionary war. Out of this mix of concerns evolved a plan which Pitt hoped might solve the Irish question by providing rewards and safeguards to all parties, Protestant and Catholic, British and Irish. Pitt's scheme was twofold. He wanted to enact a full constitutional union between Britain and Ireland, at the same time granting full civil equality to Catholics. Catholics would be placated by emancipation and the disappearance of a separate Ascendancy parliament, so reducing the momentum of separatism and nationalism. The Ascendancy Protestants would be appeased for the loss of their parliament by becoming part of the majority in an enlarged Protestant state (rather than an embattled minority in an Irish assembly dominated by emancipated Catholics). On this basis Irishmen of all shades might be reconciled to the Union, just as the Scots and the Welsh had been. Whether Pitt's plan would have achieved its intended result cannot be known. Plainly there were differences between Ireland's situation and the cases of Scotland and Wales. Nationalism was further advanced and recent events had inflicted wounds which were not easily healed. The Irish question might have remained a problem for later generations of statesmen whatever Pitt had done. Such discussions, however, can be no more than academic, since Pitt was unable to force the emancipation proposal on a reluctant sovereign and resigned the premiership instead. When the union of Great Britain and Ireland was enacted in 1800 it merely reinforced the Protestant character of the enlarged polity. Catholics were denied the promised emancipation, and the nineteenth-century British state was born in an atmosphere of crisis and betrayal.

Yet, for all these ill omens, in the early 1800s the Union prospered. Despite continuing popular protest before and after 1815 (the Luddite outbreaks, the campaign for parliamentary reform) and the assassination of prime minister Spencer Perceval in 1812, the threat of domestic revolution receded. Abroad, Britain was ultimately victorious in the wars against Napoleon and emerged from the conflict with an enlarged empire and an enhanced sense of national patriotism, built around the exploits of heroes like Nelson and Wellington. The various parts of the United Kingdom also began to be more closely knit together. In Ireland, reformist administrations at Dublin Castle, particularly under the chief secretaryship of Robert Peel, initiated beneficial measures in the fields of education, health and poor law reform. Scotland and Wales emerged from the Napoleonic period more committed to the Union too, though continuing to combine a sense of Britishness with an appreciation of and attachment to their own national cultures and traditions. In the case of Scotland, the work of Sir Walter Scott was hugely instrumental in easing the process of emotional and psychological integration. Scott's various literary and historical works encouraged an interest and pride in Scottish tradition, which suited the self-confident Scottishness of the country's elite. Edinburgh remained a national capital, and Scottish political and intellectual life retained their distinctive flavour (illustrated by the founding of *The Scotsman* newspaper). Yet Scott and the other leaders of Scottish opinion saw no incompatibility between this heightened sense of Scottish identity and loyalty to the British state. The first of Scott's novels, *Waverley*, published in 1814, made the point in fictional form. While sympathetically portraying a romanticized Highland society at the time of the Jacobite rebellion of 1745, it also conveyed the message that the future (i.e. Scott's present) depended upon Scotland embracing the union with Hanoverian England and the opportunities that came with it. Scott leant the full force of his personal reputation to the cause when in 1822 he was the principal organizer of George IV's state visit to his Scottish kingdom.

That said, not all parts of the Union were happy or contented. Ireland's Catholics, for example, remained aggrieved that they had been denied the benefits of emancipation and that many features of the Protestant Ascendancy had been preserved by the Act of 1800. In

1823, Daniel O'Connell, a Catholic lawyer, founded the Catholic Association to campaign for full emancipation. The Catholic Association quickly became a widely supported mass movement, and O'Connell was determined to use the power of popular protest to extract concessions from the Westminster government. When a by-election occurred in County Clare in 1828 O'Connell stood against the government's nominee. Benefiting from the Catholic vote (Catholics had been enfranchised on equal terms with Protestants since 1793), he scored a dramatic victory, which in turn provoked a constitutional and political crisis because O'Connell, as a Catholic, was not eligible to take his seat as an MP. If the Catholic Association repeated its ploy of running Catholic candidates at the next general election the whole Irish representative system could be thrown into chaos. Faced with this possibility, and mindful of the dangers of a deteriorating public order situation in Ireland, the Wellington government in power in Britain decided to concede defeat as gracefully as they could. Catholic emancipation was granted in 1829 and, for the time being, the O'Connellite threat receded.

The spread of O'Connellism showed that questions of religion and nationality were still important in the politics of Britain and Ireland. The issue of Catholic emancipation, moreover, was only part of a more general crisis that the British state was undergoing in the late 1820s and early 1830s. In parliament, the Tory coalition which had held power almost uninterruptedly since the 1780s was breaking up, and a general election in 1830 resulted in the formation of a Whig government. Already by this date, in addition to the Emancipation Act, parliament had in 1828 finally repealed the Test and Corporations Acts which operated against dissenters. But these concessions by the governing elite had only stimulated further pressure for change, this time in the political system itself. The campaign for parliamentary reform, which had begun in the late eighteenth century and flourished briefly in the post-war depression after 1815, revived in earnest from the mid-1820s. Political unions were formed in many parts of the country and radical agitation was widespread. The election of 1830 took place against the backdrop of a revolution in France and popular protest – notably the 'Swing' riots of agricultural labourers in the south-east of England and trade union unrest in northern districts – in addition to the reform campaign. When Grey's government attempted to contain popular protest by introducing a moderate Reform Bill this provoked hostility among the Tories and opposition in the House of Lords, which rejected the Bill and forced a further general election. The election of 1831 was accompanied by fierce expressions of popular discontent, and not until the Reform Bill was safely passed and a reformed parliament had been elected in 1832 did this popular clamour begin, at least temporarily, to subside.

What is significant from the point of view of the present study, however, is that the political battles of 1828–32 were fought out within the framework of a British state, not in opposition to it. True, there was a quasi-nationalist aspect to O'Connell's Catholic agitation, which was to become more marked in the 1830s when he launched a campaign for repeal of the Union. Scottish and Welsh politics retained their distinctive colourings. Yet increasingly, political conflicts were taking place on the British stage, with the United Kingdom parliament as their focus. The reforms of 1828–32 helped to make the political system more inclusive at all levels, by removing religious discrimination and extending the franchise.[30] Coupled with the feelings of Britishness engendered from without, and the growing economic and social integration, or at least interdependence, consequent on the Industrial Revolution, the future seemed to hold the prospect of a more unified nation within a more unitary state.

CHAPTER 2

INDUSTRIALIZATION, INTEGRATION AND PROTEST, 1830–1850

I n the first half of the nineteenth century the physical and mental landscape of Britain was transformed by a series of changes – economic, social and political – which, while they did not eliminate internal divisions, had the effect of integrating the country more completely and locating its diverse communities more firmly within a common framework of experience.[1] Yet while the consequences of industrialization and parliamentary reform drew the various parts of Britain closer together, they emphasized the differences between Britain and Ireland and the difficulties of assimilating the latter into the structures of the more centralized post-Union state. Already in the 1840s Irish nationalism was emerging as a significant force, and Daniel O'Connell had launched a mass campaign for repeal of the Act of Union. The onset of famine following the failures of the Irish potato crop in 1845–46 posed a practical and ideological challenge which the British state proved unable to meet. It is the interplay of factors behind these divergent processes of integration and estrangement that forms the subject of the present chapter.

Economic and social change

The main components of economic and social change were threefold: population growth, urbanization and industrialization. The population explosion was both cause and consequence of the other two changes. In experiencing what amounted to a demographic revolution, Britain and Ireland were part of a general European trend. The population graph took a sharp upward turn across the Continent from about the 1750s on, for a variety of reasons still debated by historians. But the effects on the British Isles between the 1780s and the 1850s were especially dramatic. In 1780 the total population of Britain and Ireland has been estimated at approximately 13 million. Between 1801 and 1851 the figure rose from 15.7 million to 27.4 million. The population of Britain roughly doubled in that time, from 10.5 to 20.9 million. All parts of the island showed similar levels of increase. The population of Wales rose from 587,000 in 1801 to 1,163,000 in 1851; that of Scotland from 1,608,000 to 2,900,000. England, however, enjoyed the largest net increase, both proportionately and absolutely (8.3 to 16.9 million), enhancing its overall preponderance within the United Kingdom as a whole from 52.7 per cent of total population in 1801 to 61.8 per cent 50 years later.[2]

Raw figures like these conceal several important trends. One such is the considerable internal migration that was taking place between different parts of the United Kingdom. For example, there were 734,000 inhabitants of Irish birth in England in 1851 (half of whom had arrived in the previous decade). Liverpool alone had an Irish population of 40,000. The population of Wales in 1851 included 140,000 people born beyond the country's borders, 115,000 of them from England, 20,000 from Ireland. The traffic was not all one way, however, since there were at the same time nearly 50,000 people of Welsh birth in Lancashire and Cheshire, and a further 18,000 in London to add to the already significant London-Welsh community. Migration, however, was not all – or even mainly – across internal national boundaries. The early part of the nineteenth century saw a net outflow of population from the United Kingdom to lands overseas, to colonies like Canada and Australia, and increasingly to the United States. There was even greater movement, at least within the countries of Britain (Ireland was a separate case), between the different regions of Wales and Scotland, and in England from the countryside to the towns and cities. It was this dramatic process of urbanization that left the greatest long-term mark on the way of life of Britain's people. In 1801 only about 30 per cent of the population of Britain lived in towns, and many of these were small communities closely linked to the surrounding rural areas. The census of 1851 revealed that for the first time a majority of Britons were town-dwellers, albeit by a small margin, and by the early twentieth century Britain was a predominantly urban nation. Over 75 per cent of its population lived in towns or cities, making it the most urbanized country in Europe. In the first part of the nineteenth century the growth of towns was fuelled by the overflow of surplus population from rural areas, and already by the 1840s some parts of the Scottish Highlands and rural Wales were registering an actual fall in population as the lure of the cities exerted its pull.

Urbanization was in one sense a unifying experience, since it concentrated people in a common environment. Yet just as every urban community had its own identity and characteristics, so the process of urban growth varied from one part of Britain to another. In England, London was sui generis the largest city in the land by a wide margin, with a population in 1801 of 1.1 million, rising to 2.6 million in 1851 and 6.6 million in 1901. As the political and administrative capital of a world-wide empire it had a unique status in Britain and beyond.[3] It set the tone of culture and fashion; it dominated the economy of south-east England as it had done for centuries. London apart, though, the most rapid urban development in England took place in the industrial centres of the Midlands and the North, indicative of the shifting balance of economic power that the Industrial Revolution was bringing in its wake. Manchester, the prototypical industrial city which seemed to observers like Frederick Engels to herald the arrival of a new social order, had been a town of fewer than 20,000 inhabitants in the mid-eighteenth century. By 1851 it had a population of over 300,000. Other northern cities underwent similarly rapid growth. Liverpool's population increased from 82,000 to 376,000 between 1801 and 1851, swollen by the Irish influx. Leeds tripled in size in the same period (from 53,000 to 172,000 inhabitants), while its neighbour and rival Bradford grew eightfold, its population in 1851 reaching 104,000.

Although towns like Leeds and Manchester had long histories, in the nineteenth century they became virtually new cities as they expanded away from their older cores. Their growth displaced previously more important urban centres like Norwich and York from their former positions in the national pecking order and effectively redrew England's urban map. Elsewhere in Britain urbanization followed different patterns. There was also rapid urban growth in Scotland, but it centred mainly on what were already in the eighteenth century the four principal cities: Edinburgh, Glasgow, Dundee and Aberdeen. Of these, Edinburgh had its character subtly altered rather than completely transformed in the early nineteenth century. Its population more than doubled (from 83,000 in 1801 to 202,000 in 1851) but it remained essentially a city of the learned professions and artisan crafts rather than heavy industry, the completion of the New Town giving it a physical appearance of leisured elegance that went well with its reputation as 'the Athens of the North'. Glasgow's metamorphosis was much more profound. In the eighteenth century it had become a major commercial port. Like Edinburgh it had an established civic identity and an ancient university. But in the nineteenth century it quickly outstripped its eastern rival in terms of size and industrial development. Between 1801 and 1851 its population quadrupled (from 77,000 to 357,000) and it became the hub of the Industrial Revolution in the west-central Lowlands. By 1901 44 per cent of Scotland's total population lived and worked in the greater Glasgow region.[4]

The impact of urbanization on Wales was even greater. Prior to the nineteenth century, Wales was a country of small towns, villages and isolated farms. It had no capital city to compare with London, Edinburgh or Dublin, no large administrative or urban centres. Cardiff, the future capital, had only 1870 inhabitants in 1801 and was no more than the 25th largest town in Wales; even the largest, Merthyr, had a population of under 8000. If Welshmen gravitated to the city, it was to London, or perhaps Liverpool or Bristol, rather than to anywhere in Wales itself. This changed during the first half of the nineteenth century. Welshmen still migrated to London or other English cities, but for the first time Wales acquired mass communities of its own in the towns and valley settlements of industrial south Wales. Cardiff's population had risen to 18,000 by 1851. Merthyr Tydfil, the 'crucible' of the Industrial Revolution in south Wales, saw its population increase from 7700 to 46,000 between 1801 and 1851.[5] Given this mushrooming growth, many of the new towns were initially unplanned and lawless places, a 'frontier society' that was often violent and lacked the disciplinary influence of urban traditions or established civic institutions. Church and chapel provided some measure of restraint. Improved policing and the gradual emergence of political and administrative structures were making their effects felt by mid-century, and incidentally making the town life of Wales more like that of England and Scotland. But for the Welsh the experience of urbanization marked an even greater break with the past, and the Welsh urban landscape retained the imprint of its origins throughout the Victorian period.

Britain in the nineteenth century was thus becoming a more urbanized nation, but its towns and cities, while showing some similarities of development, were infinitely variegated, their characters shaped by a range of economic, geographic, historical and cultural factors. The process of industrialization, though it had common features across all areas, was similarly diverse, and the history of the Industrial Revolution can be written either on a British or on a more local basis. At the macroeconomic level there were some general factors which stimulated the eighteenth-century industrial 'take-off'. The post-1707 British state presided over Europe's largest free market for goods and capital and guaranteed conditions of political and social stability in which enterprise could thrive. Britain, as the centre of an expanding empire and as the world's leading commercial and naval power, was well placed to dominate overseas trade, facilitating the import of raw materials and the export of finished goods. Population growth and the commercialization of agriculture provided labour for industry, food to feed this labour and at the same time enlarged the domestic market. Britain's involvement in the French wars of 1793–1815 gave a further impetus to industrial growth, especially in the key sectors of the industrial economy such as textiles, iron and coal.

In the development of particular industries or regions, however, local factors played a more important part. The nature of the existing industrial base, the availability of local resources like water power or mineral deposits, accessibility to communications, the quality of the labour force, could all affect the path which the economic history of any given locality took. England alone presents a varied enough picture. Yorkshire's Industrial Revolution rested heavily on the mechanization of its traditional woollen industry. Lancashire founded its burgeoning wealth on cotton, which in the space of four decades between 1780 and 1820 superseded and dwarfed woollen goods as Britain's most valuable manufactured export. Staffordshire enhanced its position as the centre of the pottery and china industry, although it also developed its coalfields and ironworks, as did parts of the Midlands, Yorkshire and the North-East. Birmingham remained largely a centre of the skilled metal-working trades, as did Sheffield, although the latter, as the 'steel city' of the nineteenth century, established a more formidable heavy-industrial base.

The pattern of industrial diversity and regional specialism was reproduced in Scotland and Wales. In Scotland's case the difference was that most industrial development was concentrated in the Glasgow–west of Scotland industrial belt. The Borders retained their traditional woollen industry, but the more dynamic sectors of the textile industry – linen and cotton – developed around Glasgow and Paisley. There were 134 cotton mills in Scotland by the early 1830s, employing over 150,000 people, and most of them were in the

Glasgow region. The coal and iron industries were similarly located mainly in Lanarkshire and Ayrshire, the opening of the Carron ironworks at Falkirk in 1759 marking the beginning of Scotland's modern industrial revolution. Other industries like chemicals (in the shape of Charles Tennant's St Rollox works) were also Glasgow based, drawing on the practical scientific expertise of the city's university. Edinburgh and Aberdeen had some limited manufacturing industry, and Dundee became the world's leading producer of jute, but Glasgow was the pre-eminent Scottish industrial city, with the Clyde's flourishing engineering and shipbuilding industries maintaining the city's momentum of growth for most of the nineteenth century.

The south Wales coalfield became the Welsh equivalent of the Glasgow region, except that the Welsh Industrial Revolution was more narrowly based than either the Scottish or English versions. The late eighteenth century development of industry in north Wales soon petered out, leaving only the coal mines of Flintshire and the slate industry of Gwynedd as major employers. There was a woollen textile industry in mid-Wales based on towns like Newtown and Llanidloes, but it too was in decline by the mid-nineteenth century, unable to compete in scale with the Yorkshire mills. (Significantly, the Newtown-born Robert Owen chose to pursue his entrepreneurial career in Scotland, at the New Lanark factories of David Dale.) It was only in the south that large-scale industrialization took hold, built on the twin foundations of iron and coal. The great ironworks of Merthyr Tydfil – Dowlais, Cyfarthfa, Plymouth, Penydarren – blossomed during the French wars and continued to pour forth their products in ever increasing quantities, at least until the mid-nineteenth century. Welsh iron output rose from 100,000 tons in 1815 to 277,000 tons in 1830 and 706,000 tons in 1847. The coming of the railways provided a further boost, the south Wales ironworks becoming the main suppliers of iron rails not just in Britain but in much of Europe and the United States as well. Coal developed alongside the iron industry, initially in its shadow, then increasingly as an industry in its own right, with nearly a third of its production of 8.8 million tons going for export by the 1850s.

Economic diversity was matched by the social and cultural diversity of the urban-industrial regions. The south Wales iron and coal industries, for example, remained very much Welsh in character, at least until the 1850s. The booming population came to a large extent from the hinterlands of Glamorgan and Monmouthshire and from the more rural areas of mid and west Wales. The census of 1851 showed that 44,000 of Merthyr's 46,000 inhabitants were of Welsh origin. In the early nineteenth century the incomers brought with them their language and a still recognizably pre-industrial culture. This evolved rapidly into an industrial culture, but retained its Welshness, so vividly celebrated in the writings of the historian Gwyn A. Williams and the novelist Alexander Cordell.[6] The existence of the south Wales safety valve for the surplus population of the country districts spared Wales the famine experience of the Irish and meant that a smaller proportion of Welsh than Irish – or, for that matter, Scots or English – emigrated overseas, thereby maintaining the cultural integrity of Wales as a nation. A similar case can be made for Scotland. Population gravitated to the central industrial region, remaking Scottish identity certainly, but not necessarily diminishing its Scottish character. In England too, long-distance migration was the exception rather than the rule, giving the industrial districts of Lancashire and Yorkshire a distinctive identity of their own. Britain could therefore be seen as a series of economic-industrial regions, following older boundaries of nationality, geography and identity, rather than an homogenized or fully integrated national-industrial state.

Yet this is only one side of the picture. The dynamics of capitalism meant that the boundaries between regions were steadily being broken down and that the different parts of the country were becoming more closely incorporated into a single, integrated British economy. This was not a wholly new development. There was an inbuilt symbiosis between the agricultural and industrial sectors that created interdependence between the countryside and the towns, sometimes over very long distances, as with the cattle droving of the eighteenth century which linked London with the rural districts of Wales and Scotland. The agricultural revolution introduced more sophisticated market mechanisms, enabling a more commercialized agricultural sector to supply the needs of an expanding urban population. The agricultural-industrial connection was only one facet of the more integrated economy that was taking shape in the eighteenth and nineteenth centuries. The commercial expansion of the eighteenth century had created a British financial and mercantile infrastructure, based on the City of London and linked to imperial trade. Within Britain itself there was considerable mobility of capital and of entrepreneurial and technological expertise. The iron industries of south Wales were developed largely by English investment.

James Watt, the pioneer of the steam engine, perfected his inventions in Birmingham rather than in his native Scotland. Since the Union, the Scots had been exploiting the opportunities of the expanded imperial state, and there was a real sense in which, at a strategic level, Britain's Industrial Revolution was being conceived on a genuinely British, if not world, scale.

This in turn was easier because improved communications were bringing all parts of Britain closer together, facilitating the more rapid movement of people, goods and ideas. Until the 1830s the main improvements were in the form of roads and canals. The 'canal age', conventionally dated from the opening of the Bridgewater Canal in 1761, had created a network of canals and navigable waterways by the 1820s. New or improved roads, many of them operated by turnpike trusts, were also a feature of the period. Scotland alone acquired 3000 miles of new roads between 1750 and 1814.[7] But it was the steam revolution and the coming of the railways that really transformed the transportation system. Between 1830 – when the Liverpool to Manchester line was opened – and 1850, over 6000 miles of railway were laid. The railways carried some 67.4 million passengers in the latter year, as well as vast amounts of freight and industrial goods. Journey times were considerably reduced. Whereas in 1750 it could take two weeks to travel from London to Edinburgh by the fastest route, in 1850 the train journey took 18 hours or less. The railways also speeded up the distribution of newspapers and postal communications. The 'penny post' system launched in the 1840s was made practical by the existence of reliable rail transport, and the number of letters handled by the Post Office quadrupled between 1839 and 1849.[8] In a variety of ways, railways were the sinews that bound the different parts of the British state together, crossing internal boundaries and representing a symbol of British engineering and industrial collaboration which had an effect on the image of Britain in the eyes of the rest of the world and among its own people. The six million visitors to the Great Exhibition of 1851 – many of whom came in specially provided trains – were participating in more than one sense in a celebration of British achievements, in a way that transcended the more localized concerns of any region or part.

Nevertheless, while Britain of the early 1850s was an economically more integrated entity, in other respects it was much less unified. Improved communications and the advance of industrialization might be breaking down some divisions, but they were putting others in their place. One consequence of the Industrial Revolution was to sharpen and generalize distinctions of social class. Disraeli, in his literary, Young England, phase in the 1840s, famously dramatized the difference between classes in his novel *Sybil* (1844) as a division between 'Two Nations – the Rich and the Poor'. Karl Marx and Frederick Engels, in *The Communist Manifesto* (1848), wrote of the ever widening gulf between bourgeoisie and proletariat which, they predicted, must lead inevitably to revolution. Neither Marx and Engels nor Disraeli captured the intricacies of the new industrial society with perfect precision, but they and other commentators were demonstrating an awareness of the way in which social structures were being remade around the polarities of middle class and working class life. Later writers have stressed the potential for cooperation as well as conflict between the classes, and have at least implicitly identified the nation as the context within which such conflicts as did exist could be resolved (as in Harold Perkin's description of mid-nineteenth century Britain as a 'viable class society' based on shared culture and ideals[9]). Yet for contemporaries the class divide could be urgent and threatening, and in some ways became more so as the nineteenth century progressed, with the rise of working class and socialist movements challenging the economic and political status quo.

In the 1830s and 1840s, however, Disraelian class divisions were arguably less important than the division – part geographical, part economic, part psychological – summed up in the title of Mrs Gaskell's novel, *North and South* (1855). The novel explored the differences between the rural south of England and the industrial north, acknowledging that there were conflicts within industrial society (notably between masters and men) while reflecting the reality that there was an even more profound divide between the industrial and non-industrial parts of the country. From this perspective, the vertically integrated community or economic interest, not its internal stratifications of class, was the central component of what, in emblematic shorthand, came to be known as the 'North–South' divide. The 'northern' part of this equation was a mental as much as a geographical construct, containing not just the north of England but, by extension, the industrial regions of south Wales and central Scotland. What was being recreated here was the old division between Highland and Lowland Britain, which had for centuries distinguished the poorer upland areas of the north and west from the fertile plains of the south and east – with the difference that in the nineteenth century (and until the depression and de-industrialization

of the twentieth) the north was increasingly the centre of economic
power and the forcing house of new ideas, partly reversing the old
Highland–Lowland relationship.[10] The struggle over the repeal of the
Corn Laws, which convulsed politics in the mid-1840s, symbolized
the clash between the representatives of the landed interest and those
of the new industrial order. Equally symbolically, it resulted in a
victory for the 'Manchester School' free traders in a manner that
reflected the shift of political and economic power. True, agriculture
remained the largest single employer of labour, and the agricultural
interest enjoyed something of a 'golden age' in the 1850s and 1860s.
But this was not to last, and the onset of agricultural depression in
the 1870s emphasized the diverging fortunes of the 'two nations' of
rural and urban Britain.

The increasing scale of economic and social activity and the
possibility of clashes of competing interests, whether of class or
region, posed a challenge for government and led inevitably to
changes in the relationship between governors and governed. Indeed,
one of the main consequences of the Industrial Revolution was to
enhance the part that the central institutions of the British state
played in the life of the community. The resulting tensions between
centre and localities were to provide a major theme in British history
throughout the modern period. In the eighteenth century the state
had only a limited role: it raised taxes to fight wars and organize
national defence; it promoted trade and supported the empire. But it
played virtually no part in large areas of national life such as education
or social welfare, which were left to the churches, to charities or local
communities. During the French wars, as has been seen, the state
assumed a more oppressive presence, through extending taxation and
suppressing popular protest, yet the period after 1815 is often seen as
'the age of laissez faire', in which minimal government became the
ideological as well as the practical rule. This view of the early Victorian state is, however, misleading. While the ideas of liberal
economics were steadily applied in the moves towards a comprehensive policy of free trade, the impulses of utilitarianism and
humanitarianism, in addition to more mundane political considerations, led successive governments in a steadily more interventionist
direction. A succession of factory and mines acts in the 1830s and
1840s regulated the conditions of women and children in the industrial workplace. Public health measures, particularly the Public Health
Act of 1848, were an attempt to improve living conditions in the new
industrial towns and reduce the threat of disease. The reforms of the

Poor Law in England and Wales in 1834 and Scotland in 1845 were important interventionist measures, which staked the claim of central government to be the directing agency of future social policy. The centre still depended on the cooperation of local authorities, and much legislation was permissive rather than mandatory. Even so, there were signs that in the face of social divisions and social problems the state was taking on a more active regulatory role, the effect of which was to offset the diversity of British society by creating a more uniform legislative framework. If Britain was, on the whole, being more united than divided by processes of economic and social change, political structures were following suit, and perhaps were stimulating the integrationist trend.

Politics and protest

The expansion of central government – with an increased legislative role for parliament and an enlarged, though by later standards still small, civil service – was accompanied by changes in the political system as the British state underwent a significant transformation in the early years of the nineteenth century, especially during the Reform crisis of 1829–32. As was noted in the previous chapter, since the late eighteenth century reforming pressures had been building up across a wide field, for greater civil and religious equality and for the extension of the parliamentary franchise. The effects of the Industrial Revolution, particularly the growth of a more self-confident and often Nonconformist middle class and the emergence of a more urbanized, industrialized Britain to challenge the institutions of an aristocratic system of government, gave the movement for reform an almost irresistible momentum. In a flurry of activity in the late 1820s and early 1830s the political and religious framework of the British state was substantially recast. The Test and Corporation Acts were repealed and Catholics were granted emancipation. The reform of the electoral system in 1832 was followed by the introduction of more representative local government in the boroughs of England and Wales and the burghs of Scotland. Governments in the 1830s made further concessions to Nonconformists, and an Ecclesiastical Commission was appointed to inquire into abuses in the established Church of England. Taken together, these reforms amounted to a more extensive remodelling of the state than anything that had occurred since the upheavals of the seventeenth century, and according to the opinions of some historians marked the end of Britain's ancien regime.[11]

The cornerstone of change was parliamentary reform, embodied in the 1832 Reform Act for England and Wales and in separate measures for Scotland and Ireland. Latterly there has been a tendency to play down the significance of the 'Great Reform' of 1832, seeing it mainly as an attempt by the Whigs to preserve the essence of an aristocratic constitution by making minor concessions rather than as a firm step on the road to democratization. There is some validity in this view. Lord Grey's Whig government was certainly aristocratic rather than democratic in complexion. Its members were driven to reform as an alternative to more extreme, perhaps revolutionary, change. Although the 1832 Act produced an electorate 50 per cent larger than at the last election of the pre-Reform era in 1831, it still only increased the total number of prospective voters in England and Wales from 435,000 to 652,000 and left four out of five adult males (and all women) beyond the pale of the franchise.[12] In any case, as Professor Gash demonstrated in his classic study, many features of pre-Reform politics perpetuated in the early Victorian period tended to nullify the importance of the extended franchise, among them the high proportion of uncontested elections, the widespread deployment of aristocratic 'influence' and the retention of the practice of open voting, which facilitated the use of bribery, treating and other similarly traditional forms of electoral management.[13]

However, while it is legitimate to acknowledge the limitations of the reforms, it would be perverse to take too negative a view of them. A 50 per cent increase in the size of the electorate was far from negligible. The introduction of standardized qualifications for county and borough voters was an important step towards the creation of a more transparent, modern voting system. There were also two other ways in which the Reform Acts of 1832 had a vital impact on the political development of the British state. The first was that in England and Wales the franchise changes were accompanied by a substantial redistribution of parliamentary constituencies. A total of 143 seats were made available for reallocation by removing or reducing the parliamentary representation of smaller boroughs, mainly in the south and west of England. These were used to increase the representation of the more populous (mainly northern) counties, and to give separate representation for the first time to expanding industrial cities like Birmingham, Manchester, Leeds and Sheffield. Wales had its representation increased by four seats, including one for

Merthyr Tydfil, a storm centre of protest in the 'Merthyr riots' of 1831.[14]

Secondly, the reforms narrowed the political gap between Scotland and the rest of Britain. Pre-1832 electoral politics in Scotland were dominated by an extremely narrow group of unrepresentative oligarchies, especially in the burghs which had been the special target of reformers since the 1780s. The total Scottish electorate in 1831 – county and burgh combined – was 4579, and there was virtually no direct popular involvement in the electoral process since in practice MPs were chosen by landowners or local burghal elites. The Scottish Reform Act of 1832 consequently had a far-reaching impact on the Scottish political system. In the words of the Whig Solicitor-General, Henry Cockburn, it gave Scotland 'a political constitution for the first time'.[15] The introduction of a new £10 occupier franchise in the burghs, together with reforms in the counties, increased the size of the Scottish electorate to 65,000 by 1832. Scotland also gained an additional eight seats at Westminster, helping to reduce the under-representation in parliament that had been a grievance of Scots since the Union. The effect of these changes no more made Scotland a democracy than they did other parts of Britain, but they did at least allow Scotland to develop a similar form of representative politics to that which operated in England and Wales. Nor were Scottish voters slow to exercise the new power that reform gave them, returning a decisive majority of Whig and radical MPs at the 1832 election in place of the 'Tory despotism' by which they had been ruled since the days of Pitt and Dundas.[16]

In this way, the reforms of 1832 and the political changes that followed from them were broadly integrationist, and after 1832 a more uniform British political system began to emerge. A party system evolved in which Whigs and Tories competed for power in electoral contests across the United Kingdom, and general elections became more 'national' both in their conduct and their content. Of course the extent of this change should not be exaggerated. Party organizations were rudimentary and fragmented, even at the end of the early Victorian period. Politics was still as much about the power and influence of territorial magnates as it was about manifestos and party machines. Many contests (where they occurred at all) were decided on local issues or by loyalty to individuals rather than in relation to any larger national concern. In the case of Scotland, moreover, it should be appreciated that, despite the assimilationist, integrationist trend, Scottish politics retained a character different in many respects from the rest of Britain. This was reflected in the establishment by the parties of separate Scottish organizations and in Scotland's distinctive electoral history in this period. Scotland remained staunchly Whig-Radical throughout the 1830s and 1840s. Even in 1841, when Peel's Conservatives were victorious in the general election in Britain as a whole, they could win no more than 22 of Scotland's 53 seats. Scottish politics differed from the rest of Britain in its subject matter too, particularly in the years before and after the Disruption of the Church of Scotland in 1843 when the affairs of the Kirk (especially the conflict over lay patronage) dominated much of the supposedly secular political debate. The relationship between Church and State, and religious questions generally, were to the forefront of politics in other parts of the United Kingdom as well, but because in Scotland the Church had for so long been the principal symbol of nationhood any rift in its affairs was bound to have a disproportionately large political fallout.[17]

Yet although Scotland retained a separate political character, this was not translated into any form of nationalist politics or a challenge to the Union, at least before the 1850s. A similar situation obtained in Wales, where Nonconformists were beginning to test their power (for example through movements such as the pro-disestablishment Liberation Society) but nationalism had not developed as a fully fledged political force. The restricted enfranchisement of 1832 may have been a factor in restraining the more rapid evolution of an alternative politics, though this is far from certain. What seems more likely is that the political classes in Scotland and Wales were content with a system that gave them freedom of expression and limited autonomy within the overall framework of a British state. Scottish affairs were actually brought more closely under central control from London in the 1830s, as the Home Office assumed an administrative role in respect of Scotland that had previously been discharged by a Scottish 'manager' or by the lord advocate. There were few protests in Wales at the abolition of the Courts of Great Sessions in 1830.

A countervailing trend which may have made the centralization of government more palatable was the extension of representative government at local level. The reform of the Scottish burghs in 1833 and the passing of the Municipal Corporations Act for England and Wales in 1835 established the principle of elective local government, with councils elected by ratepayers undertaking an increasing range of functions as the legislative revolution of the 1830s and 1840s gath-

ered pace. Cities like Glasgow and Liverpool pioneered reforming
initiatives in public health and social policy, and their councils became
the focus for new forms of civic politics that carried power and
prestige to the newly enfranchised middle classes. The industrial cities
of northern England – Leeds, Sheffield, Manchester, Bradford –
developed their own political worlds which were linked to the
national parliamentary system but in which party conflicts had a
richness and intensity that derived from local circumstances, person-
alities and concerns as much as, if not more than, from any outside
stimulus.[18] Inevitably tensions sometimes arose between centre and
locality, the product of the 'rise of the provinces' as a factor in the
national political equation. But for most of the time the relationship
was complementary rather than confrontational, and the structure of
the nineteenth-century British state is not really understood unless
the importance of the growth of local institutions as a counterweight
to – or possibly a corollary of – the expansion of central government
is given due emphasis. The permissive nature of much legislation gave
full scope to local initiative, and encouraged an independent sense of
political community at a local level. The existence of autonomy on
the basis of individual urban units may also, for a time, have provided
an alternative, maybe even a barrier, to the growth of wider regional
or national/regional loyalties by stimulating competition among
neighbours (as evidenced by the fierce rivalries between Glasgow and
Edinburgh, Cardiff and Swansea or Leeds and Bradford).

The combination of national structures with local diversity that
existed in the formal politics of the British state was also characteristic of the informal politics of pressure groups and popular protest
that were a prominent feature of the early nineteenth-century political
world. Extra-parliamentary pressure groups had begun to coordinate
their activities on a nationwide scale even before the Reform Act.
The campaign for parliamentary reform itself was a national movement, although one that since its origins in the eighteenth century had
been infinitely varied at the local level and divided into moderate and
radical wings. Agitations like the anti-slavery movement and the
Nonconformist campaign for repeal of the Test and Corporation
Acts had similarly mobilized support on a wide basis. Other forms of
protest, however, especially those linked to economic grievances,
tended to be more localized or regional in extent. The food riots of
the second half of the eighteenth century are a good example. So too
are some of the main outbreaks of popular protest of the early
nineteenth century. The Luddite protests of 1811–16 affected the

textile districts of Nottinghamshire, Leicestershire, Derbyshire and parts of Lancashire and Yorkshire. The 'Swing' riots of 1830 involved agricultural labourers in the south of England but did not spread to the northern counties. In mid and west Wales in 1839 and 1842–44 the Rebecca rioters carried out nocturnal raids on tollgates and attacked workhouses, yet their particular form of protest was not reproduced in other parts of Britain.[19] In each of these cases, while there was some similarity of method (direct action involving the ritualized, symbolic use of violence against property, or 'collective bargaining by riot'), the precise form and targets of the protest derived from local conditions and grievances: low wages, high rents and tolls, the introduction of new machinery, unsympathetic land-lords or employers.

The same was true of more sophisticated protests against the new industrial order and government policies towards the poor. In the 1830s two overlapping movements emerged in the industrial north of England, most strongly in Yorkshire, that succeeded in uniting sections of the middle and working classes, but only on a local or regional basis. One was the campaign for factory reform, spearheaded by Tory radicals like Richard Oastler (author of a famous letter denouncing 'Yorkshire slavery' in the *Leeds Mercury* in 1830). Oastler and his allies formed a network of 'short-time committees' to press for parliamentary regulation of working hours and the introduction of a statutory ten-hour day in the textile industry. The reforms of the 1830s went some way to meeting their aims, those of the 1840s a little further. But in the late 1830s the factory question was pushed into the background by a second agitation, against the New Poor Law of 1834. This measure, which began to be implemented in the north of England in 1837, was unpopular because it sought to remove 'outdoor relief' for the able-bodied poor, forcing them instead into the hated workhouse. The main complaint of the industrial districts was that the strictness of this regime was inappropriate to an econ-omy vulnerable to fluctuations of trade, where short-term outdoor relief might be cheaper as well as socially preferable to long-term incarceration. The anti-Poor Law agitation, which did achieve a more flexible administration of the Poor Laws that recognized the differ-ences between the industrial north and the rural southern counties, was another example of regional, community-based protest operating within an emerging national political-economic framework – of the accommodation of diversity in a context of integration and centrali-zation.[20]

The problems of integration and diversity were confronted by two more of the popular movements of the 1830s and 1840s, trade unionism and Chartism. Trade unions had begun to develop in the eighteenth century on a small-scale, local basis, though their growth was hampered by the passage of the Combination Acts of 1799 and 1800. Even after the Combination Laws were repealed in 1824 unions still had at best a quasi-legal status, and their members were liable to stiff penalties if they infringed the law, as the six Dorchester labourers transported for swearing illegal oaths discovered in 1834. Nevertheless, trade unionism did flourish fitfully in this period, and the early 1830s saw the first attempts to organize workers on a more comprehensive footing. In 1830 the Irishman John Doherty founded the National Association for the Protection of Labour, a more ambitious undertaking even than the Grand General Union of Operative Spinners of Great Britain and Ireland which he had launched in the previous year. Robert Owen formed the Grand National Consolidated Trades Union in 1833, and the national trade union movement achieved a significant moral victory when their campaign to reverse the convictions of the Tolpuddle Martyrs was successful in 1836. By then, however, the Doherty and Owen unions had collapsed, showing the difficulty of bringing together workers from different occupations and different parts of the country in organizations that were inadequately resourced and extremely vulnerable to the fluctuations of the economy, the hostility of employers and the vagaries of the law. The lack of a common outlook on the part of the workers themselves was also a factor in their defeat, and when more permanent national unions did emerge from the 1850s on they did so on a much more modest prospectus, serving comparatively small occupational groups of mainly skilled men. Only thus could the conflicts arising from geography and internal divisions within the working class be overcome and a labour movement be given a firmer institutional and organizational foundation.

Chartism encountered the same difficulties of binding socially and geographically diverse elements together into a movement capable of making common cause. Under the detailed scrutiny of historical research these difficulties have been made to seem insurmountable and to constitute a major reason for the movement's failure to win its objectives of democratic parliamentary reform according to the six points of the 'People's Charter'.[21] The regional variations in the composition of the Chartist movement, the divisions between 'moral force' and 'physical force' wings, the colouring of Scottish and Welsh

Chartism with the national characteristics of those countries, all seem to reflect the fragmentary nature of popular politics in early Victorian Britain. Chartism seems to be a series of episodes – the presentation of the three petitions, the Newport rising of 1839, the 'Plug Plot' of 1842, the Kennington Common demonstration of 1848 – rather than a coherently structured mass movement. Yet there is another inter-pretation, or at least a different emphasis, that can be put on the Chartist experience, for it could be argued that Chartism was the first genuinely British mass movement, building on the hesitant attempts of 1790s radicals and later parliamentary reformers to construct an oppositional force that could match the reach of the British state. Originating in disappointment at the limited nature of the 1832 Reform Acts, Chartism based itself around the programme of the Charter drafted by the London Working Men's Association in 1836,[22] which was formally adopted at mass meetings throughout the country in 1838. Local Chartist groups succeeded in electing a Chartist Convention which met in London in February 1839 and which included representatives from England, Scotland and Wales. The collection of over a million signatures for the first Chartist petition represented a tremendous feat of organization. The petition was rejected by parliament, prompting outbreaks of violence, but the movement continued to develop its structural base. The Irish lawyer Fergus O'Connor (whose presence as one of Chartism's most prominent leaders testified to the 'multi-national' aspect of the movement, and growing Irish involvement) founded the National Charter Association in 1840, using the networks already established by his newspaper, the *Northern Star*.[23] The NCA had 400 branches by 1842 and over 50,000 members. Even though it declined after the failure of the second petition, and Chartism reverted to a more fragmented condition, the campaign for the Charter and what it represented remained a powerful unifying force for popular radical-ism for the remainder of the decade, and its legacy was to be important in the creation of a popular Liberal movement in Britain in the 1850s and 1860s. The diversity of Chartism mirrored the diversity of the politics of the British state, yet by the same token it possessed a similar underlying unity. Just as, by the 1830s, there were signs that the political system was becoming more inclusive, so, after 1832, even for those still excluded from formal participation in the electoral process, it was the British dimension that was coming to the fore.

The same could be said of the other major popular agitation of the 1840s, the campaign against the Corn Laws. Introduced at the

end of the Napoleonic Wars to protect British agriculture by preventing the import of cheap foreign grain, by the 1830s the Corn
Laws were unpopular with industrialists and workers alike for the way
in which they maintained high food prices and raised costs. Free
traders had secured a modification of the laws in the 1820s, but their
demand was for complete repeal. A number of bodies emerged to
campaign for this end, including the Anti-Corn Law Associations in
London and Glasgow, which attracted widespread radical support.
The most successful of these organizations, however, was the Anti-
Corn Law League, established in Manchester in 1838 and led by
Richard Cobden and John Bright. Between the late 1830s and 1846,
when the Corn Laws were finally repealed, the ACLL waged a tireless
propaganda battle, and its leaders toured all parts of Britain to spread
their word. How much their efforts contributed to the eventual
outcome is debatable. The nature of the campaign is nevertheless
indicative of the strengthening British orientation of the political
system, not only in terms of its geographical spread but in that it
represented a consolidated British industrial interest against the
previously dominant agricultural sector.

    In its structures and practice alike, therefore, Britain in the post-
Reform era was developing a more integrated political system. There
was considerable regional diversity. There were also divisions of
party, class, religion and economic interest. But these were evolving
within a British framework and in relation to the governing institutions of a British state. Moreover, that state, while it was extending its
central authority, had also enhanced the powers of self-government
of local communities, particularly in the towns, in a way that established a partnership between centre and locality. There were
examples, too, of the willingness of central government to respond
flexibly to the needs of particular regions and to recognize national
diversities within the United Kingdom. The tacit relaxation of the
administration of the Poor Laws in response to popular protest in the
north of England was a case in point. The setting up of an inquiry
into the causes of the Rebecca riots and the subsequent introduction
of remedial measures was another. In the 1840s the Scottish Poor
Laws were reformed to take into account the diminished capacity of
the Church to provide poor relief, and a separate Scottish Poor Law
Board was established. In other areas the state and its ruling elite were
more resistant to change, notably in the refusal to consider further
parliamentary reform. They took a robust line in putting down violent
protest wherever it occurred. But the resulting tensions grew out of

the dynamics of conflict within a single political community rather than between communities that would have preferred to be separate. The integrationist process that had been at work since the eighteenth century, and which was being reinforced by the parallel economic and social changes resulting from industrialization, appeared in consequence by the middle of the nineteenth century to be pointing clearly in the direction of a more unified, unitary state, with appropriate balances between the powers of Westminster and Whitehall and the autonomy of local communities.

There was, however, one glaring exception: the developments in Britain were not accompanied by any similarly increased closeness between the political nations of Britain and Ireland. Although links existed, the union on which the United Kingdom was based remained stubbornly partial and incomplete. The experience of the 1830s and 1840s served only to emphasize differences and to harden divisions, presenting the post-Union system with a problem that potentially threatened the integrity and security of the British state itself. While in Britain peaceful integration appeared the order of the day, in Britain's 'other island' an altogether different future beckoned.

Ireland

With the benefit of hindsight, it is tempting to conclude that the political union between Britain and Ireland was bound to fail – not perhaps because it was inherently impossible for the two peoples to live together in a single political community, but because the circumstances in which the union was created, and the prejudices that existed on either side, made the establishment of that community in itself impossible to achieve. Unlike the union between England and Scotland, that between Britain and Ireland was not, even theoretically, a coming together of two independent nations. Ireland had been in effect a colonial dependency of Britain, and that status was reflected in the continuing presence of the lord lieutenant and the separate administration at Dublin Castle even after the Irish parliament had been abolished and Irish representation transferred to Westminster. Then again, the Anglo-Scottish union had explicitly underwritten the existence of Scotland's national institutions: its Church, law and education system. In Ireland those institutions either did not exist, or were the institutions of a minority of the population, like the established Anglican Church of Ireland. The Union, therefore, perpetuated a Protestant Ascendancy that had no popular roots in the majority

Irish national community. Had Pitt's original intention of combining union with Catholic emancipation been adhered to, this weakness might have been overcome and much bitterness avoided. As it was, even after emancipation was granted in 1829, the minority Irish Church retained its established status and remained a potent source of grievance. Whereas Scotland grew into the Union confident and secure in its national identity, generations of Irishmen felt compelled to seek to break the Union in order to establish theirs.

In the 1830s an alternative scenario seemed possible. The Irish Reform Act of 1832 was more restrictive than those for England, Wales and Scotland (leaving only about one in 20 Irishmen with the vote), but, coupled with emancipation and an increase in Irish representation at Westminster to 105 MPs, it opened up the chance of greater participation by the Catholic majority in the workings of the Union state. The success of Daniel O'Connell's followers in securing the largest share of Irish seats at the 1832 general election was confirmation of this, even if they were outnumbered by the combined forces of Irish Liberals and Tories. The integrationist possibilities were enhanced by the parliamentary strategy that O'Connell pursued. Although he was already expressing support for the repeal of the Act of Union, in the 1830s he shelved this demand in favour of cooperation with the Whigs and radicals at Westminster, an arrangement formalized by the 'Lichfield House compact' of 1835 by which these groups combined to oust Peel's minority government of 1834–35 from office.[24] This strategy produced a number of Irish reforms from Whig ministers, among them the Irish Church Temporalities Act of 1833 (which reduced the number of Church of Ireland bishops), the commutation of tithe payments, the reform of Irish corporations (giving some Catholics a representative voice in local affairs) and measures to promote elementary education and to extend the Poor Law to Ireland. Not all of these measures were popular, and many of them aroused controversy either for going too far or not far enough. The Irish Poor Law was imposed in the face of considerable opposition. However, the signs were that Ireland and her representatives were being assimilated into a common political system with the British nations and that the British state was willing and able to devote the necessary attention to the redress of Irish grievances and the management of Irish affairs. The fact that at the election of 1841 O'Connell's party was reduced to only 18 seats, a smaller representation than either Whigs or Tories, suggested that Irish voters were becoming reconciled to the politics of the Union and perhaps were even beginning to perceive potential advantages in becoming part of an extended British political nation.

Yet if this was true of Irish voters, it was not true of O'Connell, nor of the Catholic masses excluded from the franchise. Substantial discontent remained, in particular at the slowness with which Catholics were gaining promotion to positions of authority in an Irish administration that continued to exhibit many of the traits of traditional Ascendancy Protestant culture. O'Connell believed that this situation would only finally be changed by the repeal of the Act of Union and the restoration of an Irish parliament in Dublin with powers to control the executive and create an administrative structure more responsive to the majority view. Accordingly in 1840 he founded the National Repeal Association as a vehicle for mobilizing popular support for this objective, along the lines of the earlier movement for Catholic emancipation. The Repeal movement won the backing of the Catholic Church and rapidly acquired a mass following, encouraging O'Connell boldly to declare that 1843 would be 'the Year of Repeal' and to organize a series of monster outdoor meetings to demonstrate the strength of the demand and put pressure on the government. O'Connell's calculation, or hope, was that Peel, the new British prime minister, would respond as the earlier Conservative government had over emancipation in 1828–29, and give him what he wanted. On this occasion, however, his strategy failed. Peel's government, having already similarly withstood the Chartist onslaught in Britain, refused to give in to the menace of popular agitation in Ireland. Instead they banned the O'Connellite demonstration that was to have taken place at Clontarf in October 1843 as the climax of the Repeal campaign, leaving O'Connell either to defy the prohibition or to run the risk of a fatal faltering of momentum for his plans. Much to the disappointment of some of his followers, O'Connell decided to acquiesce in the ban and cancelled the Clontarf meeting, thereby dissipating the head of steam that had been built up. The Repeal Association went into decline and was breaking apart even before O'Connell's death in 1847.

O'Connell himself throughout his campaign had emphasized his loyalty to the crown (his organization was officially entitled the 'Loyal National Repeal Association'), and the repeal of the Act of Union did not necessarily in his eyes mean that all ties between Britain and Ireland would be broken. The Repeal movement was nevertheless the first major challenge to the unitary British state and represented the emergence of something like a mass political nationalist movement in one part of the United Kingdom. The rather diffuse formulations of O'Connellism, moreover, provided a useful umbrella beneath which a more carefully articulated nationalism could develop and garner support. In 1842 the Repealers Thomas Davis and Charles Gavan Duffy founded the journal, *The Nation*, which became the mouthpiece for the group known as 'Young Ireland'.[25] The Young Ireland faction supported the demand for a Dublin parliament but they saw this merely as a stepping stone to complete Irish independence. They differed from O'Connell in that they sought a more inclusive, republican nationalism that was less Catholic in its orientation and could appeal equally to Anglicans and Presbyterians. They were also ready to use revolutionary means to achieve their ends, representing a 'physical force' alternative to the 'moral force' of O'Connellism. In both respects they embodied the more extreme, insurrectionary tradition of nationalism established by Wolfe Tone and the rebels of 1798, who provided them with heroes and role models. After the Clontarf climbdown of 1843 the Young Irelanders were increasingly at odds with O'Connell, and in 1846 broke away from the Repeal movement to form the Irish Confederation led by John Mitchel (editor of the *United Irishman* journal) and Smith O'Brien. Confederate clubs were established among the Irish in Britain and the Confederation movement had close links with physical-force Chartism, which in its final 1848 incarnation owed much to its Irish activists. Like the Chartists, however, the Confederation nationalists found that 1848 was a year of disappointment rather than revolution, the attempted Irish rebellion leading to no more than a violent clash with police at 'Widow McCormack's cabbage patch' at Ballingarry in County Tipperary.

The growth of nationalism and the presence of a disaffected Catholic majority were instances of one way in which Ireland was moving along a special path of development in the early nineteenth century compared with the rest of the United Kingdom. There were important economic and social differences between Britain and Ireland as well. Both countries experienced rapid population growth (Ireland's population rose from approximately 4.4 million in 1790 to 8.2 million in 1841), but Ireland enjoyed a much slower rate of economic expansion. It remained a much less urbanized country. Dublin was a large city, with a population of 232,700 in 1841, and Belfast had 75,000 inhabitants at the same date, yet in total only 14 per cent of the population lived in towns of more than 1500 people. Lack of urban development reflected the lack of an industrial revolution comparable to that of Britain. There was a substantial linen industry in Ulster, but Ireland as a whole was without the resources of minerals or capital to fund heavy industrial expansion, at least until the growth of shipbuilding and engineering in Belfast in the later nineteenth century. Meanwhile traditional cottage industries were in decline, priced out by mechanization and competition from British manufactures. Ireland's economy was thus left heavily dependent on agriculture, which was partly commercialized, producing for the British market, but which also had a large subsistence-based peasant sector in which poorer families waged a struggle for existence by the farming of livestock and the widespread cultivation of potatoes which became a staple of their diet.[26]

Even in good times the fruits of this system were barely able to sustain Ireland's booming population. When crops failed, as they did periodically in the early nineteenth century, extreme hardship was the result. In the 1840s much worse was to occur.[27] From 1845 to 1849 the potato crop was attacked repeatedly by a previously unknown disease (*phytophthera infestans*) that destroyed entire plantings, depriving the rural poor of their main food supply and reducing large numbers to destitution and starvation. One consequence was an increase in emigration, both to Britain and further afield, especially to Canada and the United States. Between 1845 and 1855 the 'famine ships' took an estimated 1.5 million emigrants to the USA alone, many of them poor Catholic Irish from the southern and western districts worst affected by the potato blight. Population was reduced by more tragically direct means too. There is no agreed total for the number of deaths attributable to the crop failures, whether from actual starvation or from lessened resistance to disease. Estimates suggest, however, that as many as 1–1.5 million excess deaths might have occurred during the years 1845–51. By the time of the 1851 census the population of Ireland had been reduced by death and emigration by almost a quarter compared with the 1841 figure, from 8.2 to 6.5 million.

The famine was a seminal event in Irish history. It led to far-reaching changes in the structure of Irish society and was responsible for the enlarged 'Irish diaspora' of the mid-nineteenth century. Its legacy burned deep into the Irish memory. The causes of the famine have been variously interpreted.[28] Some contemporaries saw it as an act of God, a form of divine retribution on a sinful people. Others have categorized it as a natural, ecological disaster, made worse by the over-dependence of the Irish peasantry on the potato and by the pressure of population growth on the island's strained agricultural and economic resources. Yet both in the 1840s and subsequently, there have been those who have argued that the famine was the product of a more deliberate human agency: that it occurred as a consequence of Ireland's political subordination to Britain, perhaps even because of an active policy of 'genocide' on the part of the British state. Even historians who would not necessarily endorse the perception of the famine as a British-induced 'holocaust' have expressed the view that, while the potato blight was 'unavoidable', 'the Great Famine was largely the result of Ireland's colonial status and grossly inequitable social system'.[29] In other words, God or nature may have sent the disease that killed the potatoes, but it was the British connection that turned blight into famine because the British government allowed Ireland to starve.

The charge is not only an emotive one. It goes to the heart of questions about the Anglo-Irish relationship within the British state in the early nineteenth century. To say that the British government ignored the evolving catastrophe in Ireland would be untrue. Although the authorities in London and Dublin were slow to appreciate the scale of the problem, when realization began to dawn Peel's government responded immediately. An expert commission of inquiry was appointed and £100,000 of grain was purchased on the American market to provide emergency food supplies.[30] Peel's decision to push ahead with the repeal of the Corn Laws, despite the rift that this created in his own party, was precipitated by the need to address the Irish crisis. The Whig government which succeeded Peel used a variety of expedients to provide relief for those most seriously affected by the destruction of crops. A programme of public works between October 1846 and March 1847 offered temporary employment to 750,000 labourers to enable them to earn money to buy food. This scheme was replaced by the direct provision of food through 'soup kitchens' set up under the Destitute Poor (Ireland) Act of 1847. By July 1847 up to three million meals a day were being distributed by local relief committees funded through government loans supplemented by private charity and the efforts of non-governmental agencies such as the Quakers. The soup kitchen experiment was wound up in September 1847, though by then a more institutionalized solution to the problem of distress had been introduced in the form of the Irish Poor Law Extension Act, which led to the Irish Poor Law authorities giving relief to over a million applicants by the summer of 1849, when the famine was entering its final phase.

Individual facets of these policies can be criticized. Plainly they were inadequate to prevent the deaths and social devastation that occurred. But could more have been done to alleviate distress, and is there any evidence that government measures, whether by inadvertance or design, made matters worse than they need have been? The answer to these questions must take into account the scientific, financial and administrative limitations of the early Victorian state and the background of poverty in Ireland itself. Nevertheless, in other parts of the United Kingdom, notably in the Scottish Highlands where the potato blight also struck in 1845–49 (admittedly over a smaller area), more effective steps were taken to avert mass starvation.[31] While various initiatives were attempted in Ireland, they were palliative only. This was partly because of the difficulties of the Irish situation: poor communications, less developed local administration, and the sheer scale of the misery that had to be dealt with. But other factors were involved as well. Particularly after the advent of the Whig government in 1846, adherence to the economic ideology of laissez faire prevented interference with the export of food from Ireland even during the 'starvation year' of 1847. In the long run the government, and key civil servants like the permanent secretary to the Treasury, Charles Trevelyan, undoubtedly saw the commercialization of agriculture as the solution to Ireland's difficulties. They were reluctant to impede the operation of the free market, and the crisis of the 1840s provided an opportunity to accelerate the transition from subsistence farming. This is not to say that Irish peasants were purposely starved as a consequence, but they were seen all the same as symbolizing an outmoded and inefficient way of life. This, coupled with a more racist view of the Irish poor as uncivilized savages, which was common among educated opinion in Britain, may have earned Ireland less sympathetic treatment from the government that any area of the British mainland would have received.

There is an irony here which was not without its relevance for the future. The 'modernizing' attitude of the Whigs, which saw the demise of subsistence agriculture as beneficial even if it entailed short-term suffering, was intended to facilitate the closer integration of Britain and Ireland within the United Kingdom by making the two countries more alike. Yet in the methods by which they sought to achieve their ends they emphasized the incompleteness of the Union and drove a great wedge of bitterness into its operation. Both the soup kitchens of 1847 and the Poor Law reforms were to be funded ultimately by Ireland alone (a policy of making 'Irish property pay for

Irish poverty'). Support from the British government might have helped to foster more pro-Union sentiment, but it was not forthcoming. Meanwhile the extent to which responses to the famine were determined in London rather than Dublin highlighted the political weaknesses from the Irish point of view of being a subordinate component of the British state. The events of the 1840s demonstrated that whereas the different parts of Britain were becoming more completely integrated into a single, interdependent political and economic community, Ireland's relationship with the rest of the Union was at best one of semi-detachment. The experience of the famine did not make it inevitable that the Union would be broken, but it did make it more difficult for the Union to succeed. It remained to be seen, in the second half of the nineteenth century, whether as Ireland underwent further economic and social change it would be drawn more firmly into the British orbit, or whether the centrifugal tendencies of political nationalism would assert themselves even more strongly, thus mounting a renewed challenge to the structures and unity of the British state.

CHAPTER 3

THE CHALLENGE OF NATIONALISM, 1850–1900

I n European history, the late nineteenth century has been termed the 'age of nationalism'. Between the revolutions of 1848 and the outbreak of the First World War in 1914 nationalist ideas and nationalist movements became a major force in shaping the internal politics of European states and their external relations with other powers. In the international sphere, nationalism manifested itself in escalating economic, imperial and military rivalries. Domestically it presented a dual aspect. Where it could be identified with an existing or newly created state structure – as in France, or the emergent Great Powers of Italy and Germany – nationalism had a unifying effect, which tended to consolidate the authority of the state and entrench the position of ruling elites. Elsewhere, most notably in the Austro-Hungarian Empire, where a variety of national and ethnic groups competed for recognition and precedence, it exerted a more disruptive, centrifugal pull. The United Kingdom reflected both facets of this duality. Britain's imperial nationalism will be considered more fully in the next chapter. Here the focus will be on the rise of internal nationalisms within the British Isles, their impact upon the politics of the British state and their importance in relation to British society and culture as these were developing in the late Victorian period.

The rise of nationalism in Ireland, Scotland and Wales

The development of nationalism – as opposed to any more generally diffused sense of national consciousness or identity – in any of the constituent parts of the United Kingdom before the 1850s was, as has been seen, limited. Only in Ireland had the beginnings of a political nationalist movement been laid down, in the legacy of Wolfe Tone and the United Irishmen and the subsequent activities and writings of

the Young Ireland movement of the 1840s. Even then, nationalism as
an ideologically coherent, articulated body of opinion was a minority
tendency. O'Connell's mass agitations, including that for Repeal in
the 1840s, were not explicitly nationalist, and can be seen rather as a
continuation of earlier radical campaigns for parliamentary reform.[1]
Elsewhere in the United Kingdom nationalism was still less well
advanced. England had a historic and cultural identity, but no
nationalism. Neither Scotland nor Wales had developed nationalist
movements: the one because it was a fairly complacent component of
the British state, in which Scots and English cooperated on equal
terms, the other because its political structures had not yet reached
the point where nationalism could find proper expression. There
were defiant assertions of political Welshness in the Merthyr riots of
1831 and the Chartist Newport rising of 1839,[2] but neither in Wales
nor Scotland was there an insurrectionary, revolutionary nationalist
tradition on the Irish model. In 1848, when other parts of Europe
were experiencing nationalist-inspired revolutions in the 'springtime
of peoples', Ireland's only rising was pathetically abortive, while in
Scotland and Wales there were seemingly few who heard the nation's
call. Britain, almost alone of the European states, appeared immune
to the disruptive aspects of the nationalist contagion, representing an
alternative spirit of the age based on the creation of a modern,
centralized industrial state in which, if anything, pride in Britishness
and British achievements outweighed local or regional loyalties.[3]

Yet Britain's isolation from European trends was more apparent
than real. In the half-century after 1850 nationalism emerged as a
potentially disruptive political issue in the multi-national British
imperium just as it did in Austria-Hungary or the Russian and Turkish
empires. This was most obviously the case in Ireland where, from the
1860s, an increasingly strong nationalist movement took hold, in both
revolutionary and constitutional forms, supported by the large
expatriate Irish community in the United States. The 'Irish Question'
became a prominent, and at times decisive, feature of British politics,
from the debates over the disestablishment of the Irish Church in the
1860s to the crisis over Home Rule in the 1880s. But Ireland was not
alone in the challenge it presented to the British state. In Scotland,
and more particularly in Wales, by the 1870s and 1880s there were
stirrings of political nationalism, coupled with growing resistance to
the centralizing and Anglicizing trends inherent in the Victorian
expansion of government. There were differences as well as similarities in the Irish, Scottish and Welsh situations, but they had sufficient

features in common for them to be seen as part of a general reaction against the unitary nature of the British state and a test of its ability to satisfy or reconcile the aspirations of a variety of potentially competing national groups.

The origins of political nationalism were diverse. Nationalist movements drew their strength in part from a developed sense of cultural nationhood, in part from specific grievances that emphasized aspects of national identity or highlighted a source of conflict between subordinate national regions and the central government of the state or the institutions of an occupying power. In the British and Irish context, perhaps the most powerful focus both of identity and grievance was religion. For example, while the nationalism that developed in Ireland between the 1790s and the 1840s was not religiously exclusive – indeed, Wolfe Tone and the Young Irelanders saw nationalism as an ideology that could bridge the sectarian divide, and many leading nationalists were themselves Protestants – mass nationalism in the nineteenth century became increasingly bound up with the movement for Catholic rights. Even after emancipation, Catholic grievances remained a powerful motor for national agitation, aimed against the established 'alien' Church of Ireland and the threat that government-sponsored non-denominational elementary education posed to the culture of the Catholic majority. In 1864 the Catholic hierarchy, led by Archbishop Cullen, directly entered the political arena by forming the National Association of Ireland, which had the disestablishment of the Church of Ireland as its first objective. Admittedly the extent to which this body was nationalist can be questioned: it allied itself with British Liberals and its political purpose in Ireland was partly to rally moderate support in opposition to the more violent nationalism of the Fenians. But the demand for disestablishment amounted to a demand for 'home rule' in matters of religion, and identified the Catholic Church as a force for constitutional and political change. Moreover, although Gladstone's government did disestablish the Irish Church in 1869, the Liberals' preference for non-sectarian over denominational education (embodied in the unsuccessful Irish Universities Bill of 1873) emphasized the difficulty of realizing Catholic aspirations within the framework of what was still effectively a Protestant state and led to the collapse of the Liberal–Catholic alliance before the general election of 1874. In the later nineteenth century the Catholic Church became more unequivocally supportive of Irish nationalism, while the nationalist movement acquired a more pronounced Catholic orientation.

In Scotland the connection between religion and nationalism was more oblique, though not necessarily less significant. It lacked the sharp edge of grievance that marked the Irish case, since Scotland had its own Presbyterian Church establishment. The Kirk, as has been noted, was one of the foundation pillars of Scottish national identity in the post-Union period. When the Church of Scotland split in the Disruption of 1843 this was primarily the result of a disagreement between Scotsmen, and divisions within the Scottish ecclesiastical community, rather than of a conflict between a Scottish majority and a minority alien Church. Yet the Disruption affected perceptions of Scottish nationhood in two important ways. First, the fissure that it created in the hitherto 'national' Church focused attention on the problem of preserving a measure of institutional unity for Scotland within the British state. This was an issue that went beyond the purely religious, because of the way in which the General Assembly of the Kirk had acted almost as a surrogate parliament and because of the key role which the Church played as a provider of education, poor relief and other social services. With the Presbyterian community divided between the Church of Scotland, the rival Free Church and the separate United Presbyterians, the authority of the Kirk was weakened and a central unifying feature of Scottish life was removed.

The events of 1843 had a further consequence as well, which bore more directly on Scotland's British connection. The Disruption arose out of a conflict between the moderate and evangelical wings of the Church of Scotland, but the principal issue of dispute was that of lay patronage, the question of whether landlords should have the right to place ministers against the wishes of local presbyteries. This right had been guaranteed in law by the Patronage Act of 1712 (which many Scots saw as a violation of the terms of the Act of Union) and upheld by the Scottish courts and the British House of Lords, even in the face of a 'Veto Act' (to give presbyteries the right to veto appointments) passed by the General Assembly in 1834. In that sense, when the evangelicals withdrew from the General Assembly in 1843 they were doing so not only in opposition to the moderate establishment of the Church itself, but also to the House of Lords and Peel's government which had refused to amend the law in conformity with the General Assembly's wishes. Unlike the more radical United Presbyterians, the Free Church did not immediately press for disestablishment of the Church of Scotland. Nevertheless, there was increased disquiet at the way in which Scottish affairs were subject to ultimate regulation by an English-dominated state, with Anglican bishops in the House of Lords as part of its legislative machinery. As the state extended its role in Scottish life, discontent was likely to increase, although ironically it was Disraeli's decision in 1874 to abolish lay patronage as part of an attempt to consolidate Conservative support in Scotland that roused the real anger of the Free Church and persuaded them to throw their weight behind the disestablishment campaign in the 1880s.[4]

In Wales the correlation between religious grievance and the rise of nationalism was much more explicit. Like Ireland before 1870, Wales had a religious establishment that represented only a minority of the population. The religious census of 1851 had demonstrated that 80 per cent of worshippers were Nonconformists, most of them belonging to one of the four principal denominations of Calvinistic Methodists, Baptists, Congregationalists and Independents.[5] Yet the Anglican Church in Wales not only enjoyed the historical status of an established Church, but its privileges and influence extended over many areas of Welsh life, including education (provided largely in Church schools) and the controversial right to levy tithe payments. In reality the Anglican Church was not wholly an alien implant. Although Welsh bishops in the early Victorian period were notorious for their inability to speak Welsh, many ordinary clergy were of Welsh origin and committed to the Welsh language and Welsh culture. Nevertheless, Nonconformists – in a manner similar to Irish Catholics – were able to appropriate the national standard for their own purposes. The disestablishment of the Welsh Church provided the rallying point for early nationalist agitation, coordinated by the pro-disestablishment Liberation Society which in the 1850s and 1860s became the prime vehicle for mobilizing Nonconformist-nationalist sentiment.[6] One of the successes of the campaign was the election of the Nonconformist Henry Richard as MP for Merthyr in 1868.[7] Richard's declaration that 'the Nonconformists of Wales are the People of Wales' emphasized the link between religious denominationalism and nationalist sentiment, a link reinforced by a burgeoning and largely Welsh-language Nonconformist newspaper and periodical press and by the key role that the Nonconformist chapels played in the popular cultural life of Wales in the late nineteenth century – in rural areas and in the teeming industrial communities of the south Wales valleys alike. Significantly it was also from the same Nonconformist religious-intellectual milieu that the main leaders of the Welsh nationalist movement in the late Victorian period were drawn.[8]

Religion was not of course the only issue to fuel nationalist grievance. Economic and social discontent was another recruiting sergeant for the nationalist cause, particularly in the rural areas of Ireland, Scotland and Wales where it was exacerbated by the onset of agricultural depression in the 1870s. The 'Land Question', it is true, had a wider political importance throughout the United Kingdom, not least because of the impact of the ideas of the American land reformer Henry George, whose proposals for a radical taxation of land values were popularized in his book *Progress and Poverty* (1879), in his lecture tours of Britain and Ireland in the early 1880s and in the work of various land reform and land nationalization societies. Already the growth of Joseph Arch's National Union of Agricultural Labourers had illustrated the tensions that existed in the English countryside between farmers and their workers, and English radicals like Joseph Chamberlain made land reform a major plank of their political platform. Even so, the land question outside England had a political dimension that was lacking in the English case. This was partly because of the greater importance of agriculture in the economies of Ireland, mid and north Wales and the Highlands of Scotland, and partly because the agricultural economies of those areas were structured differently from those of England, with the crucial conflict of interest being between landlords and tenant farmers rather than between farmers and an essentially proletarianized labour force. More particularly, the landlord–tenant relationship was often complicated by differences of religion and language as well as those of social class, and tenant farmers or Scottish crofters could see themselves struggling to preserve a traditional way of life against the pressures of Anglicization and modernization as well as seeking help from a British state that seemed to be either reluctant to respond to the needs of peripheral areas or too much in the pocket of the landowners to take the needs of their tenants into account.

The land problem had been at its most acute in one sense in the Ireland of the 1840s. In the wake of the famine a substantial restructuring of landholding took place, with a reduction in the number and increase in the average size of holdings and a transfer of land ownership away from impoverished landlords who took advantage of the Encumbered Estates Act of 1849 to sell to new owners.[9] The 1850s and 1860s were a period of diversification – including a switch from arable to pastoral farming – and modest prosperity, as the peasant-dominated countryside of the pre-famine era gave way to more modern patterns of land use. Yet discontent remained. Tenant farmers, especially in the south and west of Ireland, resented the lack of any mechanism for fixing 'fair' rents and the ease with which they could be deprived of their holdings without any compensation for improvements they had made. These grievances gave rise to the Tenant Right movement of the 1850s, which received some support from the Catholic politicians of the National Association. Gladstone's Irish Land Act of 1870 partly addressed the farmers' concerns, but left others unresolved. Then, in the late 1870s, Ireland, in common with the rest of the United Kingdom, was hit hard by the agricultural depression. Prices fell, rent arrears built up and the number of evictions soared (to over 10,000 in 1879 alone). Farmers responded by joining together to resist what they saw as the harshness of the landlords, and it was in these circumstances that the Irish Land League was born.

The Land League was organized throughout Ireland from the summer of 1879 by Michael Davitt, although it was less well supported in Ulster than in the rest of the country. It waged a campaign against rent rises and evictions, using the weapons of intimidation and boycott against those who took over farms from evicted tenants. What is significant for present purposes, however, is the alliance that was forged between the Land League and the political wing of the Irish nationalist movement.[10] Davitt himself was a convinced nationalist, having been a member of the Fenian Brotherhood and in 1882 becoming a Nationalist MP. He enlisted the support of Charles Stewart Parnell, the leader of the Irish Parliamentary Party, who became the Land League's president. The confluence of personnel reflected a deeper underlying convergence, involving Irish-America as well as Irish-based nationalist groups. Indeed, the 'Land War' of 1879–82 was the product of a consciously coordinated 'New Departure' by nationalist forces in Ireland and America, which sought to use economic agitation as a vehicle for raising nationalist consciousness in Ireland. The strategy seems to have achieved some success. While the land agitation died away after the introduction of Gladstone's 1881 Irish Land Act (which established tribunals for deciding fair rents and extended tenants' rights over tenure and compensation for improvements – the so-called 'three fs'), the organizational structure of the Land League had drawn large numbers of people into political activity, and many of these transferred their allegiance to the Land League's successor, the Irish National League, established in 1882. Thus, even after the problems of rural Ireland had been addressed by legislators, the impetus imparted to nationalist politics by the land question continued to be felt.

In Wales and Scotland similar patterns can be discerned, albeit on a smaller scale. Welsh tenant farmers suffered some of the same problems as their Irish counterparts, aggravated in their case by religious and social grievances such as the payment of tithes to an Anglican establishment that was seen by the mainly Nonconformist Welsh farmers as having a particular affinity with the landlord class. Encouraged by the Irish example, in the mid-1880s they set up a Welsh Land League and launched a militant protest that became known as the 'tithe war'. The government finally responded by appointing a commission to inquire into the land question in Wales in 1893, but in the meantime the land campaign had added a further strand to the Nonconformist nationalism which was a growing feature of the Welsh political scene.

In Scotland too, the radical land reform movement took on a nationalist tinge. Here it was the crofters of the Highlands and Islands of western Scotland who provided the nucleus of unrest, their rearguard action against the long-term effects of the Clearances given fresh urgency by the depression of the late 1870s and the spread of Georgite ideas of land reform. Discontent spilled over into violent protest in outbreaks such as the 'Battle of the Braes' on Skye in 1882. At the general election of 1885 the crofters carried their protest to the ballot box, five independent MPs being elected to form a separate 'Crofters' Party' at Westminster.[11] Gladstone's Liberal government was sufficiently alarmed by this display of Highland spirit to rush a Scottish Land Act on to the statute book giving the crofters the same forms of legal protection already extended to tenant farmers in Ireland. As a result, the land question lost some of its urgency, but the problems of Highland communities provided sympathetic territory for political nationalism and many of the leaders of the land movement became active in the subsequent campaign for Scottish Home Rule.

However, specific grievances of this sort, while they may have reinforced a more widespread feeling that the interests of 'peripheral' regions were being neglected by the central institutions of the British state, do not wholly explain the emergence of nationalism – as opposed to more localized forms of regional or group protest – as a political force. In transforming a raft of grievances into 'nationalism' there were other underlying factors at work. Most obviously, the late nineteenth century was marked by a growing sense of national identity – of cultural nationalisms that could be translated into political forms. The countries of the British Isles were here being influenced by trends that were European in scope. As has been seen, the period of the French Revolution gave rise to romantic nationalism, with its rediscovery of national languages, histories and cultures, as well as to nationalistically inclined liberation movements. In the early nineteenth century the ideology of nationalism was developed by figures such as Mazzini, and in the revolutions of 1848 nationalism had been a factor in risings across the Continent.[12] Thereafter the nationalist tide divided into two streams. In Italy and Germany, once national unification had been achieved, nationalism became identified with the new state structures. Through much of the rest of Europe it remained a cultural-political movement that embodied the aspirations of 'subject' peoples for eventual statehood, or at least for national institutions that could affirm the historic status to which they felt themselves entitled. In some cases this led to early campaigns for political autonomy. Elsewhere the focus was rather on movements to secure equal rights for national languages, separate educational or religious establishments or the celebration of national traditions in literature, music and the arts. Idealized versions of the nation's past were embroidered into a 'national myth', which extolled the virtues of past greatness (real or imagined) or of particular historic figures in the national pantheon. Established nations and aspiring ones were alike in participating in this process of what has been described as 'the invention of tradition',[13] although the traditions which they invented were more likely to be conflicting than complementary.

This process of rediscovering, or re-inventing, the past was taking place in Britain and Ireland as it was in other parts of Europe, and its effect was to direct attention to the separate histories of the 'four nations' of the British Isles and to the differences between them as opposed to their common heritage. In England, historians were emphasizing the importance of the evolution of institutions such as parliament and the monarchy as central to the development of an English nation-state which was taken to subsume other parts of the British polity. As a counterweight to this, however, from the 1860s onwards, there was growing recognition of the existence of a 'Celtic' identity which supposedly highlighted the differences between the Welsh, Irish and Scots on the one side and the 'Saxon' English on the other.[14] Cultural nationalist movements were an increasingly prominent feature of the late nineteenth century. The Irish 'Gaelic revival' of the 1880s and 1890s – promoted by organizations like the Gaelic

Athletic Association and the Gaelic League – attempted to reverse the decline of the Irish language and to boost the popularity of 'traditional' Gaelic sports and pastimes. Gaelic societies were founded in Scotland (led by that of Inverness in 1871), and the Crofter movement of the 1880s can be seen as a cultural movement as well as one of economic protest.[15] Similarly, the formation of the Society for the Utilization of the Welsh Language in 1885 was part of a more widespread cultural reawakening in Wales which found its fullest expression in the success of the popular Cymru Fydd ('Young Wales') movement, in the campaign for educational improvement and in the flourishing musical and literary world of the *eisteddfodau*, which were as important to the national life of the country as was its Nonconformist chapel culture. Also characteristic of the renewed consciousness of national identity was a heightened interest in the nation's past, and the writings of historians and other scholars were instrumental in creating a sense of heritage and national pride. The 'Young Irelanders' had published 'nationalist' histories in the 1840s. At a more scholarly level, a writer such as J.E. Lloyd (whose magnum opus on the history of Wales before 1282 was published in 1911) analysed past periods of political autonomy in ways that could assume added significance in the context of contemporary debates about devolution and Home Rule. The link between past history and present sentiment was illustrated by moves to commemorate national heroes, most notably the erection of the Wallace monument outside Stirling in the 1860s to serve as a reminder of an earlier, ultimately successful struggle for Scottish independence.

Nationalist movements were the product of social and political, no less than cultural and intellectual, change. One particular social phenomenon of the nineteenth century – across Europe, and not in Britain alone – was the growth of the middle classes. It was from among these groups, particularly from the expanding professional strata of teachers, lawyers and ministers of religion, that nationalist movements drew most of their leadership and inspiration – partly because of the affinities between nationalism and middle-class liberalism as creeds of emancipation and reform, and partly because the espousal of 'national' causes gave individual members of the middle classes an opportunity to pursue sectional grievances against existing aristocratic and landed elites under cover of a more democratic agenda. But the working classes of the towns and cities were touched by similar trends. The spread of education and literacy, coupled with the formation of new urban communities and the coming of mass communication, created a constituency for nationalist ideas that went beyond the boundaries of the middle class. In Scotland and Wales certainly, perhaps to a lesser extent in Ireland, there were traditions of working-class self-improvement that placed working men and women in touch with the literary and historical debates of the day and involved them in the cultural nationalist movement. For example, the campaign to establish a national university in Wales, which was centred on the founding of the 'College by the sea' at Aberystwyth in 1872, was supported by communities throughout Wales, with many individual donations from members of the working class. The industrial communities of Scotland and Wales demonstrated their burgeoning sense of national identity in other ways too, especially through sport and other forms of popular culture. J.G. Kellas has expressed the view that in Scotland 'working class nationalism is generally related to culture and football, not politics',[16] and it is true that Scotland established a national footballing identity through the setting up of its own Football Association and football league in the 1870s and 1880s. Unity was threatened by sectarian rivalries, such as those between the Protestant followers of Glasgow Rangers and the Catholic supporters of Glasgow Celtic. But the institution of 'international' matches between Scotland and the 'auld enemy', England, from 1872 brought even these conflicting groups into accord. In Wales the rugby field and the choral society took the place of football as touchstones of national identity and became the foci of a competitive international spirit, with victories of the Welsh rugby team over the English or successes gained against English choirs giving a lift to communal self-confidence and national pride.[17]

The translation of social and cultural nationalism into political movements was made possible by the democratization of the political system and the emergence of new forms of mass politics. The Reform Acts of 1867 and 1884 extended the franchise throughout the United Kingdom, so that by the mid-1880s two out of three adult males had the right to vote in parliamentary elections. A further Act of 1872 introduced the secret ballot for elections, while the Corrupt Practices Act of 1883 imposed limits on constituency expenditure during election campaigns. The combined effect of these measures was twofold. First, by extending the vote, they enabled groups like the Welsh Nonconformists and Irish Catholics to bring their numerical strength to bear on the political process. Secondly, the influence of landed and propertied elites was reduced, and voters could exercise their franchise without fear of eviction or intimidation – something of especial significance in rural areas covered by the legislation of 1884. Politics in consequence assumed a more genuinely popular, if not yet wholly democratic, form, and discontented groups, communities and regions were able to gain representation for their interests at parliamentary level. The success of the Crofters' Party in the mid-1880s was one instance of this trend. Many of its members were reabsorbed into mainstream Liberal-radical politics, but others went on to join the Scottish Labour Party on its formation in 1888. A more significant demonstration of the potential of democratization to assist the nationalist cause was provided by Welsh political Nonconformity. Although Welsh MPs operated within the broader structures of British Liberalism, by the late 1880s they had formed a distinct 'Welsh party' in the Liberal Party at Westminster to act as a pressure group for Welsh nationalist demands.[18] The Irish nationalists, aided immensely by the quadrupling of the Irish county electorate following the 1884 Reform Act, went further still, establishing an Irish Parliamentary Party fully independent of the British party machines and supported in Ireland by the grassroots organization of the Irish National League.

It was the electoral success of the Irish Nationalists in particular that brought nationalism to the forefront of British politics in the 1880s and precipitated a constitutional and political crisis in the British state. From the election of 86 Irish Nationalist MPs in 1885, intermittently for the next three decades the Nationalist demand for 'Home Rule' was to be at the heart of the debate over how Britain was to be governed and what the future constitutional structure of the United Kingdom should be. The origins, details and ramifications of the Home Rule debate therefore deserve consideration in their own right.

Home Rule and the British state

The controversy that erupted over Home Rule in the mid-1880s had two separate aspects. It was a debate about how the British state could best be governed, in particular about whether a devolution of power from Westminster to a subordinate legislature in Ireland, and possibly to parliaments in Scotland and Wales, would improve the efficiency of government in the United Kingdom as a whole. It was also a debate about how best to respond to the challenge of domestic nationalisms, especially in Ireland, and the question of how, or even whether, the Union could be preserved in the face of devolutionary and separatist pressures. These two questions were further complicated by three additional factors: the interaction between the politics of Home Rule/devolution and the party and parliamentary politics of the existing United Kingdom state; the maze of legal, jurisdictional and fiscal difficulties that arose from the incremental way in which the British state had developed without a comprehensive written constitution; and the fact that Home Rule was part of a broader process of democratization, which included a major reform of parliamentary representation in 1884–85, extensions of representative local government in 1888–89 and 1894 in England, Scotland and Wales (1898 in Ireland), and growing pressure for a reduction in the powers of the House of Lords. Add to this the perceived connection in many political minds between the future constitution of the United Kingdom and the future of Britain's overseas empire, together with the upsurge of domestic social and labour unrest simultaneous with the rise of radical nationalism, and it will be seen that the politics of the British state were entering a period of turmoil and redefinition paralleled in the nineteenth century only by the earlier 'Reform crisis' of 1829–32.

It was events in Ireland that gave the Home Rule debate its early impetus. Ireland was the one part of the United Kingdom that had an historically recent experience of legislative devolution, in the form of 'Grattan's parliament' of 1783–1800. In the nineteenth century, the continued existence of a separate Irish administration highlighted Ireland's distinctive constitutional status, and also the anomalous state of affairs under which the actions of that devolved administration could be scrutinized only by the imperial parliament at Westminster rather than by an indigenous Irish legislature. This situation emphasized to many Irishmen the essentially 'colonial' condition of their country and, alongside the desire for better government per se, was a constant spur to constitutional reform. O'Connell's Repeal campaign of the 1840s did not seek full Irish independence, but it did aim to secure the restoration of an Irish parliament to deal with Irish affairs. Although there were variations of detail with later schemes, this remained the objective of those who in 1870 joined with Isaac Butt to found the Irish Home Government Association, which in 1873 became the Irish Home Rule League. Butt, a Protestant lawyer and former Tory MP, was perhaps an unlikely leader for what in the 1880s was to become a largely Catholic mass movement. Yet the very moderation of its prominent figures enabled the Home Rule League to win support from a cross-section of Ireland's political elite. At the general election of 1874, 59 Irish MPs were returned under the 'Home Rule' label, a figure that rose to 65 in 1880. By then Butt had been replaced as leader of the parliamentary party by the charismatic Parnell, who forged alliances between the Irish MPs and the broader nationalist movement, especially the forces of rural unrest represented by the Land League and the Irish-American community in the United States. Under Parnell's leadership the Home Rule MPs became a more tightly disciplined parliamentary force, capable of harrying Gladstone's Liberal government and systematically obstructing the work of the House of Commons. Through the grassroots organization of the Irish National League (which had 1200 branches by 1885) the Parnellites were poised to become the dominant electoral presence in Ireland once the franchise had been extended in 1884.

However, the emergence of a parliamentary Nationalist Party was not the only reason why the governance of Ireland was coming under scrutiny in the 1880s. There were also worrying signs that the existing structures of government were beginning to break down. Irish society was traditionally violent, with deep-rooted sectarian conflicts that frequently spilled over into rioting and rural 'outrages' involving arson, cattle-maiming and attacks on landlords and their property. Disorder was endemic, and only partly kept in check by the police and by the Crimes or 'Coercion' Acts employed by successive governments. In the late 1870s and early 1880s rural violence reached new peaks: 863 'outrages' were recorded in 1879, 2590 in 1880; there were 67 murders of landlords and their agents between 1879 and 1882.[19] Nor was this all. Behind the outbreaks of rural violence and sectarian rioting a more organized, political, form of terrorism was at work. The Fenians had carried out bombing campaigns in England and attempted a rising in Ireland in the 1860s. Fenianism was still a presence in the Land War of 1879–82. Terrorist splinter groups like the 'Invincibles' scored high-profile successes with acts such as the Phoenix Park murders of 1882, in which Lord Frederick Cavendish, the newly appointed chief secretary, was assassinated. There were further bomb attacks on English targets in 1883–84, to counter which the Special (Irish) Branch was set up by Scotland Yard. Even though the level of violence in Ireland itself declined after the settlement of the land question in 1881 and the discontinuation of the Land League's campaign in 1882, it still appeared as if Ireland might remain ungovernable by normal means without some basic reform of political structures that would enable an Irish executive to rule by consent rather than force.

This much was only gradually acknowledged by a section of the British political elite. Since his first election as prime minister in 1868 Gladstone had declared it to be his 'mission' to 'pacify Ireland', and he had attempted to redeem his pledge through measures of Church disestablishment, education and land reform. In 1882 he negotiated directly with Parnell (the so-called 'Kilmainham Treaty') in a bid to secure acceptance of his reforms and restore order in the countryside. Yet in political terms he still saw Ireland as exhibiting 'local patriotism' rather than fully fledged nationalism. The most that his government was prepared to offer by way of constitutional change, therefore, was the enactment of local government reform through the establishment of provincial councils or an 'Irish Central Board' with local government functions. Both schemes were rejected as inadequate by Parnell, who was beginning to sense the reinforcement of his electoral strength that would follow the 1884 Reform Act and the opportunities that might consequently arise to negotiate with whichever of the British parties most needed his support. His minimum demands were set out in a speech at Cork in January 1885 on 'the great question of national self-government for Ireland'. The least that he and his followers could ask for would be the restoration of 'Grattan's parliament', but even this, he hinted, in words that delighted his audience, might be only a first step in the 'progress of Ireland's nationhood', for 'no man has the right to fix the boundary to the march of a nation. ... No man has the right to say to his country, "Thus far and no further".'[20]

Parnell's political opportunity came as a result of a British political crisis. By early 1885 Gladstone's government was in trouble and its parliamentary position was disintegrating. In May the Irish Nationalists were able to combine with the Conservatives to defeat the government over its budget proposals, and Lord Salisbury formed a minority Conservative administration pending the preparation of a new electoral register. In its brief term of office the Salisbury government introduced an important Irish Land Act (providing £5 million for land purchase loans for tenant farmers). More tantalizingly for Parnell, the new lord lieutenant, Lord Carnarvon, made sympathetic noises in private about the possibility of Home Rule. This was enough to cause Parnell to advise Nationalist supporters in Britain to vote Conservative at the ensuing general election, after which the 86 Nationalist MPs were left holding the balance at Westminster between the minority Conservative government and the larger Liberal opposition. Here, however, Parnell's strategy of auctioning his support to the highest bidder came unstuck, since Salisbury and the rest of his cabinet overruled Carnarvon's tentative endorsement of Home Rule. Meanwhile Gladstone had been converted to the idea, a fact which was leaked to the newspapers by his son and private secretary Herbert by means of the celebrated 'Hawarden kite' in December. Gladstone's motives, and the reasons for his conversion, have been the subject of considerable speculation. The effect of the announcement was nevertheless clear. The Conservatives were confirmed in their anti-Home Rule stance, throwing Parnell into Gladstone's arms. In January 1886 Liberals and Nationalists combined to defeat Salisbury's government on an amendment to the Address, whereupon Salisbury resigned and Gladstone was called to form his third ministry, with Ireland once again at the top of his political agenda.

The short parliamentary session of 1886 was dominated by the introduction and eventual defeat of Gladstone's first Irish Home Rule Bill. When it was presented to the Commons in April the Bill proposed the creation of a parliament in Dublin which would have a total membership of 307, divided into two 'Orders'. The first Order would consist of the 28 Irish representative peers from the House of Lords, plus 75 elected members serving ten-year terms, chosen by the propertied classes. The second Order would comprise the 103 Irish MPs, together with a further 101 representatives elected on the normal parliamentary franchise. The two Orders would sit and debate together, but could vote separately, and the members of the first Order were given what amounted to a suspensory veto over legislation. Irish MPs and peers would meanwhile be removed from Westminster, even though the imperial parliament would retain control over defence and foreign affairs, currency issues, posts and telegraphs, and matters relating to the royal succession, honours and titles, and the treason laws. The Irish parliament would not be empowered to alter the Government of Ireland Act, to establish a new state Church, or to introduce protective tariffs. Nor, for an unspecified period, would it be given control over the Royal Irish Constabulary. Ireland would be expected to contribute a fixed proportion of one-fifteenth of the expenditure of the British state and would still be nominally governed by a lord lieutenant on behalf of the crown, although a separate Irish executive would be created which would be responsible to the Irish parliament and composed, in all likelihood, of members drawn from the majority party.[21]

From the outset, the measure had no realistic prospect of becoming law. Even its proponents admitted it was far from perfect, and Parnell and the Nationalists gave it at best a grudging welcome. The Conservatives were resolutely opposed, and their inbuilt majority in the House of Lords would have prevented the Bill from making any further progress even if it had been endorsed by the House of Commons. But the most crucial rifts at this stage were within the ruling Liberal Party itself. Lord Hartington, the principal leader of the party's Whig wing, had refused to join Gladstone's government when he knew that a Home Rule Bill was contemplated. Joseph Chamberlain, the party's leading radical, initially joined the government but resigned in March 1886 when the scale and nature of the measure was revealed to the cabinet. The two men together became the nucleus of opposition to the Bill on the Liberal benches, with the result that the party split in the vote on the Second Reading. Despite last-minute appeals from Gladstone, 93 Liberals voted against the Home Rule proposals, and the Bill was defeated by 343 votes to 313. This split was merely the prelude to a deeper division in the Liberal ranks. When, following the defeat of the Bill, Gladstone resigned and called a general election, he found himself opposed at the polls by many of his former colleagues. Although Gladstone retained the support of the official machinery of the party, including the National Liberal Federation, Chamberlain and Hartington improvised a separate 'Liberal Unionist' organization for Liberal MPs opposed to Home Rule. When the election was held, Gladstone and his followers suffered a resounding rebuff, winning only 191 seats.[22] The Nationalists retained their strength, but the combined totals of 314 Conservatives and 78 Liberal Unionists gave the anti-Home Rulers a large majority, and Salisbury formed a Conservative ministry with Liberal Unionist support.

The debates of 1886 demonstrated two things. The first was the difficulty of framing a workable solution to the problem of devolving parliamentary power in the context of what had hitherto been a unitary state. Under the proposed legislation, the Irish legislature would still have been constitutionally subordinate to Westminster (a status reflected in the reservation of powers and the inability of the Irish parliament to initiate constitutional change). Yet there was no clear mechanism by which that sovereignty on the part of Westminster could be exercised in practice, particularly if political conflicts

arose between the two assemblies – a not unlikely event if there was a
Nationalist majority in Dublin and a Conservative or Unionist one in
Britain. This was not merely an academic question, since disagreements on a range of issues could be foreseen, and indeed were made
more likely by other provisions of the Home Rule Bill. For example,
there was considerable criticism of the arrangements for Ireland's
financial contribution to the imperial exchequer. Parnell attacked the
proposal of one-fifteenth of imperial expenditure as too high; in any
case the arrangement left Dublin at the mercy of decisions about total
expenditure taken in London, with only limited means of regulating
the revenues of an Irish administration. The resolution of such
problems was made more difficult by the most contentious of all the
Bill's proposals, namely the removal of Irish representation from
Westminster. On one level the reasons behind the proposal are easily
understood: one of the aims of Home Rule on Gladstone's part was
to reduce obstruction in the House of Commons; it was also felt to
be anomalous that Irish MPs should be able to vote on British affairs
while British MPs would have no voice in those of Ireland. However,
the removal of Irish Members raised the spectre of 'taxation without
representation'. It also denied Ireland's elected representatives a say
in the foreign and imperial affairs of the United Kingdom (unless the
'Austro-Hungarian' solution of a joint Anglo-Irish ministerial council
was adopted). An 'in–out' solution, whereby Irish MPs would be
present for some debates but not others, was rejected as impractical,
not least because it would upset the arithmetic of government
majorities in the House of Commons. But the convolutions of the
argument emphasized the complexities of establishing devolved
representative government in any part of the United Kingdom and
were to surface again in every Home Rule debate over the next
century and more.[23]

In addition to these practical objections, the debates of 1886
showed that there was more deep-rooted opposition to the concept
of Home Rule irrespective of the form it took. This was based on a
mixture of prejudice and principle. Undoubtedly there was an
undertow of anti-Irish feeling, a mingling of racial and religious
bigotry, which was reluctant to concede that the Catholic Irish would
ever be capable of self-government. Equally there were more reasoned objections from those who believed that Home Rule would
lead inevitably to the separation of Ireland from Britain and so
precipitate the break-up of the Union. Politicians like Chamberlain
placed great emphasis on this 'thin end of the wedge' argument, and

made much of the possible consequences not just for the UK but for the future cohesion of the empire as well – a point leant weight by the founding of the Indian National Congress on a 'home rule' platform in 1885 and the strength of nationalist feeling in Egypt and among the Boers in South Africa. The imperial dimension of the Home Rule controversy became increasingly important, at least in Conservative propaganda. It had its counterpart in Ireland among the substantial minority who wished to preserve the Union in its existing form. This was especially true of Protestants in Ulster, though there was support for the Unionist position throughout Ireland and across the religious divide. Nevertheless, 1886 did raise the 'Ulster question' to a separate status within the wider controversy, and Unionists were encouraged in their opposition to Home Rule by Conservative politicians in Britain. Lord Randolph Churchill, in a speech at Belfast's Ulster Hall in January 1886, set the tone for this emotional bonding when he declared that if an attempt were made to force Home Rule on the 'loyalists' of Ulster, 'Ulster will fight, Ulster will be right; Ulster will emerge from the struggle victorious, because all that Ulster represents to us Britons will command the sympathy and support of an enormous section of our British community.'[24]

Churchill's words, with their hint of unplumbed depths of feeling on the Irish question, give a clue to the impact that the Home Rule controversy had on the domestic politics of the British state. In the crisis year of 1886 these were profound enough: the Liberal split, the fall of Gladstone's government and the defeat of the Liberals in the subsequent general election. The longer term effects were to be felt, however, well beyond the turn of the century. The Liberal party was seriously weakened by the departure of the anti-Home Rulers. Attempts at Liberal reunion in 1887 failed, and although Liberal fortunes revived briefly in the late 1880s they formed only one short minority ministry (in 1892–95) between 1886 and 1905. Even that was dominated by Gladstone's second Irish Home Rule Bill, which passed the Commons only to be unceremoniously thrown out by the .Lords. Meanwhile the Conservative–Liberal Unionist alliance was being consolidated to such an extent that the two parties formed a coalition in 1895, which held office for the next ten years. Obviously during that time other political issues obtruded, yet the realignment of parties that occurred after 1886 was largely the result of the Home Rule debate. The Home Rule–Unionist division that had become the basis of Irish politics after 1874 was effectively transferred to the United Kingdom as a whole. This was true in electoral as well as parliamentary terms, with the post-1885 electoral map of Britain showing almost two nations: a Conservative–Unionist England (especially in the south and east) and a Liberal–Nationalist Ireland, Wales and Scotland.[25] The divisions were not absolute, and were in any case much exaggerated by the first-past-the-post electoral system. The Liberals retained strong support in some urban, industrial areas of England; Unionism was a force in parts of Scotland and in Protestant Ulster. But the terminology and orientation of British politics had nonetheless undergone a significant shift, with important consequences for individual politicians, parties and the party system.

Perhaps unsurprisingly, the rise of the Nationalist Party in Ireland and the sudden prominence of the Home Rule question acted as a particular stimulus to nationalist and Home Rule movements in Scotland and Wales. In Scotland, as has been seen, political nationalism had been slow to develop. In the 1850s a short-lived National Association for the Vindication of Scottish Rights (founded in 1853) had drawn attention to Scotland's inadequate representation in the British parliament and to the absence of a separate Scottish secretary of state in the British government. The campaign for administrative and ministerial devolution had revived in the 1880s, and was partially rewarded by the appointment of a Scottish secretary and the establishment of a Scottish Office in 1885–86. The practical effect of these measures was limited. The Scottish secretaryship remained a junior post, and the Scottish Office was based in London rather than Edinburgh and had only very restricted powers and responsibilities. Certainly compared with what was being offered to Ireland they seemed very small beer. This feeling that Scotland was being treated as less deserving than Ireland, coupled with the grievances of groups like the crofters, largely accounts for the formation in 1886 of a new quasi-nationalist organization, the Scottish Home Rule Association, a body that differed from previous movements in two respects. First, its political orientation was definitely radical, whereas earlier movements (including the National Convention of 1884 which had mobilized support for a Scottish secretaryship) had been bipartisan, including Conservatives and Liberals alike. Secondly, for almost the first time since 1707, the restoration of a Scottish parliament was made the centrepiece of a political campaign. In the short term this did not develop the momentum of its Irish counterpart, and the SHRA acted as a pressure group rather than as an alternative to the existing parties, but its emergence helped to focus attention on Scottish Home Rule as a serious political issue.

In Wales, similarly, Home Rule crystallized as a political demand in the wake of the Irish example. The rise of Nonconformist radicalism as the dominant force in late Victorian Welsh Liberalism gave the Welsh 'national revival' a sharper political edge than the Scottish movement, and more akin to the Irish. The younger generation of Welsh MPs such as Tom Ellis, who was elected to represent Merioneth in 1886, and David Lloyd George, the victor in the Caernarfon Boroughs by-election in 1890, were proud to make the national question in its various forms the central focus of their brand of radical Liberal politics. Ellis, a product of the University College at Aberystwyth and New College, Oxford, was the intellectual leader of the Welsh MPs. His speeches and writings evoked the Celtic contribution to British history and the claims of Wales to national statehood.[26] Lloyd George – who, after Ellis's acceptance of office as Liberal whip in 1892, became the main spokesman for radical nationalism – was a more aggressive campaigning politician. In 1894 he led a revolt of Welsh MPs against the Liberal government because of the latter's failure to press ahead quickly enough with legislation for Welsh disestablishment. With three colleagues and a larger number of extra-parliamentary supporters, he attempted to use the Cymru Fydd organization to gain control of the Liberal Federations of north and south Wales, with the aim of subsuming both in a united body to campaign for Welsh self-government. The plan had some success in north Wales but faltered with the refusal of the south Wales Liberals to follow Lloyd George's lead and merge with their colleagues in the North. The Cymru Fydd campaign never recovered from this setback. The issue of Welsh Home Rule was revived periodically thereafter, but it never attained the centrality it had in the Irish nationalist movement and was always less important to the Welsh than issues such as disestablishment, education and even land reform.

Despite the failure of Home Rule campaigns to gather the same momentum in Scotland and Wales as they had in Ireland, they received sufficient support to show that the constitutional debate over the future of the British state went beyond the confines of what was referred to as the 'Irish Question'. The challenge of Irish nationalism was the most widespread but not the only national movement that the British government faced, and the constitutional arguments consequently acquired a British as well as an Irish dimension. Most politicians in Britain were agreed that their goal was the preservation of 'the Union', by which they meant the political integrity of the

United Kingdom. Where they differed was over whether that could best be done by maintaining, possibly even strengthening, the centralizing tendencies of a unitary state, or whether it would be better in the long run to make concessions to nationalist and devolutionary pressures. For 'unionists' (in whichever party they were found), support for the latter required something of an act of faith – a belief that nationalists could be satisfied with self-government within the United Kingdom, or with some kind of federal solution to the constitutional conundrum (loosely referred to as 'Home Rule All Round'), and that devolution was not the first step on the 'slippery slope' to separation and the break-up of the British state. The trouble was that once the change had been made, there could be no going back – hence the uneasiness of many Liberals with Gladstone's precipitate and single-minded pursuit of Irish Home Rule as the party's rallying cry in the late 1880s. Gladstone's actions raised a further point too, in that he seemed to take English Liberals for granted. While it could be argued that Home Rule for Ireland would be beneficial to Britain, and that England herself might benefit from being treated as a separate nation for political purposes, this was not necessarily a view that the English shared of their constitutional future. England had long been the hub of the British state, which was often seen as merely the English state writ large. Any dismantling of that state threatened what Lord Rosebery described as England's status as 'the predominant partner' and was therefore not likely to be popular with English voters. One of the unforeseen results of the Home Rules debates was thus to stir into life an English backlash against Celtic nationalism, complicating still further the political considerations attaching to constitutional reform. With the stirrings of this embryonic English nationalism, not only the future of the British state, but also the future of 'Britishness' in relation to the other national identities of the British Isles, moved firmly into the spotlight, and a new self-consciousness of national differences threatened to undermine the sense of shared identity that had been evident at the time of the Great Exhibition 50 years earlier.

Unity and diversity

The 'rise of nationalism' in Ireland, Scotland and Wales is an historically traceable trend, especially in the historiographies of Ireland and Wales (less so, Scotland) in the late nineteenth century. There are dangers, however, in relying exclusively on an interpretation of British history derived solely from the national histories of those countries or from other nationalist sources, since these inevitably highlight the importance of nationalism compared with other factors. They can also offer a rather one-dimensional view of the history of the British Isles as a whole. Even on the 'Celtic periphery' (if that dangerously anglocentric appellation can be used) nationalism was not necessarily a single, dominant force: where it was strong it could take a variety of political and cultural forms; elsewhere it co-existed and competed with equally important integrationist tendencies that emphasized the ties that united the different nations in a British state. The nationalist interpretation of British history does not allow for the extent to which the 'four nations' were themselves fractured or invented entities, nor usually does it give full recognition to the place of England within the Union as a nation in its own right. It is almost as if in trying to redress one historiographical imbalance – the fact that English and British history were once deemed almost synonymous – historians have gone close to the other extreme, leaving England out of the historical reckoning altogether, except as an 'anti-nationalist' deadweight in the political balance. In order to get a more rounded picture of British history, it is necessary not only to appreciate the strength of unionism as well as nationalism, but also to reintegrate the history of England into that of the wider British community. Just as the political success of the British state can be judged on the basis of how well it reconciled or accommodated a variety of social, regional and national divisions, so the cultural history of Britain is as much the story of the blending of cultures as of conflict or antagonism between them. To assess the real strength of the nationalist challenge to the British state and the effectiveness with which it was met in the late Victorian period, both a broader contextualization of the challenge itself and of other social, political and cultural trends in British history at this time are essential.

This is not to downplay the significance of nationalism and nationalist movements. In the Irish case, for example, nationalism, or at least the Nationalist Party, was the main influence on Irish politics from the early 1880s. Under Parnell, the Irish party cornered four-fifths of Ireland's parliamentary representation, winning 85 of the 101 Irish seats at the general elections of 1885 and 1886, against only 16 Unionists. At the 1886 election the extent of Nationalist dominance was emphasized by the fact that 66 of the Irish party's MPs were returned unopposed. Parnell's involvement in the O'Shea divorce case and his subsequent disgrace and death in 1891 weakened the unity of constitutional nationalism, and led to more contests between Parnellites and anti-Parnellites, but overall Ireland's loyalty to the nationalist cause remained unbroken, with the various factions retaining a combined representation of 81 MPs in 1895 and 1900, and 82 in the election of 1906. The same pattern repeated itself in the first elections to Ireland's new county councils (established by the 1898 Local Government Act) in 1899, where Nationalists took 551 seats to the Unionists' 125 (all but 39 of the latter being in Ulster). Through its newspapers and constituency organizations, the Nationalist Party established a firm hold over Irish opinion, providing an avenue of advancement for Irishmen which the British parties denied them and apparently demonstrating the strength of popular support for Irish Home Rule. The strength of the Nationalist Party, and the virtual elimination in Ireland of Liberalism as an electoral force, gave Ireland a pattern of politics different from the rest of the United Kingdom and leant confirmation to the nationalist contention that the Irish were a people struggling to be free of the colonial status forced upon them by the English-dominated British state.

Ireland was unusual in that the emergence of a political nationalist movement pre-dated some of the more obvious forms of cultural nationalism. Yet from the 1880s an explicitly cultural strand was added to Irish nationalism in the shape of the so-called 'Gaelic revival' and the writings of the Irish literary renaissance. Both emphasized the distinctiveness of Ireland's Gaelic/Celtic traditions and the consequently alien character of the English-British state. The cultural nationalist movement began to crystallize in 1884 with the formation of Michael Cusack's Gaelic Athletic Association. The GAA, which by 1901 had 10,000 members in 41 branches, encouraged the development of a muscular Irishness by fostering the revival of 'traditional' Irish sports such as hurling and gaelic football. So that the political dimension of its activities should not be mistaken, GAA members were forbidden to play 'British' sports like rugby, football and cricket, and the ranks of the GAA were closed to those whose employment identified them too closely with the organs of the British state, including members of the Royal Irish Constabulary and the Dublin police. The GAA, moreover, was only one of a number of cultural organizations that sprung up at about this time. In 1893 the Gaelic League was founded by Eoin MacNeill and Douglas Hyde, its purpose amply summed up in Hyde's November 1892 lecture 'On the Necessity for De-Anglicizing the Irish People'. The Gaelic League worked to revive the Irish language and interest in traditional Irish folklore. Meanwhile modern literary figures, notably W.B. Yeats and the other writers of the 'literary renaissance', were using a mythologized Irish past to comment on contemporary political themes; Yeats's *Cathleen ni Houlihan*, for example, looked back to the rebellion of 1798 as a symbol of Ireland's past failure to assert its independence from the dominant British state. The theme of self-sufficiency and national self-confidence in Ireland's indigenous culture was taken further by Arthur Griffith's organization Sinn Fein ('Ourselves') formed in 1905 as a cultural counterpart to the Home Rule movement, advocating the virtues of Ireland's traditional economic and social structures compared with the modernizing tendencies of the British imperial system.

Behind the open manifestations of political and cultural nationalism lay the continuing presence of the revolutionary underground, sustained by the moral and material support of 'Ireland abroad', especially the Irish-American community in the United States. Ireland's insurrectionary tradition of nationalism had begun with the rebellion of Tone and Emmett in the 1790s and early 1800s. They had provided role models for the 'Young Ireland' physical-force revolutionaries of 1848 and the Fenians of the 1850s and 1860s. The Fenian tradition extended into the late nineteenth and early twentieth centuries, embodied in the shadowy conspiracies of the Irish Republican Brotherhood. All of these groups drew support from Irish-America.[27] From the 1790s onwards, the USA provided a refuge and a base for Irish republicans. The mass emigration of the famine era not only increased the stream of 'emigrants and exiles' settling in the New World; it also heightened anti-British feeling, particularly among the Catholic Irish in America, and led to the increased mobilization of Irish-American opinion on behalf of nationalist and revolutionary movements in Ireland. The Fenians were founded simultaneously in Ireland and America; Irish-America provided weapons and leadership for the Fenian terrorist campaigns and the rising of 1867. In the 1870s Clan na Gael, a revolutionary republican organization founded in the USA by John Devoy, became the main recruiting agent for the Fenian cause. Although the Clan and other Irish-American organizations also cooperated with the constitutional nationalists and land reformers in the 'New Departure' (Parnell was feted on his speaking tour of America in 1880), tensions between the 'physical force' wing and more moderate nationalists were never far below the surface, and there were splits in the movement in the 1880s and 1890s. Nevertheless, the transatlantic character of the Clan na Gael–IRB organization did much to keep revolutionary nationalism alive in Ireland and to shape its strategy. At a deeper level, the existence of a large Irish community in America (and in other destinations of the Irish diaspora such as Australia) did much to shape a sense of Irish nationhood which existed both within and beyond the confines of the British state, reinforcing the desire for Irishness to find expression in greater political and cultural independence.

However, not all of Ireland was nationalist, and not all of those who accepted the nationalist label necessarily subscribed to that creed in its most extreme form. For example, the voters who supported the Irish party may have backed the demand for Home Rule or the establishment of an Irish parliament. This did not mean that they, or for that matter their leaders, automatically wanted to break all links with the British state or the British crown. John Redmond – Parnell's eventual successor as leader of the Nationalist Party at Westminster – defined Home Rule rather as a 'middle course between separation on the one hand and over-centralization of government on the other',[28] not inconsistent with Ireland's continued membership of a reconstituted Union. Arthur Griffith, founder of Sinn Fein, for all his espousal of Irish self-sufficiency, envisaged an 'Austro-Hungarian' solution to the problem of Ireland's constitutional future, with the creation of a 'dual monarchy' and possibly joint ministerial councils for foreign and imperial affairs. The mass of Irish voters might well have been content with a constitutional compromise that gave Ireland some autonomy but preserved a broader Anglo-Irish Union. It would certainly be a mistake to exaggerate the importance of the more extreme minority nationalist groups, or the extent to which they were representative of Irish opinion as a whole. The cultural and linguistic nationalists of the Gaelic League were a small intellectual, middle-class elite. They loomed large in later nationalist versions of Irish history, through the figures of Pearse, de Valera and others, but in the 1880s and 1890s they had little popular impact. The Gaelic Athletic Association, while more popular and broadly based, was unable to wean the majority of Ireland's games players and spectators away from 'imperialist' British sports. Similarly, although Fenianism and its traditions had a romantic appeal to the Irish heart, the experience of 1848 and 1867 (and indeed of Easter 1916) showed that Irishmen were more willing to sing about insurrection and rebellion than actually to participate in it.

In any event, nationalism of whatever kind was only one strand of Ireland's political make-up. 'Unionism' – and the sense of positive rather than simply passive loyalty to the British state and its institutions – may have been a minority tendency, but it was by no means a negligible one. Nor was it geographically or socially confined to one part of Ireland. It is true that Unionism was most organized and most vocal among the Protestants of Ulster, especially from the mid-1880s when the province became the focal point of opposition to Home Rule. The Presbyterian 'Scots Irish' were particular adherents of the Unionist cause, though it was a movement capable of linking all classes and sections of the Ulster community (for example, in the lodges of the Orange Order). Yet just as there were Catholic nationalists as well as Protestant unionists in Ulster, so too Unionism was a force beyond Ulster's boundaries in the rest of Ireland. It drew its strength, as might be expected, from the still-powerful remnants of the 'Ascendancy' class and the institutions most closely identified with them: from Protestant landowners and the Anglican Church, from the academic community centred on Trinity College Dublin, and from the organizations directly linked to the Castle administration – civil servants, local officials and the police. But there was life in Unionism 'beyond the Pale' too. There were Catholic Unionists as well as Protestant ones,[29] and the political balance between Nationalism and Unionism in Ireland as a whole may have been closer than the parliamentary election returns – based on a first-past-the-post system which discouraged contests – might at first sight suggest.

In the closing years of the nineteenth century, moreover, there were economic and social factors that were strengthening the appeal of the Union in material terms. The expansion of Belfast and, to a lesser extent, Dublin as industrial centres owed much to their links with the wider British and imperial economy. Belfast in particular, with its shipbuilding and engineering industries, depended heavily on its British connection, a fact that reinforced opposition to Home Rule. In the years before the First World War socialist activists like Larkin and Connolly attempted to give the labour unrest of industrial workers a nationalist edge, but the apparent hostility of most nationalists to the modern industrial world raised fears about the economic future of an Ireland cut adrift from British markets, capital and expertise. Nor was it in the industrial sector alone that the benefits of the Union were becoming more clearly marked. The Irish countryside was also being substantially transformed by the policies of 'constructive Unionism' pursued by the Salisbury and Balfour governments, including a series of Land Purchase Acts that provided government loans to allow tenants to purchase their own farms, the establishment of Congested Districts Boards to coordinate improvements in rural infrastructure such as harbours, roads and railways, and the creation of an Irish Department of Agriculture and Technical Instruction. Coupled with state support for the relocation of population and emigration, and the separate initiatives in cooperative farming sponsored by Horace Plunkett's Irish Agricultural Organization Society, these measures completed the work of rural and land reform begun by the post-famine Encumbered Estates Act and the Liberal Land Acts of 1870 and 1881. By the end of the 1890s the rural areas of Ireland – though still poor in places – were less unsettled and more prosperous than at any time since 1800. Even if the political case for the Union was still contested by nationalists, the economic arguments in its favour appeared strong.

The possibility thus existed that, given time, Ireland might become another Scotland, with economic prosperity undermining political separatism and reinforcing the unionist tendency. Certainly this seemed more likely than that Scotland would become another Ireland. As has already been demonstrated, Scotland was much more fully integrated into the Union state. It retained separate religious, legal and educational establishments, and its own self-sustaining civic society, yet these operated within an overall framework of support for the Union. There was a more self-conscious debate over Scottish identity, linked to expressions of cultural nationalism, in the late nineteenth century, and these led to an increased emphasis on the distinctiveness of Scotland's past and traditions. The Scottish 'Gaelic revival' was one aspect of this movement, part of a more romantic 'tartanry' that stimulated an interest in Jacobitism and the Highland clans that was also reflected in the historical novels of Robert Louis Stevenson, John Buchan and Neil Munro.[30] The 'kailyard' writers of the turn of the century mythologized the cultural distinctiveness of rural Scotland in a different way, while urban working-class Scots were busy building a new Scottish popular culture around the football field and the public house. But for all this heightened awareness of Scottishness, political nationalism remained a minority tendency, and support for outright separatism was barely voiced before the twentieth century. Scotland's political elites were fully integrated into the British Establishment and saw their country's future in British terms. The campaign for a Scottish secretaryship in the 1880s provides a good illustration. The most prominent advocate of administrative devolution was perhaps Lord Rosebery, but he was also firmly committed to Liberalism in Britain as a whole and to the maintenance of the Union. Scotland had its own political idiosyncrasies – notably the long Liberal ascendancy that was only partly broken by the defection of Liberal Unionists from the party's ranks in 1886 – but its political representatives were overwhelmingly unionist (small 'u'), and the fact that so many prominent English politicians sat in parliament for Scottish constituencies emphasized the completeness of Scotland's integration into the British state. Even on the left, where Scottish socialists like Keir Hardie and Ramsay MacDonald supported the campaign for Scottish Home Rule, the same integrationist tendencies applied. Hardie moved on from founding the Scottish Labour Party in 1888 to become first an English and then a Welsh member of parliament.[31] Ramsay MacDonald, whose political career began as secretary to the Scottish Home Rule Association, in 1924 became the first Labour prime minister of the United Kingdom.[32]

The Welsh 'national revival' was more deep seated and more political in character than Scotland's, yet, as the fate of the Home Rule movement in the 1890s amply demonstrated, it too failed to develop a truly separatist dynamic. Welsh Nonconformist nationalists were content for the most part to work within the already devolved structures of the British Liberal Party. Tom Ellis, at one time seen as a potential 'Welsh Parnell', in the 1890s became chief whip of the party during the Rosebery government. Lloyd George, who led the Cymru Fydd rebellion in the mid-1890s, was also a leading figure on the British radical stage and became a member of Campbell-Bannerman's cabinet in 1905. However, the merging of the fortunes of nationalism and radicalism should not be seen in terms of personal ambition. The fact was that the centrifugal tendencies of Welsh nationalism were arrested by a series of reforms in the late nineteenth century that recognized and safeguarded the separate identity of Wales within the British state. Measures such as the Welsh Sunday Closing Act of 1881 and the Welsh Intermediate Education Act of 1889 established the principle of Wales's legislative distinctiveness. The foundation of a national University of Wales (granted its charter in 1893), of a National Library and a National Museum, provided the country with valuable symbols of institutional nationhood, while the creation of country and district councils in the 1880s and 1890s gave Nonconformist radicals a chance to exercise power at a local level and so removed much of the practical demand for further Home Rule. The desire for disestablishment remained unsatisfied, but even this reform was Liberal Party policy, and there was every hope that a future Liberal government – especially with Lloyd George as one of its members – would be able to redeem its pledges on the issue.

In any case, as in Ireland, the idea of a uniformly nationalist Wales should not be accepted uncritically just because of dominant historiographical trends. The Liberals were politically ascendant in Wales from 1868 to 1914, but nationalism was only one strand of the Liberal movement. Then again, the Conservative Party was a less negligible force than is sometimes supposed, polling a third of the votes cast even in its electoral nadir of 1906. With the Anglican Church, the Conservatives acted as a strong counterbalance to the highly political Welshness of the Nonconformist–nationalist movement. Another factor that reduced the appeal of any form of separatist nationalism was economic and social change. Not only were the industrial districts of south Wales attracting large numbers of immigrant workers, mainly from England but also from places as far afield as Spain and Italy, but there was also a clear realization that the prosperity of the Welsh economy – the coal, iron and steel industries of south Wales, the slate industry of the north – was bound up with that of Britain and its empire. As with Scotland, economic integration offered a powerful disincentive to political change and underlined the common interests of the different parts of the British Isles. It was no coincidence that political nationalism was strongest in the more rural areas of mid and north Wales, suggesting that though its representatives claimed to speak for the whole of the Welsh people, nationalism could, on the contrary, be a divisive as well as a unifying force.

It seems unlikely, therefore, that the United Kingdom was threatened with imminent political disintegration as a consequence of the rise of nationalism in its constituent parts in the second half of the nineteenth century. Indeed, the flexibility of the governmental response to the concerns of peripheral areas, and the openness of the British political system to the influence of regional pressure groups – whether the Irish party, the Welsh MPs or Scottish crofters – suggested the existence of a good balance between centralization and devolution within the confines of a union state. Local government reform, the enactment of separate legislation for Ireland, Scotland and Wales, together with administrative devolution through the creation of the Scottish Office and a variety of boards and commissions, promoted a measure of self-government and diversification without weakening the authority of central institutions. Only in the case of Ireland, where the strength of constitutional nationalism was reinforced by revolutionary nationalist activity, and where the historical antagonism towards the Union was deeper and more recent, was there a serious threat to the gradual, evolutionary path of constitutional development which was combining a more democratically accountable central government with the establishment of locally responsible representative institutions.

As has been stressed, this is not to underplay the reality of national feeling in Scotland, Ireland and Wales. In England, too, for that matter, there were signs of a more keenly developed national consciousness in this period. Partly this was a response to the Home Rule controversy, which directed the attention of the English electorate to the differences between themselves and their Celtic neighbours, as well as to the implications for the predominant partner if the other, smaller, nations in the British polity were to receive preferential constitutional treatment. The whole debate over Home Rule forced the English to acknowledge that 'England' and 'Britain' were not synonymous, and that England had its own historic culture and identity, and perhaps its own national interests, within the larger framework of the British state.

It was no coincidence that England, like the other countries of the British Isles, had been manufacturing its own national myths in the nineteenth century, with a rediscovery of the Saxon as opposed to the Norman or Celtic past.[33] Historians like Stubbs and Maitland stressed the 'English genius' for government in their studies of constitutional and legal history. The 'Englishness' of the Anglican Church was another cohering influence on England's national life, even if it left Nonconformists in an ambiguous position 'beyond the Pale'. More inclusive was England's distinctive heritage in both high and popular culture. The late Victorian period saw cricket (a rival to football as England's national game) emerge as a mass spectator sport, with the towering figure of W.G. Grace as its supreme practitioner and the 'Test' matches against Australia appealing to England's patriotic sporting instincts. An English culture of the music halls developed, especially in London and the North. On a more elevated level, Dickens created a panorama of English society that was influential beyond his lifetime, while the works of novelists as varied as Thomas Hardy, Arnold Bennett and H.G. Wells in their different ways encapsulated aspects of Englishness for the reading public. Politically English nationalism was less explicit than the Celtic varieties (not least because England's economic, demographic and political superiority limited the room for feelings of exploitation or suppression on the part of its people). But the serious consideration of a federal future for the UK, in which an English parliament might exist alongside separate assemblies for Ireland, Scotland and Wales, and the markedly strengthened position of the Conservatives in English constituencies (where they won a majority of seats at every general election between 1886 and 1910, with the exception of 1906) indicated stirrings of concern for England's political future and a preference for a perceivedly 'English' party over one, like the Liberals, seen as being in thrall to Celtic particularists. The simultaneously increased hostility to immigrants and 'aliens' was another instance of a perceptibly less tolerant, more xenophobic mood in English life as the nineteenth century drew to its close.

That said, the picture of a United Kingdom becoming increasingly divided into contending, competing parts should not be overdrawn. The image of a British state comprising four distinct nations is at best an approximation to the truth; at worst, positively misleading. The intermingling of people and cultures across the British Isles, through migration and intermarriage, continued to erode self-contained geographical or national units. The national or sub-national territorialities within the United Kingdom were in any case riven by their own internal divisions, so that clear-cut national identities are difficult to discern. The appropriation of the national label by particular social or religious groups further muddied the waters. Thus in Ireland the Catholic majority, in Wales the Nonconformists, laid claim to being the true embodiment of their nation's heritage, while other groups, such as the Ulster Protestants, found or felt themselves to be excluded. The complex issues of identity and allegiance raised by the controversies over Irish Home Rule were only part of an even more complicated pattern of multiple identities in which different varieties of Englishness, Irishness, Scottishness and Welshness co-existed or contended with other, more localized, loyalties, or with the facets of a more comprehensive 'British' identity to which their relationship had to be worked out both in practical and emotional terms.

A further error easily made by the historians of nationalism is to assume that national identities (however these are defined) must automatically take precedence over other social and group loyalties. This is far from being the case. In late Victorian Britain and Ireland, national identities may have been becoming more clearly defined, and political nationalism was a growing force. But there were other forms of social identifier that cut across national boundaries and offered alternative priorities. The two most obvious were gender and class.

The nineteenth century, and especially the period after 1850, saw the emergence of a trinity of movements that challenged the prevailing dispensations of the Victorian social and political system in an era of democratization. Nationalism was one, challenging as it did the anglocentric orientation of the British state. At the same time, however, the embryonic women's movement was challenging the male-dominated character of the Victorian legal and political establishment in areas such as education, employment and the rights of married women, while from the 1850s and 1860s trade unions and labour movements were campaigning for improved conditions and greater political power for the working classes.[34] By the 1880s and 1890s, socialism and feminism offered an alternative prospectus for change to that proffered by the nationalists. There was, admittedly, some overlap between the various movements. Labour leaders like Keir Hardie, or the Welsh miners' leader 'Mabon' (William Abraham, MP for the Rhondda from 1885[35]), stood on platforms that combined labour and nationalist demands. Labour organizations and the early women's groups often had a local or regional rather than an all-British focus. But their growing strength and wider horizons provide a different perspective on the social and political divisions of late-Victorian Britain than one that emphasizes the role of nationalism to the exclusion of other movements.

Finally, an over-concentration on the subsidiary nationalisms within the British state underestimates the extent to which the processes of integration were working in parallel with the recognition of diversity. As Keith Robbins has demonstrated, 'blending' rather than 'ending' was the keynote of much that was happening in the nineteenth century, leading to a more organic, fully realized 'Britishness' than had existed in earlier periods. Integration was most advanced in the political and economic spheres. Politically the constitutional framework had been established by the Acts of Union of 1707 and 1800, but the progress of democratization through the Reform Acts of 1832, 1867 and 1884 had created a more genuinely integrated political system, not just at the level of the aristocratic ruling elite but in the shape of mass political parties organized on an all-British basis. True, Ireland remained semi-detached from the British party structure, although in practice Unionists and Nationalists worked with their British allies and were integrated into the Westminster parliamentary system. Elsewhere, while there were separate party organizations in Scotland and Wales, in Britain an integrated two-party system emerged in the late nineteenth century in which the

Liberal and Conservative parties competed for power on the strength of common platforms throughout the three nations and under a single leadership in which English, Scots and Welsh were all represented. Where nationalist tendencies existed, they were subsumed in the overall framework of two-party politics, just as, at least until the formation of a separate Labour Party, were the special interests of industrial workers or other sectional groups.

The state itself was also taking on a more integrated 'British' character. Already in the eighteenth century some of the main agencies of state power such as the army and navy had become all-British organizations both in leadership and personnel, a trend accelerated by the wars of the revolutionary and Napoleonic period. In the nineteenth century the state expanded in the domestic as well as the military arena. The civil service, for example, grew substantially in size during the Victorian era, and the introduction of competitive examinations and a more professional career structure in mid-century made it a genuinely 'British' body in the same way as the armed forces. As interventionist legislation increased, so the British state forged a closer relationship with its citizens in all parts of the United Kingdom. Even where region-specific legislation was introduced, London was still seen as its point of origin. This of course was precisely what fuelled nationalist support for Home Rule, but the limited support which, outside Ireland, the Home Rulers received suggested that perhaps, for the mass of the political nation, a British state was at least as acceptable as any other.

The strengthening of a British identity in politics and government was underpinned by an increasing economic integration and by a more general process of cultural assimilation. The grid-lines of an integrated British economy had been established during the first phase of the Industrial Revolution. The completion of the rail network and the further development of a regionalized yet interdependent heavy-industry economy continued the integrationist trend in the late nineteenth century, as did the increasing size of industrial companies that often had interests in more than one part of the British Isles. Inevitably the result was to increase standardization (for example in commercial practices and business law) and to create a British business class, just as the working classes were seeing that their own interests were not contained by economically arbitrary national boundaries. Not merely economically, but in other ways too, the forging of a common culture was fostered by government action. The expansion of state-sponsored elementary education from the

1870s onwards created a more universally literate working population by the turn of the century – a population literate, moreover, in English rather than the other languages of Ireland, Scotland and Wales, and so more open to the Anglicizing tendencies of mass communications represented by the popular press and, later, the early cinema. Whether the process amounted to the imposition of English culture, or whether it should be seen as marking the adoption of English as the 'British' language, is a moot point, and one obviously contested by the nationalist advocates of Welsh, Gaelic or Erse. But alongside the rise of mass entertainment through newspapers and popular literature, the common educational experience of the generations after 1880 was an important factor in contributing to the sense of British identity, even if this Britishness might be only part of a more composite picture.[36]

The situation that pertained in the British state at the end of the Victorian era was thus a complicated one. The second half of the nineteenth century had seen the rise of cultural and political national-ist movements in Ireland, Scotland and Wales, and an increasing sense of national identity in England as well. If not counteracted by other factors, the implications of these developments were plainly centrifugal, presaging the break-up, or at least the significant remod-elling, of the British state. However, it does also seem as if those counteracting, centripetal, factors were at work in the form of closer political and economic integration and the assimilation of the mass of the population into a common British culture. Except possibly in Ireland (and even there the position was far from clear-cut), the tensions between centrifugal nationalism and the integrationist tendencies of Britishness did not produce a major political crisis, and may indeed have cancelled each other out. That this was so was due in large measure to the flexible responses to nationalist pressure employed by the successive Liberal and Conservative governments from the late 1860s onwards, combining concessions to remedy legitimate grievances with firmly upholding the principle of a United Kingdom. The result was a British state which, although becoming more centralized and integrated, also provided for a democratization of local government and the legal recognition of the communal diversities of a multi-national state. By combining unity with diversity Britain's political leaders had constructed a practical accommodation between Britishness and other, competing, forms of national identity which offered at least the prospect of preserving a British state into the next century.

CHAPTER 4

NATIONHOOD AND
EMPIRE, 1830–1900

The late nineteenth century may have been the age of nationalism. It was also, unequivocally, the 'age of empire'. Between the early 1870s and the turn of the century in particular, the European Great Powers – Britain foremost among them – considerably expanded their overseas empires, thereby establishing a European primacy in world affairs only partially offset by the as yet more modest imperial excursions of the extra-European powers such as Japan and the United States of America. The impulses behind the so-called 'new imperialism' have been debated and dissected by historians, and the differing motives of the European powers analysed and compared.[1] In Britain's case the imperial dimension is an especially important part of the national history. The administration and defence of an expanding global empire inevitably exercised a powerful effect on the institutions and politics of the British state, and on the outlook of its rulers. Equally, to an even greater extent than in the eighteenth century, the existence of the empire and its multi-faceted interrelationship with British society helped to shape a sense of British national identity and provided a crucial ingredient in the development of that more generally diffused 'Britishness' that could be seen alongside the internal nationalisms of England, Ireland, Scotland and Wales examined in the previous chapter.

The imperial state

The British state was, in the nature of its creation, an imperial state. England had the beginnings of an empire before the British state was founded. Indeed, parts of the British Isles such as Wales and Ireland have been described as England's 'inner empire'.[2] But the main period of imperial growth came after the Anglo-Scottish Union of

1707 and was thus associated with the British state rather than its English predecessor. Throughout its subsequent history – at least from the expansion of empire in the eighteenth and nineteenth centuries to the decolonization and 'post-imperialism' of the late twentieth – the British state was the political and administrative hub of a world-wide imperial community, the diverse components of which were linked together by a variety of constitutional and legal ties as well as by connections of culture, sentiment and trade. The evolution of the imperial state in the nineteenth century, and the changing context of Britain's world position, provides the necessary background to a more detailed examination of the impact of imperialism on the politics, society and culture of the British nation in the Victorian period.

Britain's sustained imperial growth gathered momentum from the early eighteenth century.[3] The Treaty of Utrecht of 1713 added Gibraltar, Nova Scotia and Newfoundland to the existing colonies in North America and colonial outposts elsewhere. The Seven Years' War of 1756–63 established British predominance in Canada and India at the expense of the French, as well as bringing further gains in the West Indies. The 'first' British Empire was thrown into crisis by the events that culminated in the American War of Independence (1776–83), and there were contemporaries who believed that the loss of the American colonies would have fatal consequences for Britain's standing as a Great Power. In fact this proved to be far from the case. British trade with the USA quickly surpassed its pre-war levels, assisted by the early stages of the Industrial Revolution. Meanwhile, in the late eighteenth and early nineteenth century, Britain's imperial energies were diverted to other parts of the globe. The first settlement was established at Port Jackson (Sydney) in Australia in 1788, initially as a receiving port for transported convicts who could no longer be shipped to the Americas. But Australia, and later New Zealand, attracted non-convict emigrants too, and became valuable economic assets in their own right. The Revolutionary and Napoleonic Wars of 1793–1815 provided further opportunities for imperial aggrandizement at the expense of the French and their allies, and saw the consolidation of British power in India together with the acquisition of Ceylon, Malta and the Cape of Good Hope. In the post-war decades the march of empire continued, in Africa, Asia and the Pacific. A notable development was the forcible extraction of Hong Kong from the Chinese government as the price of peace after the first 'Opium War' of 1839–42.

The empire that emerged from this process of expansion was geographically extensive and internally varied. In extent, Britain's imperial possessions were scattered across continents, oceans and climatic zones, from North America, through the Caribbean and Mediterranean to Africa, India and Australasia. They comprised, too, different sizes and types of colony – so much so that the question has been posed whether it is possible to talk of a single British Empire at all.[4] Yet broad categories can be distinguished amid the profusion, the simplest division being between 'settlement' and 'non-settlement' colonies. The former, which eventually developed into the dominions of Canada, Australia, New Zealand and South Africa, were, like the colonies originally established in North America in the seventeenth century, primarily outlets for emigration from the British Isles (whether forced or voluntary) and consequently became part of that 'greater Britain' which was politically and culturally an extension of the mother country. Of course, the populations of these colonies were far from being exclusively British or European in origin. But the Canadian Indians, Australian Aborigines, New Zealand Maoris and Cape Colony Africans were displaced by European settlers and became subordinate peoples in their native lands. It was the Europeanization of these colonies – the imposition of new cultural and social structures rather than simply a new ruling elite – that distinguished the settlement colonies from the 'non-settlement' type, although the latter is itself an umbrella for widely differing imperial territories. They had in common that their main value to Britain was either economic or strategic rather than being an outlet for surplus population, but they varied enormously in size and character, from isolated trading posts on the African coast to the larger, more established plantation economies of the West Indies, to the vast sub-continental empire of British India, still in the first part of the nineteenth century under the rule of an East India Company whose original purpose had been the creation of trading networks in Asia and the Far East.

By the middle of the nineteenth century, Britain was the world's leading imperial power, having decisively overtaken the declining empires of the Spanish, Portuguese and Dutch, and outstripped the French. The empire – together with the world-wide naval supremacy which ensured its security and the industrial and commercial strength which the country enjoyed as a consequence of the Industrial Revolution – gave Britain an unrivalled international position and enabled the British governments of the Palmerstonian era to project an image of British power on the world stage. The possession of an empire brought burdens and responsibilities, but it also carried with it considerable benefits. The tangible benefits were mostly economic. Although most trade throughout the nineteenth century was with countries outside the formal empire, the empire nonetheless made a significant contribution to British economic growth. It accounted for up to a third of all British trade and provided access to valuable supplies of raw materials, markets for manufactured goods and outlets for investment. India was especially important in this respect and became one of Britain's largest single trading partners. But the empire was more than a testament to, or a guarantee of, economic success. It helped to shape in many less tangible ways the collective self-image of mid-Victorian Britain and to underpin that era's characteristic belief in the possibilities of progress and the uniqueness of Britain's position in the world. In part this was a simple pride in Britain's greatness, prompting comparisons with the Roman Empire and the concept of a 'Pax Britannica' enforced by the gunboat diplomacy of the Royal Navy. There was also, though, a sense that Britain was providing the rest of the world with a moral lead, for example by taking the initiative in banning the slave trade and abolishing slavery within the empire, and more generally encouraging the spread of Christianity through the work of missionary societies and their 'civilizing' activities. In this way the empire contributed to the sense of well being, harmony and optimism that have been identified as typical of the occasionally complacent, sometimes arrogant world view of Britain's elites in the mid-century 'age of equipoise'.[5]

In the second half of the nineteenth century, the imperial state entered more troubled times. There has been disagreement over how far this was accompanied by a change in the nature of British imperialism and imperial policy.[6] Some writers would draw a basic contrast between the unplanned, laissez faire imperialism of the early nineteenth century and the more formalized, coordinated expansion of the later Victorian period. The international context in which the imperial state operated was also changing, as other powers sought to clamber on to the imperial bandwagon and Britain's commercial predominance was eroded by competition from the second-generation industrial economies led by Germany and the United States – countries, moreover, that were willing to deploy protective tariffs as a means of boosting their domestic economies in contrast to the preferred British policy of free trade. Whether or not it is possible to identify any absolute discontinuity in British imperialism, it is undoubtedly the case that both the empire itself and the world in which it existed were undergoing rapid transformation in the years after 1850.

If there was discontinuity, it was not reflected in any slackening of the rate of imperial expansion, which, if anything, accelerated from the early 1860s on. In 1871 the empire (including the United Kingdom itself) covered a total area of 7.7 million square miles and had a population of 235 million people. By 1901 the respective figures were 12 million square miles – a quarter of the total land area of the globe – and 400 million people.[7] Where a change did occur was in the geographical focus of imperial expansion. Although areas of existing imperial strength were consolidated (for example, Burma on the frontier of India was annexed in 1886) and were experiencing a substantial population increase, the major area of expansion was in the hitherto relatively neglected continent of Africa. Britain already had an established presence in the Cape, and the annexation of Lagos in 1861 added to the existing outposts of Gambia and Sierre Leone in West Africa. But the largest advances occurred in the 1880s and 1890s as part of the general 'Scramble for Africa' on the part of the European powers and because of Britain's need to safeguard the recently opened Suez Canal route to India.[8] It was the latter concern that motivated the British occupation of Egypt in 1882 and, indirectly, the subsequent conquest of the Sudan in the 1890s. At the same time, for a mixture of political, economic and strategic reasons, Britain established a series of protectorates in eastern and southern Africa, including Bechuanaland (1885), Somaliland (1887), Matabeleland (1888), Uganda (1894) and British East Africa (1895). By the turn of the century, more of the map of Africa was painted British red than any other imperial colour.[9]

The expansionist impulse was thus present throughout the nineteenth century, even if its geographical emphasis and the motives behind it altered. This still leaves open the possibility that there was a change in the methods of expansion or in the nature of the empire that resulted. In some ways the continuities between the earlier and later parts of the century are still obvious. Britain's early empire had grown as a product of a combination of public and private initiative. Governments had founded colonies for specific purposes, as in Australia, and had ensured the military security of the empire and its trade routes by the use of the army and the establishment of naval bases. On the other hand, Britain's single most important imperial possession – India – had originally been acquired as a by-product of the commercial activities of the East India Company, while over large parts of the rest of the globe, such as China or South America, Britain had been content to exercise influence (what Robinson and Gallagher christened the 'imperialism of Free Trade') rather than formal control, so long as British manufacturers and investors were able to gain access to markets and raw materials.

There was a continuation of these indirect methods of expansion in the later nineteenth century. The British government licensed a number of chartered companies in the 1880s – the Royal Niger Company, the British East Africa Company and Cecil Rhodes's British South Africa Company – to spearhead the economic penetration of the African continent and provide a framework for empire. But there was also a steady extension of formal imperial control and consequently an enhanced role for the central institutions of the imperial state. The establishment of the Colonial Office as a separate department of state in 1854 was an illustration of this trend. In 1857–58, following the suppression of the Indian Mutiny, the British government took direct responsibility for ruling the sub-continent, replacing the East India Company's governor general with a viceroy responsible to a newly created India Office and Council of India in London, and to a politically appointed secretary of state. The Indian Civil Service and the Indian Army, though retaining a separate existence, became extended arms of the British state, which also increased the number of civil servants in London – in the Colonial, India and Foreign Offices – employed in the business of imperial administration. In this way, central control over the empire was increased and the structures of imperial rule became more formalized. The metropolitan government in London was also more likely to be the initiator of imperial expansion. This was most obviously the case where direct strategic interests were involved and where substantial military resources had to be committed – as for instance in the occupation of Egypt and the conquest of the Sudan. But improvements in communications, and the increasing strategic interconnectedness of developments in various parts of the world at a time of mounting imperial competition, both facilitated and required a much more interventionist approach to imperial administrations and left much less discretion to the individual judgement of the 'men on the spot'.

Yet while in some respects the central direction of imperial affairs was being strengthened, another trend of the late nineteenth century was increasing colonial autonomy, at least in regard to the settlement colonies. These were expanding both in terms of population and economic importance.[10] They were also gaining additional powers of self-government and moving towards nationhood in their own right. In 1867 the British North America Act created the Dominion of Canada as a self-governing federation within the British Empire, retaining a governor general as a symbol of a continuing link with the crown but otherwise making Canada effectively an independent state. In Australia the individual states attained responsible government between 1855 and 1890, uniting as the 'Commonwealth of Australia' in 1901 and, along with New Zealand, achieving dominion status in 1907. In South Africa, the Cape Colony was granted responsible government in 1872 and had its own domestic parliamentary system, although it was not until 1910 that it joined with Natal and the former republics of the Transvaal and the Orange Free State to create the Union of South Africa as a full dominion. The emergence of the dominions was nevertheless a major development in the history of the empire, leading to a two-tier division between the self-governing colonies and those ruled directly from Britain. This in turn led to a debate as to the future evolution of the imperial state. Could the dominions be kept in a formal constitutional and political relationship with Britain, or would they, like the American colonies before them, eventually break their remaining ties and become completely separate entities? Politically there were those, in the mother country at least, who sought to give constitutional reality to the concept of 'Greater Britain' by uniting Britain and the dominions in a formal imperial federation, perhaps even with its own imperial parliament and cabinet. The most that could be achieved in practical terms, however, was to institute regular 'colonial conferences' between the British government and its colonial counterparts to discuss matters of general imperial concern. The first of these met in London to coincide with Queen Victoria's golden jubilee in 1887, a second was held at the time of the diamond jubilee ten years later, and further conferences followed at intervals thereafter. Some useful agreements were reached on economic and defence cooperation, but no moves were made in a more federal direction.

The growth in size and complexity of the empire posed problems of management for the imperial state in terms of internal relations and responding to external threat. The working out of a successful accommodation between Britain and the emergent dominions demanded sensitivity and skill. Equally taxing were the problems of unrest in other parts of the empire and the concerns of imperial defence. In India the post-Mutiny Raj faced growing agitation from the educated Indian elite for political reform. The Indian National Congress was founded in 1885 and developed as a forum for nationalist opinion. The passage of the Indian Councils Act of 1892, which provided for the appointment of Indian members to the viceroy's Legislative Council, only whetted the appetite for further change. Britain was drawn deeper into Egyptian affairs by a nationalist revolt against foreign rule, which threatened to destabilize the khedive's government, and then to protect its interests in Egypt was driven to declare war on the Dervish empire in the Sudan. The 'River War' of 1896–98 against the Sudan, which culminated in the Battle of Omdurman, was just one of a series of frontier conflicts associated with the expansion or defence of empire in the late nineteenth century, including the Asante campaign in West Africa in 1873–74, the Zulu War of 1878–79 and the Afghan War of 1878–81. In addition to the larger conflicts, there were innumerable smaller wars or expeditions of a 'punitive' nature, for example against discontented tribesmen in southern Africa or on the North-West Frontier of India.

To the problems of internal and frontier unrest were added growing fears of external threat. In the mid-nineteenth century Britain's world position had been substantially unchallenged. Britannia ruled the waves and the British Empire had no serious rival. By the 1880s and 1890s, however, the situation had changed, potentially to Britain's detriment. Although the size of her empire had increased, so too had imperial rivalries with other European powers: the French in West Africa and Egypt, the Russians on the frontiers of India and in the Far East, Germany in Africa and the Turkish Empire. Italy, the United States and Japan were also involved in the colonial scramble and were flexing their muscles on the international stage. One consequence was that Britain's long-standing naval supremacy – on which ultimately the security of the empire and its trade routes depended – risked being undermined, as other powers embarked on programmes of naval expansion. Another consequence was that the possibility of war with one or more of the other Great Powers became more likely, creating an eventuality which, the Crimean War of 1854–56 apart, Britain had not had to contend with since the beginning of the post-Napoleonic peace in 1815. It is true that there was cooperation, or at least diplomatic agreement, between the powers on many of the ground rules of colonial expansion, especially in Africa and the Pacific. But there were still occasions when the diplomatic ice wore dangerously thin. Britain and Russia were close to conflict on a number of occasions over Afghanistan and, in 1877, over Russia's threat to the integrity of the Ottoman Empire (seen by Britain as a bulwark against Russian designs on the approaches to India). In 1898 an even more serious crisis occurred with the French over the control over the headwaters of the Nile, when British and French troops confronted each other at Fashoda in the southern Sudan. In the event, war was avoided by international diplomacy and the common sense of those on the ground, but the dangers had been apparent for all to see.

From the British point of view, what was especially alarming was that the number of potential enemies seemed to be increasing at the same time as the expansion of the empire made it more and more vulnerable to internal disruption or external attack. By the end of the Victorian period Britain was facing a classic case of what Paul Kennedy has memorably described as 'imperial overstretch'[11] – a situation in which Britain's manifold commitments around the globe were outstripping the military, naval and financial resources available to sustain them. The problem was compounded by Britain's comparative international isolation – the British Empire was not part of any of the offensive and defensive alliance systems that had grown up in Europe from the days of Bismarck and which were already dividing Europe into the two armed camps that would contest the First World War. The dangers of isolation were highlighted, and the potential for 'overstretch' emphasized, by the coincidence of crises that blew up in the 1890s, including the Fashoda confrontation with France, a dispute over the borders of Venezuela with the United States and the problems of European rivalries in China and the Far East, followed by the Chinese 'Boxer' Rebellion in 1900.[12]

The resources of the imperial state were stretched even further by the war that broke out in South Africa between Britain and the Boer republics of the Transvaal and Orange Free State in October 1899. The war was the endgame of a long struggle to establish British supremacy in the region. The Boers had originally left British jurisdiction in the Cape Colony in the 'Great Trek' of 1836, and the independence of their states had been recognized by Britain in the 1850s. Then, however, the Transvaal had agreed to annexation by Britain in 1877 in return for British military aid against the Zulus, only to rebel against British rule in the First Boer War of 1880–81 after the British had won the Zulu War of 1879. The independence of the Transvaal was restored by Gladstone's government in 1882, shortly before the discovery of gold on the Witwatersrand transformed the state's economic prospects and made possession of the territory much more of a prize. As the wealth of the Transvaal increased, the idea of forcing the Boer republics into a union with the British colonies of the Cape and Natal gathered pace, reawakening plans for a British-led federation that had first been mooted in the 1870s. For a mixture of strategic and economic reasons this was an idea that appealed both to the British government and to the politicians and commercial interests of the Cape – and especially to Cecil Rhodes, prime minister of the Cape since 1890 and the most dynamic figure in the gold and diamond industries of southern Africa as well as an ardent imperialist who dreamt of a 'Cape to Cairo' imperium under British control. Rhodes attempted to filibuster an annexation of the Transvaal in 1895, with the 'Jameson Raid' timed to coincide with a rising organized by dissatisfied English miners in Johannesburg. The raid ended in fiasco and Rhodes was forced to resign the Cape premiership, but the British government, in the persons of the colonial secretary, Joseph Chamberlain, and the newly appointed High Commissioner at the Cape, Alfred Milner, continued to pressurize Paul Kruger's Transvaal government to make concessions to Cape and 'Uitlander' interests, until finally the Boers were provoked into their own declaration of war on the British in 1899.[13]

The South African War of 1899–1902 is often seen as a turning point in the history of the British Empire and attitudes towards imperialism. It was also a supreme test for the imperial state. Britain had to mobilize a larger army than it had previously put into the field in any colonial war, and found itself faced with huge additional demands for money and materials to support the war effort. In one sense the war drew the disparate parts of the empire closer together, since Britain was backed by the dominion governments and the Indian army. Eventual victory confirmed the strength of the empire and preserved its unity. Yet while it demonstrated the robustness of imperial alliances, the war at the same time revealed weaknesses in the imperial state and forced a re-examination of its strategies and priorities. It thus had a profound impact on the politics of empire and on attitudes to the empire's future, to which it will be necessary to return as a precursor to the larger 'crisis of empire' that affected the imperial state in the post-Victorian period.

The politics of empire

The impact of imperialism on the politics of the British state can be traced on both an ideological and a practical level. Imperial issues had to be accommodated in political and constitutional theory; they also figured strongly in the electoral ebb and flow of party politics. Furthermore the imperial state had a domestic dimension that played its part in shaping a national political culture. The role of the monarchy especially as the symbol of unity for nation and empire alike was one of the main features of British imperial politics in the late Victorian period, part of a more widely diffused 'social imperialism' with which Britain's ruling elites sought to counteract and control the challenge of burgeoning democracy at home and abroad.

The ideology of empire underwent an evolutionary process which paralleled that of the imperial state. In the mid-eighteenth century, before the outbreak of the American Revolution, imperial thinking had rested on two major assumptions, one economic, the other political. Economically the prevailing doctrine was that of mercantilism, the idea that countries were in competition for finite quantities of wealth and trade and that colonies existed for the benefit of the mother country within a protected commercial relationship (exemplified and regulated in Britain's case by the Navigation Acts of the seventeenth century). The fact that colonies were locked into a closed economic system led naturally to the second, political, assumption, that they were constitutionally extensions of the central imperial state – that even where, as in North America, the colonists enjoyed a limited degree of self-government, they were still subordinate to the authority of the British parliament and the British crown.

In 1776 these assumptions were challenged by two coincident but equally epoch-making events: the American Declaration of Independence, which prefigured the breakaway of the American colonies and the break-up of the first British Empire, and the publication of Adam Smith's *Enquiry into the Wealth of Nations*, which exploded the myths of mercantilism and extolled the benefits of laissez faire and economic free trade. Over the next 50 years, the ideological attitudes to empire showed an important shift. It came to be accepted that, as the American precedent had demonstrated, whereas colonies might still be founded, their direct attachment to the mother country might be temporary rather than permanent, with every expectation that settlement colonies like Canada and Australia would develop increasing autonomy within the imperial framework, leading to a

relationship of cooperation with Britain, but not one of subordination. This caused some to doubt the value of colonies in the first
place, since the expansion of British trade with areas outside the
formal empire (including the United States) in the first quarter of the
nineteenth century suggested that a general removal of commercial
restrictions coupled with Britain's industrial and mercantile strength
would be enough in itself to ensure British prosperity. From Pitt in
the 1780s to Peel in the 1840s, British ministers became progressively
more committed to the doctrine of free trade, which was not only the
antithesis of the old mercantilist system but, taken to its logical
conclusion, seemed to remove the need for formal empire at all. The
campaigns of the Anti-Corn Law League, led by Richard Cobden and
John Bright, endowed free trade with a moral and ethical dimension
as well, again emphasizing the virtues of the voluntary cooperation of
nations and peoples against economic and political systems in which
one community was formally subordinated to another in an exploitative imperial relationship.

For this reason, the early nineteenth century is sometimes seen as
being ideologically anti-imperialist, an attitude summed up in Disraeli's oft-quoted remark about colonies as 'a millstone round our
necks'.[14] Yet, as has been seen, in reality imperial expansion continued, with varying degrees of official encouragement, even during this
supposedly anti-imperial phase. The 'imperialism of free trade' was
backed up by British power, and was only part of a world strategy
that included the acquisition of new colonies where these were
deemed economically or strategically necessary. The pure milk of
Cobdenism was never imbibed by any mid-Victorian government,
even those most practically committed to measures of free trade. By
the same token, the ideology of empire evolved with changing
circumstances, but at no point did it succumb to the ravages of inner
doubt. If anything the ideological case for empire was more strongly
developed as the century advanced, and in the process the contribution of imperialism to the idea of 'Britishness' became more strongly
marked.

This was achieved partly by a restatement of the view that the
colonies – at least the 'white' colonies of the settlement variety – were
an integral part of the larger British nation, and partly by re-inventing
the empire as a force for moral good, thus giving the imperialists a
good hymn tune with which to counter the siren songs of the
extreme Cobdenites. As has already been noted, the idea that Britain,
because of its own inherent qualities, had a unique, civilizing, imperial

mission carried genuine conviction in many Victorian minds, irre-spective of any more rapacious economic reality. The abolition of slavery within the empire in 1833 enabled Britain to claim the moral high ground, while the missionary impetus (reflected in the work of bodies such as the Church Missionary Society) was spreading the Christian message to 'heathen' peoples in its various British denomi-national forms. The empire became a laboratory, too, for other forms of social engineering and 'westernization'. In India, for example, the introduction of western education for representatives of local elites, and the use of English as the language of administration, had far-reaching effects. Ironically it was the successful inculcation of western liberal ideas into the minds of the educated minorities that later gave rise to an Indian nationalist movement, but one which was influenced as much by western as by Indian traditions.[15]

In the Asian sub-continent, and in Africa, then, the ideology of imperialism could assume a benign aspect, albeit one that rested on cruder assumptions of racial and cultural superiority. On the other hand, for the colonies in which the dominant groups were settlers of British extraction, a different ideological justification applied – summed up in the title of Charles Dilke's 1868 book, *Greater Britain* – namely that they were extensions of the British state transplanted to distant parts of the globe but retaining an organic connection with the mother country. Dilke's advocacy of this point of view, which denied that there were any inevitable separatist tendencies within the colonial relationship, was taken further by Sir John Seeley in his lectures on *The Expansion of England*, published in 1883. As a historian, Seeley felt able to place the growth of the British Empire in the context of a global analysis which compared it with earlier empires and with other imperial powers in the contemporary world. His conclusion was the superficially paradoxical one that 'Greater Britain is not in the ordinary sense an empire at all', since the foundation of colonies in places such as Canada, Australia and New Zealand had created 'not properly an empire, but only a very large state'. Moreo-ver, because of the strength of natural ties and cultural similarities, as well as through improvements in communications and the expansion of trade, far from drifting further apart, the colonies and the mother country could actually be drawn closer together: 'our colonial empire so-called may more and more deserve to be called Greater Britain, and ... the tie may become stronger and stronger'.[16]

Seeley's ideas provided an academic rationale for the imperial federation movement and the work of organizations such as the

Imperial Federation League, founded in 1884. They helped to define Britain as a global nation rather than simply as a nation-state confined to the territories of the British Isles. 'Britishness' became a more inclusive concept in consequence, since it embraced the inhabitants of the overseas dominions as well as those of Britain itself. Yet this inclusiveness also had its limits. The 'British' celebrated in this particular world view were the white ruling elites of the empire, not the African or Asian masses. Seeley himself was adamant that the 'Oriental empire' of India was distinct and separate from 'Greater Britain' precisely because its population was 'wholly foreign'.[17] In this respect his outlook was consistent with that of other British national-ists and imperialists of the fin-de-siècle period who were influenced by some of the more social-Darwinist theories of contemporary nationalism and who were apostles of the doctrine of 'Anglo-Saxon' superiority. The arch-imperialist Cecil Rhodes saw the 'furtherance of the British Empire' as his life's work, its expansion as living proof that the British were the 'first race in the world'; he even raised the possibility of the United States returning to the imperial fold and so re-uniting the 'Anglo-Saxon' peoples.[18] Many of his views were shared by politicians such as Joseph Chamberlain, who on occasion could use similar 'Anglo-Saxonist' rhetoric.[19] If such language seems only equivocally committed to a 'British' Empire as such – and Seeley, of course, wrote confusingly of the expansion of 'England' into a Greater Britain – the semantic ambiguity nevertheless under-lines the central point that for the imperialists Britain and the empire were inextricably intertwined, with the empire providing not only the vehicle through which the British ruled much of the rest of the world, but being equally important as a factor in the creation of Britain as an intellectual and political construct.

The ideology of empire was influential in shaping the identity of the British national state and provided it with an important part of its raison d'être. Imperial issues were an important part of the practical business of politics too: they occupied the minds of Britain's states-men, were debated in the electoral arena and consequently helped to promote the enlarged sense of Britishness that was characteristic of the later Victorian period. Already in the 1850s Palmerston owed much of his domestic popularity to his reputation as a staunch defender of British interests, but in the emergence of popular imperialism as in other respects the transition to a more democratic system of mass politics after 1867 was a crucial watershed. Before that, neither party identities nor democratic politics were fully developed; a broad consensus existed in the ranks of the nation's political elite on most of the major policy issues of the day, imperial and non-imperial alike. After the 1867 Reform Act this mid-century consensus began to break down and the political system went through a significant change. An enlarged electorate had to be more assiduously wooed by political leaders. The two-party system at Westminster became more clearly defined, and competing party organizations were established in the country to mobilize support. As elections became more genuine national contests, rival leaders presented more sharply differentiated party programmes to the voters in order to appeal to particular interest groups and build up a popular party base. In constructing these competing identities, domestic issues (religion, education, social reform) were obviously of considerable significance, but foreign and imperial questions were also very much part and parcel of the party battle.

Disraeli was the first political leader of the post-Palmerstonian era consciously to don the imperialist mantle. In opposition in the early 1870s he deliberately positioned the Conservatives as the 'national' party, one of whose 'three great objects' (as defined in his speech to the National Union of Conservative Associations at the Crystal Palace in June 1872) was 'the maintenance of the empire' – in contrast to the Liberals, whom he portrayed as insufficiently vigorous in their imperial resolve.[20] The Conservative government of 1874–80, over which Disraeli presided, did its best to redeem the Crystal Palace pledge, and is conventionally seen as marking the beginnings of the 'new imperialist' trend. Under the colonial secretaryship of Lord Carnarvon it adopted a forward policy in southern Africa, annexing the Transvaal and declaring war on the Zulus in pursuit of a scheme to create a South African federation. A firm line was taken against the Russians, with war being threatened in 1877 to prevent Russian expansion in the Balkans and waged against Afghanistan in 1878 to forestall the Russian threat to the North-West Frontier. Meanwhile Disraeli's instinct for the grand gesture, coupled with shrewd political calculation, prompted him to purchase a major interest in the Suez Canal (a vital link in imperial communications) and to have Queen Victoria proclaimed 'Empress of India'. By skilful diplomacy at the time of the Berlin Congress of 1878 (which followed the conclusion of the Russo-Turkish War) Disraeli and the foreign secretary, Lord Salisbury, not only secured Cyprus from the Turks but placed British influence at the heart of the European international concert. None of this perhaps was as complete a break with previous policy as it appeared, nor were all of Disraeli's initiatives uniformly successful. (The annexation of the Transvaal ended in Boer rebellion and the war of independence in 1880–81; the Afghan War was costly and inconclusive.) But the impression was nevertheless lodged in the public mind that the Conservatives were the imperial party, and they were able to draw on this feeling as a source of popular support for the rest of the century.

This is not to say that the Liberals were as lukewarm, let alone hostile, in their attitudes towards the empire as Disraeli implied. Charles Dilke, author of *Greater Britain*, was a Liberal MP and a leading figure on the party's radical wing until his career was ruined by a divorce scandal in 1886. In the 1870s the Whigs, Lords Granville and Hartington, who led the party after Gladstone's temporary retirement in 1875, supported most of Disraeli's foreign and imperial policies. In the 1880s and 1890s the party developed a more organized 'Liberal imperialist' wing that drew its inspiration from Lord Rosebery, foreign secretary in 1886 and 1892–94 and prime minister in 1894–95. Even under Gladstone, Liberal governments showed their willingness to use force if necessary to protect Britain's imperial interests, as in the bombardment of Alexandria and the occupation of Egypt in 1882.

However, while the Liberals were far from being anti-imperialist in outlook, it is fair to argue that many Liberals, especially those of a Gladstonian stamp, viewed the empire through different eyes than their Conservative opponents. The radical wing of the party was more reluctant to support aggressive policies of imperial expansion (John Bright resigned from Gladstone's government over its involvement in Egypt; Lloyd George and John Morley later opposed the South African War of 1899–1902). The Liberal Party as a whole believed in the devolution of power (at least to the white dominions) as the best way of preserving imperial unity, and their fundamental commitment to free trade made them sceptical of plans for closer economic ties based on preferential tariffs, which by the turn of the century were being advocated by some Conservatives. Liberal commitments to reduced expenditure on military and naval forces also made it more difficult for them to contemplate imperial adventures of the kind that Gladstone condemned as the worst excesses of 'Beaconsfieldism' in his Midlothian campaigns of 1879–80, with reference to Disraeli's Zulu and Afghan Wars.[21]

Conservative propaganda painting the Liberals as a party not to be trusted with the empire was leant extra resonance by particular episodes such as the death of General Gordon – killed by the Mahdi's Dervish warriors at Khartoum in 1885 because Gladstone's government had hesitated over the despatch of a relief force. The Liberal conversion to Irish Home Rule was also denounced by Unionists as threatening the break-up of the empire. These perceptions, moreover, were electorally significant, playing their part in Liberal defeats in 1874 and 1886 and in the steadily increasing support for the Conservative Party. Especially after its alliance with the Liberal Unionists following the Liberal split of 1886, the Conservative Party became the main focus of organized imperial sentiment, a development which not even the emergence of Roseberyite Liberal Imperialism could offset. Conservative Party organizations such as the Primrose League made imperialism an integral feature of the Conservatives' popular appeal, while the policies of the Salisbury governments confirmed that the empire was safe – and growing – in Conservative hands.[22] The reconquest of the Sudan in the late 1890s gave the public a textbook demonstration of Conservative imperial strategy, as well as avenging the death of General Gordon in the most emphatic manner imaginable. Under Joseph Chamberlain, colonial policy became more systematic and ambitious, notably in South Africa but also with regard to his schemes for imperial development in the tropics and the discussion of plans for closer economic and defence links between Britain and the colonies, if not for a more fully realized imperial federation. All of these issues were part of the common currency of political debate and informed the political culture of Britain towards the end of the Victorian period.

There were even more direct ways in which imperial and domestic politics interacted, such as in variants of 'social imperialism', which utilized imperial sentiment, and the promised benefits of empire, to encourage loyalty to established institutions and to consolidate the position of the existing political elite. As studies of the period have shown, this was a feature of politics across Europe, where governing regimes attempted to manipulate the forces of nationalism to bolster their authority. In France, both under Napoleon III and the Third Republic, imperial expansion and an adventurous foreign policy were used to boost the domestic popularity of governments. Bismarck, and later Kaiser Wilhelm II, used the same tactics to even greater effect in Germany, so much so that imperialism has been viewed as a vital component of the governing elite's 'strategy of integration' in the Bismarckian and Wilhelmine *Reich*.[23] In Britain too, although imperial issues could be divisive in the party political sense, imperialism was used by political leaders as a tool to reinforce support for the British state and its institutions, and the growth in the late nineteenth century of a British imperial nationalism did much to counteract the centrifugal effects of more disruptive internal nationalist movements.[24]

In all of this the monarchy played a central role, the association of 'Queen and Country' becoming the cornerstone of Victorian popular patriotism. This was a natural extension into a more democratic age of the traditional unifying role of the monarchy, yet it did not happen entirely without assistance from above. In the eighteenth century George III had been a popular monarch, but, as head of the British state, he had nevertheless become deeply embroiled in political controversy. His two immediate successors, George IV and William IV, lacked his popular appeal. The accession of Victoria began the recovery of the monarchy in public esteem, and Victoria's visit to famine-struck Ireland in 1849 and her enthusiasm for the Scottish Highlands turned her into a more representatively 'British' monarch than even George III. Then, however, following the tragic death of her consort, Prince Albert, in 1861, Queen Victoria retreated into reclusive widowhood, refusing her share of public ceremonial and losing sympathy and popularity in consequence. The early 1870s saw the only serious surge of republicanism in Britain in the nineteenth century (led, interestingly, among others, by the radical Charles Dilke, the enthusiastic advocate, in another persona, of 'Greater Britain').

It was only after the demonstrations of public rejoicing at the recovery of the Prince of Wales from typhoid in 1871 that Victoria allowed herself to be persuaded by her ministers to resume a more public role; it was from the mid-1870s therefore that the modern 'popular' monarchy can be said to have come into existence. David Cannadine has described the way in which 'the invention of tradition' gave rise to elaborately choreographed state occasions.[25] Disraeli's proclamation of Victoria as Empress of India cemented the link between monarchy, state and empire in the public mind. Thereafter the monarchy became the focus of celebrations of Britain's imperial and naval power for the rest of the century, the high points coming with Victoria's golden and diamond jubilees in 1887 and 1897. On the latter occasion especially the whole empire in microcosm paraded through the streets of London, and hundreds of thousands of Her Majesty's subjects participated directly or vicariously in the events of the summer. A Britain at the apogee of its power flaunted that power in the eyes of the world, and the figure of the Queen-Empress presided over the festivities as the personal embodiment of the unity of Britain and its empire and the recipient of affectionate patriotic tribute.

The temporary boost to patriotic feeling provided by events such as the royal jubilees with their attendant processions and reviews was reinforced by more mundane, long-term imperial propaganda by politicians and the state. The role of the Primrose League as a pro-imperial auxiliary to the Conservative Party has already been mentioned. There were other imperial organizations and pressure groups at work as well. Imperial feelings were stimulated by an educational system that promoted the officially sponsored imperial ideology in its curriculum, particularly through the teaching of subjects like history and geography. The spread of state control of education after the introduction of compulsory elementary schooling meant, moreover, that the imperial version of these subjects was taught in all parts of the United Kingdom, encouraging generations of young scholars to grow up with a background appreciation of their common British imperial identity, perhaps at the expense of an awareness of local national cultures.

The fruits of these policies can be seen, negatively, in the absence of any serious, organized opposition to imperialism in late Victorian Britain, or even of any major anti-imperial tendencies.[26] It also appears that successful imperialism, or the promise of firm imperial action, materially assisted politicians in the winning and keeping of power, and constituted an important ingredient in their electoral appeal. Disraeli's victory in 1874 owed much to the perceived weakness of Gladstone's foreign and imperial policies, whereas in 1880 the Conservatives suffered for their own failures on the imperial front (as well as because of the effects of economic depression). For the rest of the century the Conservative Party's position was buoyed up by its reputation as the imperial party – in turn a logical corollary of its stance in defence of the British–Irish Union. The most clear-cut example of the electoral potential of imperial issues was provided by the 'Khaki election' of 1900, when the Salisbury government chose to capitalize on what was believed to be imminent victory in the South African War to secure a renewal of its mandate at the polls. With the Liberal opposition divided over its attitude to the war, and thus perceived once again as unpatriotic ('a vote for the Liberals is a vote for the Boers', in the Conservative slogan), the Conservatives won a further landslide to follow their earlier victory in 1895. Not only did this demonstrate the efficacy of imperialism as an electoral weapon, but it also showed the extent to which the politics of Britain and the politics of empire were intertwined.

The imperial dimension of British politics was important for the empire, but also for the development of the British state itself. If there was such a thing as 'British' nationalism in the nineteenth century, the empire was crucial in giving it life. Enthusiasm for the empire could be used as an integrating force to strengthen the solidarity of the nation at times of internal unrest and external threat. The question that remains is how far this nationalism was the product of the political manipulation of a docile public opinion, how far there was a spontaneous popular basis to the imperial mood. In what ways did the ideology and politics of empire reflect a more widely diffused British imperial identity than could be explained by the idea of imperialism solely as a strategy designed by the ruling elite to preserve and extend the interests and institutions of the British state?

Empire and identity

The evolution of an imperial identity on the part of the British people was a complex, and not necessarily a wholly conscious, process. Before the nineteenth century, as has been seen, popular Britishness was undoubtedly stimulated by external factors, just as before the creation of a British state the English had discovered a sense of common identity through being opposed in war by the Scots, the Spaniards, French and Dutch. Even for the English of the sixteenth century, though, this identity was outward looking and expansive rather than narrowly defensive. England's naval successes and early colonies made her a potential imperial power, and the national consciousness began to respond to this awareness even while the Reformation and battles against the Armada were reinforcing insularity. By the eighteenth century the imperial mood was more fully developed, the imperial dimension of Britishness being reflected in popular culture and the growth of commercial activity associated with imperial trade as well as in more political forms. The American War, and the Revolutionary and Napoleonic Wars that followed, brought questions of imperial policy and Britain's world-power status to the forefront of public debate and ensured that the context in which popular opinions and attitudes were formed was international and imperial rather than simply English or British in character. During the nineteenth century, and especially in the Victorian period, the imperial aspect of national life was so deeply embedded in the popular mind that it was integral to the identity of the British people and their self-image. It was precisely the depth of this ingrained imperial sentiment that made 'imperialism from above' so effective as a form of political propaganda and as a means of promoting the political integration of the British state.

Any analysis of the development of Britain's imperial culture needs to proceed simultaneously on a number of levels. Among the leaders and opinion formers in society it is certainly possible to identify elite groups and interests that together constituted a self-consciously 'imperial' class. These included not only politicians and members of the aristocracy who might be employed in the imperial and diplomatic service, but also the military and naval officers who were engaged in colonial wars, garrison duties and the protection of trade routes and for whom the patriotic imperatives of 'Queen and Empire' were reinforced by the prospect of personal advancement through successful action in the imperial sphere. This combination of the 'imperial ethos' and motives of careerism and self-interest applied equally strongly to the expanding numbers of those employed in colonial administration – many of these from aspirant middle-class backgrounds who had absorbed the imperial message at public school or university and saw the empire as providing the best opportunity (literally) to make their way in the world. Organizations such as the Indian Civil Service developed carefully stratified career structures that appealed particularly to those who were equipped to be successful in the type of competitive examinations that were becoming the main method of selection for official life from the middle of the nineteenth century. Together these military, political and administrative elites created a substantial pro-imperial lobby in Victorian society, their sense of imperial duty complementing (though sometimes also coming into conflict with) the evangelical and expansionist pressures emanating from the Christian missionary societies and the powerful commercial and economic interest groups that each, in their own way, enthusiastically embraced the idea that Britain was an imperial nation. Although for the financial interests of the City of London the empire was only one among a number of areas of investment, and although there was more British trade with countries outside the empire than within it, there was a general recognition of the importance of the empire to key sectors of the economy and of the way in which Britain's imperial strength underpinned London's position as the world's leading financial centre and provided a platform for future economic growth.

However, it was not just the members of these elites who felt a direct personal investment in the fortunes of empire. Substantial numbers of members of the middle classes derived a part of their income from imperial stocks. Equally, there were significant groups of industrial workers who depended for their livelihoods on overseas and imperial trade, and who were more imperially minded as a result. The Lancashire cotton industry was heavily reliant on the empire, both as a supplier of raw materials and as an important market for finished goods. The engineering and shipbuilding industries built Britain's naval and merchant fleets, which were powered by British (and especially Welsh) coal. Railway track and locomotives were exported to India as part of a massive programme of infrastructural development. Munitions industries produced weapons for the imperial forces and colonial wars. In addition to these economic links, the empire was a source of employment in its own right – for soldiers and sailors in particular, but for a variety of other occupations as well. Through their own experience, and the ideas they communicated to family and friends, all the individuals who in their different ways 'followed the flag' contributed to the popular awareness of the empire and its importance in Britain's national life.

Another aspect of the popular connection with empire was the emigration movement. Between 1861 and 1900 over 7.5 million people emigrated from the UK, the majority of them to the United States but over one million to Australia and New Zealand, and a further 800,000 to Canada.[27] The results of this diaspora were profound. Most emigrants, whether individuals or families, left relatives behind them in the United Kingdom. Through their letters, and sometimes through return visits by themselves or their children, they formed a personal link in the chain that connected Britain with the outside world. Even for those who did not emigrate, 'Greater Britain' could be made a reality by communication with loved ones in the far-flung dominions, stimulating by suggestion the idea of the 'imperial family' to which the rhetoric of politicians often referred. The possibility of emigration was psychologically important in another sense too, in that the existence of 'new worlds', or lands of opportunity, enlarged the mental space in which individuals lived and made them more open to imperial ideas. Whether this had a uniform effect on the development of a 'British' identity is debatable. As has already been noted, the presence of large Irish (as well as Scots and Welsh) emigrant communities in the United States fed back into the growth of a heightened sense of national identity in those parts of the

United Kingdom in the late nineteenth century. The same was true to an extent of the expatriate Celtic communities of the empire, which may have identified more readily with the separate nations of the British Isles rather than with 'Britain' as a whole.[28] From the British perspective, however, it is perhaps more relevant that whatever the precise nature of the emotional and cultural interconnections that grew up, they all contributed in some way to the idea of the empire as an extension of Britain itself, with individuals being left to define 'Britain' for themselves in relation to their own circumstances and preconceptions.

Britain was integrated into a wider imperial culture, and the sense of empire permeated the fabric of British life, in other ways too. Britain exported a great deal: goods, people, religion, laws and forms of government. But the imperial relationship was a two-way one, and the empire exerted an influence on life in Britain as well. There was immigration from the empire as well as emigration to it, albeit at a lower level.[29] As a modern consumer society developed, the British found their lives being enriched by a variety of colonial imports, some of which were luxuries or works of art, others such as tea, sugar or tobacco becoming staples for the whole population and exercising a significant influence on everyday life, and even on national character. Advertisements often reflected the imperial origins of commodities, in an early form of 'Buy British' campaign. The imperial theme was built into the landscape not just on the advertising hoardings, or buildings with a direct imperial purpose, but in the choice of street names in an expanding urban environment and the frequent use of 'The Empire' as the name for new theatres, music halls or, later, cinemas. The English language gradually absorbed words from various parts of the empire, especially India. The sense of empire was further enhanced by the shared experience of contests between Britain (or England) and the imperial dominions in the sporting arena, particularly on the cricket field. Although sporting rivalries such as the England–Australia cricket tests also fostered a separate sense of colonial national identity, they were nonetheless part of a common culture that united colonies and the mother country and reinforced an awareness in Britain of the empire and its people. In other cases, sports were imported into Britain from the empire and represented a new fusion of British and imperial culture, polo perhaps being the best example.[30]

The empire was part of the cultural background of British life in fact and fiction alike. The popular literary culture of late Victorian

Britain was heavily laced with publications with imperial settings or imperial themes. This was especially true of the adventure stories for which there was an increasingly buoyant market with the spread of elementary education after the 1870s and the consolidation of a young, mainly male, readership. The novels of G.A. Henty and publications such as the *Boy's Own Paper* cultivated a taste for patriotic, empire-based stories which could then be fed further by writers like Henry Rider Haggard. Rudyard Kipling's poetry and prose conveyed the authentic flavours of empire to an even wider audience. Even works which were predominantly British in their settings often had plots that rested on Britain's imperial connections, including Wilkie Collins's *The Moonstone* and many of Conan Doyle's Sherlock Holmes stories, notably *The Sign of Four*. What is striking about these latter writings is that the empire did not obtrude artificially into stories; it was simply a natural extension of the world in which the authors worked. In an imaginative sense this would have been equally true for their readers. Throughout the educational curriculum subjects like history and geography would have been taught very much from an imperial perspective. Many of the reading classes would also have attended lectures or 'magic lantern' shows on imperial topics, or have read about the journeys of explorers or the efforts of missionaries in Africa and elsewhere, all of which contributed to the contextualization of an imperial culture.

The newspaper press played a vital role in this respect, and in terms of spreading a popular sense of empire it was significant that the expansion of the press coincided with the 'new imperialism' of the second half of the nineteenth century. The various colonial wars of the period from the 1860s onwards were reported with increasing rapidity and in increasing detail in daily and illustrated papers, with despatches from specialist war correspondents giving extra immediacy and excitement. This allowed the soldiers who led these enterprises (at least when they were successful) to emerge as popular heroes; it also gave an almost soap-opera quality to the conflicts themselves, fastening them on to the public mind as a real-life adventure in instalments and providing newspaper readers with the vicarious thrill of participation in the British imperial story. A good example of what this could mean in practice is provided by the young Winston Churchill. A subaltern fresh from Sandhurst, Churchill made his name with his first book, *The Story of the Malakand Field Force*, based on despatches written while serving with a punitive expedition on the North-West Frontier. He was one of the correspondents who advanced with Kitchener up the Nile to Khartoum in 1898, and then became hero as well as reporter during the Boer War, following his famous escape from captivity in Pretoria, having been taken prisoner while accompanying an armoured train into Boer-held territory. Churchill's reports were widely read, and the books based on them became bestsellers. He lectured lucratively on his experiences to enthusiastic patriotic audiences and used this as a springboard to launch his political career. Like Britain's other military heroes, his exploits were celebrated not only in the press but on commemorative souvenirs and even on cigarette cards (as well as in more conventional ways through the award of honours and medals), emphasizing just how far the imperial dimension could penetrate into everyday life.

Imperial, patriotic feelings were heightened in time of war, which was why Churchill was taken so enthusiastically to heart by a nation desperate for good news from the battlefield. (The relief of Mafeking, besieged by the Boers in the early stages of the war in South Africa, was greeted rapturously by public demonstrations for the same reason.) But the empire was a fact of life of which all Britain's inhabitants were aware, in one way or another, in peace and war alike. Moreover, although politicians like Disraeli and Salisbury, and writers like Seeley, referred to the empire as 'England's', imperial sentiment was genuinely British in its reach, sufficiently so to make it one of the defining characteristics of Britishness in the late Victorian period. The Scots, particularly, saw themselves as partners in the imperial project, and the large number of Scots who made their reputations as soldiers, administrators, explorers and missionaries testified to the scale of their imperial contribution, just as Glasgow and the Clyde were component parts of the larger imperial economy. The ability of Scots to blend their Scottishness with a British imperial spirit is exemplified in the life and works of John Buchan. A son of the manse, Buchan served as a young man on the staff of Milner in South Africa and ended his career as governor general of Canada. In his early novels such as *The Half-Hearted* and *Prester John* as well as in the later Richard Hannay adventures, Buchan showed his commitment to the imperial cause; he also wrote more serious works on imperial themes. But this personal imperialism (which drew him politically to the Unionist Party in Britain) was an extension rather than a negation of his Scottish identity.[31] Nor was Buchan unique, even among those who might domestically have been at odds with a British state that they felt to be insufficiently sensitive to the multi-national character of the

British Isles. The Welsh nationalist Tom Ellis, for example, was one of many who saw no contradiction in being both a British imperialist and an advocate within Britain of a local nationalist cause.[32]

The Scots and Welsh were happy to see themselves as partners in a British (though not an 'English') Empire. In the case of Ireland the situation was more complicated. Irish Unionists were able and eager to embrace a British imperial identity, and the families of the land-owning Ascendancy provided many of the empire's leading military figures. There were sufficient Irishmen serving in Britain's armed forces to give the Irish a stake in the wars of empire, and the large Irish communities in Canada and Australia provided a family connec-tion between Ireland and the British dominions. But there was an ambivalence in Ireland's relationship with the empire that did not exist, or at least was not fully articulated, in Scotland and Wales. This stemmed firstly from Ireland's perceived 'semi-colonial' status in relation to Britain, and secondly from the strength of the nationalist movement to which this subordination had given rise. Whereas in Scotland and Wales nationalists could reconcile their preferred national with a larger imperial identity, for Irish nationalists this was much more difficult, and not necessarily desirable. Thus it was that during the South African War the Irish Nationalist Party sympathized with the Boers fighting to preserve their freedom rather than with the British Empire. While it is true that there was radical criticism of the war in Britain as well – notably from the Welsh nationalist Lloyd George – the difference was that British radicals attacked the war because it sullied the honour of the empire; the Irish Nationalists attacked it because they were in conflict with the ideas and institu-tions of the empire itself.

Yet the extent of anti-imperial feeling should not be exaggerated. There were variations in the degree of enthusiasm for empire, and aspects of the imperial structure attracted criticism,[33] but the empire was integral to the sense of Britishness in the nineteenth century and those in the United Kingdom who rejected outright the British label were in a minority. The sense of belonging to a world-wide imperial community was encouraged by government propaganda and by the politics and pageantry of the imperial state, but it existed also as a more spontaneous feeling in the minds of the people, reinforced by economic self-interest, by family ties and by the popular culture that frameworked their daily lives. What is perhaps less easy to pin down is how this influenced popular perceptions of British nationhood, and how the imperial mood changed as the century progressed. The

Britishness of the imperial nation in the late Victorian period can be seen as a confident, even aggressive, assertion of national superiority, tinged with racist ideology and an assumption of Britain's God-given right to rule large areas of the globe. Yet in fact, by the end of the nineteenth century, while Britishness still implied the superiority of British character and ideas, the mood of the nation was becoming less confident about Britain's ability to preserve her pre-eminence and more defensive in outlook. Kipling's poem, *Recessional*, written in 1897 at the time of Victoria's diamond jubilee, is often taken as symptomatic of this shift, with its references to the fallen empires of the past and the dangers of hubristic over-confidence. The empire was thus undoubtedly an important factor in shaping British national identity in the nineteenth century, and fostering a spirit of national unity, but the tenor of Britishness was subject to change and mutation over time. As the Victorian age gave way to the twentieth century, both the empire and the British nation with whose fortunes it was so closely and reciprocally connected were poised to enter a new period of crisis and redefinition, in which the idea of Britishness, the integrity of the nation and the relationship between the British state and its people would be tested to the limit. Whether in these conditions Britain's imperial identity would retain its appeal, or whether it would slowly wither and die as the forces that had given it life ebbed away, remained to be seen.

CHAPTER 5

CRISIS AND CONFLICT: THE BRITISH STATE, 1900–1922

The first quarter of the twentieth century was a time of crisis and change for the British state at home and abroad. At its heart lies the multiple trauma of the First World War, yet several of the developments and trends that came to fruition after the war, and were accelerated by it, had their roots in the pre-war period and need to be studied over the longer term. In the history of the British state itself three particular developments stand out. One is the change in the relationship between Britain and Ireland, which by 1922 had led to the break-up of the Union of 1801 and the establishment of an independent Irish Free State in the south of Ireland and a separate devolved administration in the partitioned British north. A second is the continuing process of democratization represented by the reduction of the powers of the House of Lords in the Parliament Act of 1911 and the introduction of adult male, and limited female, suffrage for elections to the House of Commons in 1918. The third is the expansion of the role of central government, as the twin imperatives of warfare and welfare produced a much more interventionist, centrally powerful state, far removed from the laissez faire ideal of the mid-nineteenth century. At the same time as these changes were occurring, the attitudes and outlook of people in Britain were being affected by the international context. Patriotic and national feeling was stimulated by the approach of war, and the wartime experience encouraged a sense of national unity even while generating other problems of integration and social cohesion. Whether, as a consequence of these changes, the British people became more self-consciously 'British' is one of the main questions that this chapter will address, by considering the central events and characteristics of the pre-war, wartime and post-war periods. It will begin by examining the problems confronting the British state during the so-called 'Edwardian Crisis' before 1914. This will be followed by a discussion of the impact on British society and the state of the First World War and the relevance of the themes of nationhood and identity to the history of Britain in the immediate post-war period, with particular reference to British–Irish relations and the end of the Union.

The Edwardian crisis, 1901–14

The Edwardian era, which spanned the years between the death of Queen Victoria in January 1901 and the outbreak of the European war in August 1914, has the enduring fascination of a lost world. Ever since the publication of George Dangerfield's highly coloured account of *The Strange Death of Liberal England* in the 1930s, the period has attracted the attention of historians keen to prove or disprove the contention that Britain at this time was in an advanced state of domestic crisis which mirrored the escalating tension on the international scene.[1] This crisis has usually been cast in terms of a threefold challenge to the established social and political order represented by the sometimes violent campaigns of the suffragettes for 'Votes for Women', the upsurge of militant trade union protest associated with the ideas of syndicalism, and a right-wing 'Tory rebellion' against parliamentary government based on opposition to the pre-war Liberal administration's plans to reform the House of Lords and grant Home Rule to Ireland.[2] Much ink has been spilled on these topics, and it is not necessary to recapitulate the details of those debates here. Yet the pre-war crisis does have a bearing on our current themes, first because it was a crisis of the British state and its institutions, second because the forces of nationalism played a vital part both in the origins of the crisis and the means by which politicians and others sought to avert its more damaging consequences. Indeed, the 'Edwardian Crisis' could just as easily be seen in some senses as a 'crisis of nationalism', as the British state responded to what were perceived as external threats while struggling to preserve its unity in the face of the renewed disruption associated with domestic national discontents.

The crisis unfolded against a backdrop of uncertainty that hastened a reappraisal across all areas of foreign and domestic policy. In foreign affairs, for example, the South African War of 1899–1902 highlighted the dangers of international isolation and imperial overstretch. No foreign powers had intervened actively on the Boer side, but Kaiser Wilhelm's Germany had briefly threatened to mobilize an anti-British bloc of 'armed neutrality', and Germany's plans for naval expansion (embodied in Tirpitz's Navy Laws of 1898 and 1900) raised the spectre of a challenge to Britain's mastery of the seas on which both her commercial strength and imperial security depended. As a result of these and similar intimations of vulnerability, British foreign policy in the Edwardian period underwent considerable redefinition, emphasizing the need for more general agreements with other powers and a tightening of the bonds of imperial defence, building on the cooperation between Britain and the colonies which had seen the empire to victory in South Africa. The first fruits of this redefinition, or reorientation, of policy were shown in the Anglo-Japanese Alliance of 1902, which gave Britain an ally in the Far East and facilitated naval redeployments to home waters. The chimera of an Anglo-German alliance was pursued by Chamberlain and others, but foundered on the unreliability of the Kaiser and Germany's insistence on Britain becoming a full member of the Triple Alliance with the Central Powers. Instead, rather than risk being drawn into a war on the side of Germany against Russia and France, Britain made agreements with those powers to settle outstanding colonial differences and pave the way for cooperation against Germany. The 'Entente Cordiale' with France in 1904 and the Anglo-Russian entente of 1907 were the cornerstones of British foreign policy until 1914.[3] At the same time the Balfour government established a Committee of Imperial Defence in 1903 to formalize cooperation between Britain and the dominions to protect the empire in the event of a future conflict.

One consequence of this perception of the weakening position of Britain as a world power, paradoxical though it may seem, was the growth of a more self-conscious, if essentially defensive, British nationalism, concerned to build up the strength of the British state and its empire in the face of foreign military, economic and imperial rivalries, and also to unify the British people behind agreed agendas for change. More and more, among Unionists especially, the empire was seen as the key to Britain's survival as a great power and became the focus of British nationalist sentiment. As Joseph Chamberlain put it in 1902, 'The days are for great empires, and not for little states'.[4] He drew the conclusion that the reorganization of imperial defence arrangements should be accompanied by closer political and economic union as well. It was in pursuit of this aim that he began public discussion – at the 1902 Colonial Conference – of what by 1903 had become a fully fledged campaign for tariff reform: the transformation of the empire from a loose collection of colonies into a more organized, self-sufficient economic unit protected against foreign imports by external tariff barriers and with internal trade between Britain and the colonies regulated by a system of preferential duties. Chamberlain's proposals were highly controversial. In Britain they were unpopular because they departed from liberal free trade orthodoxy and threatened to raise the price of imported foodstuffs. Meanwhile the colonies, whose leaders did not necessarily share Chamberlain's goal of imperial federation, were equally unenthusiastic because they feared their own economies would be artificially manipulated for Britain's benefit, frustrating their industrial ambitions and relegating them to the role of agricultural suppliers to the mother country. Nevertheless, the tariff reform debate was to play a major part in British politics from the early 1900s to the 1930s. Chamberlain's resignation from the government to spearhead the Tariff Reform League in 1903, and the support he received from sectors of the business community and from sections of the Conservative rank-and-file (where protectionism had been growing in popularity since the 1880s), testified to the development of a more assertive economic nationalism committed to the defence of Britain's interests in the face of the competitive advantages that were coming to be enjoyed by rival industrial powers like Germany and the United States.

Chamberlain's schemes of tariff reform were part of a more wide-ranging nationalist impulse that galvanized British politics in the Edwardian period. The South African War had revealed other weaknesses in the military, administrative and social structures of the state that prompted a variety of proposals for reversing Britain's incipient national decline. Under the umbrella slogan of 'National Efficiency' politicians and reformers from all parts of the political spectrum brought forward ideas for improving the condition of the nation and its people.[5] Many of these related to the issue of social reform, since the unfitness of many volunteers for military service in South Africa had confirmed the fears raised by late nineteenth-century poverty surveys (notably Rowntree's *Poverty, A Study of Town Life*, published in 1901) about the 'degeneracy' of Britain's imperial race. The government appointed an Inter-Departmental Committee on Physical Deterioration to investigate the problems and recommend remedies, which it did in 1904. A more direct answer to the problem of military weakness was seen as extended compulsory military training, along lines adopted by the Continental powers. A National Service League – supported by, among others, Lord

Roberts, the former commander-in-chief in South Africa – was formed in 1902 to campaign for this end. The Boy Scout movement, founded in 1908 by another South African War hero, Sir Robert Baden-Powell, was a similar, though unofficial, attempt to improve the physical fitness and military skills of a rising generation while imbuing them with the proper imperial spirit.

In the changed conditions that followed the Boer War military-imperial patriotism and British nationalism revealed themselves in other ways too. 'Empire Day' was instituted as an annual celebration in 1904 to remind the British people of their common imperial heritage. At the same time, common interests were emphasized by a succession of international crises and fears about a future European war, including the possibility of a foreign invasion of Britain itself. In the late nineteenth century, France and Russia had been seen as Britain's most likely enemies. By the early twentieth century, however, Germany, with its unstable Kaiser and its expanding naval fleet, was coming to be seen as a more serious threat. The idea of a German invasion was graphically popularized in a series of 'invasion novels' which achieved wide circulation in Edwardian Britain, the most noteworthy (and most literate) of them being Erskine Childers' *The Riddle of the Sands*, published in 1903.[6] Popular fiction helped to create and also reflected a contemporary mood, revealed elsewhere in the pages of right-wing journals such as Leo Maxse's *National Review*, which was becoming more militarist, nationalist and even xenophobic. The National Service League's conscriptionist propaganda was paralleled by the efforts of a number of other right-wing pressure groups, for example the Navy League which pressed for more rapid naval rearmament to counter the German threat. A cruder form of 'race patriotism' came to the surface in the eugenics movement (motivated in part by a desire, influenced by late nineteenth-century social-Darwinism, to improve the country's racial-imperial stock) and in the language and prejudices of the time, including a heightened anti-Semitism and increased hostility in some areas (like the East End of London) to foreign immigrants and refugees. In a bid to assuage these feelings, and to tap into them for electoral support, the Conservative government introduced an Aliens Act in 1905 imposing restrictions on immigration and curtailing Britain's traditionally liberal 'open-door' policy towards refugees and asylum-seekers.[7]

Right-wing nationalism of this kind, emphasizing the unifying aspects of 'Britishness' in the face of a foreign threat, was a powerful factor in Edwardian political life. It was a sign of the complexity of questions of national identity within the British state, however, that in the early 1900s the fortunes of the political party most closely associated with this straightforward British nationalism were actually in decline. The end of the South African War and Salisbury's resignation from the premiership in 1902 marked the beginning of the end of the late Victorian Conservative political hegemony. Salisbury's successor, Arthur Balfour, was unable to prevent a developing rift in his party between tariff reformers and 'free fooders', and found himself facing a resurgent Liberal opposition, reunited after its divisions during the Boer War by the need to rally in defence of free trade and further boosted in electoral terms by a secret pact between the Liberal Party and the newly formed Labour Representation Committee which removed the threat of Liberals being opposed by Labour candidates at the next election. When that election occurred at the beginning of 1906 – following the resignation of Balfour's government in December 1905 and the formation of a minority administration under the Liberal leader, Sir Henry Campbell-Bannerman – its result seemed little short of revolutionary. The Conservatives reaped the full harvest of their unpopularity over issues such as the 1902 Education Act and the 'Chinese slavery' scandal in South Africa and were resoundingly beaten.[8] They and their Liberal Unionist allies won only 156 seats, while the victorious Liberals took 399, with the independent Labour wing of the 'progressive alliance' claiming a further 29.

The Liberals espoused a more tolerant, less xenophobic brand of Britishness. Their continuing commitment to free trade was evidence of the persistence of more optimistic Gladstonian attitudes to international relations, based on cooperation rather than conflict. In imperial policy the Liberals similarly favoured a conciliatory approach, recognizing the rights of the dominions to run their own affairs and adopting measures designed to appease non-British nationalists in South Africa and India. They accepted the need for army reorganization and naval rearmament but rejected excessive militarism or the introduction of compulsory military service. Domestically the alliance with the Labour Party signalled the Liberals' commitment to social reform, but they also remained the natural allies of minority nationalities within the United Kingdom, their 1906 victory benefiting, among other factors, from the hostility of Welsh Nonconformists to the 1902 Education Act which provided increased public support for Anglican schools.

Thus, even though there were broad continuities in foreign policy after 1906 (notably the signing of the entente with Russia), there were differences of style and tone. On the domestic front, the gulf between the parties was wider, and conflict deepened after 1906. The Liberal government embarked on a sweeping programme of reform, in which the 'old Liberalism' of Nonconformist radicalism was combined with a 'New Liberalism' committed to interventionist measures of welfare legislation such as the introduction of old age pensions (1908), minimum wages for low-paid workers (1909) and schemes for health and unemployment insurance (1911) which, according to some historians, laid the foundations for the 'welfare state' of the later twentieth century.[9] The Liberal programme aroused fierce Conservative opposition. While the Conservatives supported some of the aims of the social legislation (which were consistent with the broader 'National Efficiency' agenda), they would not accept that social reform should be paid for by increasing the taxation of the middle and upper classes rather than through the introduction of tariffs. Meanwhile, Liberal efforts to appease Nonconformist educationalists, land reformers and temperance enthusiasts were predictably unpopular with a party of Anglicans, landowners and brewers. The Conservatives consequently took a deliberate decision to use their inbuilt majority in the hereditary House of Lords to obstruct and amend legislation passed by the overwhelmingly Liberal House of Commons. The confrontation between the elected and aristocratic chambers came to a head in 1909 when the Conservatives in the Lords took the unprecedented step of rejecting the so-called 'People's Budget' by which the Liberal chancellor, David Lloyd George, had intended to finance the government's spending plans.[10] Asquith, prime minister since Campbell-Bannerman's resignation because of ill health in 1908, responded to the challenge to his government's authority by persuading the king to grant a dissolution of parliament and calling a general election to win popular endorsement for the budget and for the principle of a reduction in the Lords' powers.

The next two years saw some of the fiercest parliamentary and electoral battles since the debates over the Great Reform Bill in 1830–32.[11] In the election of January 1910 the Liberals lost their overall majority in the Commons (winning only 274 seats to the Unionists' 272) and remained in power only with the support of Labour and Irish Nationalist MPs. The political situation was further complicated by the death of King Edward VII in May 1910 and the accession of George V. In an attempt to find a compromise solution to the crisis, leaders of the two main parties met in a constitutional conference through the summer. Only after they had failed to find an agreed way out of the impasse over Lords reform, and after a second general election in December 1910 had confirmed the electorate's verdict of January, did the government finally, with the new king's reluctant approval, proceed with the Parliament Bill which, when it became law in August 1911, removed the Lords' right to veto legislation and gave the House of Commons guaranteed predominance in financial matters.[12]

Taken together, the Liberals' victory over the House of Lords and their programme of social reform could be seen as important both in democratizing the central institutions of the British state and extending the role of the state in the life of society as a whole. The electoral contests of 1910 also seemed to demonstrate the continuing 'nationalization' of British politics, since they were fought by two opposing national political parties on an essentially national, British, political agenda. Indeed, some years ago Peter Clarke argued that the elections of 1910 marked a crucial watershed between the 'old' politics of regionalism and religious denominationalism and the 'new' politics of class and social welfare.[13] In one sense this judgement seems borne out by the events of the pre-war period. Social and industrial issues continued to be high on the government's political agenda, not least because of the intensity of labour unrest and the number of national disputes in major industries. Other questions – from women's suffrage to naval rearmament – were national rather than local in character. There was also a continuing expansion of the role of central government and of the apparatus of the state, for example in the conciliation of industrial disputes and the policing of strikes.[14]

This did not mean, however, that regionalism and internal national variations had become irrelevant to the British state or to the workings of the British political system. The 1906 election, where one party had been victorious in all parts of Britain, was an aberration in post-1885 electoral history. In the elections of 1910 England, Scotland and Wales reasserted their separate political identities, with the Conservatives regaining their ascendancy in England while the Liberals retained their predominance in Scotland and Wales.[15] The regional imbalance between the parties reflected the different political conditions in the three countries (and indeed between different districts in each) and in turn had an influence on the programmes and policies that the parties adopted in relation to a range of political issues, not least that of the future internal organization of the British state itself. The Conservatives (or, as they more frequently described themselves in this period, the 'Unionists'[16]), with their stronger base in the English hub of the United Kingdom and their commitment to the defence of established institutions such as the monarchy, the Church of England and the House of Lords, wanted to preserve the structures of a unitary state, and consequently England's dominant role in the Union. The Liberals, conversely, although not wishing the Union to be dissolved, and pursuing policies that were in some respects expanding the power of central government, were, as the party of the periphery, more favourably inclined towards the devolution of power to the constituent parts of the United Kingdom, striking a balance between the claims of the centre and those of the regions which aimed to maintain the essential unity of the British state by recognition of its domestic diversity.

The constitutional arguments over devolution, which had been aired in the debates over Home Rule in the 1880s and 1890s, resurfaced in the Edwardian period. Ireland was again the prime focus of concern. Ten years of 'constructive Unionism' between 1895 and 1905 had not weakened the electoral appeal of the Irish Nationalist Party nor lessened its commitment to a separate Irish legislature. The return of a Liberal government in 1906 did not immediately result in constitutional change, since the Liberals of the post-Gladstonian era had adopted a more cautious 'step-by-step' Irish policy, the only fruit of which was an abortive Irish Council Bill in 1907. However, the political and constitutional crisis of 1909–11 altered the situation in two respects that placed Home Rule back at the centre of the stage. The first was that the elections of 1910 left the Irish Nationalist MPs, under the former Parnellite John Redmond, holding the balance of power in the House of Commons, making Asquith's government dependent on their support for its continuation in office. Secondly, the passage of the Parliament Act of 1911, in abolishing the House of Lords' veto, removed a major constitutional obstacle to the enactment of Home Rule in the face of Unionist opposition.

Yet Ireland was not the only factor in the devolutionary equation. In Scotland and Wales Home Rule movements re-emerged in the pre-war years, and there was discussion of possible federal solutions to the 'British' problem involving the setting up of devolved government in England or the English regions to make a reality of the proposals for 'Home Rule All Round' which had been floated since the 1880s. As far as Scotland and Wales were concerned, Home Rule was linked to nationalism, but it could also be advocated for reasons of administrative efficiency and the modernization of government. Welsh nationalism was encouraged by the scale of the Liberal electoral triumph of 1906, by the effects of the religious revivalism sweeping the principality and by the elevation of Lloyd George to the cabinet. Thereafter, however, a measure of frustration and disillusion set in. The government made no real progress towards lessening what Nonconformists saw as the unfairness of the 1902 Education Act, nor to the larger goal of disestablishment of the Welsh Church. There were minor concessions to administrative decentralization – the establishment of a Welsh Department at the Board of Education and a Council of Agriculture for Wales – but no recognition of Welsh political identity beyond the ceremonial diversion of the investiture of a new Prince of Wales at Caernarfon in 1911.[17] This lack of progress prompted the launching of the 'second' Welsh Home Rule movement, led by E.T. John, the Liberal MP for East Denbigh since December 1910, who became president of the newly constituted Welsh National League.[18] The Welsh Home Rule Bill, which he introduced in the House of Commons in March 1914, had little truly popular support, and even less chance of making legislative progress. But the ventilation of the issue alongside the debates over the Welsh Disestablishment Bill (finally introduced in April 1912) showed that the 'Welsh question' was still on the broader political agenda.

Sections of Scottish opinion were also making more assertively nationalist noises, albeit mainly from within the Liberal establishment, and the issue of Home Rule played a larger part in the politics of Edwardian Scotland than has sometimes been realized.[19] The main focus of the campaign was the Young Scots Society, formed as a Liberal ginger group after the election defeat of 1900, which had 50 branches and as many as 10,000 members by 1914. The Young Scots inclined towards the New Liberal wing of their party and were enthusiastic advocates of a progressive policy of social reform. They recognized, however, that as the role of the central British state expanded it became even less sensitive to the particular needs of Scotland. Parliament had little time to consider separate Scottish legislation, and when it did so its non-Scottish members did not fully understand the intricacies of Scottish law and institutions. This had led to difficulties in adapting housing and welfare legislation designed for England to a Scottish context. The Liberal government attempted to deal with the problem by reviving the Scottish Grand Committee in 1907, but the rejection by the Lords of two Scottish Land Bills showed the unresponsiveness of central institutions to Scottish wishes. The answer – as much for reasons of effective government as nationalism per se – seemed to be the creation of a devolved parliament in Scotland similar to that being proposed for Ireland, and it was for this that the Young Scots organized a public campaign and introduced a series of unsuccessful Scottish Home Rule Bills in the Commons between 1906 and 1914.

The option of a comprehensive devolutionary reform of the British state (or what was loosely called 'federalism' in some quarters) received support from a wide range of political opinion. The Liberal and Labour parties were officially committed to devolution in a British context (and specifically to Scottish as well as Irish Home Rule), and the principle of devolution was consistent too with the Liberal government's imperial policy, which had included the re-granting of self-government to the Transvaal and the Orange Free State and the creation in 1910 of an autonomous Union of South Africa as a dominion of the British Empire. Even on the Unionist side of the political divide there were those who were willing to consider a federal solution to the British problem, as exemplified by a series of pro-federal articles written by 'Pacificus' (F.S. Oliver) in *The Times* in 1910. Pro-federal Unionists accepted the Liberal argument that devolution would strengthen rather than weaken the British state, by improving its efficiency. They also made the connection between the pursuit of a federal agenda in the UK and the possibility of creating a larger imperial federation on the Chamberlainite model, which was not part of Liberal plans. It was here that the ambiguities of the federalist case were revealed, since it was by no means clear that there was agreement on what form of federalism was being proposed and whether it would lead to a more powerful or less powerful central government. For most Unionists this ambiguity was a crucial factor in their rejection of federal schemes for the United Kingdom, except as a political tactic to delay the prior creation of a Dublin parliament. The Unionist case was that any devolution to subordinate legislatures would undermine the sovereignty of Westminster and would be the first step towards the break-up of the Union, with fateful consequences not just for the British state but for Britain's standing in the world and the cohesion of an empire in which centrifugal tendencies were already establishing themselves, as the dominions' resistance to closer association at the 1911 Imperial Conference had revealed.

Given these differences, the adoption of a fully federal policy of 'Home Rule All Round' was perhaps never very likely in the Edwardian period, despite Asquith's assertion in the debate on the government's Irish Home Rule Bill in April 1912 that this was simply 'the first step in a larger and more comprehensive policy'.[20] Popular demand for Home Rule in Scotland and Wales was not strong enough to force politicians to act, while the desire for devolution in England or the English regions was practically non-existent. Ireland consequently became the main battleground for the devolution debate and the focal point of the arguments over the future structure of the British imperial state.

The Home Rule Bill, which Asquith introduced to the Commons in 1912, was similar in most respects to Gladstone's proposal of 1893. It provided for the creation of a two-chamber Irish parliament that would have power, through its executive, over all of Ireland's internal affairs (with the exception of certain reserved matters such as social welfare and policing), while matters of foreign policy, external trade and taxation would continue to be dealt with at Westminster, where a reduced contingent of 42 Irish MPs would sit. The lord lieutenant was to remain as the nominal chief executive authority and the representative of the crown, but in most other ways Irishmen would at last become responsible for Ireland's affairs. Even so, the measure was not without its contentious aspect. Nationalists criticized the extent of the reserved powers, and there were arguments over the scale of Ireland's proposed contribution to the imperial exchequer and the limited ability of an Irish parliament to control its own revenue. More contentious, however, was the fact that the Bill made no special provision for Ulster, where there was strong Unionist opposition to Home Rule and a fear of the consequences for Ulster Protestants of establishing what in effect was likely to be a Catholic Nationalist-dominated legislature in Dublin. The fact that the Bill denied the Dublin parliament the right to amend its own constitution or to legislate on religious establishments did little to assuage Unionist concerns. Under the leadership of Sir Edward Carson, Ulster Unionists undertook a prolonged campaign against Home Rule, in which they sought and received the staunch backing of Unionists throughout the United Kingdom.

The severity of the ensuing political and constitutional crisis over the Home Rule Bill was deepened by the complexities of the legislative process at Westminster. The Parliament Act of 1911 had removed the right of the Lords to veto legislation, but it had established a cumbersome process whereby any measure opposed by the Lords had to pass unchanged through the Commons in three successive sessions of parliament before it could become law. This meant that the Unionist majority in the Lords could obstruct the Home Rule Bill for at least two years, giving the opponents of Home Rule time to organize themselves and creating additional pressures that the Liberals had to find ways of overcoming. The resulting crisis was certainly of major proportions, and in the views of many contemporaries and historians brought the United Kingdom close to civil war by the summer of 1914.[21] The British Unionist leader, Andrew Bonar Law (who had replaced Balfour at the head of his party in 1911), raised the temperature with speeches in Belfast and Britain in the spring and summer of 1912. At Belfast on Easter Tuesday he universalized the Ulster struggle by exhorting Ulstermen to 'save the empire' by defeating Home Rule. At Blenheim Palace in July he went further, warning the Liberal government that there were 'things stronger than Parliamentary majorities' and telling his audience that 'I can imagine no length of resistance to which Ulster can go in which, in my belief, they would not be supported by the overwhelming majority of the British people'.[22] Taking their cue from Bonar Law, Carson's Ulstermen organized the signing of the 'Ulster Covenant' in September 1912, by which over 200,000 Ulster Unionists pledged to work for the defeat of Home Rule by 'all means which may be found necessary', including the establishment of a separate provisional government for Ulster and the resistance by force of any attempt by the British government to coerce Ulster into accepting a Dublin parliament against its will.

The situation was admittedly not as clear-cut as the rhetoric suggested. There was substantial pro-Home Rule feeling in Ulster (where Nationalists briefly held a majority of parliamentary seats in the nine counties following a by-election victory in 1913), just as there was a significant Unionist minority in the rest of Ireland. In the course of the Home Rule debates, moreover, various proposals were brought forward for excluding Ulster, or part of it, from the working of a Home Rule settlement, on either a temporary or permanent basis. It is possible that eventually, as the crisis reached its decisive point in 1914, some form of Ulster 'opt-out' would have been agreed as a compromise to provide a way out of the impasse. But in the meantime the seriousness of the situation escalated in ways that threatened to get beyond the government's control. The Ulster Unionists established a 100,000-strong Ulster Volunteer Force as a paramilitary political army to defend their province against Home Rule. The Nationalists responded by forming the 'Irish Volunteers' as a counterweight, and both sides began drilling and arming themselves in preparation for conflict. In Britain the Union Defence League collected signatures for a 'British Covenant', while the British League for the Support of Ulster and the Union gained the support of 100 peers and 120 MPs, and had over 10,000 members by 1914. Army officers demonstrated their reluctance to be used to coerce Ulster in the Curragh 'mutiny' of March 1914, and there seemed every prospect that the army commanders might collude with the Conservative Party and the Unionists in Ulster to deprive the elected government of the constitutional means to enforce its policies.[23] The failure of a conference of the parties at Buckingham Palace in July 1914 opened the way to a final showdown of uncertain outcome once the Home Rule Bill had been put on the statute book later in the summer.

The confrontation over Ulster was important in its own right, and in relation to the future of Ireland and the Union. It raised fundamental questions about the organization of the British state, in particular the workability of devolution in the British context as a response to the rise of Irish nationalism. It also brought to the surface complex aspects of the debate about British national identity. The Unionists in Ireland were fighting (or claimed to be willing to fight) in defence of their 'British' heritage, despite their Irish birth and domicile. Since they did not accept Liberal assurances that a Home Rule Ireland would remain an integral part of the British state, the spectre of Home Rule seemed to threaten their Britishness by forcing their incorporation into a Nationalist Ireland that they felt would inevitably slip its moorings and drift further away from the imperial government's control. Subsequent history, and the aspirations of many Nationalists for more complete self-government, suggest that Unionist fears may not have been wholly exaggerated, even if it is true that Ulster's inclusion in a Home Rule Ireland would have acted as a brake on any move towards independence. It raises the more general speculation that whereas devolution might have been an adequate response to the concerns of the Scottish or Welsh – where the demand was for greater efficiency and some sensitivity to local concerns but where loyalty to the British state itself was not an issue – it is possible that in the Irish case it could never have been more than a half-way house to the break-up of the Union.

For British Unionists, though, the Irish question intersected with perceptions of nationhood and identity in other ways too. Their sense of Britishness rested heavily on the preservation of existing state institutions, on the maintenance of the empire and Britain's place in

the world, and increasingly, in the Edwardian period, on an identification with the popular, militaristic, British nationalism represented
by the various right-wing and military pressure groups of the time.
After 1906 the Unionist community found itself on the defensive in
respect of its 'core' British identity in the face of the reforming
initiatives of the Liberal government and the rise of alternative radical
movements in the form of Labour and socialist groups and the
feminist campaigns for women's suffrage. The government continued
the Conservative policy of ententes and rearmament, but there was
concern that radical and pacifist pressure might lead to cuts in arms
spending which would endanger Britain's ability to maintain its status
in a more dangerous and hostile world. Devolution in the empire was
seen as prefiguring the break-up of the imperial state, just as Home
Rule in Ireland threatened the break-up of the Union. The reduction
in the powers of the House of Lords and the attack on the hereditary
landed aristocracy that lay behind it was seen as merely the prelude to
further assaults on the central establishment of the state, with the
battles over Home Rule and the parallel proposals for Welsh Disestablishment forming part of a rearguard action to prevent any further
undermining of 'British' institutions.

In other words, what was taking place in the fevered political
climate of the late Edwardian period was a clash of political cultures
of which Ireland was the focus but not the only cause. The so-called
'radical right' rallied to the Unionist standard because it opposed
Home Rule, but also because of its hostility to the danger which it felt
that the Liberal ministry posed to the future of Britain and the British
state.[24] This is not to say that Unionist perceptions were correct. The
Liberals genuinely believed that their policies were better suited to
improving the institutions of the state and safeguarding the interests
of the British people. The gap between the two parties may in any
case have been narrower than some of the more extreme elements on
either side would have been willing to admit. It could be argued that
politicians of both parties were seeking ways of integrating potentially
disruptive elements into the framework of a British national state;
that the disagreements between them were more about means than
about ends. But this does not mean that the conflicts of the Edwardian period were not about real issues, nor that the threatened
rebellion against Home Rule did not present a serious crisis for the
British state. How that crisis would have been resolved had it not
been for the outbreak of an even more serious conflict in August
1914 – whether it would have shattered the unity of the British state

in civil war or produced an 11th-hour compromise that left unity intact and honour satisfied – it is impossible to say.

What happened, of course, was that the internal divisions between the proponents of different futures for the British state – and different versions of 'Britishness' – were overwhelmed by the larger crisis of nationalism that engulfed the European continent. While the United Kingdom was facing the consequences of its own multi-national identity, the even more complex ethnic politics of the Austro-Hungarian Empire had boiled over in the Balkans. The assassination of the heir to the Austrian throne, the Archduke Franz Ferdinand, in the Bosnian capital Sarajevo on 28 June by a Bosnian-Serb nationalist triggered a confrontation between Austria-Hungary and her neighbour Serbia that led to the outbreak of war between the two countries at the end of July. Within a matter of days, Germany and Russia had mobilized in support of their respective allies and the First World War began. After German forces had violated the neutrality of Belgium and invaded France, Britain's Liberal govern-ment decided to commit the forces of the British Empire to the European struggle and the character of the crisis facing the British state was transformed from being a contest for national unity to one of national survival. Speculation that the Liberals were influenced in their declaration of war by the desire to provide a distraction from domestic discontents has been generally discounted by historians, but it was to prove a bitter irony that the last act of a peacetime Liberal government was to commit the country to a conflict that was so antithetical to their vision of Britishness and which could ultimately only be won by embracing the militaristic imperial patriotism of their Conservative opponents.

The First World War

The South African War had given the British people a foretaste of modern warfare, but it had not prepared them for the full horrors of 1914–18. In its scale and consequences, although concentrated into a shorter time frame, the First World War was more akin to the Revolutionary and Napoleonic Wars of 1793–1815 which it forever afterwards eclipsed in modern memory as the 'Great War'. Historians have argued about whether the war changed the direction of British history or whether it simply speeded up developments that were already in train before 1914. In fact it did both. It may have hastened the granting of female suffrage or the rise of Labour. It certainly gave

a further impetus to policies of social welfare and economic intervention. But it also wrenched debate out of its pre-war channels and tore
at the fabric of the pre-war world. Ireland might have been satisfied
with Home Rule before 1914, but by 1918 an independent republic
had become the Nationalists' minimum demand. The war also
reversed the order of pre-war politics. The Liberal Party, which in
1914 held power with Irish and Labour support, in 1918 was divided,
with the government in the hands of a Conservative majority, albeit
with Lloyd George as its Liberal premier. More than this, there were
the myriad social, economic and psychological changes associated
with the war – not least the deaths of nearly 750,000 servicemen in
military action – which left Britain a much altered place and cast for
many the Edwardian period before 'the deluge' as a longed-for
normalcy to which they were desperate to return.[25]

Whatever its ultimate effects, in its early stages the war encouraged patriotism and acted as a unifying force. Although some doubt
has been cast on the extent of popular enthusiasm represented by the
pro-war street demonstrations of August 1914, the public response to
appeals for volunteers was overwhelming, with over 300,000 recruits
coming forward before the end of August alone. Again, though there
were some individuals who withheld their support for the war, most
of the official organizations of the country – churches, political
parties and other bodies – rallied to the government. The divisive
conflicts of the pre-war period were apparently set aside for the
duration. The suffragettes suspended their campaign of militancy and
urged men and women alike to devote themselves to war service. The
TUC called for an immediate end to trade disputes and backed a
national military recruiting campaign, enlisting the labour movement
behind the war effort. Perhaps most dramatically of all, the outbreak
of conflict in Europe, and Britain's involvement in a Continental war,
temporarily lifted the threat of civil war in Ireland. The Ulster
Unionists seized their opportunity to demonstrate loyalty to king and
country by responding with alacrity to the trumpet's call. So too, if in
more measured vein, did their Nationalist opponents. John Redmond
accepted that while the Home Rule Bill should complete its parliamentary progress to the statute book, it could not be implemented
until after the end of the war. Nevertheless, in a dignified and
statesmanlike speech to the House of Commons in August 1914, he
pledged his and his party's support for the war, a gesture to which he
personally gave practical effect by appearing on recruiting platforms
in Ireland. Both Ulster Volunteers and Irish Nationalists thus soon

found themselves fighting side by side in defence of an empire of which Ireland was still very much an integral part.

The spirit of national unity also seemed more in evidence in party politics than it had in the febrile and partisan atmosphere of the late Edwardian years. The main parties concluded an electoral truce at the outbreak of war, undertaking not to oppose each other at by-elections while the war lasted. However, this did not mean that all party political activity was automatically suspended. The Conservatives criticized Asquith's decision to carry through the final stages of the Home Rule Bill after the war had begun. The appointment of Lord Kitchener to the cabinet as secretary of state for war, and the sharing of confidential information with opposition leaders, did not disguise the fact that for the first months of the war the government remained Liberal in its composition. Indeed, it was a crisis in party politics in May 1915 – triggered by the Conservatives' threat to force a general election in protest at what they saw as the Liberals' mishandling of the war – that forced Asquith to form a coalition government.[26] Even then, most of the key posts were reserved for Liberals, and much of the internal politics of the coalition continued along party lines. Not until Lloyd George replaced Asquith as prime minister in December 1916 did a more genuine 'government of national unity' emerge, bound together by the prime minister's personality and the subordination of internal differences to the pursuit of victory. In many ways the rise to the premiership of Lloyd George, the Welsh radical in place of the English Asquith, symbolized the unifying effect the war had on the British nation, with Conservative ministers happy to serve under the former 'pro-Boer' in the national cause. Lloyd George did his best, too, to spread the unifying effects of his government beyond Britain's shores. The British dominions, which along with the rest of the empire had been committed to war by Britain's declaration in 1914, were invited to participate in an 'Imperial War Cabinet', and the South African Jan Christian Smuts became an influential member of the coalition government.

The spontaneous mood of national unity that blossomed in the summer of 1914 was sustained by the growth of a more widespread sense of common identity based on the unifying nature of wartime experience. This was not simply an extension of pre-war patriotism into a wartime context. It had more to do with the transforming effects of the war itself. The millions of men who served in the war were drawn from all quarters of the United Kingdom, from all classes and occupations. Their local or regional affiliations might be preserved within the army's structure, in the 'Pals' battalions' of Kitchener's army, in Scottish, Irish or county-based regiments, or in the separate Welsh division that Lloyd George persuaded Kitchener to establish to appeal to the national pride of the Principality. But as the war went on, the scale and rapidity of army expansion deprived most units of direct territorial links and an exclusive recruiting base. The needs of the war, meanwhile, removed volunteers and conscripts from familiar surroundings and transplanted them into a new environment in which often they travelled widely in their own country for the first time before being shipped to the killing fields of France and the Dardanelles. In all of this, the soldier's most immediate loyalties would be to friends and fellow soldiers in his own unit, but the widening horizons opened up by the war, and the sensation of being part of a larger national struggle, could also produce feelings of pride in belonging to a British nation that was greater than the sum of its parts. As John Davies has written in respect of the Welsh soldiers' experience in the First World War, 'By suffering alongside Geordies and Brummies, Cockneys and Scousers, Micks, Jocks and Aussies, the Taffs became part of a new brotherhood: to become a soldier was to assume a new nationality'.[27]

A similar sense of being submerged in a common struggle took hold on the Home Front. This derived from a variety of causes: concern for family members engaged in the fighting and the collective empathy engendered by the publication of casualty lists and the arrival of War Office telegrams for the bereaved; the mobilization of civilian labour, including large numbers of women, for war-related work, often at some distance from their homes; the disruption of everyday life occasioned by the domestic privations of war or the absence of loved ones or servants from the family home. Naturally, too, the war pervaded everyday discourse – in the workplace, the shop or the school, as well as church or chapel on Sundays – and popular leisure and entertainment, in books and magazines, theatres, cinemas and music halls, clubs and public houses. New forms of activity were generated by the war itself, such as the work of war charities or the early branches of the Women's Institute (the first of which was formed on Anglesey in 1915).

The natural bonding effects of war were directly encouraged by a state that realized that the morale of the masses would be a crucial ingredient in any eventual British victory. Lloyd George and other leaders spoke of the justice of the war and Britain's national obligations. Government ministers worked closely with a cooperative press to ensure that as favourable a view as possible was presented of the war's military course and the heroism of British forces on land and sea. Despite some confusion over its organization, propaganda was seen as a vital weapon in the war effort. A Department of Information – employing the talents of such luminaries as John Buchan, Arnold Bennett and Lord Beaverbrook – was established to exercise a coordinating role, and for the first time the possibilities of the cinema as a medium for propaganda were exploited alongside more traditional methods.[28] The aim of propaganda was not only to stimulate British patriotism but also to fan the flames of hostility towards the enemy. In the early stages of the war the press whipped up anti-German feeling with stories of alleged atrocities carried out by 'the Hun' against civilians in Belgium and France. Events such as the sinking of the liner *Lusitania* by a U-boat, or the death of civilians in the German naval bombardment of Scarborough, could be used for the same purpose. In the same way, fear of the 'enemy within' could act as a unifying force by appealing to prejudice and xenophobia. There had been numerous 'spy scares' even before the start of the war, and the government had set up a new security service (MI5) to deal with counter-espionage and subversion.[29] At the outbreak of war a more general internment of enemy nationals was organized under the Aliens Restriction Act of August 1914, and this gave the green light to violent public attacks on foreigners (or individuals with foreign-sounding names) who in many cases had been living and working in Britain in all innocence for most of their lives. The hounding of the distinguished scholar Professor Ethé from his university post at Aberystwyth was just one instance of this irrational and negative outburst of 'Britishness'.[30] The decision of the royal family to change its name from Saxe-Coburg-Gotha to Windsor was another concession to the popular mood, completing the 'nationalization' of the monarchy which had paralleled the growth of the British state.

Loyalty to the state was not merely encouraged by propaganda and hatred of the enemy. It was enforced by more coercive means. The Defence of the Realm Act (DORA) introduced at the outbreak of war gave the authorities sweeping powers to regulate the life of the country and to suspend civil liberties. On the industrial front, the Munitions of War Act of 1915 enabled the government to ban strikes and to impose restrictions on the free movement of labour, to ensure the maintenance of essential war production. Both measures were justified by the overriding primacy of the needs of the state in wartime compared with the rights of the individual, even where this conflicted with inherited assumptions about individual liberty that had been integral to nineteenth-century British social and political thought. The move away from traditional liberalism was emphasized by two further assertions of state power. One was the extension of government control over industry and the economy, which went beyond the modest interventionism of the pre-1914 Liberal govern-ments and involved the state taking control (albeit temporarily) of key industries like the mines and the railways. The second was the imposition of military conscription. As the levels of voluntary recruitment to the army fell behind the insatiable demands of the generals, compulsory enlistment was finally accepted as a necessary step. Its introduction in 1916 marked another giant blow to the voluntary principle and underlined the ability of the state to impose its authority on the community at large.

However, the enforcement of unity included carrot as well as stick. The corollary of extended state control of industry was the extension of state provision for social welfare. The wartime coalitions introduced legislation to limit rent and price rises resulting from the inflationary effects of the war. Under the aegis of the newly estab-lished Ministry of Munitions a variety of measures regulated the conditions of workers and imposed minimum standards of health and safety. The participation of the Labour Party in the Asquith and Lloyd George governments after May 1915 assured that workers' interests were not neglected. Politicians were also keen to strengthen the sense of common purpose by promising the redrawing of the boundaries of the national state on a more inclusive social and political basis at the war's end. A Ministry of Reconstruction was set up in 1917 to coordinate planning for post-war initiatives in health, housing and welfare reform, encouraging workers and soldiers to look forward to 'a fit land for heroes to live in'. A parallel reform of the electoral system meant that the post-war state would be founded on the more democratic basis of citizenship. In place of the old voting qualifications linked to property, the 1918 Reform Act introduced universal suffrage for men over the age of 21 and women over 30, in the process tripling the size of the electorate from 7.7 million in 1910 to 21.3 million in 1918.[31]

The picture that emerges is thus of a more united 'United King-dom' than had existed before the war, with the war leading to a lessening of, or providing a distraction from, pre-war discontents and fostering the growth of a shared sense of Britishness alongside the creation of a more powerful central British state. Yet while this picture is not entirely false, it is not wholly accurate either. Just as in the earlier 'Great War' of 1793–1815 radical oppositional and internal nationalist movements survived despite the prevalent patriotic conservatism, so in the First World War there were cracks in the facade of national unity that suggested deeper lines of social and political cleavage.

Certainly there was a continuation of political conflict. The three main British parties officially supported the war effort, but there was not complete agreement between them on how the war should be waged or what its aims were. Internal disagreements occurred within the coalition government, especially in 1915–16 over the issue of conscription. After December 1916 the Asquithian Liberals had withdrawn from the coalition and constituted themselves as a 'patriotic' opposition to Lloyd George. A more serious divide opened up between the Labour Party and the coalition. Although Labour remained a formal participant in the Lloyd George administration until the armistice in 1918, from 1917 onwards Labour was organizing as a fully independent party intent on mounting a separate challenge to the other coalition parties at a post-war general election. The reasons for Labour's assertion of independence are complex. They stemmed at least in part, however, from the differing perspectives that Labour brought to bear on the war itself. Henderson, the Labour leader, resigned from Lloyd George's government in 1917 because of the refusal of his cabinet colleagues to allow him to attend an international socialist conference in Stockholm which had been called to explore the possibility of a compromise peace. His party included those like Ramsay MacDonald and others on its ILP wing who had initially opposed the war and who were the allies of radical-pacifist Liberals in anti-war organizations such as the Union of Democratic Control and the No Conscription Fellowship. These bodies had never generated mass support, but they indicated the survival of a liberal-internationalist school of political opinion amid the state-sponsored patriotic nationalism of the period and kept alive a tradition of dissent in foreign policy that could be traced back to the Foxite opposition to the Revolutionary Wars of the 1790s.[32] By 1917–18, moreover, Labour critics of the war could draw on much more widespread feelings of war-weariness, which threatened to breach a patriotic consensus committed to 'victory at all costs'.

In addition to political differences, the war years also saw a continuation of economic and social protest. The mass labour unrest of the late Edwardian period died down in the early stages of the war but it did not entirely die away. Despite the TUC's initial support for the war and the 'Treasury Agreement' that Lloyd George negotiated with the unions in March 1915, there were still serious disputes, including strikes of miners on the south Wales coalfield and workers in the Clydeside engineering industries. These disputes were mainly industrial in origin and were not necessarily symptomatic of an anti-patriotic mood. Over 40,000 Welsh miners had volunteered for military service by the end of 1914, and when Keir Hardie died in 1915 the successful candidate in the ensuing by-election in Merthyr was the extreme pro-war C.B. Stanton.[33] However, there were signs, particularly among the trade union rank-and-file, of increasing dissatisfaction with the government's wartime policies. In January 1916 two-thirds of the delegates to the executive committee of the South Wales Miners' Federation voted in favour of a strike if the government introduced conscription.[34] In the engineering industries skilled workers were unhappy at the 'dilution' of the workforce with semi-skilled and unskilled labour. Shop-floor militancy increased in the latter stages of the war and the number of strikes and stoppages rose from 532 in 1916 to 1165 in 1918, with the total of working days lost increasing from 2.4 to 5.8 million.[35] There was hostility towards the enhanced role that employers had been given in the wartime administration of industry, and a sense of outrage at the profits that were being made in a 'bosses' war'. The hardening of working-class attitudes towards the existing regime was encouraged by the example of the Russian Revolution, and in June 1917 a conference of socialists and trade unionists in Leeds called for the establishment of soldiers' and workers' councils on the Russian model. The Labour movement as a whole did not follow this revolutionary line, but the Labour Party's distancing of itself from the coalition, and its adoption of an explicitly socialist programme (*Labour and the New Social Order*) for the 1918 election, was evidence of the emergence of an alternative view of Britain's future to the one being offered by the incumbent rulers of the state.

It is true that these changes probably signalled a struggle for power within the state rather than a desire to overthrow the existing state structure altogether. Similarly, although there were strong regional concentrations of discontent (south Wales and Clydeside being the obvious examples), this had not apparently led to an increase in competing internal nationalisms to challenge the overriding wartime loyalty to the British state. Wales and Scotland were generally as supportive of the war as was England. There may have been some enhancement of local national consciousness as a result of the wartime experience, but this was not necessarily at odds with a larger British patriotism. If anything, the war was breaking down internal geographical barriers, replacing them either with a more generalized 'Britishness' or with horizontal socio-economic divisions based on class. Separate histories of England, Scotland and Wales during the First World War can be written, but they have an element of artificiality about them because of the increased importance of the British context.[36]

As in the 1790s, though, this was not the case in the 'other island' of the British Isles, where the war brought out the full contradictions of Ireland's position in relation to the British state. To begin with, as has been seen, Unionists and Nationalists alike had given their support to the war, and Ireland had supplied over 150,000 recruits to the army by April 1916. But Ireland was not as wholly committed to the war as the other parts of the United Kingdom. After the initial surge, recruitment levels lagged behind those of Britain and were particularly sluggish in rural areas. Among Nationalists especially there was opposition in principle to the idea of fighting 'Britain's war' and there were those who argued that, far from supporting Britain's cause, Nationalists should exploit the wartime emergency to secure independence, in line with the old adage that 'England's extremity was Ireland's opportunity'. Some, notably Roger Casement, were ready to take an even more pro-German line and to enlist German backing for an Irish rising, in much the same way that Wolfe Tone had turned to the French Directory in the 1790s. The upshot was a widening split in nationalist ranks between Redmond's constitutional supporters and the more extreme, revolutionary elements of the nationalist movement. The latter were the progenitors of what, in retrospect, was the seminal event of wartime Irish history, the Dublin Rising of Easter 1916.

The Easter Rising had its roots in the nineteenth century and the Edwardian period: in the Fenian revolutionary tradition which had created the IRB, in the pre-war struggle for Home Rule that had spawned the Volunteer movement and Connolly's Irish Citizen Army, and in the Gaelic revival and the cultural separatism of leaders like Patrick Pearse.[37] In 1914 an IRB-influenced minority within the Volunteers split from Redmond over the issue of support for the war,

and a minority within a minority began laying the plans for armed
rebellion. The idea of a rising was partly an attempt to seize power,
but more a symbolic act of 'blood sacrifice' which kept alive the
tradition of a 'rising in every generation' as a protest against Ireland's
subordination to British interests. As a practical plan it was a failure
before it began because of the seizure of weapons by the authorities
and confusion among its leaders. Even as a symbolic act it failed
immediately to win the support of the Irish people, merely ensuring
that the central parts of Dublin were laid waste in fighting the British
forces. Nevertheless, the Rising was an important turning point in the
relationship between Ireland and the British state, and provided an
impetus to events that led to the subsequent war of independence
after 1918. The declaration of a republic by the rebels provided a
programme for an independence movement that could claim 'constitutionally' to be acting in the name of the Irish people and their
provisional government. Of even greater significance was the decision
of the British authorities to carry out the judicial execution of the
Rising's leaders – an act that led to a revulsion of feeling in favour of
the rebels and created a climate of opinion in which a more intransi-
gent, republican nationalism could thrive.

The last two years of the war saw three main developments in
Irish politics. The first was the failure of renewed British attempts to
secure a constitutional settlement of the Irish question on the basis of
some form of Home Rule. In the wake of the Easter Rising, and
encouraged by the American government with whom they became
formal allies in 1917, the British tried a variety of expedients to reach
agreements with the Irish parties, all to no avail. Lloyd George was
employed as a special negotiator in 1916. In 1917 an 'Irish Convention' met to consider constitutional proposals. But no agreement was
reached. The failure of these attempts was linked to two further
developments. One was that Irish opinion began to abandon support
for the constitutional Nationalist Party and its moderate stance of
cooperation with the British government. The death of John
Redmond in 1918 was a factor here, yet even before Redmond's
death the Nationalist Party was in decline, as its performance at by-
elections in the latter part of the war confirmed. By contrast, Sinn
Fein was emerging as a major force on the Irish political landscape,
and this was the other main trend of the post-Rising period. Sinn
Fein had been only a minority party in 1914. After the Rising it
benefited from its more uncompromising anti-British stance, its
public identification with the imprisoned rebels and the unpopularity

of British plans to extend conscription to Ireland. Aided by this substantial swing in the popular mood and by the presence in its ranks of heroes of 1916 like Eamon de Valera, by 1918 Sinn Fein had become the main voice of nationalist Ireland. At the general election of December 1918 Sinn Fein won 73 Irish seats, compared with the old Nationalist Party's seven. The difference between the old order and the new in Irish politics was demonstrated when the Sinn Feiners refused to take their seats at Westminster, establishing instead a separate parliament (the Dail) in Dublin which, in defiance of the British government, they proclaimed to be the elected assembly of a sovereign Irish republic.

Yet while the triumph of Sinn Fein presaged further trouble between Britain and Ireland, the other outcomes of the war were more equivocal as far as the British state was concerned. The war had extended the role of the state, establishing a new relationship between state and people, and the common experience of wartime had engendered a mood of national unity that had heightened a collective sense of 'Britishness'. On the other hand, domestic conflicts had not been entirely eradicated, especially on the industrial front, and the emergence of the Labour Party threatened to disrupt the pre-war political system already weakened by the Liberal split. At the election of 1918 the appeal of national unity seemed to prevail. Lloyd George's coalition government of Conservatives, Liberals and 'National' Labour, basking in the reflected glory of 'The Man Who Won the War' and capitalizing on the patriotic euphoria of victory over Germany, swept back to power, winning 478 seats against only 63 for Labour and 28 for the Asquithian Liberals. In England and Scotland, Coalition candidates polled more than half the votes cast, ironically falling below the 50 per cent mark only in Lloyd George's Wales. Ireland apart, the British appeared politically more unified in the new democracy ushered in by the 1918 Reform Act than at any point since the transition to mass politics had begun in the mid-nineteenth century. What was still unclear was whether this unity was more than skin-deep, and whether the strategies of national integration that had worked during the war would be equally effective in the altered conditions of peacetime. Only once those questions had been answered could the true impact of the First World War on the British people be fully assessed.

1918–1922: The search for national unity

The war had severely tested the British state, its people and its institutions. Lloyd George's government after 1918 faced a number of unresolved problems: the problems of peacemaking and an uncertain international and imperial situation; the management of the domestic transition from war to peace, complicated by economic depression and social and labour unrest; the search for stable political frameworks in the new conditions of electoral democracy and with the party system in a state of flux. The key to all these problems, from the government's perspective at least, lay in somehow preserving the wartime spirit of cooperation, of 'Country before Party', and extending its operation in the social and political spheres. The need for unity in the face of internal strife and external danger became the leitmotif of the Coalition's appeal. As Lloyd George himself put it in a speech at the Manchester Reform Club in December 1919, 'National unity alone can save Britain, can save Europe, can save the world'.[38]

In one respect, however, the achievement of 'national unity' required the acceptance of a more limited territorial definition of the British state. In 1919 the Sinn Fein 'government of the Irish republic', headed by de Valera but with Michael Collins emerging as an increasingly influential figure, launched a 'war of independence' against British rule. The old IRB/Volunteer movement, transformed by Collins into a more disciplined, tightly organized Irish Republican Army, embarked on a campaign of guerrilla warfare against British forces and governing institutions in Ireland, exposing to violence and intimidation Irish supporters and officials (such as police officers and civil servants) of the British state. Backed by Irish-American money and weapons, the IRA offensive effectively nullified British authority over large areas of southern Ireland and made the achievement of any form of political stability an almost impossible task. Collins and other IRA leaders became popular heroes, while de Valera (sprung from Lincoln gaol in a daring raid masterminded by Collins) took on himself the role of international statesman and self-styled 'President of the Republic' in an extended tour of Irish-American supporters in the United States in 1919–20.

The Lloyd George government responded to the Irish troubles with a twofold strategy that was a familiar combination of coercion and concessions via constitutional reform. The latter (supported now, ironically, by the Unionists who were a majority in Lloyd George's cabinet) involved the passage of the 1920 Government of Ireland Act that provided for the setting up of two 'Home Rule' parliaments – one in Dublin, the other in Belfast – and the creation of a 'Council of Ireland' to serve as a link between the separate devolved administrations in the north and south. At the same time attempts were made to defeat the IRA campaign by military means. The Restoration of Order Act of August 1920 gave the authorities sweeping emergency powers. Virtual military rule was instituted in parts of the country, and the 35,000 regular soldiers of the Irish garrison and 10,000 members of the Royal Irish Constabulary were reinforced by special 'Auxiliary' units of ex-officers and the 'Black and Tans' (so-called because of the colour of their uniforms) recruited from among recently demobilized ex-servicemen. IRA attacks were met with arrests and reprisals, terror with counter-terror, and the towns and by-ways of Ireland became the setting for an increasingly dirty war as the British forces strove to fulfil the government's pledge to 'take murder by the throat' and suppress the obstacle that the IRA/Sinn Fein rebellion presented to peaceful constitutional progress.

Neither the military nor the constitutional strategies worked. Despite some heavy losses (176 policemen and 54 soldiers were killed in 1920 alone) and occasional successes, the military authorities were unable effectively to counter the IRA threat. Indeed, the policy of reprisals, and the unofficial brutality of the 'Auxis' and the Black and Tans in particular, deflected attention from IRA outrages, handed a propaganda weapon to Sinn Fein and exposed the government to criticism from liberal opinion in Britain and condemnation in America. Meanwhile, at least in the south of Ireland, the Government of Ireland Act of 1920 proved a dead letter. Whereas pro-Unionist Ulster duly elected its new parliament in May 1921, in the rest of Ireland the opportunity for elections was used merely to confirm the electoral mandate of Sinn Fein and consolidate the authority of the Dail. The southern Home Rule parliament thus did not come into existence, and the Council of Ireland – which Lloyd George had hoped might conciliate moderate nationalists by preserving an all-Ireland dimension to the constitutional settlement – was similarly still-born. The results of the 1921 elections, and the army's continuing inability to restore full British rule, finally persuaded the prime minister that the only way permanently to resolve the situation was to deal directly with Sinn Fein. Informal contacts with the republicans had been taking place for some time, and the speech in which George V at the opening of the Belfast parliament in June appealed to all

Irishmen 'to pause, to stretch out the hand of forbearance and conciliation, to forgive and forget'[39] was part of a carefully choreographed peace process. Sinn Fein and the IRA agreed to a truce with the British, and in July de Valera met Lloyd George in London. Detailed negotiations later in the year – led on the Irish side by Michael Collins and Arthur Griffith – eventually produced the 'Anglo-Irish Treaty' of December 1921.[40]

The Treaty settlement reshaped the relationship between Britain and Ireland more profoundly than any other measure since the Act of Union, perhaps even more than the Union itself. It gave de facto independence to the south of Ireland by creating a 26-county Irish Free State with dominion status within the British Empire. This went further than any of the previous Home Rule proposals and marked a decisive step towards separate statehood, with only vestigial (though symbolically important) links to the British crown through the presence in Dublin of a governor general and the swearing of formal loyalty to the crown as part of the Irish parliamentary oath. On the other hand, the 1921 agreement also accepted the partition of Ireland and the continuing status of Northern Ireland as an integral component of the United Kingdom. The idea of an all-Ireland council, which had been contained in the 1920 Act, was dropped, thus recognizing the reality that for the foreseeable future there would be two Irelands, one British, the other not. This was too much for some nationalists to swallow, and even leaders of the pro-Treaty faction like Collins saw it only as an interim arrangement – the ultimate aim of Sinn Fein still being a united, republican Ireland fully independent of Britain. It was over the tactical question of whether the Treaty was an acceptable first step on this road that a split in the Sinn Fein ranks occurred, de Valera rejecting partition and holding out for an immediate republic while Collins argued that the Treaty was the best deal that could be achieved in the absence of practical means of renewing the armed struggle. The Treaty was accepted by a narrow majority in the Dail but de Valera and his followers (including elements of the IRA) refused to acknowledge the legitimacy of the new Free State government and embarked on a fresh civil war to secure its overthrow. In this they failed, although not before Collins himself had fallen victim to their guns. In the late 1920s de Valera had to accept Collins's more gradualist constitutional strategy to work his way back to power and edge the Free State closer to independence, though even he was unable to end partition.[41]

The Anglo-Irish Treaty and the settlement that followed thus formalized the division of Ireland and ended the Union. In a sense this was true not just for the south but for the north as well. Northern Ireland became effectively a self-governing state – technically within the United Kingdom (its MPs still sat at Westminster) but politically separate, with its own party system, its own prime minister, cabinet and civil service and with little or no interference in its internal affairs by successive British governments from the 1920s to the 1960s. It was almost as if Ireland had ceased to exist for British politicians, after 120 years of attempting to integrate it into the Union state. Likewise, after 1922 the Irish question ceased to be a factor in British politics. The considerably reduced Irish representation in the House of Commons rarely made its presence felt (and then only as a wing of the Unionist Party), and Irish issues were deemed to be properly a matter for the Northern Irish government, unless they involved the discussion of relations between Britain and the Free State. The absence of an Irish nationalist party at Westminster for the first time since the 1870s inevitably made parliament more British in its outlook as well as in its composition, and further enhanced the 'Britishness' of the British state, with Northern Ireland a constitutional appendage to the unitary part of the United Kingdom and virtually a separate province of the crown.

What is perhaps remarkable is the apparent lack of interest that these far-reaching constitutional changes seemed to arouse in Britain, at least compared with the overcharged atmosphere of pre-1914. The explanation for this, and especially for the lack of serious opposition to the Irish settlement, lies partly in the changed political conditions on both sides of the Irish Sea. In Britain the Unionists were now the dominant group in the government. They backed the Treaty because it preserved the status of Ulster as part of a modified Union, while recognizing that nationalist feeling in the rest of Ireland made any more broadly conceived Unionist position simply untenable. In the end, therefore, they were willing to negotiate the diminution of the United Kingdom because there was no practical alternative. Perhaps they realized too that their position as a party would be strengthened by the removal of nationalist MPs from the Commons and the consolidation of the Union around its British core.

The lack of resonance that the Irish question had in post-war Britain was also connected with other changes that had weakened internal nationalisms and made the contest between nationalism and unionism less central to British political life. These changes were both hastened by and reflected in the decline of the Liberal Party. Before 1914 the alliance between Liberals and Irish Nationalists had been the principal means by which Irish concerns were transmitted to the heart of the British state. The Liberal Party also provided an organizational framework that enabled Welsh and Scottish nationalists to gain political leverage on the British stage, thus embodying in a single movement the internal national diversities that were such an important part of late Victorian and Edwardian politics. In 1918, however, the Liberal Party was split: its Lloyd Georgite wing had temporarily embraced unionism, while the Asquithians, for the moment, were no longer credible contenders for power. In any case, the final shape of the Irish settlement was of such a nature – more nationalist than unionist – that it would have been difficult even for a united, pre-war Liberal Party to have opposed it. But even had this not been so, the nationalist impulses from Scotland and Wales that had given life to that earlier Liberalism no longer had the same vigour. Economic and social change had brought industrialization and urbanization, continuing the drain of population from rural areas and lessening the impact of the land question from which nationalist movements had drawn a lot of their strength. The rise of an urban working class, consolidated in consciousness by the war, had undermined the leading political and cultural roles of the professional middle classes so vital to pre-war liberal-nationalist movements – incidentally increasing the gulf between the social structures of Scotland and Wales and those of nationalist Ireland, and emphasizing instead their common experience with that of England. Finally the war had had its effect on the other main bastion of pre-war nationalism, religion. In particular, it had led to divisions between pro- and anti-war groups that had damaging consequences for denominational unity and may also have caused a more general loss of religious faith. The churches remained important in their local communities, but the energy and self-confidence of their political activities – already weakening before 1914 – never regained their former levels, and though religion might still be important in national cultures it became more marginal to political debate.[42] Perhaps the best illustration of this was the general absence of excitement that greeted the final implementation of Welsh Disestablishment in 1920, when the measure that had been the mainspring of the late Victorian Welsh national revival was enacted with none of the controversy it had earlier generated.[43]

The unionist tendency in politics, and the reduced prominence of Irish, Scottish and Welsh 'questions', was reinforced by the wartime encouragement of British national feeling and the expansion of the role of central government. The Lloyd George coalition did its best to build on these wartime foundations. There was a continuation of policies of social reform – in education, housing, and the extension of national insurance. The 1918 Reform Act had created a new, British, political system on more democratic lines, which reduced the influence of pre-war minority groups. Much of the post-war political debate anyway was about external rather than internal issues – the peace settlement, the future of the empire, the creation of a League of Nations – which emphasized 'British' concerns. It is true that in other circumstances the debate over post-war reconstruction in Europe, especially the idea of a peace settlement founded on self-determination and the rights of small nations, could have struck a separatist chord in parts of the United Kingdom, but outside Ireland this was hardly the case. The political, economic and social integration of the British state seemed to be proceeding apace, and the solution of the Irish question appeared to make unity in the rest of the United Kingdom easier to achieve.

That said, national unity remained in some respects an aspiration rather than a reality. In straightforward political terms it was always a suspect slogan once the wartime truce was over and ordinary party political activity had been resumed. As has been seen, Labour opposed the 'national' government at the 1918 election and polled over 20 per cent of the vote. Between 1918 and 1922 Labour's electoral challenge strengthened, and even the Asquithian Liberals underwent a revival in their fortunes (illustrated by Asquith's victory at the 1920 Paisley by-election following his defeat at East Fife in 1918). The Labour/Liberal recovery represented a revival, too, of regional politics – Labour especially building its strength in the industrial heartlands of northern England, south Wales and the west of Scotland. This did not necessarily give it a 'nationalist' appeal similar to pre-war Liberalism, but it introduced a geographical dimension to anti-Coalition politics that indicated the limitations of 'national unity' as a rallying cry. Moreover, the growth of the Labour Party's political strength in particular geographical areas coincided with a return to large-scale industrial unrest in those same regions, where the onset of post-war depression, coupled with government decisions such as the return of the coal mines to private control and cutbacks in public expenditure on welfare measures provoked disputes that dwarfed even those of pre-1914 in their scale and ferocity.[44]

By 1920–21 the Coalition's claim to represent the spirit of national unity looked increasingly threadbare to supporters and opponents alike. Lloyd George had tried to develop a new political appeal that would fuse British nationalism with social reform in an integrationist social imperial programme similar to that advocated by the pre-war national efficiency movement.[45] His hope was that the blending of Liberalism and Conservatism would render existing party divisions redundant and enable him to construct a new centrist alliance that would ensure his own survival in power. There were two problems with this scenario. One was that the Coalition's view of national unity became increasingly exclusive. In particular it became more and more anti-Labour, dependent on mobilizing 'moderate' Britain against the 'enemy within' as manifested by socialism and the trade unions. If this did not disqualify the government from claiming the 'national' label, the Coalition faced a second problem in its own internal disunity. Lloyd George's proposal for a 'fusion' of the Conservative Party and the Liberal Coalitionists was rejected by his own Liberal followers in 1920. The Conservative rank-and-file meanwhile were becoming restive at being led by a nominal Liberal in whom their confidence was being eroded by events. Accepting Lloyd George's leadership had always had the expediency of a flag of convenience – hoisted initially because he was felt to be a popular war leader, then in 1918 because he offered the best chance of victory in the general election. But while senior Coalitionists like Austen Chamberlain (who succeeded Bonar Law as Conservative leader in 1921) became more supportive of Lloyd George, the majority of Conservatives, their hostility fuelled by scandals over the sale of honours and differences over foreign policy, did not. The result was the overthrow of the Coalition at a meeting of Conservative MPs at the Carlton Club in October 1922, which forced Lloyd George's resignation and a general election held on more conventional party lines.

The political consequences of this will be dealt with more fully in the next chapter. However, the fall of the Lloyd George Coalition brings to a close a distinct period in the history of the British state. Most obviously, the years between 1900 and 1922 saw the endgame of the Victorian battles over the Irish question, climaxing in the partition of Ireland, the establishment of a devolved government in the north and the separation of the south from British rule. Partly as a corollary of these changes, partly as a result of the wider impact of the First World War and of other factors, the character of the British state itself also altered. It became internally more homogeneous, and the importance of regional nationalisms was diminished by the effects of closer integration. The role of the state was expanded and its political base democratized. British patriotism grew and the sense of 'Britishness' was stimulated by the common experience of war. Throughout the period, national unity was the goal of politicians in both the two main pre-war parties. There were Liberal and Conservative variations on this theme before 1914. The war fused the Liberal and Conservative approaches in the person of Lloyd George. Neither in Lloyd George's definition nor in the more general sense was 'national unity' fully achieved, but arguably the creation of 'one nation' within the framework of the British state had been brought perceptibly closer.

CHAPTER 6

ONE NATION? 1922–1964

To what extent did Britain become more completely 'one nation' after 1922? There was continuing political, economic and social integration. The experience of the Second World War, perhaps even more than the First, enjoined a more cohesive sense of Britishness. The completion of political democratization together with the extension of a comprehensive system of social welfare and the nationalization of large sections of the country's industrial base encouraged citizens and workers to identify more directly with the central institutions of the British state. Yet for all that, differences and divisions remained. For much of the inter-war period it seemed that there was not one nation in Britain but two, as economic and political divergence occurred between a prosperous south and a depressed north and west, between what Hugh Kearney has described as 'Inner' and 'Outer' Britain. Then again, although the separate cultures of Scotland and Wales – and England too – were being moulded and assimilated in a British context, the distinctive national identities of those countries remained a latent political force. Even if the trends of the period seemed to point persuasively in a 'one nation' direction, the acceptance of a centralized, unitary British state was still conditional rather than permanent, and a range of alternative futures was conceivable if, for whatever reason, the late nineteenth-century 'nationality question' were to re-emerge. With the benefit of hindsight, the decades between the 1920s and the 1960s offer an atypical interlude of stability in the domestic relations of the British nations with their central government, not the solution to the problems of nationhood and identity which many contemporaries assumed.

Politics

The political history of the period reflects the 'one nation/two nations' theme. Between the wars, the confusion of three-party politics in the 1920s resolved itself in the 1930s into a confrontation between a Conservative-dominated 'National Government' and a Labour opposition confined largely to its depressed industrial heartlands – a pattern of politics, in the words of one historian, 'based, unequivocally and unapologetically, on class and regional divisions'.[1] The Churchill Coalition of 1940–45 – in which Labour was a full partner – restored a more genuine sense of national unity and created a new political consensus that enabled Labour to move decisively beyond its heartlands to claim outright power in the post-war landslide. From then until the 1960s British politics operated within the framework of a reconfigured two-party system in which centralization and unionism were the driving impulses, and both parties subscribed to their own variants of a social and geographical 'one nation' philosophy.

The unionist trend was exemplified by the electoral dominance that the Conservative (and Unionist) Party established in the inter-war period. Apart from the brief interludes of Labour government in 1924 and 1929–31, the Conservatives were the majority party at Westminster from 1918 until 1945. They were the main supporters of the Lloyd George Coalition between 1918 and 1922, before regaining power in their own right by winning 345 seats at the general election of 1922 and 419 seats in 1924. As the core component of the National Governments of the 1930s their triumph was even more complete. In 1931 they won 473 seats and polled 55 per cent of the total vote; despite slipping from this peak in 1935 they retained a comfortable majority and still managed to poll nearly half the popular vote.[2] It is true that the workings of the electoral system on occasion exaggerated the Conservatives' strength (in 1922, for example, their parliamentary majority was obtained with only 38.5 per cent of the votes cast); also their support was not evenly distributed across Britain as a whole. They depended heavily on the more prosperous south and east of England and the Midlands to boost the numbers of their MPs, whereas in Wales they remained a minority party throughout the 1920s and 1930s, their best performance being the winning of nine seats (and 28.4 per cent of the vote) in 1924. It has been argued, moreover, that under Baldwin in particular the Conservatives became increasingly 'English' in their outlook, in an ideological replication of psephological reality. Yet this underestimates the extent to which the party could legitimately claim a larger British identity. The Conservative record in Scotland was much better than their performance in Wales, and they were the majority party there between 1924 and 1929, and again from 1931 to 1945. Membership of the Glasgow Unionist associations rose from 7000 in 1913 to 32,000 in 1929 – higher than that of the entire ILP.[3] Scottish Conservatives remained an important element in Conservative politics at the British level and their strength indicated that, while regional disparities might persist, the Conservative Party was still a powerful unifying factor in the politics of the British state.

Labour, by contrast, was much more regional in its roots. Although it expanded rapidly in the 1920s – winning 142 seats in 1922, 191 in 1923 and 287 in 1929 (increasing its share of the vote from 29.7 per cent to 37.1 per cent in the process) – the Labour Party remained largely reliant on its support in the industrial areas of northern England, Scotland and Wales. But whereas from 1922 Labour was the largest party in Wales both in seats and votes, never falling below 40 per cent of the poll, only in 1929 did the party win more English seats than the Conservatives (226–221) and even then on a lower percentage of the popular vote (36.9 to 38.8).[4] The electoral defeat of 1931, following the resignation of the second minority Labour administration and the formation of the National Government, revealed the inter-war regionalization of Labour's support even more starkly, with 16 of its 52 seats being won in Wales, where the Labour poll of 44.1 per cent was almost half as much again as its UK figure of 30.8 per cent. The gap closed slightly as Labour recovered some of its former strength in 1935, but it was not until 1945 that Labour could claim a national, British, standing comparable to the Conservatives.

However, the regionalized nature of Labour support did not make Labour a regional party per se. If it had particular sectional interests they were those of social class rather than geography, reflecting the origins of the Labour Party as a trade union pressure group and its institutional links with industrial workers. In any case in the 1920s, under MacDonald's leadership, the party was trying to shed its sectional image and establish itself as a national party by appealing to a broader social constituency and to all regions of Britain. In practice it became as unionist as the Conservatives, seeking to gain and exercise power within the context of a unitary British state. Thus, despite the fact that MacDonald himself and MPs like Thomas

Johnston had earlier been enthusiastic advocates of Scottish Home Rule, devolution did not figure in the programmes of the first two Labour governments and was quietly shelved as an aim of party policy.[5] Electoral calculations may have played their part in this, since devolution would have reduced the number of Scottish MPs and so make the return of a Labour government at Westminster less likely. The replacement of MacDonald by a succession of English leaders in the 1930s – Henderson, Lansbury and Attlee – may also have strengthened the unionist perspective. But the underlying reality for most Labour politicians was that the economic and social objectives to which they were committed were more important than constitutional reform, and seemed more achievable through the agency of a centralized British government than through the creation of devolved assemblies.

The belief in the efficacy of a stronger central government had been growing for a number of years. The Liberal ministries of the Edwardian period had expanded the role of the state, and the process continued during the First World War. Even though some wartime controls were abandoned after 1918, the pressure for state intervention to offset the effects of economic depression and improve social welfare remained considerable. International influences encouraged the trend. The development of the planned economy in the Communist Soviet Union and the corporate state in Fascist Italy emphasized the importance of state institutions and central economic management – a message echoed in different ways by the spread of Keynesian economic thinking and the policies of FDR's 'New Deal' in the United States. The idea of centrally coordinated intervention within the framework of a British state was absorbed not only, as will be seen, by the Labour and Conservative Parties, but also on the extremist fringes of the political system where the ideological examples of the European dictatorships exerted their strongest pull. The Communist Party of Great Britain, founded in 1920, although its limited support was regionally concentrated (in London, south Wales and the industrial districts of central Scotland), aimed at revolution on a British plane rather than focusing just on local or regional concerns. At the opposite end of the political spectrum, Oswald Mosley's British Union of Fascists, formed in 1932, based its appeal on a Mussolini-style corporatism adapted to British conditions and combined this with a British imperial nationalism that assumed not just the political integrity of the British state but the common identity of the British people as well.[6]

The result was that while there were still considerable regional variations in the political map, these were variations within a British system rather than at odds with it. This is not to say that there were not parties or groups that had a more regionalist, decentralizing agenda. For instance, the ILP, though affiliated to the Labour Party, retained a separate political organization and developed an increasingly regionally focused identity, based on Glasgow and the Clyde. The Clydeside MPs combined a commitment to socialism with a fierce sense of Scottishness, which became all the more pronounced when the British state was in Conservative hands. Some members of the ILP were sympathetic to the idea of a Scottish parliament which might be more responsive to the needs of the Scottish working class than a remote assembly at Westminster dominated by the English bourgeoisie. Yet while the ILP, drawing on the legacy of Keir Hardie and the Scottish Labour pioneers of the 1890s, could have developed a more nationalist dynamic, the overriding claims of class solidarity and the need to work alongside English and Welsh socialists in the British Labour movement prevented it from taking this path. The most successful of the Glasgow ILP-ers, John Wheatley, demonstrated the benefits of the integrationist approach when, as a member of the first MacDonald government, he introduced the 1924 Housing Act – a measure informed by his knowledge of Scottish conditions but enacted as a British reform by a British government. Significantly, when the ILP disaffiliated from Labour in 1932 and attempted to carve out a separate electoral niche it fared badly at the polls and confirmed the extent to which the political system was becoming the preserve of the major British parties.

The experience of the Liberals illustrates another aspect of the interaction between regional and national politics and the increasing dominance of British politics by the centralist two-party system. In the 1920s the Liberals were fighting a rearguard action to salvage their identity as a potential party of government following the damage wrought by the wartime split. As late as the general election of 1929 they fielded over 500 candidates in a last, desperate bid for at least a share of power. Yet despite the reunion of the Asquithian and Lloyd Georgite wings of the party in 1923 their prospects of success were fading fast. They won 158 seats in the 1923 election but were pushed into third place behind the Conservatives and Labour; in 1924 their representation crashed to only 40 seats and rose to only 59 in 1929 (even though on the latter occasion they polled nearly a quarter of the popular vote). The party, which before 1914 acted as the main conduit for the national grievances of Scotland and Wales within the British state, and itself espoused the policies of devolution and federalism, thus virtually disappeared from the centre of British political life. It retained a diminished presence as the party of the periphery (six Liberals, including the veteran Lloyd George, won seats in Wales at the 1935 election, when the Liberals' total tally was only 21) and continued to support a policy of Home Rule for Wales and Scotland. But its marginalization in the politics of the second half of the inter-war period reflected very clearly the reduced importance of nationalist and regional grievances of the kind that had played such a prominent part in late Victorian political debate.[7]

As the Liberal Party declined, new nationalist groupings emerged in Scotland and Wales, but they remained very much in the nature of minority movements. In Wales the nationalist party, Plaid Genedlaethol Cymru, was founded at a meeting held during the Pwllheli eisteddfod of 1925. It gathered support only slowly (its membership was no more than 2000 in 1939) and achieved little electoral success. Its sole candidate at the 1929 election – Lewis Valentine in Caernarfonshire – polled only 609 votes. In some respects the lack of progress at the polls was not a major worry, since Plaid Cymru's initial focus was more cultural than political, its main concern being the preservation of the Welsh language. But even after the party had adopted a more conventional programme of political autonomy its fortunes failed to pick up. Indeed, the more clear-cut pro-independence platform and the emphasis of the party's president, Saunders Lewis, on the unique virtues of Welsh-speaking Wales may have prevented the party from appealing to less exclusivist forms of Welshness which could still find a congenial home in the declining, but in Welsh terms more powerful, Liberal Party, at least in the north and west of the country. Lewis's Catholicism and his apparent sympathy for right-wing nationalist movements on the Continent (notably in Spain) may also have kept at a distance nationalistically inclined potential supporters still imbued with the heritage of the Welsh Nonconformist radical tradition. Plaid Cymru thus remained little more than a debating society for Welsh-speaking students and intellectuals (although the importance of this role as a 'forerunner' for a later expanded nationalist movement should not be overlooked). The only occasion when its activities touched a more populist chord was when Saunders Lewis, Lewis Valentine and D.J. Williams carried out an arson attack on an RAF bombing school under construction at Penyberth in Caernarfonshire in 1936. The transfer of the trial of the arrested arsonists from Wales to the Old Bailey in London, and their imprisonment after refusing to give evidence in English, briefly became a cause celebre in radical circles and raised the hackles of a national consciousness temperamentally disposed to see itself as the victim of English oppression. But the politics of Welsh nationalism were small beer when set against the world events of economic depression and approaching war, and on neither of these larger themes did Plaid Cymru have a credible alternative to offer to an electorate accustomed to look to London and the London-based parties for political leadership and solutions.

What was true of Wales was also true of Scotland, except that it could be argued that whereas in Wales the nationalist movement was less vigorous than in the era of the 'national revival' before 1914, in Scotland the post-war period saw a definite, if limited, advance in the direction of nationalist politics. The Scottish Home Rule Association had been revived in 1917 by Roland Muirhead and Thomas Johnston. It looked initially to the Labour Party to deliver devolution, but the Labour leadership's inertia prompted more nationalist elements in the SHRA to seek an alternative strategy. In 1928 Muirhead joined forces with John MacCormick and members of other nationalist groups (including the Scottish National Movement and the Scottish National League) to found the National Party of Scotland, which subsequently, in 1934, merged with the Scottish Self-Government Party (formed in 1932) to become the Scottish National Party, the direct ancestor of the modern SNP. The individual strands of this new movement are difficult to disentangle.[8] MacCormick and Muirhead are perhaps best described as moderate nationalists – MacCormick a romantic, Muirhead, as a former 'Young Scot' and member of the ILP, closer to the political mainstream. Both saw the NPS, and later the SNP, as essentially a vehicle for pressurizing the other parties, mainly Labour, into granting Home Rule. They were willing to cooperate in a 'broad front' (symbolized by the all-party Scottish Convention movement) with other pro-Home Rule forces, and in the 1930s contemplated an electoral pact with the Scottish Liberals. The merger with the Scottish Self-Government Party, which created the SNP, brought them into alliance with a more Conservative-inclined grouping, and at the same time forced them to purge the NPS of more extreme separatists associated with the Gaelic cultural wing of the nationalist movement. Given the complexity of the internal politics of Scottish nationalism, it is perhaps not surprising that its electoral impact was less than decisive. At the 1931 election the NPS contested five seats and lost its deposit in four (although it did win 14 per cent of the vote in Inverness); in 1935 the SNP's eight candidates polled an aggregate of 29,000 votes (just over 1 per cent of the Scottish total). As in Wales the electorate was not yet ready to turn to nationalist politics as the answer to Scotland's problems and preferred to stick with the established British parties.

The established parties were not entirely insensitive to the special needs of Scotland within the British state. Thomas Johnston continued to campaign within the Labour Party for an active commitment to establish a legislative assembly for Scotland, and in 1937, while serving as Labour's spokesman on Scottish affairs, became president of the London Scots Self-Government Committee. Meanwhile Walter Elliot, the secretary of state for Scotland in the National Government from 1936 to 1938, though not willing to endorse electoral devolution, took the decision (on the recommendation of the Gilmour Committee) to relocate the main departments of the Scottish Office from London to Edinburgh, giving Scotland at least a devolved administration – and civil service – in St Andrew's House, if not yet a devolved parliament. This, however, was as far as British governments were prepared to go in altering the structure of the political system of Britain's unitary state. Even the administrative devolution within the Scottish Office was far from complete, since the chief political power in Scotland was wielded by a secretary of state who was a member of a London cabinet rather than an independent political figure who headed an entirely separate Scottish executive (giving Scotland at best a status analogous to that of Ireland within the Union of 1801–1920, rather than any larger measure of executive independence). The degree of central control if anything increased rather than diminished in subsequent years as Scotland was integrated more fully into the central planning framework of British policy. As secretary of state from 1941 to 1945, Johnston created an advisory 'Council of State' for Scotland, the membership of which was drawn from his surviving predecessors in office, but did not initiate any moves towards legislative devolution. Admittedly the special circumstances of wartime were perhaps not conducive to radical constitutional change, but it may be too that, having held office, Johnston came to believe that the benefits of intervention from above outweighed, or rendered unnecessary, the democratic advantages of a Scottish parliament of which earlier he had been such a staunch advocate.[9]

The events of the late 1930s and early 1940s in any case strength-ened the 'British' dimension of British politics and increased the importance of central institutions. In particular, the outbreak of the Second World War in September 1939 and the formation of the wartime coalition in May 1940 transformed both the internal and external context of political authority, with 'national unity' again becoming the key theme. The government over which Churchill presided from 1940 to 1945 was a genuine 'national' government – including all three of the main British political parties – in contrast to its more dubiously labelled predecessors under MacDonald, Baldwin and Chamberlain. Its elements gelled, moreover, into a more harmo-nious team than the Asquith or Lloyd George equivalents of 1915–18. There were naturally some internal tensions and disagreements, but on the whole the description of the coalition as representing a 'wartime consensus' is not inaccurate. There was unity on the main thrust of military strategy, the defeat of Hitler being the overriding objective. A consensus also emerged on the need for domestic reform, embodied in the Beveridge Report of 1942, the Butler Education Act of 1944 and a plethora of white papers on social insurance, health care and employment policy.[10] Ministers were also agreed on seeing the war from a British perspective and running it through the central agencies of an expanding state. The number of civil servants almost doubled between 1939 and 1945 (from 387,000 to 704,000) and government expenditure rocketed from £1000 million to £6000 million in the same period.[11] Apart from occasional rebellions by backbench MPs, the government faced little real opposition. A general election was delayed until after the end of the war in Europe, and in the meantime an electoral truce ensured that the coalition partners were not in competition with one another at the polls. Popular dissatisfaction with the government could find an outlet at wartime by-elections only by voting for candidates repre-senting minor parties – a factor which undoubtedly contributed to the SNP's first victory in a parliamentary contest with the return of Dr Robert McIntyre in the Motherwell by-election of April 1945.

Certainly the SNP's success did not presage any major nationalist electoral advance. When the general election was held a few weeks later in July 1945, after the break-up of the coalition in May, McIntyre lost at Motherwell and none of the SNP candidates, nor those of Plaid Cymru in Wales, won a seat. The election also marked the near demise of the Liberal Party, which polled 9 per cent of the national vote but won only 12 seats. There was thus a clear shift even more firmly in the direction of a British two-party system, at least in terms of votes cast and seats won. Between them the Labour and Conservative parties secured 603 of the 640 seats in the new parliament and 87.6 per cent of the popular vote.[12] The significance of this was understandably overshadowed for contemporaries, however, by the distribution of support between the two major parties themselves. The Conservatives, despite having Churchill as their leader, slumped to their first electoral defeat since 1929, with only 210 MPs in the new House of Commons. Labour, on the other hand, broke fresh ground, securing an overall majority at Westminster for the first time in its history, its 393 seats giving it a landslide victory comparable to the great Liberal triumph of 1906. Like the Liberals in 1906, Labour appeared at last to have made the crucial breakthrough of adding an English majority to those that it had already achieved in previous elections in Scotland and Wales, in 1945 becoming the largest party (both in votes and seats) in all parts of Britain, and even winning one seat (via an independent Labour candidate) in Northern Ireland.

The Attlee governments of 1945–51 carried on the work of expanding the role of central government and extending the field of action of the British state. Whether this marked a continuation of a wartime consensus, or whether it represented a more partisan socialist departure, is debatable, but the practical results were the same in either case. There were some limited concessions to regionalism. For example, a 27-member 'Council of Wales' was appointed to advise the government on Welsh issues. But the government was not otherwise sympathetic to the devolutionary principle, and refused to consider the possibility of a secretary of state for Wales to parallel the arrangements in Scotland.[13] Aneurin Bevan, the Party's most prominent Welshman, was a firm believer in centralism and central planning, and, like Labour opponents of devolution in the 1970s, saw any reduction in the powers of the central British state as a likely hindrance to the process of social and industrial reform. The consequence of these attitudes, married to the statist ideologies of the wartime and inter-war periods, was that the 'Labour revolution' of the late 1940s was based almost entirely on the principle of 'nationalization' at an all-British level. This was literally true in the area of industrial policy, where basic industries such as coal, the railways, electricity and gas supply, road haulage and iron and steel were taken into state ownership on a model that relied on the creation of national boards such as the British Railways Board or the National Coal Board which might be operationally regionalized but which were nonetheless subject to a central planning regime determined in Whitehall and Westminster. The same was true of the expansion of social welfare provision through the National Insurance and National Assistance Acts of 1946–48 and the creation of a National Health Service. Regional authorities and local community links might be established or preserved, and in Scotland and Northern Ireland would be mediated through local administrations, but it was the British state that was identified as the main provider in structural and financial terms.[14]

The defeat of the Labour Party at the general election of 1951 and the return of the Conservatives to power did not substantially alter the direction of government policy, which again has led to discussion of the existence of a 'post-war consensus' in succession to that of 1940–45. This concept has in turn been challenged, on the basis that politics continued to have a partisan aspect and that on certain issues the policies of the Labour and Conservative parties were far from identical – disputes over the nationalization of iron and steel and over foreign policy providing cases in point.[15] It may perhaps be more accurate to say that partisanship existed, but within a consensual framework. By the 1950s both parties were committed to the idea of a mixed economy and the welfare state. Both believed in maintaining the constitutional status quo and governing through strong central institutions. Both had bases of support that were socially diverse and geographically varied. In that sense the 'One Nation' Conservatism of Eden, Macmillan and Butler was mirrored by the 'One Nation' Labourism of Gaitskell, Bevan and Harold Wilson. The party system in the 1950s became an even more comprehensive duopoly between two British parties, the two-party share of the general election vote rising from 89.6 per cent in 1950 to 96.1 per cent in 1955 and falling only slightly to 93.2 per cent in 1959. Labour remained nearly twice as strong as the Conservatives in Wales, but in England and Scotland there was a more even balance of forces which fluctuated from side to side with the swing of the electoral pendulum.

Between the 1920s and the early 1960s, therefore, the politics of the British state had undergone significant change. A fragmented and regionalized party system had been replaced by a two-party system integrated at an all-British level – a process simplified by the disappearance of the Irish Nationalists from Westminster after 1918 but also due to the coalescence of British electoral opinion into Labour and Conservative camps. At the same time the role of central government and the scale and scope of the activities of the British state had increased dramatically, especially in relation to the management of industry and the provision of social welfare. Whatever view is taken of the 'consensus' debate in its various forms, there was clearly an underlying trend that operated irrespective of the party complexion of the government of the day, and suggested at least a measure of practical agreement if not total unanimity or accord. In all these ways the political divisions of class and region that had loomed so large in the 1920s and early 1930s seemed to have become less significant by the 1950s and 1960s. England, Scotland and Wales retained their own distinctive political characteristics, and the main parties maintained separate organizational structures in Scotland and Wales. Administratively, too, Scotland was different from the rest of Britain because of the expanded role of the Scottish Office and the emergence of an Edinburgh-based civil service. Yet none of these differences had led to any substantial support for nationalism or separatism, and the momentum in favour of the closer political convergence of the various parts of the British state seemed strong.

Economics

The combination of regional diversity and national integration was as applicable to the economic history of Britain as to the political, with a similar pattern of divergence between the wars being followed by convergence during and after the Second World War. The basic economic geography of Britain as the first industrial nation had been established in the nineteenth century as the development of regional industrial economies integrated into a larger national, imperial and global matrix. Thus the Lancashire cotton industry produced goods for India and Africa as well as for domestic and European markets. The south Wales coal industry (where production expanded from 16 million tons in 1870 to 56.8 million tons in 1913) was heavily geared to the export trade, while the prosperity of the shipyards of the Clyde, Belfast and the Tyne depended on the maintenance of Britain's world-wide maritime supremacy and the buoyancy of international trade. Britain itself formed a compact and tightly organized economic unit, in which specialized regional producers contributed to the success of the country as a whole. Prosperity, it is true, was not universal, nor was economic growth necessarily smooth. Agriculture suffered in the late nineteenth century from falling prices and increased foreign competition. Manufacturers were concerned about the trading threat presented by industrial rivals like Germany and the

United States (hence the support in some quarters for the introduction of tariffs). And for at least a third of the population (as Booth and Rowntree had demonstrated) a century of industrialization had brought nothing better than a life of grinding poverty, barely offset by the social reforms of the pre-war Liberal governments. That said, Britain before the First World War was still one of the world's wealthiest nations. Her traditional industries were booming in the Edwardian period and newer industries were beginning to develop. The income from overseas investments and invisible earnings was huge, and London remained the centre of the world's financial system. Economically the British state was integrated into a world economic order in a way that minimized the impact of internal differentiation, even if for regions and local communities economic specialization had a more formative effect on lifestyle, culture and experience.

The First World War brought a further boom for war-related industries, but its longer-term effects were more damaging and disruptive. Normal patterns of investment and production were distorted, the government was left with a heavy burden of increased indebtedness and the interruption to international trade led to a crucial loss of overseas export markets for key industries like coal and textiles. The problems of the economy worsened in the post-war period as wartime prosperity collapsed and depression hit the country in 1920–21. Unemployment rose sharply, from 2.4 per cent of the insured workforce in 1919 to 17.8 per cent in 1921, putting over two million people out of work and giving a foretaste of what was to come in the late 1920s and 1930s.

The ups and downs of the economy were accompanied by rising levels of industrial unrest. Already before 1914 labour discontent had become a serious economic and political problem. In the worst year of the pre-war unrest, 1912, 40.8 million working days were lost through stoppages; national strikes in the coal industry, the docks and the railways became a regular occurrence as workers strove to achieve wage increases that would keep pace with rising prices. After the war the context was different, but the contests that took place were if anything more bitter. The trade union movement had expanded its membership during the war, from 4.1 million in 1914 to 8.3 million by 1920. In 1919 the unions tried to use their enhanced strength to win a share of post-war prosperity: engineers on Clydeside struck in favour of a 40-hour week; the miners demanded a 30 per cent wage increase, a six-hour working day and the nationalization of the mines.

The government and employers made some concessions but they also resisted union demands, and their hand was strengthened by the economic downturn of the early 1920s. The total of working days lost in 1921 reached 85.8 million (more than twice that of 1912) but the tide was turning against the unions as unemployment rose and membership began to decline.[16] The experience of the miners provides the most graphic illustration of changed circumstances. In 1920 they secured a pay increase by strike action. But in 1921 the government returned the mines to private control and the miners were forced to accept pay cuts. Relations between owners and men continued to deteriorate as markets contracted and by 1925 the owners were again seeking wage reductions and an increase in working hours. On this occasion a threatened strike, together with sympathetic action by railway and transport workers, forced the government to intervene by promising a temporary subsidy and appointing a Royal Commission under Sir Herbert Samuel to make recommendations on the future of the industry. However, the report of the Samuel Commission failed to provide a basis for agreement between the parties and the 'General Strike' of May 1926 was the result.

The General Strike – in which one and a half million workers in the transport, power generation and printing industries, together with engineering and shipbuilding workers, were called out on strike by the TUC in support of the miners who, under the leadership of A.J. Cook, had rejected the owners' terms – has rightly been seen as the major event in the industrial politics of the inter-war years. It showed the extent to which the battle between capital and labour had become national in scale, with the government exercising the role of referee and guardian of the community interest by ensuring the maintenance of essential supplies and services. In its origins and outcomes it had another dimension as well, in that it grew out of the plight of a traditional heavy industry – one of the cornerstones of Britain's nineteenth-century industrial success – being pushed into decline by altered economic conditions. This aspect was underlined by the failure of the strike. On 12 May the TUC, after an assurance from the government that it would back a negotiated settlement, decided to call off the sympathetic action, though the miners remained on strike until October when they were forced by economic necessity to go back to work on the owners' terms.

From this perspective, it is less the national aspect of the General Strike that attracts attention than the fact that it highlights the particular problems of the older industrial regions, centred on the coalfields and textile districts, which were finding it most difficult to cope with increased foreign competition and the loss of world markets. As the depression of the 1920s turned, after the Wall Street Crash of 1929, into the deeper slump of the 1930s the areas in which these older industries were located – predominantly the 'Outer Britain' of northern England, Scotland, Wales and Northern Ireland – suffered disproportionately heavily, in a way which emphasized the regionalized character of the British economy as opposed to its national integration. Unemployment rose across the UK, from 1.2 million in June 1929 to 2.5 million in December 1930 and 2.9 million in 1931. But the overall statistics do not reveal the differential experience of particular groups of workers or parts of the country. In 1931, when the national level of unemployment was 23 per cent, among miners it was 35 per cent, among steel workers 48 per cent and among shipbuilding workers 62 per cent. Viewed geographically, whereas the unemployment rate for Britain as a whole was 23 per cent, in Scotland, Northern Ireland and the north of England it was 27 per cent, while in Wales it was 36.5 per cent. In Merthyr, where the Cyfarthfa ironworks had closed in 1922 and the furnaces and mines were either idle or working well below capacity, nearly 62 per cent of the workforce was unemployed, a figure exceeded by only a few blackspots such as the shipbuilding town of Jarrow in the north-east of England, where over two-thirds of the insured population were out of work.[17]

Of course the effects of depression were not confined to the areas of traditional heavy industry. But in other parts of Britain – especially in the south-east of England and the Midlands – the depression was not of the same depth or duration as in the north-east, Scotland or south Wales. Recovery set in earlier, based on greater economic diversity and the growth of new industries producing consumer goods for the domestic market and high technology products such as aeroplanes and motor cars. Consequently by 1934, Oxford, the city of dreaming spires but also the site of the William Morris car factory at Cowley, had an unemployment rate of only 5 per cent, while the rate in Abertillery in south Wales was 50 per cent. Since higher rates of employment have their own multiplier effect, industrial growth in London and the south-east generated further economic activity in construction and related occupations and in the service sector, making the gap between the 'two nations' of inner and outer Britain even wider. The rate of new house building was 50 per cent higher in

England in the 1930s than in Scotland, with England having a higher proportion of owner occupiers and mortgage holders, most notably in the expanding suburbs and dormitory towns on the metropolitan fringe of London. Generally, too, as the inter-war period progressed, comparisons between the new Britain and the old were in favour of the former in relation to other indices of prosperity such as wage and salary levels, health and life expectancy, educational attainment and social mobility. Aesthetically, culturally and environmentally the more dynamic growth areas of the south and east had huge advantages over the industrial 'waste lands' of the north and west.

Government policies made some attempt to bridge the gap and bring help to those most in need. The Special Areas (Development and Improvement) Act of 1934 provided for the appointment of regional commissioners whose brief it was to encourage economic diversification in depressed areas such as south Wales, Scotland and Tyneside, and government funds and tax incentives were offered to employers willing to locate new enterprises in the regions in question. The Commissioner for the Scottish Special Area disbursed more that £4 million between 1935 and 1938, while in south Wales 1938 also saw the opening of the new Treforest trading estate near Pontypridd. Such schemes had only a limited impact on the problems of deep-seated structural unemployment, yet equally the government could argue that they were only part of a more systematic industrial and economic strategy. The National Governments of the 1930s, having taken office in the depths of the economic crisis, gradually evolved a coherent economic plan. Tariffs were introduced to protect domestic markets and (via the 1932 Ottawa agreements) to promote 'Empire Free Trade'. Measures were also brought in to facilitate the rationalization and modernization of run-down basic industries, including the Cotton Industry Reorganization Act of 1938 and the nationalization of mining royalties to provide a fund for restructuring the coal industry. These initiatives fell short of the outright public ownership of heavy industry being advocated by the Labour Party, or the ambitious public works programmes suggested by Lloyd George as a way of reducing unemployment and kick-starting economic recovery. On the other hand, they did reveal the beginnings of a more ambitious regional policy than any previous government had attempted. Together with Neville Chamberlain's careful handling of public finances at the Exchequer, the early stages of rearmament and the acceleration of economic activity in the south-east of England, they helped to create the conditions for a gradual recovery that between 1932 and 1939 reduced the unemployment figure by over a million.

This, however, was too slow for the inhabitants of the depressed areas themselves, where dissatisfaction and ultimately desperation manifested itself not only in electoral support for the Labour Party as opposed to the National Government, but also in other ways. There was direct-action protest from the working classes through support for the Communist-led National Unemployed Workers Movement, through the 'hunger marches' from places like Jarrow and south Wales to London, and through more violent outbreaks such as those in the Rhondda in February 1935 in protest against the administration of the local Unemployment Assistance Board and the hated 'means test' which could determine eligibility for relief. At a higher level, local authorities attempted to use their powers to influence government or stimulate schemes for self-help. The Convention of Scottish Burghs established the Scottish National Development Council in 1930, and in 1936 the industrialist Sir William Fairchild set up the Scottish Economic Committee to investigate the problems of the Scottish economy and advise on solutions. For many individuals in the depressed parts of Scotland and Wales, though, the response to the collapse of traditional industries and the bleakness of the immediate economic prospect was simply to move elsewhere, and the 1920s and 1930s saw larger-scale internal migration within Britain probably than any decade since the mid-nineteenth century. Between 1921 and 1940, 430,000 people left Wales, most for the Midlands and south-east of England, and between 1925 and 1939 the population of Wales fell from 2,736,800 to 2,487,000, with every county except Flintshire experiencing a net loss.[18] There was a similar drift southward from Scotland (and parts of northern England) as the younger unemployed moved in search of work and a better life, just as the Irish had in the famine years of the 1840s.

Despite the efforts of the government and the movement of individuals, economically Britain remained a deeply divided nation until the Second World War. If anything, the partial recovery of the mid to late 1930s made the division between the 'two nations' even more pronounced, with the inhabitants of the 'new Britain' of southern England gaining only occasional glimpses of the depths of poverty in other parts of the country from newsreels and newspapers, published reportage (George Orwell's *The Road to Wigan Pier* was published in 1937) and episodes like the 'Jarrow Crusade'.[19] In the depressed areas themselves, for those who stayed behind and even for those who left, the psychological wounds ran deep. Unemployment and poverty shaped the character and collective memory of a whole generation, strengthening a sense of the separateness of those regions from the rest of Britain. In Scotland and Wales this could have led to anti-English feeling (again as in the example of nineteenth-century Ireland), yet if this was so, as has been seen, it did not translate into simple nationalism. Prosperity was seen as being bound up with the British, and world, economy. Political protest found its voice in support for the Labour Party and demonstrations of class solidarity with fellow workers and trade unionists in other industrial regions, rather than in support for the nationalist parties. There were nevertheless strong feelings about what was perceived as the neglect of the interests of regions by central government, which strengthened the demand for political change and for a new attitude on the part of the British state.

Only with the coming of the Second World War was this divergence between the two nations halted, as the economic basis of national unity was rebuilt alongside the emerging political consensus. The war, with its demand for war materials and manpower, led to full employment and revitalized the depressed industries such as coal, steel and shipbuilding whose products were once again crucial to the war effort and to the life and death of the nation in the struggle against Nazi Germany. New factories were established to meet the demand for armaments, vehicle and aeroplane parts and all the other multifarious components of the war machine. A policy of geographical dispersal of plants to reduce their vulnerability to air raids also acted as a means of reviving the depressed areas, as well as providing a potential foundation for post-war diversification. Scotland and Wales both benefited from this; their local economies, and that of Northern Ireland, were also stimulated by the expanded presence of military bases, particularly with the build-up of American forces in the UK from 1942 on in preparation for the D-Day landings. Agriculture received a boost from the increased wartime demand for home-grown food to offset the U-boat threat to imports, and this too benefited farmers and rural communities, from the prosperous districts of southern and eastern England to the hill farmers on the margins of northern and western Britain. Finally, to an even greater extent than in 1914–18, there was a sense of central direction and planning behind the economic side of the war effort, with the state taking over control of war-related industries, taking on increased responsibility for the direction of labour, the provision of welfare and the rationing of supplies, and for promoting scientific and technical research. The establishment by Thomas Johnston, the secretary of state for Scotland, of the North of Scotland Hydro-Electric Board, and the investment in improvements to roads and harbours, showed that some of the wartime initiatives might be expected to bring peacetime benefits too, and so lessen the division between the prosperous south and depressed north which had become a staple feature of the inter-war years.

The promise of economic improvement was at least partly fulfilled under the post-war Labour governments, which continued the wartime regime of central planning and extended the boundaries of state control. Nationalization of basic industries such as coal and the railways, and of public utilities like gas and electricity, created a more integrated national industrial base and opened the way for much-needed public investment to assist recovery in run-down sectors of the economy. The Distribution of Industries Act of 1945 was an important step in the direction of a more effective regional policy, providing funds and incentives for the diversification of economic activity in the pre-war depressed areas by encouraging the development of manufacturing and light engineering alongside the more traditional, but declining, heavy industries.[20] In south Wales alone, 179 new factories – 112 of them government-sponsored – were opened between 1945 and 1949 on industrial estates such as those at Bridgend, Hirwaun and Fforestfach. A variety of new industries were introduced into the valleys, including the manufacture of vehicle components, electrical goods, chemicals and textiles. By the mid-1960s manufacturing employed 30 per cent of the Welsh workforce, compared with only 10 per cent before 1939.[21] The immediate post-war years also saw a general expansion of employment in the public sector, not just in the newly nationalized industries but in the variously expanding organs of local government, the health and welfare systems and education. In the late 1940s these advances were tempered by crises and setbacks, notably the fuel and power crisis of 1947–48 and the devaluation of the pound. But the general economic and industrial record of the Attlee governments was one of improvement, with unemployment rates of under 3 per cent (considerably better that the inter-war average) and the huge disparities between the fortunes of inner and outer Britain being ironed out by returning prosperity and a carefully targeted programme of regional development and economic aid.

Burgeoning affluence underpinned the 'one nation' political consensus of the 1950s and early 1960s. During the 13 years of Conservative government from 1951 to 1964 unemployment continued at the low levels of the late 1940s, averaging 2.5 per cent and reaching a post-war low of 360,000 in 1960. The 1950s witnessed a consumer and housing boom as rising incomes and an improving standard of living spread the 1930s prosperity of the suburban south-east to other parts of the country. At the macroeconomic level, the Conservative governments continued broadly the policies of the post-war Labour administration. Harold Macmillan, who served as minister of housing and chancellor of the Exchequer before becoming prime minister in 1957–63, had been a supporter of what he called the 'Middle Way' between the wars, and he and his colleagues readily embraced the idea of a mixed economy and extended welfarism that had become current during and after the war. There was some concern in the late 1950s about the level of inflation, rising public expenditure and Britain's declining international competitiveness, but this was not allowed too much to detract from the 'feel good' mood of what in retrospect was seen as an economic golden age.[22] The theme of central planning continued to figure largely in the minds of those on both sides of the party-political divide. The Churchill and Macmillan governments moved in what has been seen as a 'corporatist' direction by attempting to involve employers and trade unions in government economic planning, notably in the National Economic Development Council (NEDC) established in 1962.[23] The Labour opposition meanwhile, led by Harold Wilson after Hugh Gaitskell's death in 1963, was committing itself to encouraging the 'white heat of technological revolution' and devising a comprehensive economic and industrial policy in the form of a 'National Plan'.

In this brave new post-war world, regional economic and social differences of course remained. A careful observer could still see the outlines of the 'two nations' of the inter-war period beneath the layers of prosperity created after 1945, and the lineaments of the old division would re-emerge more harshly as the tide of affluence receded in the 1970s and 1980s. The accelerating decline of traditional heavy industries from the mid-1970s once more emphasized disparities between 'north' and 'south', which economic diversification over the previous quarter of a century had not been able to eradicate or disguise. In Scotland and Wales the folk memories of the depression years remained strong, and were waiting to be reawakened in a younger generation by the ending of the post-war boom. Economics and politics would interact to provoke not only an end to the post-war consensus, but also a renewed interest in nationalist or regionalist solutions. In the process, attitudes and identities would also come under scrutiny, with a new sense of the divisions that existed in and between the societies of Britain, as opposed to their common bonds and outlook. Inevitably this raises an important retrospective question in relation to earlier trends. It has been seen that between 1922 and 1964 the politics of the British state became more integrated, and that government intervention and rising prosperity had produced a less divided and more centrally coordinated national economy. But were these shifts in the direction of 'one nation' irreversible trends or mere transient phenomena? Did the idea of 'Britain' exist now as the prime focus of nationhood and identity, or was the concept of 'one nation' less deeply ingrained than the political and economic record would suggest?

Identities

The 'Festival of Britain', staged in the summer of 1951 during the last days of the Labour government, was seen by its ministerial initiators as having a twofold purpose: to lighten the mood of a public still living under the shadow of post-war austerity while at the same time celebrating British achievements in the contemporary world in a self-conscious emulation of the Great Exhibition of exactly 100 years earlier. Inevitably perhaps, it combined the futuristic with the nostalgic. Its main site, on London's South Bank, was dominated by the pre-space age futurama of the 'Skylon' and the 'Dome of Discovery'. Yet at the opening ceremony the bands played 'Land of Hope and Glory', and many of the exhibitions and displays highlighted the historic origins of Britain's institutions and the technological triumphs of the Victorian era. Historians have pointed out that this duality reflects the character of Attlee's Britain – shaped by the legacy of its past yet striving towards a new modernity.[24] They have less frequently explored the extent to which the idea of Britain itself was a meaningful one for the millions the Festival was intended to entertain and inform, and indeed whether identification with Britain and a sense of Britishness had increased or diminished between the Great Exhibition of 1851 and the Festival of Britain a century later.

Identities are composed of a variety of ingredients, including a sense of community or place, loyalty to particular institutions or ideologies, shared aspects of common experience and culture. As has been seen, a growing sense of Britishness had emerged in the nineteenth century as Britain steadily became more integrated as a political, economic and cultural entity. The process continued in the twentieth century, hastened by the First World War and reinforced by subsequent events and economic and social trends. A number of factors played their part in forging a more unified, homogeneous British identity. Of central importance was the spread of a more standardized educational system and the expansion of the mass media. By the end of the 1940s, following the Butler Education Act of 1944, all parts of England and Wales had a common structure of primary and secondary education. Scotland retained its own system and qualifications, but throughout Britain minimum levels of literacy had become universal, and the key elements of an inherited common culture (including at least some Shakespeare and probably 'English' history) were being imparted to successive generations of scholars. The non-scholarly mass media may have been of even greater significance in promoting cultural homogenization. The national newspaper press continued to expand its circulation in the early part of the period, from about three million copies a day in 1918 to ten million a day by 1939. The main bulk of sales were accounted for by mass-circulation papers like the *Daily Express* (two million copies), the *Daily Mail* (1.5 million) and the *Daily Mirror* (one million), alongside broadsheets like *The Times*, *Telegraph* and *Guardian*.[25] Although there were successful newspapers like *The Scotsman*, the *Western Mail* or the *Yorkshire Post* which operated on a more regional basis, the provincial press had entered a prolonged decline, and even those regional papers that survived dealt heavily in national as well as local or regional news. Their daily readers were thus kept aware of the British (and indeed the wider international and world) context of their community life, and made to feel, however vicariously, part of the day-to-day history of the British state.

As agents of cultural assimilation the media of radio, film and television outstripped even print-based forms as the communications revolution of the twentieth century gathered pace. Radio broadcasts began in Britain in the early 1920s. The British Broadcasting Corporation (BBC) was established in 1926 and exercised a virtual monopoly over the air waves until after the Second World War. Its output of music, news, educational programmes, drama and light entertainment – all carefully vetted for their edification quotient by the puritanical Scottish director general Sir John Reith – created an entirely new bond of unity between homes and regions the length and breadth of Britain. Seventy-one per cent of all households had radio licences by 1939, allowing not only the programmes but also the BBC's version of 'standard English' to be heard nightly by almost three-quarters of the population, exceeding even the newspapers in the size of its audience. The only serious rival to radio as a popular medium between the wars was the cinema, especially after the introduction of 'talking pictures' in the 1920s. Glasgow alone had 127 cinemas by 1929. By the end of the Second World War cinema attendance had reached a weekly total in excess of 20 million.[26] Since the same films and newsreels were shown in all parts of the country, here again was a major step towards the creation of a common, media-centred popular culture. In due course the leading role of the cinema in this respect – and of radio too – would be supplanted by television, but this transition did not get properly under way until the 1950s. Even so, there were already ten million TV sets in Britain by 1960 and the potential of television as a culturally unifying force was already clearly apparent.

Improved communications were having a unifying effect in physical as well as cultural terms. The role of the national railway network in this respect has already been noted as a significant factor in the Victorian period. The railways continued to be socially and economically important in the twentieth century, reaching their furthest extent (over 20,000 miles) between the wars and becoming even more national in their orientation, first through the grouping into four large companies – the Great Western; London, Midland and Scottish; London and North Eastern; and Southern – in 1921 and then as 'British Railways' after nationalization by the Labour government in 1947. But after the First World War railway travel faced increasing competition from the roads, both for freight and especially for passengers – the latter more likely to able to benefit from the alternatives offered by the motor bus or the private motor car. The number of motor cars increased from 579,000 in 1924 to 2,045,000 in 1938; the number rose even more sharply in the consumer boom of the 1950s, and by 1970 had reached a total of 12 million.[27] In little more than half a century the automobile had gone from being a rich man's luxury to a realizable material ambition for most of the middle classes and many of the working classes. The precise connection between increased personal mobility and questions of identity is difficult to establish, and for firm conclusions to be drawn would require detailed analysis of journeys and travelling distances for which accurate data probably does not exist. At the very least, however, improved communications opened up the possibility of wider horizons. Longer journeys were made on holidays and at other times as coach and motor tours became more popular; in the inter-war years railway package tours and charabanc trips to the seaside towns of Yorkshire and Lancashire, the 'Cornish Riviera' and the north Wales coast came within the reach of larger numbers of people as the introduction of paid holidays extended the bounds of working-class leisure. The shrinking of geographical distance inevitably encouraged an enlarged sense of the reality of 'Britain' for the mass of the population, just as tours of the mountain regions of Wales, the Lake District and the Scottish Highlands had done for the intrepid poets, artists and travellers of the late eighteenth and early nineteenth centuries.[28]

To the enlarged sense of cultural community and the enhanced sense of place as unifying factors must be added a closer and more intimate relationship between individual citizens and state institutions. Some established institutions, admittedly, were losing influence rather than gaining it, as in the case of the Churches whose congregations were being thinned by secularization and generational change. But since the differences between Churches emphasized divisions within the British state rather than its unity, it is possible that – in a reversal of the argument that Protestantism was a foundation of Britishness in the eighteenth century – their decline may have removed barriers to closer identification with the state, perhaps even promoting a secular British identity in place of narrower denominational ties. Whether this was so or not, in other ways the secular state had a larger and more comprehensive presence. With the enfranchisement of women over 21 in 1928, Britain had become a parliamentary democracy based on universal suffrage, in which all citizens had the right to participate in choosing their elected governors. The advent of the full welfare state after 1945, and especially the inauguration of the National Health Service, further encouraged a positive identification with state structures, and significantly the NHS was to be seen as one of the distinctive features of 'British' society for the rest of the century. It was not just the innovative departures that stimulated loyalty to state institutions, however. The monarchy retained, even surpassed, the popularity it had attained in the last years of Queen Victoria. This owed much to the personal qualities of the monarchs themselves, yet it also derived from a symbiotic relationship between old institutions and new. The broadcasting of royal events by the BBC – from the first Christmas radio broadcast by George V to the televising of the coronation of Queen Elizabeth in 1953 – gave the monarchy a greater immediacy in its contact with the population at large than ever before and allowed individuals to identify more personally with the monarch as the head of the British nation and the symbol of its unity.

As in the narrower fields of politics and economics, so as a factor in shaping a national British identity in the broader cultural sense, the Second World War was of considerable significance, both for those who lived through it and for those subsequently influenced by the myths and memories it left behind. From the study of previous wars – the Revolutionary and Napoleonic Wars of 1793–1815, the First World War of 1914–18 – it has been seen that the experience of struggle against a common enemy engendered patriotism and national unity. In the circumstances of the Second World War these feelings were evoked not just by the events themselves – the drama of Britain standing alone against Hitler in 1940, the direct involvement of the civilian Home Front in the military conflict during the Blitz, the day-to-day sharing of anxieties and frustrations as the fortunes of war ebbed and flowed – but by the way in which these events were interpreted for the general public by politicians and the media, pre-eminently by the speeches and broadcasts of Winston Churchill, whose sonorous phrases gave form to the nation's history even as it happened, but also by the newspapers, newsreels and radio broadcasts that presented the events of the war in patriotic terms that encouraged among their audience a sense of participating in a common struggle. It was from these same sources, and from the countless later war films, memoirs, novels and adventure stories, that a collective memory of the war was manufactured which kept alive stereotypical images of the Battle of Britain or the Battle of the Atlantic, recreating the 'Dunkirk spirit' and extolling the national qualities of stoicism, determination and sheer bloody-mindedness that had seen Britain through, even when other countries had fallen beneath the Nazi yoke or stood aside from the conflict until forced to intervene by external assault.[29]

It has become fashionable to attempt to explode the myths of the 'People's War' and to stress the limits of national unity, social solidarity and common endeavour behind the supposed wartime consensus. While this, like all debunking, is an exercise that can be taken too far, it is justifiable to insist that there are alternative memories that deserve to be recorded, to ensure a more rounded historical picture. Similarly, with the larger question of 'Britishness' in the middle years of the twentieth century, although the image of the united, self-reliant Britain of the early 1940s is an important cultural reference point, it does not tell the whole story, or at least does not reveal its full complexity. A 'British' identity was still more difficult to define than the simplified verities of wartime propaganda or the post-war consensus might suggest. It was also constantly evolving, partly because of the impact of the war itself, partly because of the interaction of longer-term social, economic and cultural trends.

One obvious way in which the cultural independence of Britain was being eroded, and the insularity of Britishness modified, was through the increasing importance of American influences on British life. The heroic 'ourselves alone' version of the Second World War ignores the degree to which Britain's survival, and her eventual share in victory, depended on American support: the economic and military assistance of lend-lease, America's role in protecting the Atlantic convoys, and, finally, the part played by American soldiers, sailors and airmen in bringing about the defeat of Germany and Japan. It is true that individual Britons actively resented the American presence, and the growing inferiority of Britain within the Atlantic relationship that it represented.[30] Anti-Americanism of this kind could actually reinforce insularity and the determination to preserve 'traditional' British cultures and customs. Yet already since before the war Britain had been succumbing to the embrace of American cultural imperialism, especially the products of Hollywood's film studios which provided the staple fare of cinema programmes and drew their audiences into the transatlantic cultural orbit through the escapism of an Astaire musical, the comedy of Laurel and Hardy or the historical sweep of *Gone with the Wind*. Britain's film industry did its best to compete, and the government encouraged its efforts by requiring cinemas to show a quota of home-produced films, but the pressures of the market were ultimately too strong to resist. The same applied after the war, to begin with, in the field of popular music and the burgeoning world of youth culture, as successive waves of innovation swept across the Atlantic, dominated from the late 1950s by the regal presence of Elvis Presley. Local imitators such as Cliff Richard gave the new music a domestic gloss, but only with the advent of The Beatles in the 1960s did Britain successfully reverse the direction of cultural traffic and carve out a distinctive identity for itself in the rapidly changing global scene.[31]

If a unified sense of Britishness was eroded by external influences it also continued to be variegated by internal divisions of region, religion, gender and class. Of these, religion was a less important factor in society generally than it had been in the nineteenth century; the relationship between gender and national identity remains to be fully explored. In all parts of Britain, however, class identities remained strongly differentiated and were reflected in the existence of a variety of class-based cultures and sub-cultures. The overall shape of the class structure was recognizably similar in the first half of the twentieth century to that of the Victorian period. The aristocracy and landed interest were in economic decline after the First World War, but a distinct 'upper class' retained its place and influence at the top of the social pyramid. The middle classes continued to expand along with the suburbia that became their distinctive habitat, with the industrial working class still making up the bulk of the population, notwithstanding the depression of the 1930s.[32] Part of the 'myth' of the Second World War was that class distinctions were dissolved in the crucible of war, paving the way for a more meritocratic, egalitarian post-war society based on universal access to secondary education and the opportunities for enhanced social mobility offered by changing employment patterns and the benefits of the welfare state. In reality, the 'democratization' of society in this way was less dramatic. Working-class children were much less likely than their middle-class counterparts to go to grammar schools, even after the 1944 Education Act, and university entrance remained the preserve of an educational 'few', at least until the 1960s. In terms of occupation, housing and leisure the divisions between classes remained considerable, even if full employment and post-war prosperity steadily narrowed the gap between working- and middle-class incomes. This is not to say that, during the Second World War and after it, middle and working class alike did not think of themselves as British. But the Britains they inhabited could be radically different in their ideas, values and assumptions, as well as in the physical realities of their lifestyles and environmental and material cultures.

Alongside the different class-based identities, and interwoven with them, the geographical regions of Britain continued to exhibit their own separate national identities, even if these lacked the immediate political force of the period before 1914. The character of these nations was also changing. In Wales, for example, the vigorous, self-confident Nonconformist nationalism of the late nineteenth century had become more defensive, inward- or backward-looking. Wales had become an even more fractured society in social and cultural terms, and 'Welshness' – even in the depression years – was coming for many to be represented by the working-class culture of the south Wales valleys rather than the rural *gwerin* of the west and north. The fall in the number of Welsh speakers (from 43.5 per cent of the population in 1911 to 36.8 per cent in 1931) was evidence of a general cultural shift as well as the purely linguistic Anglicization that was taking place in the decades after the First World War. Yet this process should not be seen in wholly negative terms. The tension between the old Wales and the new had a culturally creative effect that, in the longer run, helped to fashion a more comprehensive Welsh identity. The leaders of Welsh-speaking Wales, in their determination to preserve a living language, fostered a flourishing literary movement, centred on journals like *Y Llenor*, edited from 1922 by W.J. Gruffydd, and the stories and novels of writers such as Kate Roberts and Saunders Lewis. *Urdd Gobaith Cymru*, a Welsh-language youth movement, was successfully launched in 1922 to promote Welsh culture, in its broadest sense, among a younger generation. The formation of Plaid Cymru in 1925 was part of this same 'cultural nationalist' movement, which in 1927 won some success when a report of the Welsh Board of Education encouraged the teaching of the Welsh language in schools.

At the same time, a parallel 'Anglo-Welsh' culture was developing which extended the debate about the nation's future and gave it an urban, industrial as well as a rural dimension. The writings of Caradoc Evans and Dylan Thomas attacked, in their different ways, the narrowness of traditional Nonconformity. Idris Jones, especially in his collection of poems, *Gwalia Deserta* (1938), explored the impact of the depression of the 1930s. Such work was important not just in addressing contemporary themes but in doing so in a form that was distinctively Welsh while being accessible to English as well as Welsh speakers (as, later, were the poems of R.S. Thomas).[33] In this way, a national Welsh identity was not only preserved but extended, since it could appeal to all sections of the Welsh community across the linguistic divide in similar fashion to the more familiar unifiers of sport and song. A sense of national unity was also encouraged by the success of Welsh national institutions, especially the University of Wales, which, from its humble Victorian origins had become a powerhouse of scholarship and research, in addition to providing a cadre of graduates for teaching and other professions and for the expanding public sector. The establishment of a separate Welsh region of the BBC in 1937, with studios at Cardiff, Swansea and Bangor, was another symbolic recognition of the national status of Wales, which also helped to unify the country by broadcasting in both the national languages.

Scotland experienced its own crisis of identity between the wars, as the self-confidence built on industrial success and imperial pride withered with the onset of depression. Nevertheless, as in Wales, out of adversity there developed a measure of national renewal. In the literary field this came in the form of the 'Scottish renaissance' of the 1920s and 1930s, a movement that brought together writers such as 'Hugh MacDiarmaid' (Christopher Murray Grieve), 'Lewis Grassic Gibbon' (James Leslie Mitchell) and Neil Gunn whose poems and novels probed the contemporary Scottish dilemma and sought to reawaken national identity by a revival of Scots and Gaelic culture.[34] Their ideas had only a limited impact, just as the political nationalism of the SNP remained a minority force. In a wider sense, though, the depression of the inter-war period, by emphasizing the economic and social differences between Scotland and England, focused attention on Scotland's distinctiveness and encouraged a broad cross-section of Scottish opinion – politicians, academics, industrialists and trade unionists – to think in more specifically Scottish terms. The transfer of the administrative apparatus of the Scottish Office to Edinburgh after 1937 reaffirmed the existence of Scotland as a national political entity and the status of Edinburgh as the nation's capital. Together with the other 'national' institutions of the law, the Church and the universities – to which should be added the Scottish press and broadcasting media – the St Andrews House bureaucracy consolidated the fabric of the self-sustaining 'civil society' that had distinguished the unique position of Scotland within the British state since the Union. Perhaps even strengthened by the vicissitudes of the depression, and by the need to confront the challenges of the twentieth century, Scottish national identity remained strong, and beneath the umbrella of political unionism 'Scottishness' continued to provide a unifying cement in an otherwise economically and socially divided national community.

Nor was it only the smaller nations of Britain that showed signs of national awareness. England, too, especially in the inter-war period, was becoming more analytically conscious of its own identity, while continuing to foster distinctive cultural movements in music, literature, art and the media. Writers of the stamp of J.B. Priestley (in his *English Journey* of 1933) and George Orwell explored facets of the

English experience and the impact of the depression on English society, while the Conservative leader Stanley Baldwin was pre-eminent among those who celebrated the quintessential virtues of traditional Englishness (for example in his essays *On England*, published in 1926). Defining England, or at least isolating any single version of 'Englishness', remained problematic. This was partly because of the size and diversity of England itself, and the number of its internal regional and social divisions. (Was the *real* England that of Baldwin's rural idyll, Betjeman's southern suburbia or the industrial north; was it Yorkshire, London, Cornwall or Kent?) Yet, on a smaller scale, Scotland and Wales were similarly diverse. What added an extra dimension to the English problem was the greater difficulty of establishing a separate English identity within the structure of the British state. The Scots and Welsh were able to embrace their own national identities and, in most cases, a British identity as well, though maintaining a difference between the two. The division between Englishness and Britishness was much more blurred, since England's historical role as the predominant partner in the British state had obviated the need for clear-cut distinctions. Baldwin's 'Englishness' could thus easily embrace the Scots and Welsh (indeed, many of his utterances on the theme were drafted by the Welshman Thomas Jones[35]), whereas the Welshness of, say, Saunders Lewis was by definition much more exclusive. English identity may have been stirring in Britain between the wars, but its emotional and cultural geography was still confused – a state of affairs further clouded by the resurgence of dual English/British patriotism during the Second World War and the renewed emphasis on the integrationist trends of 'one nation' after 1945.

Perhaps in another way, however, the cases of England, Scotland and Wales were not so dissimilar after all. Politically and economically the advantages of union seemed, by the 1950s, to have won out over those of independence, and returning prosperity had apparently healed the wounds that had threatened to divide inner and outer Britain into 'two nations' in the 1920s and 1930s. A strong central state and closer economic integration co-existed with a degree of political differentiation and a more diversified but still regionally specialized national economy. In a similar fashion, England, Scotland and Wales, and the regions within them, preserved their own identities while being more closely integrated into a British cultural community through the personal experience of individuals and the effects of the new mass media, especially radio and television. The existence of a stronger British state, particularly in the years after the Second World War, helped to foster a common British identity, albeit one that was itself being reshaped by external influences, from America and elsewhere. In the sense that Englishness, Scottishness and Welshness, and other internal identities as well, could all be seen as variations of 'Britishness', the 'one nation' of political propaganda could be said to have become a reality. As long as political stability was accompanied by economic prosperity, and the British state could be counted a success in domestic and international terms, there was no reason for these identities to be in fundamental conflict. On the other hand, the experience of earlier years, and the conditionality of any arrangements dependent on economic criteria, suggested that times could change. If this were so, the persistence of strong regional identities within what was still a multi-national British state could bring renewed pressure for constitutional reform and call the validity of a common identity of Britishness into question once more.

CHAPTER 7

DEVOLUTION AND THE TROUBLES: THE BRITISH STATE, 1964–2000

Between the partition of Ireland in 1921–22 and the Labour victory in the general election of 1964 the British state enjoyed a long period of constitutional stability. The reach of the state expanded, and the party system was recast into a Conservative–Labour duopoly, but the basic fabric of the parliamentary structure remained remarkably intact. From the early 1960s on, however, the constitutional settlement of 1922 came under increasing strain. Instability in Northern Ireland led first to the suspension of the Stormont regime and then to a 30-year search for an alternative framework for the government of the province that would satisfy both sides of a divided community and bring an end to the problem of terrorism. In Scotland and Wales the rise of the nationalist parties and other political pressures forced the issue of devolution back on to the agenda, with the abortive attempt to legislate for change in the 1970s being followed, 20 years later, by the establishment of a Scottish parliament and a Welsh assembly. The return at the end of the 1990s to a form of devolved government in Northern Ireland completed the most substantial overhaul of the constitutional machinery of Britain's multi-national state since the Acts of Union of 1707 and 1800. This chapter will examine the factors that led to these changes, the nature of the changes themselves and their implications for the development of the British state and its politics.

The re-emergence of nationalism

The 1960s were in many respects not unlike the 1880s – a time of political and social change, in which growing economic uncertainty

followed a generation of prosperity, and movements of radicalism
and protest were challenging a staid status quo. In 1963–64 13 years
of Conservative rule came to an end in an atmosphere of scandal and
satire which assisted Labour recovery and Liberal revival. By the
second half of the decade the confident mood of post-war affluence
was registering the tremors of doubt as unemployment began to rise,
inflation and industrial unrest increased and the government was
forced into a costly and ultimately unavailing effort to prevent the
devaluation of the pound. More generally, society was responding to
what Arthur Marwick has described as the decade's 'cultural revolution'.[1] If these broader themes of political radicalism, social
permissiveness and cultural awakening recalled, however distantly, an
earlier era, so in a more direct way did the return of nationalism to
the centre of the political stage, with the re-emergence of movements
of nationalist protest in Ireland, Scotland and Wales. The precise
circumstances of their reappearance were of course different in each
case, but there were sufficient similarities and common features for
them to be seen as part of a wider crisis of governance within the
British state that was particularly acute in the late 1960s and 1970s,
though not resolved (and then perhaps not finally) until nearer the
end of the century.

As in the nineteenth century, Ireland became the most violent and
immediate cause for concern, surprisingly so to British opinion given
the apparent quiescence of Irish affairs in the preceding decades.
Since the settlement of 1921–22, the Irish question had been in
virtual abeyance as a factor in British politics. After the end of the
civil war in 1923 the Irish Free State consolidated its independence.[2]
Following the victory of de Valera's Fianna Fail in the 1932 elections
the remaining ties with Britain were loosened by the adoption of a
new constitution in 1937 (which made Ireland a republic in all but
name[3]) and finally severed altogether by the formal declaration of a
republic and Ireland's decision to leave the Commonwealth in 1949.
The process was not without some friction. De Valera instituted a
trade war with Britain in the 1930s; his government negotiated
uncompromisingly to secure the return to Irish control in 1938 of the
three 'Treaty ports' reserved for the Royal Navy in 1922 and then
demonstrated its international autonomy by remaining neutral in the
Second World War. Yet although the 1937 constitution laid claim to
the Northern counties as an integral part of the national territory of
Ireland, de Valera made little sustained effort to end partition.
Indeed, he used the power of the state to suppress his former allies in

the IRA, and Churchill's suggestion that the division of Ireland might be ended in return for Eire's participation in the war against Germany was not taken up. The IRA, forced underground, did mount its own offensive both in Britain and against targets in the North in the late 1930s and again in the 'Border War' of 1956–62. But their activities did not make much practical impact, nor did they do much to re-establish the future of Ireland as an issue in the minds of the British public.

Internal developments in Northern Ireland similarly attracted little British attention. Under the Government of Ireland Act of 1920 a system of devolved government had been set up in the province, giving Northern Ireland its own elected parliament and a structure of prime ministerial cabinet government based on the Westminster model. The links with London were not entirely broken. The Northern Ireland government controlled most of the province's internal affairs, but foreign policy, external trade and military matters remained the preserve of the United Kingdom administration, as did key areas of fiscal policy such as income tax and customs and excise. Northern Ireland retained 13 seats in the House of Commons (reduced to 12 after the abolition of the Queen's University seat in 1948) and the UK parliament was still the sovereign body, with theoretical power to legislate for Northern Ireland and the sole right to amend the Northern Ireland constitution. In the main, however, Northern Ireland was governed by London on a fairly loose rein. There were annual negotiations between the two governments on the appropriate level of Northern Ireland's budget (most of which was provided by the UK Treasury), and the principle was laid down that there should be 'parity' between Northern Ireland and other parts of the United Kingdom in areas such as welfare provision and social security. Otherwise relations between London and Belfast were based on giving the Northern Ireland government maximum freedom to manage its own affairs. Between 1922 and 1969 there was no Westminster legislation on 'transferred' areas of responsibility that had been devolved to Stormont; the convention was even accepted that the House of Commons did not debate, or expect British ministers to answer questions on, matters that were officially the preserve of the Northern Ireland government. By the same token, the reduced contingent of Irish MPs at Westminster played a much less conspicuous role in British politics than had their predecessors before 1918, although as Unionists they mostly sided with their natural allies in the Conservative Party.

However, the absence of serious disagreements between London and Belfast did not mean that problems were not building up in Northern Ireland itself. Indeed, the 'sleeping dogs' attitude of successive British governments from the 1920s onwards, which permitted the internal politics of Northern Ireland to take shape with the minimum of outside interference, contributed in no small measure to developing tensions. These, in turn, were inherent in the structure of the Northern Ireland state and the circumstances of its creation. In 1920, it will be recalled, the intention of the British government presided over by Lloyd George had been to establish two Irish parliaments – one in Belfast, one in Dublin – which would be linked through a Council of Ireland in an all-Ireland relationship that would facilitate an early, and it was assumed inevitable, reunion of the divided island. To this end the six-county Northern Ireland had deliberately been created with a substantial Catholic minority (including Catholic majorities in the counties of Fermanagh and Tyrone) to provide it with a nationalist leaven in an otherwise Unionist Protestant enclave. Temporary partition would assuage immediate Unionist fears of nationalist domination, while nationalist opinion in north and south would be appeased by the withdrawal of British rule. In the medium to longer term, cooperation between Dublin and Belfast would pave the way for a united Ireland. In the meantime, minority rights in the north would be protected, principally by constitutional provisions to prevent discrimination on religious grounds and by the introduction of proportional representation for elections to the Belfast parliament and for local elections in Northern Ireland to ensure the Catholic community at least a share of political power.

This perhaps always over-optimistic scenario was invalidated from the outset by the south's rejection of the 1920 Act. Instead the 26-county Free State evolved into de Valera's Catholic republic, the Council of Ireland never came into existence and Northern Ireland was left to survive as best it could as an isolated outpost of the United Kingdom separate from the main currents of British political life. One consequence of this turn of events was that the Northern Irish Unionists, who had been forced to accept Home Rule against their will (preferring to remain fully integrated in the Union), now seized on the institutions of the new mini-state as their most reliable bulwark against absorption by the south. Accordingly they sought to use their numerical superiority in Northern Ireland to recreate a modified form of Protestant Ascendancy and to consolidate their hold on political and community power. In 1922 and 1929 respectively proportional representation was abolished for elections to local councils and the Northern Ireland parliament. The combination of a first-past-the-post system and the redrawing of local ward boundaries to give added weight to Protestant votes reinforced Unionist dominance across the province while also frustrating the emergence of new parties that might have bridged the sectarian divide.[4] With the Catholic majority represented at Stormont only by the remnants of the (often abstentionist) Nationalist Party and a handful of independents who had no hope of becoming a government, Northern Ireland became a one-party state in which the majority deployed their power systematically to promote the interests of their Protestant supporters. There was widespread institutionalized discrimination against Catholics and Catholic areas in housing, education and employment. Northern Ireland was policed by the Protestant-dominated Royal Ulster Constabulary, whose authority was augmented by Special Powers legislation that included extended powers of arrest and internment. Against none of these measures was there any protest or intervention from London, even though outbreaks of sectarian rioting such as those in Belfast in 1935 showed the continuing depths of communal tension. The Unionists' virtual monopoly of parliamentary representation meant that the Catholic nationalist minority lacked spokesmen at Westminster, and their occasional protests or calls for reform went unheeded or unheard. In 1949, following the declaration of the Irish Republic, the Attlee government passed an Act confirming that there would be no change in the status of Northern Ireland as part of the United Kingdom without the consent of the Northern Ireland parliament, but there was no attempt to ensure that the province's political institutions were as fully representative as had originally been intended in 1920.

It was only in the 1960s that Catholic discontent was mobilized with sufficiently organized effect to prompt a more constructive response. The changing social context of the time was important in producing a more educated, articulate Catholic middle class (rather as the 1790s had given birth to a more radical Catholic Committee and to the United Irishmen), while the more liberal atmosphere of the decade, and especially the example of the American Civil Rights movement, provided inspiration and organizational models. As a result of this conjunction of factors a number of protest movements emerged to press for an end to discrimination and for specific reforms in housing, education and local government. The Campaign for Social Justice was founded in 1964, joined in 1967 by the more broadly based Northern Ireland Civil Rights Association (NICRA) which brought together a wide range of political, community and trade union groups. Lobbying, demonstrations and protest meetings were complemented by more vigorous electoral activity, the new mood symbolized by the election of Gerry Fitt as MP for West Belfast in 1966 and the return of three 'civil rights' candidates in the 1969 Stormont elections. Moreover, although the civil rights movement was not wholly or explicitly nationalist, the spread of popular political activity based on Catholic grievances undoubtedly boosted the nationalist cause. Republican groups supported organizations like NICRA, according to some critics making it little more than an IRA front organization. Another manifestation of the same trend was the formation in 1970, by Gerry Fitt and John Hume, of the Social Democratic and Labour Party with the objective of campaigning for an end to discrimination but also 'to promote the cause of Irish unity based on the consent of the majority of the people of Northern Ireland'.[5]

The campaigns of the 1960s produced a response but they also provoked a crisis. The early signs were encouraging. The appointment of Captain Terence O'Neill as prime minister of Northern Ireland in 1963 ushered in a more liberal phase of Unionist rule, in which O'Neill committed himself to reforms to redress Catholic grievances as well as to plans for economic development across the province. In 1965 he took the bold step of inviting Sean Lemass, the new taoiseach of the Irish Republic, to Belfast for talks about future cooperation between north and south. O'Neill's programme of liberalization was also welcomed in London, where the Wilson government elected in 1964 showed itself willing to invest heavily in regional aid, and where the Campaign for Democracy in Ulster was gathering the support of Labour MPs for political and social reform.

Yet the consequences of this modest thaw only served to confirm de Tocqueville's dictum on the French Revolution, that a conservative regime is at its most vulnerable precisely at the moment when it initiates change. By the summer of 1969 Northern Ireland was spiralling into a crisis that threatened a breakdown of law and order and seriously endangered the Unionist regime. At the risk of over-simplification, three elements to the crisis can be distinguished. One was that the promise of change encouraged some reformers to demand even more, and militant groups like the student-based People's Democracy (which emerged as an Irish child of the more widespread student protests in Europe and America in 1968) adopted a more aggressive, confrontational approach which even affected existing organizations such as NICRA. A second was that this lurch to the left provoked a still more powerful right-wing Unionist backlash which drew on deeply embedded currents of fear and antagonism within the Protestant community. These had resurfaced at an early stage in the struggle, notably at Dungannon in July 1968 where a NICRA demonstration had been met by a counter-demonstration orchestrated by the Reverend Ian Paisley and groups such as the Ulster Constitution Defence Committee and the Ulster Protestant Volunteers. In October 1969, when a NICRA march went ahead in Londonderry despite a government ban, there were clashes between marchers and the RUC which provoked condemnation in London and led to the appointment of a commission of inquiry. In January 1969 a People's Democracy march from Belfast to Derry was attacked by Protestant loyalists and off-duty 'B-Special' police at Burntollet Bridge, and this led to further riots in other parts of Northern Ireland as sectarian animosities flared and the efforts of politicians were drowned by the violence on the streets.

The inability of politicians to halt the slide to violence, and in particular the growing instability of the Unionist government, provided the third element in the crisis. O'Neill's position was weakened by the groundswell of hostility to his reform plans from within Unionist ranks. Although a comfortable Unionist majority was returned in the Stormont elections of February 1969, at least a dozen of the 39 Unionists elected were opponents of O'Neill. A wave of bomb attacks on public buildings in April – blamed on the IRA but actually the work of anti-O'Neill loyalist paramilitaries – proved the final straw and O'Neill resigned, to be replaced by James Chichester-Clark. Chichester-Clark tried to press ahead with reform, but as summer progressed the main priority was to end the violence. The Protestant 'marching season' in July and August led to large-scale rioting in Belfast and Derry which the police were unable to control. In an attempt to contain a dangerously disintegrating situation, after emergency consultations between Belfast and London, the Northern Ireland government was finally driven to call for the deployment of British troops as a peace-keeping force.

The events of 1968–69 marked not only the re-entry of the British government into Irish politics but also the beginning of a 30-year recrudescence of Ireland as a problem for British politicians. Furthermore, although the future of Northern Ireland was to some extent a self-contained issue (and the direct impact of Northern Ireland on party politics in Britain was much less than that of the Irish question in the 1880s or 1912–14, because of the limited presence of Irish MPs in the Commons and the fact that the British parties maintained a largely bi-partisan approach to Irish affairs), it was also part of a wider problem of governance emerging at the time. The upsurge of unrest in Northern Ireland in the late 1960s coincided with – and may have been connected to – the re-emergence of nationalism as a political force in Scotland and Wales. Together these movements presented the Wilson government and its successors with a much more complex series of choices about the constitutional future of the United Kingdom and the political management of the British state, reactivating a debate about the relative merits of centralism versus devolution which had languished since the First World War and even calling into question the unity of the United Kingdom itself.

In Wales the renewal of nationalism as a movement came from a variety of sources. An important factor that linked the nationalism of the 1960s with that of earlier periods was concern for the Welsh language. Despite the spread of Welsh-language education and the vitality of Welsh literary culture, the number of Welsh speakers showed a steady fall – from 909,261 (36.8 per cent of the population) in the census of 1931 to 656,002 (26 per cent) in 1961.[6] For traditional nationalists and for a younger generation of students and intellectuals, improving the status of Welsh as a language was a key objective. Their chosen vehicle for pursuing their goal was Cymdeithas yr Iaith Gymraeg (the Welsh Language Society) which was formed in 1962 and which immediately embarked on a consciousness-raising campaign of public demonstrations and direct action, the most widely noticed tactic of which was the painting out of English versions of place-names on road signs and public buildings. A small minority of activists followed a more militant path still by engaging in outright terrorist activity through organizations such as the Free Wales Army, which briefly attracted some public sympathy with bomb attacks on the unpopular Tryweryn dam project in the early 1960s.[7] The main forum for nationalist politics, however, remained Plaid Cymru, led from 1950 by its charismatic new president, Gwynfor Evans, who was determined to replace the party's exclusivist image with a more broadly based popular appeal. To this end he redefined Welshness by identifying 'common membership of the Welsh community rather than language or descent [as] the test of nationality in Wales',[8] and emphasized the need to address social and economic as much as linguistic or cultural issues if the party was to win support in south Wales as well as in the remoter parts of the west and north. The party extended its organizational base and gradually carved out an electoral niche. At the general election of 1951 it ran only four candidates and polled a mere 0.7 per cent of the Welsh vote; in 1964 23 candidates totalled 4.8 per cent of the votes cast. Its real breakthrough, though – and the one which registered on a British and not just a Welsh level – followed the general election of 1966. In July 1966 Gwynfor Evans won the parliamentary by-election in Carmarthen which followed the death of Labour's Megan Lloyd George. Plaid Cymru candidates also ran Labour a close second at two further by-elections in hitherto safe seats in Rhondda West (March 1967) and Caerphilly (July 1968). After long years on the whimsical fringe of Welsh politics, nationalism seemed once again to be firmly on the move.

Scottish nationalists enjoyed a similar upturn in their fortunes. Scottish nationalism lacked the linguistic and extremist dimension of the Welsh movement, although there were episodes of direct action such as the removal of the Scottish coronation stone (the 'Stone of Destiny') from Westminster Abbey by four nationalist students at Christmas in 1950 and subsequent attacks on pillar boxes bearing the legend EIIR after the accession of Queen Elizabeth (Scotland's first) in 1952. In the late 1940s, however, the Scottish Convention movement, led by the former SNP stalwart John MacCormick, had demonstrated the strength of support for some kind of Home Rule – a petition launched by the Convention's Scottish National Assembly in 1949 in the form of a 'Scottish Covenant' attracted two million signatures – and the neglect of Scotland's claims by the British parties provided an opportunity that nationalists could exploit. By the early 1960s the SNP, like Plaid Cymru, was becoming a more broadly based, professionally organized mass party. It increased the number of its branches from 20 in 1962 to 140 in 1965 and 470 in 1969. It also became progressively more ambitious in its electoral strategy, fielding 23 candidates in the 1966 election compared with only two in 1955 and increasing its share of the Scottish vote from 0.5 to 5 per cent in the process.[9] In 1962 its candidate William Wolfe polled particularly strongly in the West Lothian by-election won by Labour's Tam Dalyell, taking over 10,000 votes. But, as with Plaid Cymru in Wales, it was in the 1966 parliament that the SNP's first significant post-war breakthrough occurred. After claiming 28 per cent of the vote in the Glasgow Pollock by-election in March 1967, in November of the same year the SNP won its first parliamentary contest since 1945 when Mrs Winifred Ewing took Hamilton from Labour. In the Scottish local elections of May 1968 the SNP polled 34 per cent of the vote and gained over 100 seats, giving it, among other successes, the balance of power in Glasgow. At the general election of 1970 the SNP's 65 candidates won 11 per cent of the popular vote, and although the Hamilton seat was lost to Labour there was a compensating victory in the Western Isles.

It is true that much of the sudden increase in nationalist support reflected a short-term protest vote rather than a widespread desire for separation or independence. The SNP's performance in 1970 actually came as a disappointment to the party since it represented a sharp falling away in its electoral strength from the peak of two years earlier. Even so, the stirrings of discontent on the periphery could not be ignored by politicians at the centre. The Labour government was especially vulnerable to the nationalist challenge because of its dependence on Scottish and Welsh constituencies for a British majority, but electoral considerations also prompted a Conservative response. Labour had already tried to preempt the nationalist upsurge in Wales by the creation in 1964 of the Welsh Office in Cardiff and the appointment of the prominent Welsh MP James Griffiths as secretary of state. The Welsh Office gradually assumed similar administrative and executive powers to those already exercised by the Scottish Office in Scotland and was an important move towards a unified governmental structure for the principality.[10] In 1967 the government introduced a Welsh Language Act that extended bilingualism as a policy and made increased provision for the use of Welsh for official purposes. There was greater reluctance on the part of the Labour establishment, however, to move from administrative to representative devolution. Jim Griffiths and his successor Cledwyn Hughes were sympathetic to the idea of an elected 'Welsh Council' as part of a more comprehensive local government reform. But devolution was opposed by George Thomas, who replaced Hughes as secretary of state in 1968, and by the Labour Party in Scotland, where the staunchly unionist Labour secretary of state William Ross believed that any constitutional change would be seen as a concession to the nationalists that would encourage separatism and endanger Labour's hold on power. In fact it was the Conservatives who seized the initiative in Scotland, when the 'Declaration of Perth' made at their Scottish conference by the party leader Edward Heath in 1968 appeared to commit them to the principle of an elected Scottish assembly, for which a committee under the former premier Sir Alec Douglas Home was then deputed to work out a plan. The Labour government meanwhile temporized by setting up a Royal Commission under Lord Crowther 'to examine the present functions of the central legislature and government in relation to the several countries, nations and regions of the United Kingdom' without committing themselves in advance to any preferred outcome.[11]

The irony was that as politicians began once again to consider the possibility of devolution in Britain, in the one part of the United Kingdom that already had devolved government the devolutionary principle was in danger of being undermined or discredited because the constitutional settlement in Northern Ireland was becoming increasingly unworkable. Between 1969 and 1972 the situation deteriorated in almost every conceivable respect. The ruling Unionist regime was destabilized by defections and internal divisions. In March 1971 Chichester-Clark's brief premiership ended in resignation and he was replaced by Brian Faulkner, but Faulkner could do little to heal the breach between reformers and hardliners. The fragmentation of Unionist politics was accelerated by the formation of the Paisleyite Democratic Unionist Party. By this time, however, Stormont was becoming an increasing irrelevance as political battles transferred to the streets. Protestant paramilitaries were engaged in terrorist acts and sectarian violence from an early stage in the Troubles. In the winter of 1969–70 the militant spirits in the Catholic nationalist community responded by forming the 'Provisional IRA' to defend Catholic areas and to wage a retaliatory republican offensive against loyalist groups, the Northern Ireland state and the British 'occupation'.[12] The 'Provos' rapidly took over from the old IRA (which had pursued a more political strategy in the 1960s and was felt to have been discredited by its failure to protect Catholics in the riots of 1969) as the main purveyor of the nationalist armed struggle. In 1970–71 the cycle of violence and counter-violence took dreadful hold, with neither the Stormont government nor the British Army able to bring it to an end. As an act of desperation in 1971 the Northern Ireland government introduced the internment without trial of suspected terrorists, but this only prompted further violence and the withdrawal in protest of the SDLP from Stormont. The army, meanwhile, having in 1969 been initially welcomed by Catholics as a protecting force, came to be seen more as an oppressive arm of the Protestant state. Nationalist opinion was alienated by heavy-handed army searches of Catholic estates in the Lower Falls area of Belfast and in Derry. The shooting, by soldiers of the Parachute Regiment, of unarmed demonstrators on 'Bloody Sunday' in January 1972 was the final stage in the estrangement between the army and the Catholic community, which had already led the IRA to identify soldiers as legitimate targets in their guerrilla war. The killing of the first British soldier in the Troubles in February 1971 was a clear indication that the Provos were moving over from defence to attack, and that they were willing to confront the full might of the British state in order to destroy the hated Stormont regime.

In these circumstances the only solution that the Conservative government which had taken office in Britain in 1970 could come up with was to take over the reins of power itself. The Northern Ireland government was suspended in March 1972, the Stormont assembly prorogued and a system of 'direct rule' instituted under William Whitelaw as secretary of state. Northern Ireland was thus brought into a status equivalent to that of Scotland or Wales, having a devolved administration but with its chief executive being a cabinet minister in the London government. The aim, rather as with the original Act of Union, was to placate nationalists by removing them from the grip of a discriminatory Protestant regime while reassuring Unionists that they were still an integral part of the British state. Yet although the imposition of direct rule seemed to signal the end of the devolutionary experiment in Northern Ireland, and perhaps to make it less likely that devolution would be implemented in either Scotland or Wales, in reality it did nothing of the kind. Direct rule was seen as at best a temporary expedient. The anticipated report of the Royal Commission on the Constitution would reawaken debates that had died away after the Conservative victory in the 1970 election. In any case by 1972–73 the nationalist parties in Scotland and Wales were on the verge of further breakthroughs, and the need to confront the problems of Northern Ireland after a long period of neglect had focused attention on the anomalies by which the constituent parts of the United Kingdom were governed. Far from being the end of the devolutionary path, therefore, the suspension of Stormont was merely the beginning of a new search for a constitutional framework for the British state that would allow the peoples and nations of Britain and Ireland to live together in a more peaceful and harmonious way.

Northern Ireland

The political and constitutional conundrums presented by Northern Ireland, Scotland and Wales were similar but not the same. Each was a small unit in comparison to its English partner, each contained nationalist minorities who wanted to break away or gain autonomy from the British state and unionist majorities who preferred to remain part of the United Kingdom, with or without devolved government. Yet behind the broad similarities lay important differences. Scotland and Wales were more fully integrated into the British system. Northern Ireland by contrast had a separate political geography, based largely around the sectarian religious divide. In Ulster it was the Unionists who supported devolution (which they saw as a restoration of Stormont). Nationalists preferred direct British rule to Protestant Irish rule, though their long-term aims were irredentist – to be allowed to join the Irish Republic in a 32-county Irish state. The politics of Northern Ireland were also overlain by the politics of terrorism in a way that was never seriously the case in Scotland or Wales. The three regions were part of a larger question of governance, but it makes sense to consider them separately before standing back to look at the bigger picture.

The situation in Northern Ireland after 1972 was especially troubled. Stormont had been suspended and direct rule imposed. This was seen as only a temporary solution, yet alternatives were not easy to find. Any settlement needed to address the problems of violence, the creation of political structures acceptable to both sections of the community, and the 'Irish dimension' of Northern Ireland's existence. It also faced a series of obstacles not easy to overcome, including Protestant/Catholic tensions, the incompatibility of extreme unionist and extreme nationalist demands and the difficulty of finding a workable compromise between them. If the restoration of a Protestant state was impossible, and any move towards a united Ireland impractical, in many ways direct rule was the 'least worst' option.

The full intractability of the problem was amply illustrated by the failure of William Whitelaw's attempts as secretary of state to effect a settlement between 1972 and 1974. Whitelaw held secret talks with leaders of the Provisional IRA in 1972 but these produced no agreement because of the IRA's insistence on an immediate British declaration of their intention to withdraw from Northern Ireland and on an all-Ireland referendum on Irish unity.[13] Having failed to reach agreement with the terrorists or to prevent a renewal of the armed struggle, Whitelaw next tried to harness moderate opinion in favour of a new constitutional compromise for the devolved government of the province. The 1973 Northern Ireland Constitution Act abolished the Stormont parliament and replaced it with a 78-member Assembly to be elected by the single transferable vote system of proportional representation. The devolution of power, however, was to be contingent on the formation of a 'power-sharing executive' that would include representatives from the two main political communities. The Act confirmed that Northern Ireland would remain part of the United Kingdom unless 'a majority of the people of Northern Ireland' decided otherwise (thereby offering some reassurance to the Unionists), although a parallel agreement negotiated between the British and Irish governments at the Sunningdale conference in December 1973 moved some way to recognizing the need for an Irish dimension that would appeal to nationalists by providing for a Council of Ireland comprising seven members each from the Northern Ireland Executive and the government of the Republic.[14]

This carefully constructed house of cards collapsed in the first half of 1974. In 1973 nationalists had shown their disaffection by boycotting a poll on the future of Northern Ireland (which consequently produced the meaningless verdict that 98.9 per cent of those voting wanted to remain in the UK). In 1974 it was the turn of the Unionists to resort to tactics of non-cooperation. Elections to the new Northern Ireland Assembly in June 1973 had already revealed a split in Unionist ranks, with 24 Faulknerite moderates being more than cancelled out by 26 anti-Faulkner Unionists, including eight representatives of Ian Paisley's DUP and seven from William Craig's ultra-Protestant 'Vanguard' movement. The Ulster Unionist Council approved Faulkner's participation as head of the power-sharing executive with the SDLP's Gerry Fitt as his deputy by the narrow margin of 377 votes to 369. The anti-Faulknerites then joined the other anti-executive parties in forming a United Ulster Unionist Council to oppose the embryonic Faulkner–Fitt government and to condemn the Sunningdale Agreement which they saw as a sell-out to the nationalists. In the United Kingdom general election of February 1974 the anti-Sunningdale Unionists won 11 of the 12 Ulster seats. The real measure of their popular support in the Unionist community was demonstrated, however, by the 'General Strike' in Northern Ireland in May 1974, organized by the Ulster Workers' Council and backed by loyalist paramilitaries, which brought the province to a virtual standstill. Faced with opposition to its existence on such a scale the power-sharing executive lost any credibility it still had. Faulkner resigned as chief executive, the assembly was prorogued and the reins of direct rule were resumed by the London government.

Admittedly the chances of success at this juncture were not helped by the concurrent political instability in Britain, where the defeat of the Heath government in February 1974 and its replacement by a Labour Party that in opposition had made statements appearing to confirm that a united Ireland was the long-term objective of its policy, had inevitably exacerbated Unionist fears.[15] Yet even without this additional complication the underlying divisions in Ulster society bedevilled attempts to make constitutional progress under governments of both parties. The Labour government sponsored the election of a Northern Ireland Convention in 1975 to discuss possible constitutional models, but it failed to reach agreement and was dissolved the following year. The Thatcher governments after 1979 similarly tried various expedients without conspicuous success. The Northern Ireland Act of 1982, introduced by secretary of state James Prior, provided for the election of a new assembly and the novel concept of 'rolling devolution' whereby powers would be transferred to the new body and its executive in proportion as agreement was reached across the inter-communal divide. But since the SDLP and other nationalist parties refused to participate in the assembly, no transfer was possible and the assembly was finally dissolved in 1986. By this time controversy had broken out over another Conservative initiative, the Anglo-Irish Agreement of 1985. The Agreement, signed by Margaret Thatcher and the Irish prime minister, Garret Fitzgerald, sought to recognize the Irish aspects of the Ulster problem by creating an 'Inter-Governmental Conference' to deal with matters of mutual concern. It was precisely this Irish dimension that antagonized Ulster Unionists who were united in their opposition, which they demonstrated by collectively resigning their parliamentary seats at Westminster and forcing a raft of by-elections.[16] Contacts between the British and Irish governments continued under the auspices of the IGC and by other means, though without at this stage leading to any decisive change of atmosphere in Northern Ireland or any diminution of the terrorist threat.

The problem of Northern Ireland was less of a source of conflict in British politics in the 1970s and 1980s than the issue of Home Rule had been in the nineteenth century because Labour and Conservative politicians adopted a broadly bi-partisan approach to Irish affairs.[17]

Developments in Northern Ireland nevertheless had an impact on the British state in other ways. One was the cost in money and man-power of maintaining a large-scale security operation in Northern Ireland, with at times a quarter to a third of the army's peacetime strength being deployed in Ulster in addition to increased numbers of police, intelligence and undercover anti-terrorist officers. Even this large expenditure of resources could not stop the bombers getting through or a rising total of deaths and injuries in terrorist incidents and paramilitary sectarian violence. Eventually more than 3000 people died in Northern Ireland as a result of the Troubles. The IRA and offshoot republican groups like the Irish National Liberation Army also carried out high-profile terrorist attacks on the British mainland against army bases, shopping and business centres and against Britain's political leaders. In the last category were the IRA bomb attack on Brighton's Grand Hotel during the Conservative Party conference in 1984, which came close to killing Mrs Thatcher and several senior figures in her cabinet, and a spectacular mortar attack on Downing Street in February 1991, early in the premiership of Mrs Thatcher's successor John Major. Inevitably these and other incidents – often involving widespread loss of life and damage to property – forced the state to take protective measures. The 1974 Prevention of Terrorism Act (renewed annually despite left-wing criticism that it infringed civil liberties) gave the authorities special powers for dealing with suspected terrorists, including banning their entry into Britain. In Northern Ireland internment was revived intermittently in an attempt to limit terrorist activity, and non-jury trials (the so-called 'Diplock courts') were introduced in terrorist cases to speed up the machinery of justice and prevent the possible intimidation of jurors. Censorship was imposed, preventing the voices of terrorists or their supporters being broadcast on radio or television.

None of these measures fully answered the terrorist threat, and politically they may have been counterproductive in that they reinforced the propaganda image of Britain – in the eyes of Irish nationalists and their sympathizers, particularly in the United States – as a repressive power in Northern Ireland, whose presence was the root cause of the Irish conflict. Yet, as the various initiatives of the period had shown, the roots of the problem lay not so much in British intransigence as in the nature of Northern Ireland and the divisions of its community. The Northern Ireland that had been created in 1921 was an artificial construct. The loss of its separate government in 1972 did not alter its anomalous position within the United Kingdom, since although its government by direct rule under a secretary of state made it appear on a par with Scotland and Wales, unlike those two countries it did not possess a historic national status (institutional or cultural) and remained a province of the British state in the island of Ireland.[18] In the absence of a common 'Northern Irish' heritage, Northern Ireland's inhabitants had to define their national identity in relation to a larger whole, whether Irish or British, and Northern Ireland existed in a kind of limbo-land between Britain and its southern Irish neighbour. The anomaly would have been resolved by the eventual union envisaged by the Lloyd George settlement, or by the British withdrawal demanded by Irish nationalists and the 'Troops Out' movement. But neither option seemed practical politics in the face of Unionist opposition and the threat of sectarian civil war. Even the cautious attempt of the Thatcher government to involve the Irish Republic in discussions over Northern Ireland through the Anglo-Irish Agreement had provoked a Unionist backlash that revealed the emotional depths of historic suspicions and placed an apparent veto on constitutional change.

Beneath the appearance of a static conflict akin to the stalemate of trench warfare, however, there were some more hopeful signs emerging from the very tangle of fractured identities that made progress so difficult to achieve. It was, and is, common shorthand to talk of the 'two traditions' in the make-up of Northern Ireland, based on a Catholic/Protestant, nationalist/unionist, Irish/British divide. The reality of this division is hard to gainsay. Most Protestants were Unionist (and vice versa), and most Catholics supported either the nationalist SDLP or republican parties such as Sinn Fein. These divisions were reinforced by segregation in housing, education and employment, as well as by the myths, organizations and rituals that shaped communal life. Yet the relationship between the two traditions and the larger entities of 'Irishness' and 'Britishness' was not entirely straightforward. Probably most Catholics perceived themselves as Irish, even if they were not actively dissatisfied with their citizenship of the British state. But the position of Protestant Unionists was more equivocal. They proclaimed their Britishness in their loyalty to the Union and the crown. However, as they showed in the period before 1914 and again in 1974, that Britishness was of a particular Ulster variety, which justified them in opposing the United Kingdom government (or anyone else) if they felt that the interests of Protestant Ulster were threatened, for example by the forced introduction of power-sharing or the implementation of any changes that could lead to Ulster's eventual incorporation in an all-Ireland state.[19] It was this paradoxical ambiguity of the Ulster-British identity that could lead even Unionists to stress their Irishness rather than their Britishness and which suggested that, in the right circumstances, the kaleidoscope of multiple identities that existed in Northern Ireland could be shaken to produce outcomes that were more consensual than confrontational.

A common sense of Irishness could, on occasion, transcend sectarian and political divisions.[20] A deeper unity in the north, overshadowed through 30 years by the violence of the Troubles, was represented by the heartfelt desire of individuals and communities of both traditions for forms of peaceful co-existence that could provide the conditions for a quiet life and a safe future. Initiatives such as the founding of the non-sectarian Alliance Party and the Peace Movement of the 1970s attempted to give organizational form to this more widespread feeling, as did experiments in co-education for Catholics and Protestants and similar community-based projects. Alongside paramilitary gang warfare, normal life continued and moderates on both sides searched for a way forward that acknowledged the historic duality of Northern Ireland without being disabled by it. The impetus for a new reformism in the 1980s and 1990s came not just from accumulated war weariness but was a response to changes in the wider context. Britain and the Irish Republic established increasingly friendly relations, both through bilateral agreements and through their cooperation in international bodies such as the EEC (which they joined at the same time in 1973). From the 1970s on, with the final retirement of de Valera from political life, the Republic embarked on its own programmes of modernization and liberalization which made it seem less of a bogey to all but the most unreconstructed of hardline Unionists. Finally, and perhaps most compellingly, processes of social and demographic change were altering the complexion of Northern Ireland itself. The census of 1991 revealed that Catholics made up 43.1 per cent of the population (compared with about 35 per cent in 1922), and that they were actually a majority among younger age groups.[21] Upward social mobility was gradually eroding the effect of past discrimination (Catholic students comprised 65 per cent of the population of Queen's University in Belfast) and redressing the historic imbalance between the two communities in wealth as well as numbers. While these changes may again have intensified the fears of more reactionary Protestant elements, other Unionists saw the need to use their remaining strength to negotiate a new constitutional settlement before their position eroded further.

Gradually, through the 1980s and early 1990s, the various elements of what came to be described as the 'peace process' were put in place. Nationalist politicians in particular engaged in creative attempts to break the deadlock by broadening the terms of the Northern Ireland debate. The SDLP, although it boycotted the 1982 Assembly, participated in a 'New Ireland Forum' sponsored by the Dublin government. More dramatic in its impact was a shift in strategy among republicans. The IRA and its political allies in Sinn Fein had committed themselves in the 1970s to a policy of armed struggle: the removal of British rule in Ireland by force. In the early 1980s, without abandoning the concept of armed struggle, Sinn Fein, under the leadership of Gerry Adams, entered on a more directly political path. Impressed by the success of popular campaigns to mobilize support for IRA prisoners on hunger strike against internment in 1981 (which included the election of one of the hunger strikers, Bobby Sands, as MP for Fermanagh and South Tyrone at a by-election), Adams recognized the potential for building a Sinn Fein electoral base in Northern Ireland which would not only enable it to challenge the SDLP for leadership of the nationalist community but would give the republican movement moral authority in any negotiations with the British government and a valuable propaganda appeal among sympathizers in the Irish Republic and the United States. Adams himself was elected as MP for West Belfast in 1983, although he followed the traditional abstentionist policy of refusing to take his seat at Westminster. The emergence of Sinn Fein as a constitutional party was to be a key factor in engaging the IRA in the political process and bringing about a ceasefire, a goal which began to be discussed in the 'Hume–Adams' talks between the SDLP and Sinn Fein from 1988.

By the early 1990s changes in politics were taking place in an increasingly encouraging international environment. The governments headed by John Major in Britain and Albert Reynolds in the Irish Republic were kept informed of the progress of the Hume–Adams talks and were taking their own soundings about the scope for fresh initiatives. Their efforts were encouraged by the administration of Bill Clinton, who took office as president of the United States at the beginning of 1993. Clinton had a keen interest in Irish affairs and had promised Irish-American lobbyists during the presidential campaign that one of his first acts as president would be to appoint a 'peace envoy' to Northern Ireland.[22] He was dissuaded from what could have been seen as a provocative move by Albert Reynolds, but only on the understanding that the British and Irish governments were themselves at a delicate stage in negotiations which could lead to a real breakthrough in the direction of peace.

The first fruits of these discussions came in the form of the Downing Street Declaration of December 1993, a statement by the governments of Britain and Ireland that was intended to establish a basis for constitutional progress by clearing away obstacles to change. A carefully worded document promised 'a new political framework' for the whole of Ireland. Britain emphasized that it had 'no selfish strategic or economic interest in Northern Ireland' and that it was 'for the people of the island of Ireland alone ... to exercise the right of self-determination on the basis of consent, freely and concurrently given, north and south, to bring about a united Ireland, if that is their wish'.[23] The Irish government, for its part, indicated a readiness to change the constitution of the Republic by giving up their claim to the six counties of Northern Ireland (which Unionists found offensive) and accepting that any settlement must include a respect for the liberties and traditions of 'both communities' in the north.

The Declaration was important in demonstrating the determination of both governments to try to bring peace to Northern Ireland, and it seemed in the summer of 1994 as if it might succeed in doing so when, in August, the IRA announced 'a complete cessation of hostilities', followed by a similar ceasefire by loyalist paramilitaries in October. Thereafter, however, progress was slower than the Declaration's signatories might have wished. This was partly because of a political crisis in the Irish Republic which led to the fall of the Reynolds government and its replacement by a coalition under John Bruton. A more serious barrier was the reluctance of the British government to enter into negotiations with Sinn Fein without assurances that the IRA ceasefire was permanent. Unionists in Northern Ireland were in any case suspicious of any proposed settlement that appeared to involve doing a deal with republican terrorists. They rejected 'Framework Documents' which were tabled early in 1995 proposing a power-sharing assembly for Northern Ireland and the creation of new north–south bodies. A Major government that was now dependent on Unionist MPs at Westminster, and whose right wing was opposed to any appeasement of the IRA, was in no position to force the pace of negotiations or to override Unionist fears. The visit of President Clinton to Northern Ireland in November 1995 imparted, briefly, a renewed momentum to the peace process, and in January 1996 the report of a commission headed by the American senator George Mitchell suggested a structure for all-party talks and parallel discussions on the 'decommissioning' of terrorist weapons. But these wisps of optimism were blown away in the following month when the IRA, its patience with the politicians exhausted, revoked its ceasefire and carried out a bomb attack on the Canary Wharf financial centre in London in which two men died.

A resumption of progress proved impossible until after the United Kingdom general election of May 1997. The election demonstrated the growing strength of Sinn Fein and the SDLP in Northern Ireland, who between them claimed 41 per cent of the vote.[24] More importantly, it brought to power in Britain a Labour government under Tony Blair which was not dependent on Unionist support. Behind-the-scenes discussions produced a renewal of the IRA ceasefire in June 1997, and all-party talks were instituted shortly afterwards. The outcome of these was the Good Friday Agreement, concluded in Belfast on 10 April 1998, which provided a comprehensive framework for the political future of Northern Ireland in both a British and Irish context.[25] There were three main elements in the proposed constitutional arrangements. At their heart was a devolved Northern Ireland Assembly with 108 members (elected by proportional representation) and a multi-party executive to guarantee power-sharing. An 'Irish dimension' was ensured by the creation of a north–south ministerial council (in addition to other cross-border bodies), while there was also to be a 'British–Irish' Council, comprising representatives of the British, Irish and Northern Irish governments, together with members from other devolved assemblies elsewhere in the British Isles. Other provisions of the agreement included a promise by the political parties involved to use their 'best efforts' to achieve the decommissioning of paramilitary weapons, the appointment of an independent commission to consider the future of the RUC, and a programme for the accelerated release of paramilitary prisoners still in detention. The Irish government reaffirmed its willingness to amend its constitution to relinquish its automatic claim to the territory of Northern Ireland, thereby recognizing the right of Northern Ireland to remain part of the United Kingdom for as long as its people chose to do so.

The Agreement was approved by referendums in Northern Ireland and the Republic in May 1998. In the Republic the 'Yes' vote was 94.3 per cent, in the north 71.1 per cent. The anti-Agreement voters in Northern Ireland were mainly Unionists (especially in the DUP and the smaller UK Unionist Party) opposed to negotiations with 'Sinn Fein/IRA' and to the establishment of formal links with the Republic, though they may also have included extreme republicans who saw any deal involving a recognition of the legitimacy of Northern Ireland as a betrayal of their ideals. In elections to the new Northern Ireland Assembly, pro-Agreement parties (David Trimble's Ulster Unionists, the SDLP, Sinn Fein and the Alliance Party) secured a comfortable majority, although the 20 DUP and five UK Unionist members could hope to gain enough support from dissident official Unionists to delay the complex process of forming an executive. In fact the process was made still more difficult by outside events. The summers of 1998 and 1999 saw a series of street confrontations over the rights of Protestant Orangemen to parade during the marching season, leading to a particularly bitter dispute at Drumcree. Meanwhile IRA splinter groups attempted to derail the 'peace train' by resuming a terrorist campaign, most tragically with the bombing of the busy shopping centre of Omagh on a summer Saturday afternoon in August 1998. This in turn strengthened the determination even of pro-Agreement Unionists not to enter an executive with Sinn Fein until the decommissioning of IRA weapons had begun. Eventually the Unionist leader and first minister designate, David Trimble, agreed to a partial compromise on his strict 'no guns, no government' line to allow an Executive to be formed with Sinn Fein membership in November 1999, but even then the absence of a breakthrough on decommissioning caused a suspension of the Executive in February 2000 and it was only restored later in the year after protracted negotiations on all sides.

Despite the difficulties of its birth, the new Executive represented a substantial constitutional change in the government of Northern Ireland. Apart from certain reserved matters (such as security policy) which remained the concern of the secretary of state, all other areas of internal policy were devolved to the Executive and Assembly, giving Northern Ireland politicians responsibility for running the province's affairs for the first time since 1972. Moreover, unlike the old Stormont regime, the Good Friday settlement ensured that any government would be a multi-party executive with cross-community support. In the executive formed by David Trimble and his SDLP deputy, Seamus Mallon, Unionist and SDLP ministers sat in cabinet with members of Sinn Fein and the DUP (though the Paisleyites refused to play a full part in collective discussions involving Sinn Fein). Whether in the longer run this would be a permanent solution to the political problems of the province remained to be seen. The ultimate objectives of Unionists and Nationalists were still very different, and even short-term disagreements over areas of policy were bound to occur. In the Unionist community especially, any moves towards a united Ireland, or a closer relationship with the south, were likely to reawaken old suspicions. Again, too, the early history of the new regime suggested that, while the visible problems of terrorism had been at least temporarily curtailed, a persistent, if lower, level of communal and sectarian violence continued. The debate about the long-term future of Northern Ireland was thus far from over. History could not be stood on its head overnight. The re-establishment of devolved government on the basis of a genuine compromise between the 'two traditions' nevertheless amounted to a significant achievement for all concerned, building on a new relationship between Britain and Ireland to create a possible solution to the most difficult internal problem that had faced the British state in the final part of the twentieth century.

Scotland and Wales

In Ireland, Home Rule had become a majority demand in the nineteenth century. Northern Ireland, though mainly Unionist, had a devolved government from 1921, and even after the suspension of Stormont in 1972 the restoration of devolution was an aim of policy until it was finally achieved in 1999–2000. The pattern of constitutional development in Scotland and Wales was very different. Despite fitful Home Rule movements before 1914, Liberal support for the principle of 'Home Rule All Round' and some discussion even among Conservatives of the possibility of federalism, there had been no move to dismantle Britain's unitary state or to reduce the role of the Westminster parliament. What had emerged instead was a system of administrative devolution (similar in some ways to the Dublin Castle regime in post-Union Ireland) that decentralized the functions of the executive without weakening the authority of the central government. The process began in Scotland with the creation of the Scottish Office in 1885 (which Gladstone described, perhaps misleadingly, as 'a little mouthful of Home Rule'[26]), the elevation of the Scottish secretaryship to a secretary of state in 1929 and the transfer of the Scottish Office from London to Edinburgh in the 1930s. Wales followed suit more slowly, not acquiring the Welsh Office and a secretary of state until 1964, although thereafter the size and scope of the department expanded rapidly so that 20 years later the Welsh Office employed over 2000 civil servants and controlled a broad swath of policy areas, from agriculture, industry and roads to housing, education and local government.[27]

The system was not without its defects or critics. Although it brought decision-making closer to the national communities of Scotland and Wales, it lacked democratic accountability. The secretaries of state and their junior ministers usually represented Scottish and Welsh constituencies, but they were responsible to the UK parliament rather than to their own national assemblies. It was difficult for Westminster properly to scrutinize their actions, even with separate question times and committees. Equally, ministers had such a wide range of portfolios that it was difficult for them to avoid what Bogdanor has described as 'executive overload',[28] and important decisions were being left to civil servants. Another criticism was that the system gave secretaries of state only limited freedom to pursue a distinctive national policy. They were responsible for representing the interests of their countries in cabinet; some, like Thomas Johnston and William Ross in Scotland, were adept at bending colleagues to their views. More often, however, their status was too junior to carry real weight at the UK level, and they had simply to follow the dictates of British policy decided in London. The result was a system of devolution which paradoxically fostered centralization rather than genuine diversity. Nor did it necessarily provide good or stable government. Aside from perpetuating anomalies in the British state (such as the fact that Scotland had its own legal system but not its own legislature), it also generated discontent. The existence of the Scottish and Welsh Offices stimulated a national political consciousness by focusing attention on Edinburgh and Cardiff while denying that consciousness full democratic expression through a representative assembly. As in Ireland in the nineteenth century, there was a danger that the division between 'Castle' and people would promote a colonial mentality that provided a breeding ground for nationalism or separatism.

These factors helped to make a case for representative as well as administrative devolution on a number of grounds: democratization, efficiency, the recognition of the national distinctiveness of Scotland

and Wales within the larger British state. In the eyes of devolution's opponents, however, the arguments were far from conclusive. Harking back to the Irish example, they warned that devolution would encourage nationalism rather than appease it, and so might lead to the break-up of the United Kingdom which most devolutionists claimed to want to prevent. They emphasized the practical difficulties of any devolutionary scheme, particularly the problem of defining the respective powers of any devolved assemblies and the sovereign Westminster parliament, together with the greater anomaly that could be created if Scotland and Wales had their own parliaments but England did not. They could also point to the absence of any incontrovertible evidence of a popular majority in favour of change – in sharp contrast to the repeated Irish electoral verdicts in favour of Home Rule that had driven Gladstone into the constitutional quagmires of devolution in the 1880s. This appreciation of the obstacles to reform merely served to confirm the overwhelming view that reform was unnecessary. As has been seen, at least from the 1920s to the 1960s, British political opinion was predominantly unionist, and the unionism of the Conservative and Labour Parties was expressed in terms of their belief in a unitary British state and a strong central government. Under nationalist electoral pressure and for tactical political reasons, the Wilson government appointed a Royal Commission on the Constitution and the Conservatives flirted with the idea of an elected Scottish assembly. But neither move signalled a deep-seated conversion to devolution or a lessening of their centralist unionist resolve.

Anti-devolutionist politicians were reassured by the failure of the nationalist parties to achieve a more substantial success in the general election of 1970 and by the apparent durability of the unionist two-party system. The incoming Conservative government abandoned any putative plans it might have had for constitutional reform, embarking instead on a reorganization of local government in England, Wales and Scotland which was plainly seen as an alternative to regional devolution rather than a preliminary or complement to it.[29] But events forced devolution back on to the agenda. The publication of the report of the Royal Commission on the Constitution in 1973 (completed by Lord Kilbrandon following the death of Lord Crowther in 1972) was not a decisive influence. It appeared at a time of mounting crisis at home and abroad, and its findings were not sufficiently unanimous to command widespread attention compared with more urgent matters.[30] Neither of the major parties included devolution proposals in their manifestos for the February 1974 general election. The improved performance of the nationalists in 1973–74 nevertheless refocused attention on the constitutional future of Scotland and Wales as a political issue. The SNP won Glasgow Govan from Labour in a by-election in November 1973. In the following February, Plaid Cymru won two seats (Caernarfonshire and Merioneth) at the general election, while the SNP won seven (gaining four from the Conservatives and two from Labour compared with 1970). At the second election in October 1974 the nationalist advance continued. Gwynfor Evans regained Carmarthen for Plaid Cymru to take his party's total of seats to three and their share of the Welsh vote to 10.8 per cent. The SNP gained another four seats from the Conservatives to increase their tally to 11, their share of the Scottish vote rising from 21.9 per cent in February to 30.4 per cent in October.

The nationalist successes of 1974 occurred in the context of a bigger political and constitutional crisis. It has already been seen that the spring of that year witnessed an explosion of protest in Northern Ireland that brought about the collapse of the power-sharing Executive and the failure of the Sunningdale agreement. In Britain, equally far-reaching political upheavals were taking place. The election of February 1974 was called because the Heath government found itself in open confrontation with the miners and other trade unions over its industrial relations policy. An election was intended to settle the question of 'Who Governs Britain?' and to provide a firm mandate against union militancy, but it did not produce the answer the Conservatives wanted. Rather it revealed a new, less class-oriented political picture in which the Conservative–Labour two-party system was partly submerged by a strong Liberal revival (which garnered six million votes though only 14 seats) and the nationalist victories in Scotland and Wales. The re-emergence of a more variegated regional/national pattern of politics posed problems for the main parties, especially for Harold Wilson's Labour government which, with 301 seats to the Conservatives' 297, was struggling to establish itself in power despite not having an overall parliamentary majority. Wilson was keen to call a second election to consolidate his position (as he had in 1966 after a narrow victory in 1964) but, like Gladstone in the 1890s, realized that he needed to appease the forces of nationalism if he was to succeed. The position in Scotland was particularly worrying, since although most of the nationalist gains had come in Conservative constituencies, the SNP was also emerging as the main challenger in Labour-held seats. With these considerations in mind, devolution rapidly became a Labour priority and a white paper proposing elected assemblies for Scotland and Wales was published in September 1974 before the country was summoned once again to the polls.

Labour's conversion to devolution was thus more the product of expediency than conviction, and as such perhaps reaped the reward it deserved. The October election result emphasized the importance of finding the right response to the nationalist challenge but at the same time made legislative success unlikely. Labour's fortunes, like those of the Liberals in 1892, were tied to the minority parties (Scottish and Welsh Nationalists, Liberals and Northern Irish MPs) who had their largest representation in the Commons since the 1920s; its own slim majority dwindled steadily and was fissured on the devolution issue by backbench opposition, particularly from some Scottish and south Wales Labour MPs. The government compounded its difficulties by tactical errors. The Scotland and Wales Bill introduced in 1976 to provide for devolved assemblies in Edinburgh and Cardiff was a cumbersome and poorly drafted measure which, although it passed its second reading by 294 votes to 249, quickly became bogged down by parliamentary obstruction and had to be withdrawn.[31] A second attempt to legislate with separate Bills for each of the two countries (introduced under the protective umbrella of a Liberal–Labour pact after the government had lost its Commons majority) was more successful, at least insofar as the Scotland and Wales Acts reached the statute book in 1978. But to achieve this partial victory the government had to concede the principle of a referendum before the measures could be implemented, and they suffered a further defeat when, on the amendment of an expatriate Scottish MP, George Cunningham, a clause was inserted to the effect that in addition to attaining a simple majority, at least 40 per cent of those qualified to vote would have to vote in favour for the devolutionary settlement to go ahead.

The referendums held in Scotland and Wales on 1 March 1979 were a disappointment for the government. Devolution in Wales was overwhelmingly rejected by 956,330 votes to 243,048. The Scottish vote was a narrow 'Yes' (1,253,502 votes to 1,230,937), but the margin of victory was not sufficient to allow the reform to proceed, since only a third of the electorate had voted in favour. The significance of these results has been much debated.[32] In one sense they had nothing to do with devolution at all, being a verdict on a Labour government unpopular for other reasons, notably its economic policies and the industrial unrest of the 'winter of discontent' of 1978–79. On the other hand, they did appear to demonstrate the strength of unionist, anti-devolutionist feeling, particularly in Wales, but also in parts of Scotland such as the Borders, Dumfries and Galloway and Orkney and Shetland which voted 'No' to register their mistrust of an Edinburgh parliament likely to be dominated by Labour's urban elite. Then again, even those who supported the principle of constitutional change were divided or lukewarm in their attitudes towards the specific measures on offer. The proposed Welsh assembly was dismissed as a mere 'talking shop' which would have little real power and would simply be an expensive third tier of local government on top of the already much-criticized restructuring of county and district councils in 1974. In Scotland, where the parliament would have had wider powers, it still fell short of the independent legislature that the nationalists wanted, while the Liberals (freed from the constraints of the Lib–Lab pact) were critical of the retention of a first-past-the-post electoral system instead of some form of proportional representation. With so many divisions among its supporters, it was easy for Conservative opponents and Labour dissidents to expose the weaknesses and contradictions of the government's plan, relying on electoral apathy and a mood of 'safety first' among the voters to do the rest.

The devolution debacle led to the defeat of the Labour government on a motion of no confidence in the Commons and to a general election in May 1979 in which Conservative unionists were victorious over devolutionists and nationalists. The SNP fared particularly badly, losing nine of its 11 seats and seeing its share of the poll fall from 30 to 17.3 per cent, pushing it back into third place (behind Labour and the Conservatives) in terms of votes and fourth place (behind the Liberals) in terms of seats. Plaid Cymru lost Carmarthen, and its share of the Welsh vote also fell, from 10.8 to 8.1 per cent. In Britain as a whole, meanwhile, 1979 marked the beginning of a remarkable period of Conservative hegemony, with Mrs Thatcher's government being re-elected by landslide majorities in 1983 and 1987 and her successor John Major scoring a narrower yet decisive win in 1992 to give the party 18 years of uninterrupted power. During that time there was a return to the centralist policies of the earlier post-war years. The Scotland and Wales Acts were repealed and faith was placed once again in direct rule by secretaries of state who were junior ministers in the London cabinet. Some, like Peter Walker in Wales, were given limited freedom to experiment with their own policies, but generally their administrations had to follow the course laid down by the prime minister and adhere to the Thatcherite consensus. Although in the exceptional case of Northern Ireland the re-establishment of devolved government was considered, elsewhere the tendency of Thatcherism was to weaken local government rather than strengthen it, as was illustrated by the abolition of the Greater London Council and the imposition of closer control of local authority finance. Indeed, notwithstanding the programme of privatization of nationalized industries and public utilities, a case could be made for arguing that the Thatcher governments of 1979–90 were responsible for a greater centralization of power within the British state than any that had held office since the Second World War.

It would be wrong, however, to exaggerate the scale of the Conservative success, or the extent to which it represented the uncontested triumph of an assimilationist unionist trend. On the contrary, in the 1980s and 1990s the pattern of politics in Scotland and Wales continued to diverge from that in England, and this development was if anything accentuated by the impact of Conservative policies. One obvious difference was that Scotland and Wales sustained genuinely four-party systems of politics, compared with the three-party system in England. The SNP and Plaid Cymru faced some retrenchment after their high-water mark of 1974, but they remained serious players in the game and nationalism offered a distinctive alternative to the varieties of unionism articulated by the other parties. Moreover, nationalism prospered in a political environment that was more consistently anti-Conservative than the rest of Britain. The Conservative majorities of the 1980s were built on the party's strength in England and on the vagaries of a non-proportional electoral system which allowed the Conservative Party after 1983 to achieve a Commons majority of 144 on only 42.4 per cent of the popular vote. But the imbalance was even more pronounced in Scotland and Wales where at no point in the years of Conservative government between 1979 and 1997 did the Conservatives have a majority of seats or electoral support. In their best year, 1979, they won 31.4 per cent of the votes in Scotland and 22 of the 71 Scottish seats; in Wales they took 32.7 per cent of the votes and 11 out of 38 seats. By 1992 their representation had fallen to six seats and 28.6 per cent of the votes in Wales, 11 seats and 25.7 per cent of the vote in Scotland (a performance outranked in awfulness only by that of 1997, when they failed to win a single seat in either country). Labour, by contrast, remained the dominant party in both Scotland and Wales throughout the period, faring significantly better there in its electoral nadir of 1983 than in all but its most loyal English heartlands.[33]

The significance of this divergence in relation to the devolution debate was emphasized by the inability of the non-Conservative majority in Scotland and Wales to prevent the election of a Conservative UK government, and consequently their inability to resist the unpopular policies of the Thatcher regime. The idea that their countries' lack of political autonomy had exposed them to English exploitation was an established part of the nationalist critique. In the 1970s the SNP had based its campaign for independence around the economic benefits which it argued Scotland had been denied because control of the revenues generated by North Sea oil ('Scotland's oil') was vested in a government south of the border. In the 1980s the economic agenda was more defensive, as heavy industries like coal, steel and shipbuilding continued their long decline, but this if anything only made the sense of grievance more acute and strengthened the appeal of some form of self-government as an antidote to Conservative indifference. The miners' strike against pit closures in 1984–85, though it highlighted the solidarity between Scottish, Welsh and English miners, added fuel to the sense of Scottish and Welsh alienation from the government in London. Policies of privatization were more unpopular in Scotland and Wales, which were more dependent on the nationalized public sector, than they were in England. The decision of the Thatcher government to introduce the controversial Community Charge, or 'Poll Tax', as a replacement for local rates in Scotland before the rest of Britain, convinced Scots that they were being used as a laboratory for Thatcherite experimentation, possibly as a punishment for not having voted Conservative in larger numbers. The antipathy of the Scots to what Mrs Thatcher represented was felt by the prime minister herself when she received a frosty reception for her party-political harangue to the General Assembly of the Church of Scotland in May 1988 and was then greeted by a booing crowd symbolically brandishing red cards when she attended the Scottish FA Cup Final between Celtic and Dundee United at Hampden Park.

What emerged from these grievances was not necessarily nationalism in the narrow party sense (though Plaid Cymru won four seats at the 1992 general election and the SNP, while returning only three MPs, won 21 per cent of the Scottish vote). Nor was there automatically an increase in support for separatism (though one opinion poll in 1992 suggested that 50 per cent of Scots wanted independence). Nevertheless, as politics in Scotland and Wales took a different course from that in England, voters in those countries were beginning to view issues in their own national, rather than British, terms, and more consciously national political cultures were beginning to evolve. The process was encouraged by the work of academics, intellectuals and the media from the 1960s on in stimulating debates about Scottish and Welsh history and national identity and by changes in the external context – notably the rise of regionalism in the European Union and the collapse of the Soviet empire in Eastern Europe – which held out the possibility of smaller nations having a viable role in a new international political framework. At the very least the result was a growing consensus behind national Scottish and Welsh political objectives and support for greater institutional recognition of the different nations within the British state. In Wales this was still more likely to be expressed in cultural rather than constitutional terms – as in the successful campaign to establish a Welsh-language television channel, S4C, in 1982 – but even in the Welsh Labour establishment the long dark night of Thatcherism brought a more sympathetic attitude towards devolution. The Scots were more committed still to the restoration of a Scottish parliament. A Campaign for a Scottish Assembly had been launched following the referendum of 1979, pointing out that Scots had voted for devolution only to be denied by a Tory majority at Westminster. In 1987 a Scottish Constitutional Convention was established with the backing of the Labour and Liberal Parties, churches, trade unions and other public bodies from across Scotland to produce a blueprint for reform which (in the words of the CSA's *Claim of Right for Scotland*, published in July 1988) would resolve the 'crisis of identity and survival' facing Scotland by restoring the link of consent between governors and governed removed by the election results of 1979, 1983 and 1987.[34]

The varied political responses to these developments reflected differing views about the future of the British state and offered a reprise of arguments that had been aired periodically since Irish Home Rule had first become an issue in the 1880s. The Conservatives were staunch for maintaining the Union in its existing form and came closest to a theory of British nationalism with which to underpin the logic of a unitary state. John Major made opposition to devolution one of the main planks of his 1992 election campaign. At the other extreme, the nationalists in Scotland and Wales sought independent statehood for their countries, although the SNP went further than Plaid Cymru in linking this unequivocally with separatism. The Liberal and Labour Parties joined the Conservatives in wanting to preserve a British state, but sought to do so by a Gladstonian recognition of the diversity of its constituent parts rather than by a rigid resistance to change. The Liberals favoured a thoroughgoing federalist solution similar to that sketched out before 1914, with separate parliaments not only for Scotland and Wales but also for England or the English regions. Labour moved pragmatically in a similar direction, though giving priority to those areas where the pressure for reform was greatest. When John Smith, a pro-devolutionary Scot who had been ministerially responsible for the legislation of the 1970s, succeeded the former anti-devolutionist Neil Kinnock as Labour leader in 1992 he accepted the desire for a Scottish parliament as 'the settled will of the Scottish people' and committed the party to completing the 'unfinished business' of the Wilson and Callaghan governments. Although Smith's premature death in 1994 removed a personal and patriotic supporter of the devolutionary cause, his commitment to reform was in turn endorsed by his successor, Tony Blair, so that in the general election of 1997 the electorates of Britain were given a clear choice of options for their constitutional future.

While it would be fanciful to claim that Labour's subsequent landslide victory (and the Conservatives' worst defeat since 1906) turned entirely on constitutional questions, the 1997 election marked a watershed in the devolutionary debate. For the first time since 1974 a government had come to power with majorities in all three countries of Britain, and in Scotland and Wales pro-devolution and nationalist candidates had swept the board. Armed with this mandate the Labour government immediately set about honouring its promise to hold referendums on its devolution proposals before legislation was introduced. When these took place in September the Scottish result was an overwhelming victory for the 'Yes' campaign – 1,775,045 Scottish voters (74.3 per cent of those who voted, 44.7 per cent of the electorate as a whole) voted in favour of a Scottish parliament, only 614,000 (25.7 per cent) against. On a second question as to whether the parliament should have tax-varying powers there was also a clear majority in favour (1.5 million to 870,000). The contest in Wales was much closer. In a referendum deliberately held a week later than that in Scotland to allow a bandwagon effect to develop, 559,419 votes were cast in favour of a

Welsh assembly, 552,698 against.[35] In both Scotland and Wales, however, a comparison between the 1997 results and those of 1979 shows the extent to which opinion had moved in a pro-devolutionary direction, with the Scottish poll especially demonstrating a high level of enthusiasm for self-government and a growing national confidence in Scotland's ability to manage its own affairs.

It could perhaps be argued, too, that Scottish enthusiasm was greater not just because of a more highly developed sense of Scotland's intrinsic nationhood, but also because the Scottish parliament was to be a more powerful body than the proposed Welsh Assembly. The Scotland Act provided for a parliament of 129 members (elected by a mixture of first-past-the-post and proportional representation) which would sit for a fixed four-year term. It was to have wide legislative and some tax-raising powers, its writ running in all areas except those such as the constitution, foreign affairs, defence, the currency, immigration, broadcasting and social security, which were specifically reserved to Westminster to ensure uniformity throughout the United Kingdom. From the parliament an executive would be chosen, headed by a first minister, which would take over most of the functions of the Scottish government from the secretary of state, whose office would continue only in a reduced form to represent Scottish interests in the British cabinet. Scotland was thus to get a real measure of Home Rule, bringing the Scottish nation into a direct political relationship with a Scottish state for the first time since 1707.

Wales, on the other hand, was to be given a more limited form of devolution. Under the terms of the Government of Wales Act a 60-member 'National Assembly' (not 'parliament') was to be established, elected on the same quasi-proportional system as its Scottish counterpart but having only executive control over areas of responsibility specifically transferred from the secretary of state (the opposite of the reserved powers approach applied to Scotland) and no primary legislative or tax-varying functions. The first secretary (not 'minister') of the Welsh executive would consequently, at least to begin with, be in a less powerful position than the head of the Scottish executive, and more dependent on the secretary of state and the British government for legislative support. This differential treatment was justified on the historical grounds that Wales, unlike Scotland, did not have a separate legal system or a recent tradition of independent statehood, and that since 1536 Westminster had effectively been the Welsh parliament. The arrangement in any case reflected the closer integration of Wales and England within the British state. But these arguments did little to convince those who believed that Scotland and Wales should have been accorded equal status and that Wales was being treated as a 'second-class' nation.

In practice, though, these differences were probably less important than the new era of politics that the creation of a Scottish parliament and the National Assembly of Wales inaugurated. For the first time in three centuries, Scotland had a government and parliament of its own. Wales had a truly national government for the first time ever. More than that, the constitutional changes consolidated the distinctive patterns of Scottish and Welsh politics, partly through the proportional aspect of the electoral arrangements for the new institutions and partly through the operation of the four-party system in its immediate national rather than a UK-wide context. Thus when the first elections to the new bodies were held in May 1999, Labour emerged as the largest party in both cases (winning 56 seats in Scotland and 28 in Wales) but without a majority in either. In Scotland, Labour's leader and first minister designate, Donald Dewar, responded to this situation by forming a coalition with Jim Wallace's 17 Liberal Democrats. In Wales the coalition option was rejected and Labour formed a minority administration, first under Alun Michael and then under Rhodri Morgan, but agreed to work as far as possible on a consensual basis with other parties.[36] Already this was a departure from the more adversarial Westminster model, even if it fell short of the formal power-sharing arrangements required in Northern Ireland. The other major respect in which the election results departed from British precedents was in the performance of the nationalist parties. Both the SNP, with 35 seats in the Scottish parliament, and Plaid Cymru, with 17 seats in the Welsh Assembly, were returned as the second-largest parties and therefore became the main opposition to the ruling executives in their respective countries. Their electoral success (especially dramatic because less expected in the case of Plaid Cymru) was an important step on the way to creating 'national' political systems in relation to the devolved institutions, as well as a significant foretaste of the way in which the politics of devolution might differ from those of the old unitary British state.

Taken together, the devolutionary measures enacted in Scotland, Wales and Northern Ireland in 1997–99, and the creation of the 'Council of the Isles', unquestionably amounted to a major change in the way the British state was governed. As Vernon Bogdanor has written, they offered 'a chance of realizing the underlying theme of

Gladstonian thinking – recognition both of the various and distinctive national identities within these islands, but also of the close and complex links between them'.[37] But it was still too soon to say how well the new arrangements would work or in what direction they would develop. It was likely that the devolved governments would gradually grow in power and authority, but it was unclear whether this would weaken the Union (by reducing the role of central government) or strengthen it (by permitting greater diversity within a unifying framework). In addition to this general centrifugal/centripetal argument, there were other specific factors to be considered. In Northern Ireland, for example, there was the likelihood of pressure from the nationalists to move towards a united Ireland, which Unionists might ultimately be unable, or unwilling, to resist. On the British mainland, the possibility existed of conflict between the devolved governments and the central power, particularly if they were drawn from different parties and if nationalist oppositions attained power in Scotland or Wales committed to renegotiating the constitutional settlement. The chances of confrontation would be further increased if a reduction in the number of Scottish and Welsh MPs at Westminster (promised as a corollary of the devolution process) made the return of a Labour government more difficult and strengthened the hold of the Conservative Party and English MPs on the central institutions of the state. Even without this situation arising, the 'English Question' remained unresolved. Did England need a parliament or a constitutional identity of its own? Should the quasi-federal 'union of nations' be extended to a more genuinely federal 'union of regions', and would this be acceptable to the Scottish and the Welsh? The liveliness of the debates surrounding these and other issues in the wake of their reforms suggested that the Blair government had concluded one chapter of the century-long devolutionary saga only to open up a more uncertain future for the British state and its peoples.

CHAPTER 8

BRITAIN, EUROPE, THE WORLD

The constitutional reforms described in the previous chapter effected a substantial adjustment of the internal relations between the central institutions of the supra-national British state and the nations and regions of the Celtic periphery. While this new accommodation was being reached with the forces of domestic nationalism, changes had also been taking place in the external context. In the closing years of the twentieth century Britain was coming to the end of its long history as an imperial power; it had joined, and was gradually yet inexorably being more closely integrated into, the community of nations which became the European Union, and was being subjected to the same processes of economic and cultural globalization that were shaping the rest of the world in the age of the information-driven technological revolution. From both within and without, therefore, the traditional role and functions of the British state were being challenged. Its sovereignty was under threat and, for some, its very reason for existence was called into question. In this atmosphere of uncertainty, as Britain crossed into the new millennium and the imperial state gave way to its post-imperial successor, the core features of British identity were being re-examined as never before. To understand the debate in its full complexity, it is necessary to have some appreciation of the significance of the loss of empire, the rise of 'Europe' and Britain's changing relationship with the world community before reaching any conclusions about the nature of Britishness in the contemporary world or the future history of the British state in the twenty-first century.

The end of empire

The British state that had emerged in the eighteenth and nineteenth centuries was an imperial state, and the existence of an expanding empire had been integral to a sense of British national identity in the Georgian and Victorian periods. In the early twentieth century, as has been seen, there was some lessening of the mood of imperial self-confidence in the face of the setbacks experienced in the South African War and the growing threats to Britain's industrial and naval supremacy. Imperial nationalism became more defensive in consequence, as evidenced by Chamberlain's schemes for tariff reform and imperial federation and the general emphasis on the consolidation of the empire rather than its further expansion. Yet despite this change in the imperial mood, perhaps in some ways because of it, the empire continued to provide a patriotic rallying point, both symbol and cement of Britain's national unity. By the end of the century, however, the situation was very different. The empire that once covered a quarter of the world's surface had mostly gone, and Britain's international position as a Great Power had correspondingly declined. What impact did these changes have on the outlook of the British people and their national self-image? Indeed, if Britain had become a nation largely through its possession of an empire and its sense of imperial mission, could the patriotic idea of nationhood that had grown up with the British imperial state survive their loss?

The final retreat from empire did not occur until after 1945 but the roots of imperial decline have to be sought much earlier.[1] All of Europe's imperial powers were severely tested by the First World War. Germany lost its colonies as a consequence of defeat. The multi-national empires of Austria-Hungary, Russia and Turkey collapsed amid military failure and internal revolt, the latter often inspired by the desire for self-determination among subject peoples. Britain experienced its own variant of the general crisis with rebellion in Ireland, though, as a victorious power, it maintained its cohesion better than the other states. The empire supported the war effort and the dominions were represented in the imperial war cabinet. After the war the empire was expanded by the acquisition of former German and Turkish territories mandated to it by the peace settlements and the League of Nations. With the other European powers seriously weakened by war and revolution, and the United States retreating into isolationism after its wartime foray on to the world stage, Britain was seemingly unchallenged as the only global power, and the empire over which it presided reached its furthest extent.

Nevertheless, the imperial state was not without its problems. The war had left Britain heavily indebted, its economic strength weakened by the disruption of world trade, the effects of post-war depression and the decline of export-oriented heavy industries. Economic retrenchment forced a reappraisal of military and naval commitments which had a bearing on Britain's ability to discharge its responsibilities as an imperial power. The size of the army was quickly scaled back to its peacetime level, despite the burden of extra colonies. More illuminating was Britain's agreement to the Washington Naval Treaty of 1921, accepting that the United States should have parity with the Royal Navy in capital ships, in a ratio of 5:5:3 with Japan. The abandonment of the traditional 'two-power standard' (by which Britain had maintained a navy at least as large as its two closest rivals combined), while it could be justified by post-war conditions (Germany had scuttled its navy at Scapa Flow, and both the USA and Japan had been Britain's wartime allies), reflected both a change in the distribution of naval power and a partial resignation by Britain from its commanding world role.

In the meantime unrest was growing in the empire itself. The situation in Ireland has already been described, but there were plenty of other trouble spots. In India the Congress movement, with Gandhi as one of its leaders, launched a post-war campaign for self-government. Indian opinion was inflamed by the British army's massacre of demonstrators at Amritsar in 1919 and scarcely mollified by the Montagu–Chelmsford reforms that gave Indian representatives a limited role in provincial governments. A nationalist revolt in Egypt forced Britain into granting the country independence (albeit under continuing British tutelage) in 1922, while the RAF was used to quell disturbances among rebellious tribesmen in Iraq. Nor were relations between Britain and her dominions, though less violent, necessarily free from friction. Anti-British feeling was a factor in the Irish Free State and among sections of the Afrikaner political community in South Africa. Elsewhere the independent-mindedness of the dominions was demonstrated by their insistence on separate representation at the post-war peace conference and at the League of Nations. In Australia, and to a lesser extent New Zealand, a 'Gallipoli factor' was also in operation, expressed in a reluctance to be drawn automatically into Britain's future quarrels (for example during the confrontation with the Turks over Chanak in 1922[2]). Another factor distancing the

Australasian dominions from British policy was the Washington Naval Treaty, which not only reduced Britain's capacity to defend the Pacific empire but also – by simultaneously ending the Anglo-Japanese alliance – increased the potential threat to dominion security.

The growth of dominion nationalism, as well as the growing strength and self-confidence of the dominions in economic and political terms, led to a redrawing of the imperial constitution and to a formal transition from 'Empire' to 'Empire and Commonwealth'. At the 1926 Imperial Conference a new definition of dominion status, drafted by A.J. Balfour, was agreed on. It stressed that the dominions were 'autonomous communities within the British Empire, equal in status, in no way subordinate one to another in any aspect of their domestic or external affairs, though united by a common allegiance to the crown, and freely associated as members of the British Commonwealth of Nations'.[3] The agreement was given constitutional form by the Statute of Westminster in 1931, which recognized the equality of the dominion parliaments and removed the right of Westminster to legislate for the dominions or override their laws. Britain thus became a partner of the dominions rather than their political or constitutional superior, the notion of its place as 'mother country' receding to a cultural or historical plane. The formal recognition of dominion independence did not preclude continuing cooperation, as shown by the Ottawa economic agreements of 1932 and joint planning for imperial defence. But it did mean that the Chamberlainite dreams of imperial federation, and the idea of the empire as an extension of the British state, were dead. The dominions had become Britain's allies rather than colonies, and were developing their own national identities and regional concerns. Britain's own relationship to her empire and her role in the world had also shifted, though in ways that had not yet been fully assimilated into the national consciousness.

Perhaps neither the pace of this change nor the immediacy of its impact on national psychology should be exaggerated. For its people, as indeed in reality, Britain remained an imperial power throughout the inter-war period. The British Empire Exhibition at Wembley in 1924–25 was attended by 27 million visitors. The links between Britain and the empire continued to be strengthened by emigration and were reinforced by improvements in communications through radio services and the development of imperial air routes as well as by the increased importance of the empire in British overseas trade during the depression. The dominions had become independent but they remained part of the 'imperial family', while Britain retained direct control of considerable parts of Africa, Asia, the Middle and Far East, the Caribbean and many smaller territories. The continuing significance of the empire was reflected, too, in the prominence attached to imperial questions such as tariffs or the future of India in domestic political debate. The latter, admittedly, also reflected some of the growing imperial uncertainty, since the possibility was being canvassed that at some point India might attain independence as a self-governing dominion. But the 1935 Government of India Act, which provided for elected administrations only at the provincial level, showed that independence was still a distant prospect as far as the official mind was concerned. A similar recognition of emerging dangers combined with a determination to maintain the imperial status quo for as long as possible was demonstrated by the thrust of British foreign policy. Awareness of Britain's inability simultaneously to fight a war in Europe and protect its empire was one of the main influences behind Neville Chamberlain's attempts to appease Italy and Germany in the 1930s, his hope being that a European settlement would enable Britain to deploy its limited military resources to deter the challenge of an increasingly aggressive Japan in the Far East.[4] The safety of the home islands was of course paramount, but British politicians were still thinking on a global scale and were seeking to minimize any reductions in Britain's world position by any means they could.

It was the failure of Chamberlain's appeasement strategy that precipitated a crisis of the imperial state in the early 1940s. Superficially it might be thought that Britain gained some benefits from the Second World War by being on the winning side. As has been seen, the wartime experience did encourage patriotism and national unity. Britain's defiance of Hitler in 1940 and her part in his eventual defeat were real achievements that buoyed up national esteem and contributed hugely to the post-1945 national myth, especially in the heroic version of events presented in Churchill's six-volume history, *The Second World War*, which became a popular bestseller. It is now recognized, however, that the war was also crucial in sapping Britain's residual strength as an imperial power – or at least in laying bare the material weakness behind the imperial facade.[5] Wartime defeats in North Africa and the Far East destroyed the image of invincibility on which much of Britain's imperial authority had rested. The British experience at the hands of the Japanese – the sinking of the *Prince of*

Wales and the *Repulse*, the loss of Burma, Malaya and Hong Kong, and the surrender of 130,000 British troops in the supposedly impregnable fortress of Singapore – was especially traumatic. Britain's moral and military superiority in the eyes of the Asiatic peoples was completely undermined, and not even the eventual defeat of Japan (achieved in any case largely by American forces and the use of the atomic bomb) could restore Britain's lost prestige. Imperial rule was temporarily re-imposed on the recaptured territories, but the Japanese victories and the new perception of British weakness greatly strengthened colonial nationalism in India and other parts of Britain's Asian empire and made the permanent restoration of authority virtually impossible.

The 'retreat from empire' began almost as soon as the war was over. Already in India, Gandhi, Nehru and the Congress Party had used the wartime emergency to mount a 'Quit India' campaign and had extracted from the British a promise of self-government at the war's end. Post-war protests by Congress and Jinnah's Muslim League hastened the granting of independence in 1947 and the partition of the Raj into a Hindu-dominated India and a Muslim state of Pakistan. The concession of independence to Ceylon and Burma in 1948 completed the dismantling of the Asian empire that Britain had built up over two centuries. As far as Britain was concerned, this first phase of decolonization was partly a practical recognition of the impossibility of sustaining the Indian empire against the wishes of the colonial people given the limited option of force that was available. It also reflected changing attitudes towards the concept of empire itself. British imperialism in India had rested on a fiction of consent that could no longer be maintained, but there was also a growing anti-colonial mood, especially on the political left. Among Labour MPs elected in the landslide of 1945 there was a strong undercurrent of support for colonial nationalist movements, which breached the hitherto-prevailing pro-imperialist consensus. American influence was a further factor. Although the Atlantic Charter agreed by Churchill and Roosevelt in 1941 had carefully excluded the British Empire from its general espousal of the right to self-determination, the broad thrust of American policy was anti-imperialist, and this was a view they were keen to promote at the expense of their British allies.

Yet, once again, the pace of change should not be overestimated. In retrospect the Second World War can be seen as a watershed in Britain's history as an imperial nation, and the relinquishing of power over the Asian sub-continent wrenched the jewel from the imperial crown. At the same time, India was a special case. Since the 1930s Britain had committed itself to the eventual granting of self-government; the post-war troubles had speeded up the timetable. But this was not seen as meaning that the rest of the colonial empire would automatically or immediately follow suit. Indeed, in the 1950s British governments showed a renewed determination to preserve the empire; for example, when they used military force against nationalist insurgents in Malaya and the Mau Mau revolt in Kenya. More generally, Britain still acted as a great power on the international stage. The Attlee government that gave independence to India (and evacuated Palestine to allow for the establishment of the independent state of Israel) still conceived of Britain as one of the 'Big Three' in global terms, with the United States and the Soviet Union. Ernest Bevin as foreign secretary played a key role in the formation of the United Nations, and Britain became one of the permanent members of the UN Security Council. The onset of the 'Cold War' in the late 1940s revitalized the wartime 'special relationship' with the United States and led to Britain becoming the main European pillar of NATO as well as a participant, as part of the UN force, in the Korean War. That Britain was still committed to a global role was emphasized by the Attlee government's decision to build a British atomic bomb and by its sharp increases in conventional military spending, together with the retention (until 1960) of conscription to permit a larger than usual peacetime establishment for the armed services.

The determination to retain a world role after 1945 has sometimes been described as a 'delusion of grandeur' on Britain's part.[6] This is to overstate the case: Britain's world role remained real enough, and the British state retained global responsibilities. But the country's capacity to sustain that role was diminishing and the effective field for action was becoming more circumscribed. The Suez crisis of 1956 is often identified as the point at which these new realities were forced home.[7] The failure of the Anglo-French attempts to seize the Canal Zone following President Nasser's unilateral nationalization of the Suez Canal, and the subsequent humiliating withdrawal of their forces under the eyes of a hostile and unsympathetic world, certainly demonstrated the limits of British power. In another way, however, this only confirmed what had been acknowledged since the beginning of the century, and arguably even in the heyday of 'gunboat diplomacy' in the Victorian era, namely that it was easier to act with international support than without it, and that the preparation of public opinion at home and abroad was an important ingredient of a successful military adventure. What Suez did emphasize – coming as it did simultaneously with the Soviet suppression of the Hungarian uprising and an American presidential election – was the extent to which the traditional concerns of European imperialism had become subsumed, or even overtaken, by the broader ideological and geopolitical struggle between the superpowers, and that Britain was no longer an equal player in that league. In 1956 the Eden government had decided to act in Egypt without ensuring the backing of their American allies, and they came badly unstuck as a consequence – a pattern increasingly likely to be repeated as the altered balance of world power asserted itself in the changed circumstances of the postwar world.

The controversy aroused by Suez also reflected the 'wind of change' (in Harold Macmillan's phrase) which, by the late 1950s, was blowing more strongly against western colonialism in Africa and beyond. Independence for the Indian sub-continent had been followed by the successful Communist revolution in China in 1949 and anti-colonial risings in French Indo-China which subsequently became the Vietnam War. Adjusting its policies to the prevailing climatic conditions, Britain abandoned outright resistance to nationalist movements in what was left of its empire and instead embarked on a programme of decolonization that enabled it to transfer, mostly peacefully, its former colonies to independent rule. Between 1957 and 1970 most of the remaining British colonies in Africa, the West Indies and the Mediterranean became independent states (as did Malaya and Pacific islands like Western Samoa, Fiji and Tonga), leaving only a few special or problem cases (such as Rhodesia, which declared illegal independence under a minority white government in 1965 and did not become fully independent as Zimbabwe until 1980, and Hong Kong, which finally reverted to Chinese rule in 1997) and a handful of scattered possessions or dependent territories as the physical remnants of a once-global empire. The relinquishment of empire was accompanied by a scaling down of Britain's military and naval forces. Conscription ('National Service') was ended in 1960, in 1968 the decision was taken to withdraw British forces from 'east of Suez', and the numbers of those in the armed services steadily declined: the army from 900,000 troops in 1950 to 163,681 in 1979, the navy from 140,000 to 72,000 in the same period, with a comparable reduction in the size of Britain's naval fleet.[8] Britain continued to act militarily on behalf of the United Nations and NATO, and

retained its own 'independent' (though American-supplied) subma-
rine-based nuclear deterrent. But the 'end of empire' and a
considerably reduced military capacity were tangible evidence of
what, to many, was palpably a process of national decline.

What effect did these changes have on the British state, its people
and their sense of national identity? At the risk of seeming paradoxical, it can be argued that the results of the retreat from empire were at
once limited and profound. Obviously the transition from being an
imperial to a 'post-imperial' power had major consequences, not least
for the imperial state and its ruling elite. At the centre, as the imperial
state contracted so did the governmental machinery that had supported it. The India, Colonial and Dominion Offices either
disappeared altogether or were absorbed into the 'Foreign and
Commonwealth Office'. The separate ministries of War and the
Admiralty were subsumed in a single 'Ministry of Defence'. There
was an even more dramatic dismantling of the apparatus of colonial
rule in the former colonies themselves, drastically shrinking the ranks
of colonial administrators, policemen and civil servants, and depriving
a class of people who for generations had been 'bred to empire' of an
outlet for their energies. As the era of planters and proconsuls passed
into history, the empire, which had been famously denounced in the
early nineteenth century as a 'system of outdoor relief for the
aristocracy' no longer fulfilled that role, nor did it offer opportunities
for the aspiring middle class either. The passing of what might be
termed the 'imperial upper class' was in turn bound up with the
increasingly egalitarian tendency of post-war British society as a
whole, as the decline of deference and respect for established
authority interacted with a loss of confidence on the part of a
traditional governing elite who suddenly had much less to govern.

The dwindling of the imperial state affected the nation's collective
self-image in other ways too. The fact that decolonization was
achieved largely by cross-party consensus did not mean that it was
either popular or uncontroversial. In some respects the empire
became a more divisive issue in relation to British identity in the
course of its decline that it had ever been in its pomp. There had, of
course, been earlier conflicts over imperial policy, mainly between the
free-trading, decentralist views of the Liberals and the preference of
Conservative tariff reformers for a more centralized federal empire.
The wisdom and morality of specific actions had been debated, for
instance at the time of the South African War or in the decision to
abolish slavery and the slave trade. But for most of its existence, the

moral validity of the empire as an institution had never been widely challenged, because the empire was simply taken for granted as part of the British way of life. Even in the 1950s, as decolonization gathered pace, most politicians were converted to the abandonment of empire by pressure of necessity rather than political conviction. However, the process of disengagement stimulated a more explicit debate between the political extremes about the nature of the British Empire and the implications of its loss. On the right, in the Conservative Party and elsewhere, there were those who regarded the empire as the nation's greatest achievement, the loss of which could be fatal to the future of the British state and Britain's standing as a world power. Conversely, on the left, the end of empire was viewed by some not just as necessary but as long overdue. For them, imperialism was morally repugnant, and a belated retreat from colonialism was the only way to begin to expunge the British nation's guilt for its past misdemeanours.

Ambivalence about the nature of the imperial legacy and uncertainty over the future fed the more general sense of national decline that had become embedded in political and academic discourse by the early 1960s. For all the tinsel and glitter of the 'swinging sixties' – the temporary uplift provided (for some) by England's victory in the 1966 football World Cup and the early promise of Harold Wilson's 'second industrial revolution' – the prevailing mood of the decade was one of mounting frustration as the optimism that had greeted the dawn of what had been billed as a 'new Elizabethan era' in the 1950s gave way to a more realistic appreciation of Britain's reduced circumstances compared with the Victorian period or even the inter-war years. An awareness of Britain's declining position as a world power was underlined by a relative deterioration of the United Kingdom's place in the global economy, the devaluation of the pound, and by domestic economic problems – poor industrial relations, low productivity and inadequate technological innovation – which became identified as components of a 'British disease'. The failure of the 1964–70 Labour governments and their Conservative successor in 1970–74 to reverse the trend of economic decline or to prevent rising inflation, unemployment and industrial discontent reinforced the pessimistic mood and fostered a more introspective focus on the country's problems, just as the rise of domestic nationalisms and the upsurge of unrest in Northern Ireland was seen in some quarters as presaging the 'break-up of Britain' altogether.

In the wake of the withdrawal from empire, therefore, a picture could well be built up of a nation and people beset by a new sense of self-doubt and consequently turning inward on themselves and abandoning the outward-looking global perspective that had been a distinguishing characteristic of 'Britishness' since its origins in the more expansive age of the eighteenth century. On the other hand, this may be to go too far. Apart from the fact, as has been noted, that Britain continued to be a prominent, if only middle-ranking, power on the international stage, it was also true that the loss of empire only impinged itself relatively slowly on the psychological make-up of the British people. This was partly because, even after most of the colonies had been given their independence, the illusion of empire was sustained by those (like Hong Kong or Gibraltar) that remained, and by the organization of the Commonwealth which, with its important cultural and political links, seemed to offer the perpetuation of empire by other means. Only, as in the 1980s, when Britain became isolated in the Commonwealth over issues such as sanctions against the apartheid regime in South Africa was the illusion exposed, and even then the residual ties with Commonwealth countries and former dominions – notably in the sporting arena in cricket and the Commonwealth Games – preserved aspects of the imperial community of a former age. And when reality became too much, fantasy could always take over. Ian Fleming, in his James Bond novels, lamented imperial decline yet created a character who managed to transcend it.[9] Bond's individual qualities, both in the books and on screen, enabled Britain still to punch above its weight against the big battalions of the superpowers (another version of Harold Macmillan's concept of a special relationship in which Britain acted Greece to the USA's Rome). Meanwhile, in the realms of fact rather than fiction, although the reality of Britain's diplomatic and military activities during the Cold War may have been more low key, they still kept open a window on the wider world and prevented the development of a totally introverted domestic national outlook.

In any event, while the main business of decolonization was complete by the early 1970s the problems and legacies of empire remained, and individual issues like Rhodesia and Hong Kong were a concern for the British state as late as the 1990s. On occasion, politicians were able to draw on the full emotions of an almost jingoistic patriotism to support quasi-imperial adventures. The best example of this is the Falklands War of 1982, when the Conservative government of Margaret Thatcher despatched a naval and military task force to recapture the Falkland Islands in the South Atlantic which had been occupied by Argentina in pursuit of its own long-standing territorial claim.[10] The resulting military victory owed something to the diplomatic support of the Reagan administration in Washington, but it was widely seen at the time as an assertion of British power and a successful attempt to counteract the downward spiral of national decline. It brought back into mainstream politics, albeit briefly, some of the traditional pro-imperial sentiments that were associated with the right wing of the Conservative Party and smaller groups from the 1950s such as the British Empire League. Such sentiments, it is true, were, in their extreme form, those of a minority. They were balanced on the left by a condemnation of Britain's imperial past and by peace movements opposed to Britain's position in NATO and its status as a nuclear power. But the Falklands experience showed that the patriotic imperatives that had underpinned the growth of an imperial state were far from dead, that the British lion could still roar and that perhaps, at heart, the British considered themselves an imperial people still.

Nostalgia for the days of empire was sustained in other ways, notably in fictional form in novels, films and television serials. Paul Scott's quartet of novels, *The Jewel in the Crown*, about life in India under the Raj, was not only widely read in its original published form but became a hugely popular television dramatization. From the 1960s a series of cinematic epics – including *Zulu* (centred on the Battle of Rorke's Drift during the Zulu War of 1879), *Lawrence of Arabia*, and *Khartoum* (featuring Charlton Heston as General Gordon) – kept the image of empire alive in ways which compensated for its corporeal decline. So too, though in a different way, the survival of the monarchy, and the role of the Queen as head of the Commonwealth and head of state of a number of Commonwealth countries, still suggested to many people the idea of an imperialism transmuted into a late twentieth-century form. That this was constitutionally inaccurate, and that it was strongly contested, for example by the vocal republican movement in Australia, made little impact on popular perception. Through the popularity of the Queen herself, the Queen Mother and – in life and death – of Diana, Princess of Wales, the monarchy in late twentieth-century Britain not only acted as a unifying influence on the domestic nation but also, through its international dimension and the panoply of apparently timeless (though often recently invented) pageantry that surrounded it, kept alive a subconscious vestige of the imperial monarchy of an earlier era.[11]

If this comes close to saying that Britain had lost its empire without fully ceasing to be an imperial power, this may not be too far from the truth. In the half-century from the end of the Second World War, certainly from the mid-1950s, the imperial state had undergone a substantial dismantling, but imperial attitudes – a sense of innate superiority, varieties of racism – remained part of the national psyche, as did the imperial patriotism reactivated during the Falklands War and a nostalgia for empire demonstrated by the popularity of books and films on imperial themes. Thus the memory of empire continued to act as a unifying influence even after the empire itself had ceased to exist. The tearful emotionalism of the final ceremonial withdrawal from Hong Kong in 1997 testified to the longevity of imperial feeling, in which even the manner of decolonization – peaceful and with due formality, rather than a messy military rearguard such as those fought by the French and Portuguese – became a new source of national pride. The British Empire passed away, but its influence on 'British-ness' remained significant, at least for those of the older generation. For younger Britons, especially those who had grown up in the post-colonial era and who had not themselves felt the trumpet's call, the reality may have been rather different. But this did not necessarily mean that they were more insular in their outlook in consequence. The empire, even at its height, had only ever been a part of Britain's global dimension, and that wider aspect of Britishness remained alive in the late twentieth century. As Britain took its first tentative steps towards a European rather than an imperial future and responded creatively to the globalization of culture and the economy, it remained a fully active participant in the international community, and in that respect the post-imperial state was less different from its imperial predecessor than might at first be supposed.

Britain and Europe

'Europe' – meaning Britain's relationship with the European Economic Community/European Union – became the most divisive issue in British politics in the late twentieth century. Membership of the European Union, and questions such as whether to participate in a single European currency, had implications for the British state at all levels: political, legal and constitutional, fiscal and economic, historical and cultural. For Britons who had traditionally defined their own identity in terms of the differences between themselves and their Continental neighbours there was a real dilemma about whether it was possible to be both 'British' and 'European' at the same time. Constitutionally this resolved itself into a debate about how far it was possible to preserve the national sovereignty of a British state within a supra-national European framework. The arguments that raged between the pro- and anti-European camps in British politics were thus not simply about the merits or demerits of specific legal, economic or political issues. They constituted in a very real sense elements of a much broader debate about the nature of Britishness and the future prospects of British national statehood.

British suspicions of Europe were deeply ingrained, almost to the extent of making them a national characteristic. The abiding aim of British foreign policy had been to prevent any one European power from becoming dominant on the Continent and from posing a threat to the British Isles or the British Empire.[12] The wars of the eighteenth, nineteenth and twentieth centuries – against the Spanish, the French and the Germans – had been fought with this end in view, and the European powers had been seen more as rivals than allies. The maintenance of Britain's freedom from entangling European alliances had been the cornerstone of Salisbury's policy of 'splendid isolation' in the late nineteenth century, and the fact that departure from it in the Edwardian period and again in the 1930s had led to British involvement in the First and Second World Wars and the destruction of Britain's standing as a world imperial power seemed retrospectively only to confirm the wisdom of the Salisbury formula. This is not to deny that Britain was part of Europe in the broader cultural, political and diplomatic sense, nor that there were individuals and organizations that fostered a Continental connection – from the philosophers of the Enlightenment to socialist internationalists and others of more recent times. But the fact remained that for many of its inhabitants Britain was an island in more than the geographical sense, separated from the Continent by long-standing differences of language, religion and historical experience as well as by the billowing waves which in the national myth Britannia ruled and which had not been crossed successfully by foreign invaders since the Normans in 1066.

The mythology of Britain's 'island story' was a factor in the ambivalence of British attitudes towards Europe after 1945. The problems facing Europe after the Second World War were severe. The Continent's shattered economy had to be rebuilt. There was a need to prevent the recurrence of national rivalries which could lead to further war. And, in addition to the search for political stability and Franco-German rapprochement, by the late 1940s the onset of the Cold War had emphasized the importance of cooperation for the defence of Western Europe against a possible threat from the Soviet East. In all of these areas Britain showed its willingness to work with the Continental powers. The British played their part in joint defence arrangements not only through their founding membership of NATO but also through the military commitments of the Brussels Pact of 1948 and the Western European Union of 1955.[13] Economically, Britain participated in the Organization for European Economic Cooperation (OEEC) established in the late 1940s to administer American 'Marshall Aid' as part of a European Recovery Programme. On the political front, Britain encouraged improved relations between the Western zones of occupied Germany (which became the Federal Republic in 1949) and her former enemies, especially the French. British parliamentarians joined the 'Council of Europe' to debate the Continent's political future, and Churchill – only leader of the Opposition in Britain after 1945 but still an influential figure on the European and world stage – even apparently endorsed the idea of a 'United States of Europe' constructed on federal lines.[14]

Here, however, ambivalence soon revealed itself. British politicians, Churchill included, were fully prepared to encourage closer integration among the other European nations, but they did not envisage Britain being more than a sympathetic bystander to the project. In their eyes Britain's situation was fundamentally different from that of other Western European countries. Britain was not a defeated or occupied country with a broken economy; nor was she a small nation reliant on the goodwill of powerful neighbours. Despite her post-war problems Britain remained a genuine world power, with a large empire and the strongest industrial base of any of the European countries. It followed that her concerns were not merely European, but global. As well as being part of a European community, Britain had imperial responsibilities and, through the 'special relationship' with the United States, had a key role as America's principal ally not only in Europe but throughout the Cold War world. Britain's strategy had thus to be conceived on a global scale, as a series of 'interlocking circles' (imperial, American, European) of which, at least in the late 1940s and early 1950s, the European was still seen as the least important.

This assumption that Britain still had a world role outside Europe, as well as a more traditional suspicion of European entanglements, helps to explain Britain's unwillingness to be involved in successive moves towards closer economic integration that were launched in Europe from the late 1940s on.[15] Britain refused to join the European Coal and Steel Community (ECSC) formed by France, West Germany, Italy, Belgium, the Netherlands and Luxembourg in accordance with the 'Schuman Plan' in 1951. In 1955 the British government sent only a diplomatic observer to the Messina Conference that prepared the ground for the Treaty of Rome of 1957 by which the same 'Six' formed themselves in 1958 into the European Economic Community (EEC). By declining to participate in the EEC from the outset, the British consequently denied themselves the chance to shape its institutions and policies (such as the Common Agricultural Policy) from the inside, and the hesitancy, even hostility, of the Attlee and Churchill governments to these developments has been criticized by 'pro-Europeans' ever since.[16] Yet the decisions not to participate were guided at the time by rationality as well as prejudice. Britain's newly nationalized coal and steel industries were the largest in Europe in 1951 and were only likely to be held back by the pooling of resources with an ECSC in which the other members had a vested interest in making up ground at Britain's expense. On the larger question of the EEC, this was viewed mainly as a political mechanism for improving relations between France and Germany (which Britain supported), and few British politicians expected it to bring major economic benefits, or even to succeed at all. In any case, in the early 1950s Europe was still much less important as a trading partner to Britain than were the countries of the Commonwealth, economic relations with which were likely to be harmed by British membership of a purely European tariff bloc.

By the late 1950s these circumstances, and consequently political attitudes, were beginning to change. The process of decolonization was under way, and changing trading patterns were reducing the importance of the Commonwealth and increasing that of Europe in British overseas trade.[17] For political reasons, Britain was under pressure from the United States to play a more active role in European affairs and to join in the work of European integration. Finally there was the carrot that the EEC, far from being the failure that British sceptics had predicted, was developing into a successful organization contributing to the increasing prosperity of its member nations. Germany especially was enjoying the early stages of its post-war 'economic miracle', while by the end of the 1950s Britain was feeling the effects of European competition and beginning to lose the momentum of its own post-war boom. The attempt to create a British-led alternative to the EEC in the form of the European Free Trade Association (EFTA) in 1959 was at best only a partial success and persuaded the Macmillan government that the time was right for a British application for EEC membership, which was duly made in 1961. Yet whereas in 1955 the 'Six' would have welcomed British participation, opinion in the 1960s was no longer unanimously in favour of British admission. President de Gaulle's France in particular was suspicious of Britain as an American 'Trojan horse' in the European Community and may have feared, in nationalistic terms, that Britain would try to usurp French leadership of the EEC. Personal pique may also have added the satisfaction of revenge to the General's veto of British membership in 1963, and to his equally resolute 'Non' when Britain was refused membership for a second time following an application by Harold Wilson's Labour government in 1967.

There was perhaps a certain irony in the fact that Britain had become more European only to be rejected by the Europeans. But the debate over entry into the 'Common Market' had also opened up divisions in British politics, both between parties and within them. Hugh Gaitskell as Labour leader had played the nationalist card when he opposed Macmillan's application for EEC membership on the grounds that it would signal the end of 'a thousand years of history'.[18] Gaitskell's verdict was not necessarily the definitive Labour view. In 1967, as has been seen, Labour sponsored its own application for British membership. Yet the fault lines in the party ran deeper over Europe than over almost any other issue. While the Conservative government of Edward Heath was successfully negotiating British entry into the EEC in 1970–72 (with Britain finally becoming a member in January 1973, along with Ireland and Denmark), Labour revealed its internal fissures. Tactical considerations, as well as an awareness of the strength of 'anti-Europe' feeling in the party, led Wilson to oppose Heath's European legislation on the grounds that the terms negotiated were detrimental to Britain's interests, but this did not stop a number of Labour pro-Europeans – including the party's deputy leader and future president of the European Commission, Roy Jenkins – from defying the party line and voting in the Commons for the principle of British entry. The 1974 elections that brought Labour back to office were fought, as was shown earlier, on a number of questions of governance, of which Europe was clearly one. Labour entered the elections committed to renegotiate the terms of British membership and to put the results of those negotiations to the British people in a referendum – a pledge that was sufficient for the Conservative anti-Marketeer Enoch Powell to resign his Wolverhampton seat and urge the electorate to vote Labour.

Wilson and James Callaghan, Labour foreign secretary and Wilson's successor as prime minister in 1976, duly effected a largely cosmetic redrawing of the terms of British membership of the EEC, and in 1975 the electorate was asked to approve remaining in the Common Market on those terms. The result was an emphatic 'Yes' which appeared to settle the question once and for all. A total of 17,378,000 people (67.2 per cent of those who voted) were in favour of continuing membership, only 8,470,000 (32.8 per cent) against. What was more, all the constituent parts of the United Kingdom recorded a majority for membership (England 68.7 per cent, Wales 65.5 per cent, Scotland 58.4 per cent, Northern Ireland 52.1 per cent), with only Shetland and the Western Isles voting 'No'.[19] On closer inspection, though, the evidence for a genuinely pro-European majority is less clear-cut. The referendum campaign was weighted heavily in favour of the 'Yes' camp, with a majority of the Labour cabinet and the leadership of the Conservative and Liberal Parties backing it, while opponents of membership appeared as an unlikely alliance of mavericks and extremists from left and right. Business and the media were firmly on the 'Yes' side, and it was probably easier in any case to persuade voters to support a status quo (however recently established) than to get them to approve a withdrawal from Europe before they knew whether the promised economic benefits of membership were going to materialize or not. All this suggests that the referendum result should be seen as a conditional verdict rather than a deep-seated conversion. It left open the possibility that if Europe could not deliver economic prosperity, or indeed if the EEC evolved in ways that were seen to threaten Britain's interests, then the argument over continued membership could be rejoined.

This was precisely what happened over the next two and a half decades as Britain's relations with the European Community continued to be an issue both inside Britain and between Britain and her European partners. The Thatcher governments of 1979–90 – and especially the prime minister herself – were much more antagonistic towards Europe than either their Conservative or Labour predecessors. Mrs Thatcher's premiership began with a fierce row over what she considered excessive British contributions to the Community budget. Although she supported the Single European Act (which by 1992 had completed the work of creating a single 'internal market') and the enlargement of the Community (to include the former dictatorships of Greece, Spain and Portugal), the 'Iron Lady' made it clear in her Bruges speech of 1988 that she was opposed to closer political and monetary union. It was her vehement restatement of this view after Britain had temporarily joined the Exchange Rate Mechanism of the European Monetary System in 1990 that was a significant factor in the internal party revolt that led to her fall from office, as more 'pro-European' elements in the Conservative Party – Michael Heseltine, Kenneth Clarke, Douglas Hurd and, more equivocally, the new prime minister, John Major (who claimed to want to put Britain 'at the heart of Europe') – moved into the ascendant.[20] However, it was not only the Conservative Party that faced internal disruption in the 1980s because of European affairs. Under the anti-Marketeer Michael Foot, the Labour Party had abandoned its support for the EEC and at the 1983 general election campaigned for British withdrawal – one of the reasons why some Labour pro-Europeans split from the party to found the SDP. Under Foot's successor (and future European Commissioner) Neil Kinnock, Labour abandoned its outright anti-EEC stance, but the party remained deeply divided. Of the three main British parties only the Liberals were consistent advocates of British membership of the EEC from its inception and unambiguous advocates of closer European integration.

For Labour and the Conservatives the internal debates continued from the 1980s into the 1990s. The stakes were raised by the determination of the Continental powers, especially France and Germany, to push ahead with the integrationist agenda. Increasingly, as the decade went on, the central issue became that of the adoption of a single European currency. The Maastricht Treaty of 1991 restated the EEC's commitment to economic and monetary union and prepared the way for the transition from an 'Economic Community' to a fully unified Europe. John Major signed up to most of the provisions of the treaty, but crucially negotiated an 'opt-out' for Britain as regards membership of the single currency. After the narrow Conservative victory in the 1992 general election the 'Euro' (as the new currency was to be called) became the focal point of the battle between pro-Europeans and 'Euro-sceptics' within the Conservative Party, with Major's official 'wait and see' policy reminiscent of Balfour's desperate attempts to keep his party united during the tariff reform versus

free trade controversy of earlier in the century. Disunity over European policy played its part in the Conservatives' landslide defeat in
1997, when a large number of Conservative candidates lost votes to
the anti-Europe United Kingdom Independence Party and the
Referendum Party backed by the multi-millionaire Sir James Gold-
smith. Tony Blair's 'New Labour' Party was more successful in riding
the Euro tiger, its leaders intimating that a Labour government would
not recommend joining a single currency unless the conditions were
right (another version of wait and see) and in any case promising a
referendum before any final decision was taken. Nevertheless, the
currency issue divided both the major parties, and opinion polls
showed steady majorities against British membership, indicating once
again, despite the 1975 referendum result, that most British people
were still reluctant Europeans at heart rather than out-and-out
enthusiasts for the European cause.

Throughout its twists and turns the debate about Europe had two
dimensions. One was the practical: how much could Britain gain, or
how much was it losing, from membership; the second was ideological: whether Britain was committed in principle to the European
project, and if so with what kind of objective in view. Related to this
were questions about how far Britain was prepared to go in supporting further integration, and the implications of this for national
sovereignty. Politically opinion could be divided into three camps.
The idealistic pro-Europeans – mainly the Liberals, plus some in the
Conservative and Labour Parties – favoured full economic and
political integration (though not necessarily a 'European super-state').
They were in favour of the single currency and the adoption of
common policies and institutional structures, albeit within a 'federal'
framework that allowed maximum autonomy to individual states and
regions (the principle of 'subsidiarity'). A larger group – embracing
the mainstream of the Conservative and Labour Parties – were
pragmatic Europeans. They supported British membership of a
European Community because it had economic and political advantages for Britain (and the alternative seemed to be international
isolation), but they were opposed to too close a political integration
and often unenthusiastic about a single currency, their ideal being a
Europe of clearly defined nation-states cooperating only for certain
agreed purposes but otherwise pursuing their own policies and
preserving their separate institutions. This last preference was taken
further by the final group, the anti-Europeans, who felt that Britain
was losing more than she was gaining from Europe and wanted a

loosening of ties with the EU or perhaps even withdrawal. The anti-Europeans, or Euro-sceptics, occupied the extremes of right and left in the Conservative and Labour Parties, and formed their own organizations such as the UK Independence Party. Here the arguments about the preservation of 'national sovereignty' were shouted loudest, in ways which could often strike a populist electoral chord.

The sovereignty issue was symbolic, and was important for perceptions of national identity, but in reality Britain's political freedom of action had been limited from the time of her accession to the Treaty of Rome, and membership of the EC/EU had had a considerable impact on the operation of the British state. Partly this was because membership of any international organization, including NATO or the UN, involved an element of compromise, since policies had to be decided in discussion with fellow members. But the European Community, with its central institutions of the European Commission, the European Parliament and the Council of Ministers, was a more overtly interventionist body, whose decisions impinged directly on the domestic affairs of member states as well as the orientation of their foreign policy.[21] It was true that individual states could protect their 'vital interests' by use of the veto in the ministerial council, but as the Community expanded and the integrationist pressures increased so the veto itself came under threat. In any case, it was a weapon that, like the opt-out, had to be used sparingly if the Community institutions were not to be permanently logjammed by disputes. For the most part, once policies had been agreed at Community level they had to be implemented by member states, which meant that national parliaments and national ministries became rubber stamps and executors of actions determined by the Community as a whole. Following the institution of direct elections to the European Parliament in 1979, European politics also took on a more supra-national character, even if most electorates still thought in national terms and national governments sought to restrict the power of a rival, European, political authority. The creation of a European Central Bank and the successful launch of the Euro as a common currency by 11 of the 15 EU member states in 1999 presaged further European intervention in the internal affairs of the participating countries, with interest rates, exchange rates and other key economic policies being decided at the European rather than the national level.

If, in some ways, membership of the EU eroded the 'Britishness' of the British state, what effect did it have on the British people? For those who were hostile to or suspicious of 'Europe', the controversies surrounding membership of the EU may well have strengthened their sense of British national identity, encouraging an at times xenophobic reaction against the Brussels 'Eurocrats' and Britain's European partners. These attitudes were reflected by politicians but they were widely held too in sections of the tabloid newspaper press and among the public at large, as the declining popularity of Europe in opinion polls after 1975 confirmed. In these quarters, being British or European were clearly alternatives rather than complementary components of a composite national/continental identity. This, however, was not the whole story. While for some, hostility to Europe strengthened a sense of Britishness, for others – perhaps particularly among the younger generation for whom the Second World War was history rather than memory – it was possible to be both British and European at the same time: a sense of common cultural experience encouraged by foreign travel, familiarity with foreign languages and foreign food, and the easy acceptance of developments such as the opening of the Channel Tunnel. Their sense of Britishness was not necessarily diminished thereby, but it was a Britishness informed by an awareness, even an embracing, of Britain's European context and heritage.

The 'Europeanization' of Britain also, however, impinged on national identities within Britain as well as on the concept of British- ness as a whole. If Britain was, as some have claimed, an invented nation, linked to a particular state structure and a specific historical time period, it was possible that as the foundations of that state were worn away – by the end of empire and Britain's absorption in Europe – the common British identity assumed by the anti-Europeans would once again be submerged by the resurgence of separate domestic national cultures. To some extent, as we have seen, this was already happening in 1990s Britain, with the revival of nationalism in Scot- land and Wales, the implementation of policies of political devolution and the consequent debate about the place of England and English- ness within the British state. But these issues plainly had a European as well as a British dimension. The SNP had already used the slogan 'Independence in Europe', arguing that Scotland could be a viable independent state within the EU just as countries of a similar size like Denmark or the Irish Republic were. In Wales, Plaid Cymru had always looked to European models of regionalism within a larger framework, which again the EU could satisfy, with or without an intermediate British tier. The limited rapprochement between north and south in Ireland had been assisted by their common membership of the EU, and perhaps more hindered than helped by Northern Ireland's historical connection with the British state. It was fully possible, in other words, to conceive of a situation in which the constituent parts of the United Kingdom might see their futures in a European instead of a British context, leaving England perhaps to rediscover its separate identity as a European nation alongside the French, the Spanish and the Germans, rather than being constrained by its responsibilities to the other parts of the UK.

This is not to say that, even within a more integrated European Union, the British state did not have a role to play. Although the Scottish, Welsh and Northern Ireland administrations established their own contacts at European level, and their domestic ministries became involved in implementing EU laws and directives, it was still at the British level that the main business between the UK and the EU was conducted. Issues of foreign affairs and defence, and perhaps crucially that of the currency, were explicitly reserved to Westminster by the terms of the devolution settlements. In that sense, the Westminster parliament remained sovereign, at least in the UK, if not necessarily in the wider arena. Of course, how these constitutional arrangements will evolve in the future is impossible to predict. Some commentators have posited the retention of a United Kingdom government as a kind of 'mezzanine' or intermediate authority between the internal national or regional administrations and the European level. Others are clearly of the opinion that, if the process of European integration proceeds, and particularly if at some point Britain decides to join the Euro, then the need for a British state in its present form will wither away. Much will depend too on whether, in an age of competing regionalization and globalization, the British continue to see themselves as British at all, and it is to this aspect of the nature of 'Britishness' in the late twentieth and early twenty-first century that attention must finally be turned.

Global British

Who were the British in the late twentieth century and what was their outlook on the world? It might be thought that the end of empire and the divisions over Europe would have encouraged insularity and a narrowing of national horizons. Yet one of the main features of the British state throughout its history was its global dimension. Since its formation in the eighteenth century, Britain had taken on a world role, established communities overseas and transmitted British ideas and values to many parts of the world. In return, British society had been shaped by global trends and influences that had had their effect on the life and culture of the British Isles. These external influences did not cease to operate on Britain simply because of the dismantling of the British Empire and the reduced presence of the Union flag in foreign parts. Indeed, the complex legacy of empire, Britain's involvement in international organizations such as the EU and the UN, and above all the globalization of culture, economics and markets, together with the information revolution of the latter part of the twentieth century, probably meant that Britain was being shaped more by outside forces in this period than at any other time in its history.

The global dimension of British society was revealed most obviously after the Second World War by its increasingly multi-cultural nature. Multi-culturalism of course was nothing new as far as Britain was concerned. British society had developed through the intermingling of a multiplicity of indigenous and imported cultures and contained a plurality of religious, linguistic and ethnic groups. Although Britain since the eighteenth century had been mainly a net exporter of people, there had also been considerable immigration which had enhanced the multi-cultural mix. Within the British Isles the movement of large numbers of emigrants from Ireland to Britain has already been documented. Britain also acted as a refuge in the nineteenth and twentieth centuries for those fleeing repression and poverty in continental Europe. Significant numbers of Jewish immigrants arrived in Britain and established distinctive communities in London's East End and in other places such as Leeds and Glasgow. There was immigration by Germans, Italians, Russians, Poles and others from Eastern Europe. During the period of the Second World War over 100,000 Poles came to Britain to flee the Nazis, and many of them not only fought with British forces during the war but stayed to make their homes in Britain when the war was over.

With the exception of the Jews, however, these early immigrant groups came in relatively small numbers and, despite linguistic and other problems, were assimilated easily enough into the host community. After 1945 the nature of the immigrant stream changed: immigrants came in larger numbers and exhibited more obvious differences of colour, religion and culture.[22] Britain already had a small black community before the 1940s, but it was not until the war brought large numbers of black American GIs to the country before D-Day that colour-based racial tensions became an issue. Only after the war did the black and Asian population in Britain itself begin to grow rapidly through successive waves of immigration. The arrival of the *Empire Windrush* with over 400 immigrants from Jamaica marked the beginning of a large influx of West Indians as the post-war economy exerted its demand for cheap, unskilled labour. In the 1950s there began a substantial inflow of immigration from India, Pakistan and other parts of the Asian sub-continent, while from the 1960s political change in Africa brought fresh waves of Asian immigrants as they fled unsympathetic regimes in Kenya and Uganda. By 1971 there were 705,000 people of West Indian or Asian origin living in Britain. In 1996 the total ethnic minority population had grown, by immigration and indigenous increase, to over 3.2 million, the largest groups being Indians (877,000), Pakistanis (579,000) and black Caribbean (477,000), but the total also included 281,000 black Africans and 126,000 Chinese as well as many smaller ethnic groups.[23]

Although these numbers were still small compared with the total UK population of over 50 million, their impact on British society was increased by the concentration of ethnic minority communities in particular urban areas. Thus London, the Midlands and parts of West Yorkshire like Leeds and Bradford acquired substantial Asian and West Indian populations and consequently developed a much more overtly multi-cultural character than England as a whole, while immigrant and ethnic minority settlement in Scotland and Wales was at a much lower level still, and in Northern Ireland virtually non-existent. Where minority communities did take root they quickly transformed the local cultural landscape. Asians retained traditional forms of dress and their own languages. They brought religions such as Hinduism and Islam into the English Midlands and the textile districts of West Yorkshire. In some districts they were strongly enough represented in local populations to elect their own councillors and establish separate schools for their children. There was also an impact on local economies. In the 1940s and 1950s West Indian immigrants and some Asians were prepared to take low-paid jobs in the public service sector, and their presence as bus conductors or hospital porters became almost as common a cultural stereotype as the Chinese restaurant, the Indian tandoori or the Asian corner shop. But Asians especially demonstrated educational and business abilities that enabled them to succeed also at a higher professional and economic level. In these ways an assimilationist interface was created between the host nation and ethnic minorities who preferred a degree of domestic or cultural separateness but were nonetheless keen to integrate into the wider regional or British community, though this ideal was more easily achieved at times of rising prosperity than economic depression. When unemployment began to increase from the late 1970s the West Indian minority in particular was disadvantaged by poor educational opportunities and its position on the less skilled fringes of the labour market, and the urban riots of the 1980s in places like Brixton stemmed in large measure from the accumulated frustration of the young black population.

As the more fully developed multi-cultural society emerged, so did a form of 'hyphenated' Britishness, in which immigrants or their descendants could identify themselves with their area of ethnic origin and the British state in which they lived. London's Notting Hill carnival, for example, thus became a flamboyant celebration of a dynamic British-Caribbean culture rather than a lament of emotional exiles for the loss of a distant homeland. But the process of acculturation was not without its problems, not least in the resistance it encountered from the overt and subliminal racism of other sections of British society. Thus the Conservative politician of the Thatcher years, Norman Tebbit, denied the possibility of hyphenated Britishness in his infamous 'cricket test', which confusingly appeared to deny West Indian or Asian Britons the right to call themselves British unless they supported the English (sic) cricket team. More serious, and more sinister, was the organized expression of racist attitudes by those who favoured an exclusively 'White British' definition of national identity. Racist attitudes had long been a factor in British politics, from the 'Scottophobia' of the 1760s and the anti-Irish feeling of the nineteenth century, to the patronizing attitudes towards colonial subject peoples of the Victorian period and the anti-Semitism that impelled the Conservatives to introduce the Aliens Act of 1905 and later resurfaced in the 1930s in Mosley's British Union of Fascists. After 1945 it was the black and Asian populations that became the targets of racist attacks. Mosley's 'Union Movement' of the 1950s and groups like Colin Jordan's White Defence League stirred up racial animosity towards immigrant communities, portraying them as an economic threat to the interests of British workers. The National Front, founded in 1967, favoured a policy of forced repatriation of 'immigrants', ignoring the fact that many in the ethnic minorities had actually been born in Britain. Moreover, although the NF and its successor, the British National Party, were minority movements, they tapped into a more widely diffused racism that also touched the mainstream political parties. In 1968 the Conservative front-bencher and Wolverhampton MP Enoch Powell won wide-spread popularity for broaching a discussion of the problems of racial tension arising from continued immigration with the classical allusion to the 'rivers of blood' that might flow unless remedial action were taken. In characteristically populist vein, Mrs Thatcher later admitted in a television interview that she understood the fears of white Britons who were afraid of being 'swamped' by an expanding Asian and West Indian population.

The attitude of the British state to the problems of race and Britishness was apparently clear-cut even if in practice it often seemed more equivocal. In the 1960s and 1970s a series of Race Relations Acts were passed, officially making racial discrimination illegal and setting up first a Race Relations Board and later the Commission for Racial Equality to monitor problems and improve inter-communal relations. At the same time, some restrictions were placed on immigration from the early 1960s on, to attempt to regulate the flow of incomers and so reduce possible flashpoints of tension. Both measures could be defined as a liberal regulation of a multi-cultural society, though the Immigration Acts were attacked in some quarters as themselves reflective of racist attitudes on the part of the state since they applied mainly to immigrants of African or Asian origin. Criticism was also levelled at official agencies such as the police for what even some policemen admitted were forms of 'institutionalized racism', for example in the differential treatment of white and black suspects and the systematic harassment of young black Afro-Caribbean males. Even at the end of the twentieth century, when the ethnic minorities were more fully represented in the professions, politics and the media, as well as in activities such as professional sport, much informal discrimination clearly remained, and at both the public and private level racism was still a feature of Britain's multi-cultural society.[24]

On the other hand, these individual criticisms should not detract from an appreciation of the extent to which British society had genuinely become more multi-cultural in character, nor from the important fact that as far as the state was concerned citizenship – irrespective of race, colour or creed – had become the criterion of Britishness, rather than any narrower definition. This was one way in which the open, global Britishness of the nineteenth century was preserved in the twentieth, but there were other respects in which the British remained a global people throughout our period. The concept of 'Greater Britain' was perhaps less valid than it had been during the

Victorian imperial era, as colonies had attained independence and the former dominions had not only become fully independent states but were evolving their own national identities based on other forms of multi-culturalism. Yet the ties that remained between Britain and her former empire were still a part of the British national persona. Even with the development of steadily closer economic and political links with continental Europe, the cultural, sporting and other connections between Britain and the Commonwealth were an important manifestation of global Britishness, albeit in a world much transformed since the late nineteenth or early twentieth centuries. The extent of Commonwealth immigration to Britain after 1945, and the keenness of immigrants to claim rights of British nationality, both testified to the enduring strength of the bond between Britain and the former imperial territories and helped to maintain it.

British society was being shaped by external influences in other ways too. In the post-war world the process of cultural homogenization and economic globalization developed apace, aided in the final part of the twentieth century by the communications revolution based on satellite systems and the internet. As a result, Britain became a corner of the global village to an extent that outstripped her exposure to international trends from the trading days of empire and the Pax Britannica. Within this transformation several strands can be identified. Culturally, America became an even more important influence than it had been between the wars, partly because of the reversion to the United States of Britain's former place in world affairs, the leading part the USA played in organizations like NATO and the presence of so many Americans in Britain especially at the height of the Cold War, but also because of the almost hegemonic influence of American popular culture, through films, television and the 'cultural imperialism' of the Coca-Cola society. As transatlantic travel increased, more Britons had direct experience of American society and were able to absorb at first hand its culture and mores, while American intellectuals and politicians also influenced aspects of Britain's economic and political thinking, notably during the Thatcher and Blair administrations. Influences from other parts of Europe paled beside this cultural version of the special relationship among the 'English-speaking peoples'. From the 1960s more Britons took holidays, or lived and worked, in continental Europe, and there were examples of cultural transfer, for example in increased consumption of Italian food or French wine. But it was a significant parallel to political debates about Britain's future in relation to the EU that in this American–European competition for cultural influence the American elements appeared to be those which were more widespread in their effect.

Still, however, it may be more appropriate to think in terms of a variety of global influences rather than of a single pull being exerted from any one particular geographical direction. Economically Britain was an integral component of a world-wide inter- and multi-national web of relationships. With the decline in London's central role in world finance, Britain's financial markets responded to the impulses sent out from the stock exchanges in New York, Frankfurt, Tokyo and Hong Kong. British industry became increasingly dominated by multi-national companies, with the privatization of state utilities and previously nationalized industries creating new opportunities for foreign takeovers and with American and Japanese firms especially seeing Britain as a profitable entry-point into tariff-free European markets. The rising profile of Asian companies in Britain, not to mention the virtual dominance of the Japanese and others in the field of imported electrical goods, was a nice example of reverse imperialism compared with the nineteenth century, but one that also had a cultural impact with Japanese-run factories in Britain's former industrial heartlands like south Wales and the north-east of England. And if Britain was guided by international forces in much of its manufacturing industry, and responding to global trends, the same was true to an even larger degree in the brave new world of electronic communications and the internet. In the mobile phone business Britain was one of the leading players, but the virtual monopoly established by Bill Gates's Microsoft Corporation over computer software and the internet was once again a major external influence on British society, just as the communications possibilities of the internet opened up in a more positive way the prospect of a genuinely global culture in which local, national and regional variations were steadily subsumed.

Given the extent of its global dimension, and the increasing cosmopolitanism of life in the early twenty-first century, how far could a distinctively 'British' society be said still to exist? This question underlay much of the uncertainty reflected in the academic and political debates about the nature of 'Britishness' from the late 1970s on. A sense of the erosion of British national identity may have been heightened, paradoxically, by the success of English as the common language of the international community. Whereas historic nations like the French, the Germans or the Spanish preserved their national distinctiveness through their language and language-based culture, using English for external purposes, the British were denied this duality of approach and consequently were more open to penetration by the predominantly English-language global culture.[25] 'Britishness', moreover, had developed alongside a British national state. By the late twentieth century the nation-state, at least at the British level, was under threat from two directions: from a European Union which was taking over some of its functions, and from the internal nationalist and devolutionary pressures which were emphasizing Scottish, Welsh, English or Irish identities rather than those of a British nation and a British state. The socially solvent effect of the declining importance of other historic factors of identity in British life – religion, a common class structure, even the weakening of family and community ties in an increasingly mobile and unstable world – also had an unsettling effect as far as an easy identification of the characteristics or facets of contemporary Britishness was concerned.

That said, neither the impact of a cosmopolitan global culture nor the culturally divisive effects of reviving domestic nationalisms should be overplayed. Britain retained a distinctive presence and identity in European and world affairs. The British state, notwithstanding the impact of internal devolution and pressures for closer integration within the larger structures of the European Union, continued to provide a unifying political framework for the United Kingdom and its citizens. In relation to that state, citizenship and nationality were synonymous terms. Yet a British national identity arguably went deeper than its purely legal forms. It represented the shared cultural and historical experience of people who inhabited a common geographical space and were governed by common laws, institutions and customs. Like any community, the British state had its own internal divisions, and there were those who would have preferred to reject membership of that community altogether. But for most groups and individuals this resulted in layers of multiple or hyphenated identity rather than rigidly exclusive or conflicting ones. Even in a global age, 'Britishness' provided a means of distinguishing a majority of those who lived in Britain from most of the rest of the world outside it. The British throughout their existence were a global people, but they were no less British for all that.

CONCLUSION

From the inception of the United Kingdom of Great Britain and Ireland in 1801 the history of the British state exhibited important continuities, but its development was not an entirely straightforward linear process. Across the nineteenth and twentieth centuries there were forces both of convergence and divergence at work. There was a steady expansion of the role of central government, especially in the provision of social welfare and in state intervention in the economy. Industrialization and the communications revolution of the Victorian period were powerful integrating factors, uniting disparate regional economies into a national industrial framework. The process of democratization and the rise of mass politics also had a unifying effect, enabling citizens to identify directly with the institutions of a central British state and creating political parties and other organizations that operated at an all-British level with the Westminster parliament and the Whitehall bureaucracy as the primary focus of their attention.

At the same time, democratization created opportunities for divergence as well as convergence. Parallel with the extensions of the parliamentary franchise went the creation of elective systems of local government. Powerful local authorities could work in partnership with central government but they could also on occasion confront it, and the state had therefore to contend with and contain tensions between the centre and the provinces. A more fundamental tension was created by the multi-national character of the British state itself. As has been shown, Ireland was never fully integrated into the structure of a unitary British state, retaining a devolved administration in Dublin after 1801 and then, with the rise of nationalism in the nineteenth century and the revolution of 1916–22, loosening its bonds with Britain still further, culminating in the establishment of a separate Irish Free State and the creation of a devolved parliament in

Northern Ireland after the First World War. Although Ireland was in some ways a special case, the democratic pressures for a decentralization of state structures also operated in Wales and Scotland, in varying degrees of strength, from the mid-nineteenth century onwards. Initially they were contained by a policy of concessions on specific issues of grievance, or in the case of Scotland by the administrative devolution embodied in the Scottish Office. By the late twentieth century, however, electoral devolution had been brought on to the political agenda, with the resulting establishment of the Scottish parliament and the National Assembly of Wales by the Blair government in 1999.

What these changes (and the simultaneous restoration of devolved government to Northern Ireland after a quarter of a century of direct rule) meant for the future of the British state has already been discussed. The reforms did not transform the United Kingdom into a federal state. They were at best 'quasi-federal', the picture being complicated by the fact that each of the assemblies had different powers, and by the absence of 'England', as an entity or a grouping of regions, from the constitutional reform process. Indeed, England's lack of a definite constitutional status of its own within the British state was both seized on as an anomaly and seen as reflective of the extent to which the devolutionary measures were a series of responses to particular historical problems rather than part of a comprehensive constitutional modernization of the British state. Thus Northern Ireland was dealt with as part of, or the legacy of, the long-standing 'Irish Question'; the granting of a parliament with legislative powers to Scotland reflected Scotland's historic status as a nation prior to the Union and the legal distinctiveness of Scotland within a British state; Wales, having been assimilated into English governing structures since 1536, was given belated recognition of its national character without the full measure of autonomy accorded to the Scots or the Irish. The establishment of the 'Council of the Isles' was an attempt to give these changes the appearance of an overall 'British dimension', although whether its role was to serve as a meeting place for partners in a common enterprise or a mechanism for enforcing conformity of policy from the centre (or, given the participation of the Irish Republic, simply as a bargaining counter in the Irish peace process) was not entirely clear.

The success of any political structure is ultimately determined by the degree to which it reflects the identity of the community it is intended to serve. Despite the description of Britain as an 'invented' nation and the late twentieth-century uncertainties about Britain's future, for much of the post-1800 period the political institutions of the British state were underpinned by a growing sense of British national identity, the product of domestic integration and the expanded role of central government which created a developing awareness of national community. Yet even when the feeling of 'Britishness' was at its height, it existed alongside, or in competition with, other historic national identities, as well as the separate though interconnected identifiers of religion and class. In political and cultural terms these multiple identities could be antagonistic or mutually reinforcing depending on circumstances. For much of the nineteenth and twentieth centuries it was possible to be both Welsh or Scottish and British. A keen commitment to Scottish or Welsh national cultures was perfectly compatible with support for the Union and membership of the British state. In Ireland these dual loyalties were more problematic, with nationalists choosing to be Irish rather than British while only Unionists were willing to embrace their own particular version of the dual identity. In England, for much of the time, the duality of identities was not explicitly an issue, although an English national cultural identity was preserved within the British state even if England's economic and demographic dominance of the state meant that this identity rarely expressed itself in political form, except when devolution of power to other parts of the United Kingdom stirred the latent forces of English nationalism into passions that were normally confined to the sporting or social arena.

In many ways it was the quiescence of England, as much as the forbearance of the minority nationalities, that made the British state work. There was enough in common between the countries of Britain at least (Ireland may have been different) to make the Union a partnership of culture as well as convenience, while the structures of government proved flexible enough to allow for internal national differences and the redressing of grievances on the part of particular social or regional groups. But the fact that England did not have a separately embodied constitutional existence was the key to this process, since it forced England's political interests to be submerged in the larger British enterprise and helped to avert the possibility of direct confrontation between a 'dominant partner' and the smaller British nations. The fact that the English were dealing with a British state partly governed by the Scots, the Welsh and the Irish (just as the Scots, the Welsh and the Irish themselves were) was an essential part of the system of international compromise on which the British state was based. Whether this arrangement would survive a situation in which the smaller nations had their own governments but England did not was one of the unanswered questions of the devolution process, although it must be admitted that the difficulties of giving England its own government and still maintaining the system of compromises on which the British state depended were equally perplexing.

The other complication as Britain entered the twenty-first century was the changing international context outside the British Isles. From the eighteenth century Britain had existed as an imperial state and its internal unity was cemented by the benefits to be derived from the common imperial enterprise and the need to defend the state against external threat. The importance of these external factors in shaping and stimulating British national identity – indeed, in creating a sense of British nationhood – has been demonstrated time and time again: in the wars of 1793–1815, in the celebration of empire in Victorian Britain, and in the First and Second World Wars as well as during more recent conflicts. The loss of empire after 1945, and especially after 1960, removed the bond of imperial unity, even if the imperial legacy continued to influence Britons of an older generation and contributed to an ongoing global role for the British state. Britain's membership of the European Community, as has been seen, had a more contradictory effect, stimulating an insular Britishness among the opponents of European integration but weakening the allegiance to the idea of a strong British state among those who supported closer integration or who felt that the main relationship should be directly between the constituent parts of the UK or its regions and 'Europe', cutting out the British middle man. In this context the issue of whether Britain should join the 'Euro' assumed an even greater symbolic than economic importance, since the loss of a British currency would weaken the argument for a British state, or at least deprive it of one of its main surviving badges of statehood.

The importance of such questions serves merely to underscore the need to view the history of modern Britain in multi-national terms and to attempt to relate the debate about the future of 'Britishness' to the historical evolution of the British state. National identities have been a central influence on the pattern of British history since 1800. This is true not only where nationalist or separatist movements have emerged to challenge the state, or when the issues of Home Rule and devolution have occupied the centre of the political stage. In a more comprehensive way the whole political history of the United Kingdom has been shaped by its internal national or regional divisions. The relationship between Britain and Ireland is the most obvious example, from the famine of the 1840s to the Home Rule struggles of 1886–93 and 1912–14, the ending of the Union in 1921 and the Northern Ireland 'Troubles' of post-1969. But in mainland Britain too, internal national divisions have been influential in determining the political character of the state. From the 1860s the Liberal Party emerged as the party of the periphery, embodying a form of what Hugh Kearney has christened 'ethnic politics', a role later assumed by Labour. The Conservatives, from the time of Disraeli and Salisbury onwards, were predominantly an English party, despite the at times strong support for Unionism in other parts of the United Kingdom, especially Scotland and the north-east of Ireland. Devolution versus centralization, and the extent to which political structures should reflect national and regional diversities, became a major issue in political debate with – apart from the 'unionist consensus' between the major parties in 1922–64 – the dividing line between the parties reflecting their different foci of regional strength. In the late nineteenth and again in the late twentieth centuries there were Welsh and Scottish 'questions' alongside the Irish Question in British politics, emphasized by the emergence of Plaid Cymru and the SNP as significant third parties in the mid-1960s. There was also, throughout the period, a connection between domestic politics and external questions of national identity, in that the encouragement of imperialism and patriotism at a British level (the appeal in other words to a 'British' nationalism) was a weapon in the electoral battle and a means by which the Conservatives especially could disguise their weakness outside their main bases of support in the south and east of England.

This is not to say that the history of Britain can be written entirely in terms of nationalism and national identities, but certainly in any genuinely 'British' history these themes must be given their due place. In this respect the history of Britain is similar to that of the other major European powers, where questions of nationhood and identity were constant preoccupations for politicians and commentators throughout the nineteenth and twentieth centuries. The British attempt to construct a 'national' state that included several national minorities as well as regional tensions and separatist movements was one that was replicated in a number of other countries, just as the rise of regionalism and devolution within a European context and the threat that it poses to the older national states is far from being a uniquely British problem. Different countries have had differing degrees of success in solving these problems. The multi-national Austro-Hungarian Empire collapsed in the face of rising nationalism at the end of the First World War, as did the Russian/Soviet Empire in Eastern Europe in 1989. Spain has struggled with the separatist movement in the Basque country, while the artificial nature of Yugoslavia was overwhelmed by the ethnic savageries of the Balkans after the withdrawal of Tito's controlling hand. Germany, for all its traumas of unification, division and reunification, has established the kind of stable federal structure that has eluded Italy (where the north–south divide is as great as in the unification period of the 1860s), whereas since the revolution of 1789 the French have favoured strong central institutions in a unitary national state.

For each country, questions of nationhood and identity have presented their own problems. Britain's difficulty has been to reconcile the institutions of what for much of the modern period was a centralized unitary state with the multi-national realities of the political communities of the British Isles. For a time in the nineteenth century it seemed as if the solution might be to concentrate on building a British identity to match the British state, but while the peoples of Britain were for the most part content to be citizens of a British state they did not see themselves solely as part of a British 'nation'. Accordingly rather than try to create a nation to match the state, from the late nineteenth century the attempt was made to reform the state in ways that could more accurately reflect national diversities. The process has continued to the present day, with the result that a British state has been preserved intact. Whether, as a consequence, 'Britishness' remains a meaningful badge of identity has been the subject of much debate. Certainly the artificial, eighteenth-century Britishness based around loyalty to an exclusively Protestant state has become less and less relevant in a more religiously tolerant and increasingly secular society. Ethnic or racial definitions of Britishness founder on core contradictions between a 'Celtic' and an 'Anglo-Saxon' British past, and in any case are limiting and divisive in the multi-cultural Britain of the twenty-first century. If Britishness is to survive, therefore, it can only be in a form of symbiotic relationship with the state with which its history has been intertwined – an umbrella identity reflecting a mingling of other identities in a common marketplace, a cultural community with shared values and traditions and a common relationship to a body of historical and political experience and the institutions in which they are embodied. The question of whether this will be enough to sustain the British as a people, or ever again to bring them close to being a nation, remains to be seen. All that can safely be said is that, given the mutability of concepts of nationhood, it is likely that the political balance between state structures and the multiple nationalities of the British polity will need further adjustment. Rumours of the impending death of Britain may be exaggerated, but, as it has done throughout its existence, the British state will have to adapt in order to survive. 'Britishness' will be redefined in the process, but the importance of national identity as a factor in British history seems set to endure for the foreseeable future.

NOTES

Introduction

1. For example, R.F. Foster, *Modern Ireland, 1600–1972* (London, 1988); John Davies, *A History of Wales* (London, 1993); T.M. Devine, *The Scottish Nation, 1700–2000* (London, 1999).
2. These points are made in Peter Clarke, *Hope and Glory: Britain 1900–1990* (London, 1996).

Chapter 1: Britons and Britishness

1. Linda Colley, *Britons: Forging the Nation, 1707–1837* (London, 1996).
2. *Ibid.*, p 5.
3. For a general perspective on this debate see E.J. Hobsbawm, *Nations and Nationalism since 1780* (Cambridge, 1990). A fuller bibliographical guide is contained in Raymond Pearson, *The Longman Companion to European Nationalism, 1789–1920* (London, 1994).
4. Davies, *A History of Wales*, pp 231–8.
5. For recent surveys see Mark Kishlansky, *A Monarchy Transformed: Britain, 1603–1714* (London, 1996); Martyn Bennett, *The Civil Wars in Britain and Ireland, 1637–1651* (Oxford, 1997).
6. Early parliaments also had a variety of other judicial and legislative functions.
7. The Act of 1536 gave Wales 26 MPs, increased to 27 in 1543.
8. Colley, *Britons*, pp 122–40. The title of Wilkes's paper was also an ironic response to the pro-government organ, *The Briton*, edited by Tobias Smollett, a Scot.
9. On this theme see David Hempton, *Religion and Political Culture in Britain and Ireland* (Cambridge, 1996).
10. Some of these restrictions could be circumvented by 'occasional conformity' but this was in itself a controversial practice, for obvious reasons.
11. Christopher Hibbert, *King Mob* (London, 1958) provides a graphic account of the riots. For a more analytical appraisal see George Rudé, 'The Gordon Riots: A Study of the Rioters and their Victims', in Rudé, *Paris and London in the 18th Century* (London, 1970), pp 268–92.

12. There are similarities with the anti-Catholic *Kulturkampf* initiated by Bismarck after the unification of Germany in the 1870s.

13. Simon James, *The Atlantic Celts* (London, 1999), pp 44–8; Geraint H. Jenkins, *The Foundations of Modern Wales, 1642–1780* (Oxford, 1987), chapter 6.

14. Hugh Kearney, *The British Isles: A History of Four Nations* (Cambridge, 1989), p 197.

15. Gwyn A. Williams, *Madoc: The Making of a Myth* (London, 1979), chapter 3.

16. Kearney, *The British Isles*, p 170.

17. John Derry, *English Politics and the American Revolution* (London, 1976).

18. Ian R. Christie, *Wars and Revolutions: Britain 1760–1832* (London, 1982), pp 128–39.

19. Foster, *Modern Ireland*, chapter 11. Technically the constitutional changes repealed the Declaratory Act of 1719 and granted the Irish parliament legislative autonomy by amending Poynings' Law, though, as Foster notes, there is room for doubting whether the extent of the changes was not more apparent than real.

20. Hobsbawm, *Nations and Nationalism*.

21. The strength of popular conservatism is examined in H.T. Dickinson, 'Popular Conservatism and Militant Loyalism, 1789–1815', in H.T. Dickinson (ed), *Britain and the French Revolution, 1789–1815* (London, 1989), pp 103–26.

22. On the popular radical movement see Albert Goodwin, *The Friends of Liberty* (London, 1979).

23. Roger Wells, *Insurrection: The British Experience, 1795–1803* (Gloucester, 1983) takes the revolutionary character of the disturbances more seriously and provides an excellent detailed account, following in the path of E.P. Thompson, *The Making of the English Working Class* (London, 1963).

24. Neil Davidson, *The Origins of Scottish Nationhood* (London, 2000), pp 152–9; Christopher Harvie, *Scotland and Nationalism* (3rd ed, London, 1998), pp 9–10; Devine, *The Scottish Nation*, chapter 10, provide commentary on Burns and the background to the Scottish radical movement. Burns's poem, with its opening line 'Scots, wha hae wi' Wallace bled' was a linking of the themes of nationalism and freedom couched in the form of an appeal by 'Bruce to his troops on the eve of the Battle of Bannock-burn'.

25. Gwyn A. Williams, *Artisans and Sans Culottes* (London, 1968), pp 65–6.

26. Gwyn A. Williams, *The Search for Beulah Land* (London, 1980).

27. Quoted in Henry Boylan, *Wolfe Tone* (Dublin, 1981), p 16. The fullest biography of Tone is Marianne Elliott, *Wolfe Tone: Prophet of Irish Independence* (New Haven and London, 1989).

28. Marianne Elliott, *Partners in Revolution: The United Irishmen and France* (New Haven and London, 1982).

29. The full story of the rebellion is told in Thomas Pakenham, *The Year of Liberty* (London, 1969).

30. The franchise reforms were comparatively limited, however, and in Ireland some Catholics actually lost the vote through changes in the property qualifications. For a fuller consideration of reform and its impact, see below, chapter 2.

Chapter 2: Industrialization, Integration and Protest

1. Keith Robbins, *Nineteenth-Century Britain: England, Scotland and Wales, The Making of a Nation* (Oxford, 1988) explores these themes across the century as a whole.
2. Christopher Harvie, 'Revolution and the Rule of Law (1789–1851)' in Kenneth O. Morgan (ed), *The Oxford History of Britain* (Oxford, 1988), p 477.
3. Asa Briggs, 'London, the World City' in the same author's *Victorian Cities* (London, 1968), pp 311–60.
4. Olive and Sydney Checkland, *Industry and Ethos: Scotland, 1832–1914* (Edinburgh, 1989), pp 13, 34–54.
5. Davies, *A History of Wales*, p 351.
6. Especially Cordell's trilogy of novels, *Rape of the Fair Country* (1959), *The Hosts of Rebecca* (1960) and *Song of the Earth* (1969).
7. Bruce Lenman, *Integration and Enlightenment: Scotland, 1748–1832* (Edinburgh, 1981), p 117. The work of the Scottish engineer Thomas Telford on roads and bridges throughout Britain symbolized the integrating effects of the early nineteenth-century communications revolution.
8. Derek Beales, *From Castlereagh to Gladstone, 1815–1885* (London, 1969), p 109.
9. Harold Perkin, *The Origins of Modern English Society, 1780–1880* (London, 1969).
10. Kearney, *The British Isles*, pp 197–8, 206–7.
11. J.C.D. Clark, *English Society, 1688–1832* (Cambridge, 1985).
12. The Act established a uniform 40-shilling freehold franchise in the counties of England and Wales and a £10-householder franchise in the boroughs. For studies of the Reform Act and its impact see John Cannon, *Parliamentary Reform, 1640–1832* (Cambridge, 1972); Michael Brock, *The Great Reform Act* (London, 1973); Martin Pugh, *The Evolution of the British Electoral System, 1832–1987* (London, 1988).
13. Norman Gash, *Politics in the Age of Peel* (2nd ed, Brighton, 1977).
14. Gwyn A. Williams, *The Merthyr Rising* (London, 1978).
15. Quoted in Norman Gash, *Aristocracy and People: Britain 1815–1865* (London, 1979), p 154.
16. The two best accounts of Scottish politics in the period are I.G.C. Hutchinson, *A Political History of Scotland, 1832–1924* (Edinburgh, 1986) and Michael Fry, *Patronage and Principle: A Political History of Modern Scotland* (Aberdeen, 1991).
17. G.I.T. Machin, *Politics and the Churches in Great Britain, 1832–1868* (Oxford, 1977) is the standard work on this theme.
18. Derek Fraser, *Urban Politics in Victorian England* (Leicester, 1976). In the later nineteenth century political organizations in the provinces transferred their activities on to a national scale, as for example did the National Liberal Federation, originally founded in Birmingham. By the end of the century elected county, parish and district councils were also developing another dimension of local politics.
19. On the detail of these protests see George Rudé, *The Crowd in History, 1730–1848* (London, 1981) and John Stevenson, *Popular Disturbances in England, 1700–1870* (London, 1979).
20. J.T. Ward (ed), *Popular Movements, 1830–1850* (London, 1970) contains chapters on both movements. Ward's longer study, *The Factory Movement, 1830–1855* (London, 1962), makes it clear that the movement for factory reform had

support from areas outside the north of England, such as Glasgow and Dundee in Scotland.

21. The regional variations of Chartism were first emphasized in Asa Briggs (ed), *Chartist Studies* (London, 1959). A more recent study is Dorothy Thompson, *The Chartists* (London, 1984). D.J.V. Jones, *Chartism and the Chartists* (London, 1973) is good on social and regional aspects.

22. The 'Six Points' of the Charter – universal male suffrage, secret ballot, equal electoral districts, annual parliaments, payment of MPs, abolition of the property qualification for MPs – had originated with the Westminster Association of the 1780s.

23. To emphasize the Irish connection, the *Northern Star* had been the title of a paper published by the United Irishmen in the 1790s. There were parallels between Chartism and the O'Connellite Repeal movement in Ireland. (See below.)

24. Oliver MacDonagh, *O'Connell: The Life of Daniel O'Connell, 1775–1847* (London, 1991) explores all aspects of 'The Liberator's' career, including the politics of the 1830s.

25. Richard Davis, *The Young Ireland Movement* (Dublin, 1987).

26. Cormac Ó Gráda, *Ireland Before and After the Famine: Explorations in Economic History, 1800–1925* (Manchester, 1988) delineates the features of the Irish economy. K.T. Hoppen, *Ireland since 1800* (London, 1989) is also very good on economic themes.

27. Christine Kinealy, *A Death-Dealing Famine: The Great Hunger in Ireland* (London, 1997) is the best recent summary of its topic.

28. *Ibid.*, pp 1–15.

29. Kerby Miller, *Emigrants and Exiles: Ireland and the Irish Exodus to North America* (Oxford, 1977), p 286.

30. Some relief supplies were also sent by Irish-American groups in the USA, and the US government provided facilities for their transport.

31. For a comparison with Scotland see Devine, *The Scottish Nation*, pp 413–21.

Chapter 3: The Challenge of Nationalism

1. Edward Norman, *A History of Modern Ireland* (London, 1973), p 53.

2. Williams, *Merthyr Rising*; D.J.V. Jones, *The Last Rising: The Newport Insurrection of 1839* (Oxford, 1985).

3. For wider comparisons with 1848 see E.J. Hobsbawm, *The Age of Capital* (London, 1985), pp 21–40.

4. Fry, *Patronage and Principle*, pp 94–6.

5. Kenneth O. Morgan, *Rebirth of a Nation: Wales 1880–1980* (Oxford, 1980), p 14.

6. Ieuan Gwynedd Jones, 'The Liberation Society and Welsh Politics', *Welsh History Review*, vol 1, no 2 (1961), pp 193–200.

7. Kenneth O. Morgan, *Wales in British Politics, 1868–1922* (3rd ed, Cardiff, 1980), pp 23–5.

8. Morgan, *Rebirth of a Nation*, pp 33–6.

9. Foster, *Modern Ireland*, pp 334–7.

10. Paul Bew, *Land and the National Question in Ireland, 1858–1882* (Dublin, 1980).

11. D.W. Crowley, 'The "Crofters' Party", 1885–92', *Scottish Historical Review*, October 1956, pp 110–26.

12. Though, as in Britain, nationalism also drew upon a variety of other social, political and economic grievances.

13. Eric Hobsbawm and Terence Ranger (eds), *The Invention of Tradition* (Cambridge, 1983).

14. Matthew Arnold was an influential figure in this debate.

15. James Hunter, 'The Politics of Highland Land Reform, 1873–1895', *Scottish Historical Review*, 53 (1974), pp 46–63, and 'The Gaelic Connection: The Highlands, Ireland and Nationalism, 1873–1922', *ibid.*, 54 (1975), pp 178–204.

16. Quoted in Harvie, *Scotland and Nationalism*, p 19. On the wider importance of sporting differences and national identity, see Richard Holt, *Sport and the British* (Oxford, 1990), pp 236–79.

17. On sport in Wales, see Holt, *ibid.*, pp 246–53. The Welsh national affinity with choral singing is analysed in its historical context by Gareth Williams in *Valleys of Song: Music and Society in Wales, 1840–1914* (Cardiff, 1998).

18. Morgan, *Wales in British Politics*, pp 111–19.

19. Norman, *Modern Ireland*, p 203.

20. Reported in *The Freeman's Journal*, 22 January 1885, quoted in Grenfell Morton, *Home Rule and the Irish Question* (London, 1980), p 88.

21. Details in Morton, *ibid.*, pp 34–5. See also Alan O'Day, *Irish Home Rule, 1867–1921* (Manchester, 1998).

22. However, the margin in votes between pro- and anti-Home Rulers was narrower, 1.34 million to 1.42 million.

23. Vernon Bogdanor, *Devolution in the United Kingdom* (Oxford, 1999), pp 19–42 contains an extended discussion of the political and constitutional issues.

24. Quoted in Morton, *Home Rule and the Irish Question*, p 95.

25. Henry Pelling, *Social Geography of British Elections* (London, 1967).

26. T.E. Ellis, *Speeches and Addresses* (Wrexham, 1912). On Ellis's career generally the fullest biography is Neville Masterman, *The Forerunner* (Swansea, 1972).

27. Thomas N. Brown, *Irish-American Nationalism, 1870–1890* (Philadelphia, 1966).

28. Quoted in Bogdanor, *Devolution in the United Kingdom*, p 20.

29. John Biggs-Davison and George Chaudaray-Best, *The Cross of St Patrick: The Catholic Unionist Tradition in Ireland* (Bourne End, Bucks, 1984).

30. For example, R.L. Stevenson, *Kidnapped* (1886) and *Catriona* (1893); John Buchan, *A Lost Lady of Old Years* (1899); Neil Munro, *Doom Castle* (1901) and *The New Road* (1914).

31. Kenneth O. Morgan, *Keir Hardie: Radical and Socialist* (London, 1975).

32. David Marquand, *Ramsay MacDonald* (London, 1977).

33. R.C.K. Ensor, *England, 1870–1914* (Oxford, 1936), pp 161–2.

34. On the various strands of the women's movement, see Philippa Levine, *Victorian Feminism, 1850–1900* (London, 1987); on labour movements, E.H. Hunt, *British Labour History, 1815–1914* (London, 1981) is a good guide.

35. E.W. Evans, *Mabon* (Cardiff, 1959).

36. At an elite level a similar point could be made about the unifying effect of public schools and the universities, although national differences were also reflected in the higher educational institutions of the four nations.

Chapter 4: Nationhood and Empire

1. A convenient summary is provided in James Joll, *Europe since 1870* (London, 1976), chapter 4. See also E.J. Hobsbawm, *The Age of Empire* (London, 1987), chapter 3.

2. J.R. Seeley, *The Expansion of England* (London, 1883), pp 9–10. For a modern view, see Kearney, *The British Isles*, chapter 7.

3. Recent surveys include, Lawrence James, *The Rise and Fall of the British Empire* (London, 1994) and Denis Judd, *Empire* (London, 1996).

4. C.C. Eldridge, 'Sinews of Empire: Changing Perspectives' in C.C. Eldridge (ed), *British Imperialism in the Nineteenth Century* (London, 1984), p 168.

5. The mid and late century mood is imaginatively explored in James (Jan) Morris, *At Heaven's Command: An Imperial Progress* (London, 1973).

6. Paul Kennedy, 'Continuity and Discontinuity in British Imperialism, 1815–1914' in Eldridge (ed), *British Imperialism*, pp 20–38.

7. Donald Read, *The Age of Urban Democracy: England 1868–1914* (London, 1994), pp 183, 350.

8. On the 'Scramble' and the reasons behind it, see Thomas Pakenham, *The Scramble for Africa* (London, 1991) and R. Robinson and J. Gallagher, *Africa and the Victorians* (London, 1981).

9. In territorial extent the French were Britain's nearest challengers.

10. For example, the population of British North America increased from 1,282,000 in 1832 to 3,689,000 in 1871, that of Australia from 52,000 in 1825 to 1,647,000 in 1870. Read, *The Age of Urban Democracy*, p 183.

11. Paul Kennedy, *The Rise and Fall of the Great Powers* (London, 1988).

12. J.A.S. Grenville, *Lord Salisbury and Foreign Policy* (London, 1970).

13. Thomas Pakenham, *The Boer War* (London, 1982), part 1, deals with the background to the war, as, in a more narrowly diplomatic way, does A.N. Porter, *The Origins of the South African War: Joseph Chamberlain and the Diplomacy of Imperialism, 1895–99* (Manchester, 1980).

14. Quoted in Ian Machin, *Disraeli* (London, 1995), p 6. The comment was made in 1852, before Disraeli reinvented himself as the apostle of imperialism in the 1870s.

15. Even Gandhi began his professional career as an English-educated barrister.

16. Seeley, *Expansion of England*, pp 296–8.

17. *Ibid.*, p 301.

18. Cecil Rhodes to W.T. Stead, 14 August 1891, quoted in M.E. Chamberlain, *The Scramble for Africa* (London, 1974), p 135.

19. Denis Judd, *Radical Joe: A Life of Joseph Chamberlain* (Cardiff, 1993), p 202.

20. *The Times*, 25 June 1872. Disraeli's other two objects were to 'maintain the institutions of the country' and 'the elevation of the condition of the people', thereby prefiguring the agenda of later nineteenth-century Unionism as developed by Salisbury and Chamberlain.

21. Gladstone resigned the premiership in 1894 rather than accept increases in naval expenditure.

22. Martin Pugh, *The Tories and the People, 1880–1935* (Oxford, 1985), pp 87–93.

23. See, for example, Hans-Ulrich Wehler, *The German Empire, 1871–1918* (Leamington Spa, 1985), pp 170–81, and the same author's 'Bismarck's Imperialism, 1862–1890', *Past and Present*, 48 (1970), pp 119–55.

24. Social imperialism as a component of British politics is considered in M.E. Chamberlain, 'Imperialism and Social Reform', in Eldridge (ed), *British Imperialism*, pp 148–67, and in Bernard Semmel, *Imperialism and Social Reform* (London, 1960).

25. David Cannadine, 'The Context, Performance and Meaning of Ritual: The British Monarchy and the "Invention of Tradition", c.1820–1977', in Hobsbawm and Ranger (eds), *The Invention of Tradition*, pp 101–64.

26. A.P. Thornton, *The Imperial Idea and Its Enemies* (London, 1959).

27. Keith Robbins, *The Eclipse of a Great Power: Modern Britain, 1870–1975* (London, 1983), p 22.

28. In Australia, Irish emigrants and their descendants reproduced rivalries from their home country and identified with Unionist or Home Rule factions in the UK according to their respective loyalties.

29. Martin Pugh, *State and Society: British Political and Social History, 1870–1922* (London, 1994), pp 82–4; James Walvin, *Passage to Britain: Immigration in British History and Politics* (London, 1994).

30. Holt, *Sport and the British*, pp 209–10.

31. Andrew Lownie, *John Buchan: The Presbyterian Cavalier* (London, 1995); Janet Adam Smith, *John Buchan* (London, 1965).

32. Masterman, *The Forerunner*, pp 148–60.

33. Thornton, *The Imperial Idea*; Bernard Porter, *Critics of Empire: British Radical Attitudes to Colonialism in Africa, 1895–1914* (London, 1969).

Chapter 5: Crisis and Conflict

1. George Dangerfield, *The Strange Death of Liberal England* (London, 1935). At about the same time the French historian Elie Halevy, in the final volume of his history of the English people in the nineteenth century, *The Rule of Democracy, 1905–1914* (revised ed, London, 1952) wrote of the coincidence of 'domestic anarchy' and 'international anarchy' in the British history of this period.

2. A recent summary of these topics is provided in David Powell, *The Edwardian Crisis: Britain 1901–1914* (London, 1996).

3. Zara Steiner, *Britain and the Origins of the First World War* (London, 1977) traces the evolution of foreign policy and the factors that shaped it.

4. Speech at Birmingham Town Hall, 16 May 1902, *The Times*, 17 May 1902.

5. G.R. Searle, *The Quest for National Efficiency* (Oxford, 1971)

6. On the wider phenomenon of invasion literature, see I.F. Clarke, *Voices Prophesying War* (Oxford, 1992), pp 93–130.

7. Read, *Urban Democracy*, p 473.

8. The fullest study of the result is A.K. Russell, *Liberal Landslide* (Newton Abbot, 1973).

9. Derek Fraser, *The Evolution of the British Welfare State* (2nd ed, London, 1984), chapter 7.

10. Among the controversial proposals in the budget was a 'super tax' on those with incomes over £5000 a year and a series of taxes designed to tap the

'unearned increment' from land. For full details, see Bruce Murray, *The People's Budget* (Oxford, 1980).

11. These are described in Roy Jenkins, *Mr Balfour's Poodle* (London, 1954) and Powell, *The Edwardian Crisis*, chapter 2.

12. Powell, *The Edwardian Crisis*, pp 57–8.

13. P.F. Clarke, *Lancashire and the New Liberalism* (Cambridge, 1971).

14. David Powell, *British Politics and the Labour Question, 1868–1990* (London, 1992), pp 36–8.

15. In 1906 the Liberals outperformed the Unionists in all parts of Britain, winning 306 seats to the Unionists' 122 in England, 58 seats to the Unionists' ten in Scotland and winning all but one of the Welsh seats (the other went to Labour). In January 1910 the figures were as follows: England – Liberals 188, Unionists 233; Scotland – Liberals 58, Unionists 9; Wales – Liberals 27, Unionists 2. For a fuller analysis, see Neal Blewett, *The Peers, the Parties and the People: The General Elections of 1910* (London, 1972).

16. The Conservatives and Liberal Unionists merged their separate party organizations in 1912.

17. Morgan, *Wales in British Politics*, chapter VI. On the investiture of 1911, see John S. Ellis, 'The Prince and the Dragon: Welsh National Identity and the 1911 Investiture of the Prince of Wales', *Welsh History Review*, 18, 2 (1996), pp 272–94.

18. Morgan, *Wales in British Politics*, pp 255–9.

19. Richard J. Finlay, *A Partnership for Good? Scottish Politics and the Union since 1880* (Edinburgh, 1997), pp 51–66.

20. Quoted in Morgan, *Wales in British Politics*, p 258.

21. *The Times*, 27 July 1914, referred to the impasse over Ireland as 'one of the greatest crises in the history of the British race'. The development of events is described in A.T.Q. Stewart, *The Ulster Crisis* (London, 1967) and, from the government's perspective, in Patricia Jalland, *The Liberals and Ireland: The Ulster Question in British Politics to 1914* (Brighton, 1980). See also Powell, *The Edwardian Crisis*, chapter 5.

22. *The Times*, 29 July 1912.

23. I.F.W. Beckett (ed), *The Army and the Curragh Incident, 1914* (London, 1986).

24. A. Sykes, 'The Radical Right and the Crisis of Conservatism before the First World War', *Historical Journal*, 26 (1983), pp 661–76; Gregory D. Phillips, *The Diehards* (Harvard, 1979); E.H.H. Green, *The Crisis of Conservatism: The Politics, Economics and Ideology of the British Conservative Party, 1880–1914* (London, 1995).

25. Arthur Marwick, *The Deluge: British Society and the First World War* (2nd ed, London, 1991) and Trevor Wilson, *The Myriad Faces of War* (Oxford, 1988) provide surveys of the war and its domestic impact.

26. Cameron Hazlehurst, *Politicians at War: July 1914 to May 1915* (London, 1971); John Turner, *British Politics and the Great War: Coalition and Conflict, 1915–1918* (Yale, 1992).

27. Davies, *History of Wales*, p 514.

28. Michael Sanders and Phillip Taylor, *British Propaganda during the First World War* (London, 1982); G.S. Messinger, *Propaganda and the State in the First World War* (Manchester, 1992).

29. Christopher Andrew, *Secret Service* (London, 1986), chapter 2.

30. E.L. Ellis, *The University College of Wales, Aberystwyth, 1872–1972* (Cardiff, 1972), pp 171–3.

31. The genesis of this measure is dealt with in Martin Pugh, *Electoral Reform in War and Peace, 1906–18* (London, 1978).

32. A.J.P. Taylor, *The Troublemakers: Dissent over Foreign Policy, 1792–1939* (London, 1957).

33. Morgan, *Rebirth of a Nation*, p 173.

34. Davies, *A History of Wales*, p 517.

35. Henry Pelling, *A History of British Trade Unionism* (London, 1976), p 294.

36. This is reflected in some of the older general works such as J.D. Mackie's *A History of Scotland* (2nd ed, London, 1978) which merge their countries with the rest of Britain after 1914, although more recent works have emphasized the separateness as well as the similarities of the Scottish and Welsh experience compared with England.

37. For the background to the Rising, see Foster, *Modern Ireland*, pp 471–84.

38. Quoted in Kenneth O. Morgan, '1902–1924' in David Butler (ed), *Coalitions in British Politics* (London, 1978), p 25. The standard history of the post-war coalition is Kenneth O. Morgan, *Consensus and Disunity: The Lloyd George Coalition Government, 1918–1922* (Oxford, 1979).

39. Quoted in Norman, *Modern Ireland*, p 282.

40. Lord Longford, *Peace by Ordeal* (London, 1962) offers a detailed history of the Treaty negotiations, based on first-hand sources.

41. See below, chapter 7.

42. G.I.T. Machin, *Politics and the Churches in Great Britain, 1869–1921* (Oxford, 1987), pp 324–31; Stephen Koss, *Nonconformity in Modern British Politics* (London, 1975). There were, however, some local cases where sectarianism still had a significant influence on political loyalties, for example in Liverpool and Glasgow where Catholic–Protestant tensions were deeply ingrained and anti-Irish feeling was also a factor.

43. Morgan, *Wales in British Politics*, pp 286–91.

44. Powell, *Politics and the Labour Question*, pp 70–2; Chris Wrigley, *Lloyd George and the Challenge of Labour* (Hemel Hempstead, 1990).

45. G.R. Searle, *Country Before Party: Coalitions and the Idea of 'National Government' in Modern Britain, 1885–1987* (London, 1995), chapters 4–6.

Chapter 6: One Nation?

1. Kenneth O. Morgan, 'The Twentieth Century', in Morgan (ed), *Oxford History of Britain*, p 611.

2. Robert Blake, *The Conservative Party from Peel to Thatcher* (London, 1985), p 371.

3. Christopher Harvie, *No Gods and Precious Few Heroes: Scotland since 1914* (Edinburgh, 1993), p 90.

4. F.W.S. Craig, *British Electoral Facts, 1885–1975* (London, 1976), pp 11–15.

5. Johnston revived his commitment to devolution in the 1930s, as to some extent did MacDonald. See below.

6. On Mosley and the BUF see Robert Skidelsky, *Oswald Mosley* (London, 1975) and Richard Thurlow, *Fascism in Britain* (London, 1998).

7. Chris Cook, *A Short History of the Liberal Party* (London, various editions).

8. The fullest analysis is R.J. Finlay, *Independent and Free: Scottish Politics and the Origins of the Scottish National Party, 1918–45* (Edinburgh, 1994).

9. Harvie, *Scotland and Nationalism*, pp 29–33.

10. There were, however, differences between the parties on the pace and scale of reform, with Labour showing greater urgency on the domestic agenda.

11. Pugh, *State and Society*, p 229.

12. Craig, *Electoral Facts*, p 21. The Conservative total includes a small number of 'National Liberals' who by this time were effectively members of the Conservative Party.

13. Morgan, *Rebirth of a Nation*, pp 376–9.

14. Kenneth O. Morgan, *Labour in Power, 1945–1951* (Oxford, 1984).

15. For a general discussion of the 'consensus' debate, see David Dutton, *British Politics since 1945: The Rise and Fall of Consensus* (Oxford, 1991).

16. Powell, *Politics and the Labour Question*, pp 66–70.

17. Arthur Marwick, *A History of the Modern British Isles, 1914–1999* (London, 2000), pp 69–71; James Hinton, *Labour and Socialism: A History of the British Labour Movement, 1867–1974* (Brighton, 1983), p 120; and, more generally, John Stevenson and Chris Cook, *The Slump* (London, 1977).

18. Davies, *A History of Wales*, p 578.

19. In some cases unofficial forms of social censorship were at work. For example, it was not until 1940 that the film version of Walter Greenwood's powerful novel of the depression, *Love on the Dole* (1933), finally reached the cinema screen.

20. The Act had its origins in the latter days of the wartime coalition. Morgan, *Labour in Power*, pp 182–4.

21. J. Graham Jones, *The History of Wales* (Cardiff, 1990), p 146.

22. On the 'golden age' theme, see Marwick, *Modern British Isles*, p 202.

23. Keith Middlemas, *Power, Competition and the State*, vol 1 (London, 1986).

24. Kenneth O. Morgan, *The People's Peace: British History, 1945–1989* (Oxford, 1990), pp 75–6; Peter Hennessey, *Never Again: Britain 1945–1951* (London, 1992), pp 425–8.

25. Clarke, *Hope and Glory*, p 116.

26. Jeremy Black, *Modern British History since 1900* (London, 2000), p 97.

27. Marwick, *Modern British Isles*, pp 65–6.

28. It is possible, however, that much of this mobility was regional or sub-regional rather than national, although again there may be significant differences between pre-1939 and post-1945.

29. Angus Calder, *The People's War: Britain 1939–1945* (London, 1969) provided the first detailed academic study of the British 'Home Front' during the war years.

30. For an analysis of the impact of American influences on British society during the Second World War and some of the problems of the Anglo-American relationship, see David Reynolds, *Rich Relations: The American Occupation of Britain, 1942–1945* (London, 1996).

31. Arthur Marwick, *British Society since 1945* (2nd ed, London, 1990), pp 131–3.

32. On the general processes of social change during the century, see Harold Perkin, *The Rise of Professional Society* (London, 1989).

33. Morgan, *Rebirth of a Nation*, chapter 9.

34. Harvie, *Scotland and Nationalism*, pp 102–11.

35. E.L. Ellis, *TJ: A Life of Thomas Jones, CH* (Cardiff, 1992), p 296.

Chapter 7: Devolution and the Troubles

1. Arthur Marwick, *The Sixties: Cultural Revolution in Britain, France, Italy and the United States, c1958–1974* (London, 1998).

2. For a recent survey, see Alvin Jackson, *Ireland, 1798–1998* (Oxford, 1999).

3. The post of governor general was abolished and replaced with that of president. The parliamentary oath of allegiance had already been abandoned.

4. The abolition of PR for the Northern Ireland parliament in 1929 was an attempt to prevent the fragmentation of Unionism and the growth of the Northern Ireland Labour Party.

5. Quoted in Marwick, *Modern British Isles*, p 227.

6. Davies, *A History of Wales*, p 644.

7. Roy Clews, *To Dream of Freedom: The Struggle of MAC and the Free Wales Army* (Talybont, 1980).

8. Quoted in Bogdanor, *Devolution in the United Kingdom*, p 159.

9. Devine, *Scottish Nation*, p 572.

10. As such it may have promoted a more national political culture, which in turn may have encouraged nationalism in a form of 'revolution of rising expectations'.

11. Bogdanor, *Devolution in the United Kingdom*, p 171–2.

12. On the IRA, see Tim Pat Coogan, *The IRA* (London, 1997) and J. Bowyer Bell, *The IRA, 1968–2000* (London, 2000).

13. Tim Pat Coogan, *The Troubles* (London, 1996), pp 173–9.

14. Bogdanor, *Devolution in the United Kingdom*, pp 103–4; D.G. Boyce, *The Irish Question and British Politics, 1868–1986* (London, 1988), pp 113–14, 150–1.

15. Whitelaw's replacement as secretary of state as a result of a government reshuffle at a crucial stage in negotiations had also not helped matters.

16. The propaganda effect of the tactic was somewhat offset by the loss of a seat to the SDLP.

17. There was, however, some support from left-wing Labour MPs for Sinn Fein and the republican movement.

18. In this context the six-county Northern Ireland state should be distinguished from the nine-county province of Ulster, which had a historic identity and had for a long time, at least until the Plantations of the seventeenth century, been the most Gaelic part of Ireland. Jonathan Bardon, *A History of Ulster* (Belfast, 1992) gives a good perspective on the relationship between the two entities.

19. James Loughlin, *Ulster Unionism and British National Identity since 1885* (London, 1995).

20. As, on a comparatively trivial level, in sports such as rugby union.

21. Coogan, *The Troubles*, p 514.

22. Conor O'Clery, *The Greening of the White House* (Dublin, 1996). See also Andrew J. Wilson, *Irish America and the Ulster Conflict, 1968–1995* (Belfast, 1995).

23. Marwick, *Modern British Isles*, p 359; Coogan, *The Troubles*, pp 439–40.

24. Sinn Fein's share was 17 per cent, the SDLP's 24 per cent.

25. Bogdanor, *Devolution in the United Kingdom*, pp 105–9.

26. Quoted, *ibid.*, p 111.

27. Davies, *A History of Wales*, pp 665–6.

28. Bogdanor, *Devolution in the United Kingdom*, p 114.

29. The reforms created a two-tier system of district and (enlarged) county and metropolitan councils in England and Wales, district and regional councils in Scotland.

30. Bogdanor, *Devolution in the United Kingdom*, p 175.

31. *Ibid.*, pp 174–83.

32. For further analysis see John Boschel, David Denver and Allan Macartney (eds), *The Referendum Experience* (Aberdeen, 1981) and David Foulkes, J. Barry Jones and R.A. Wilford (eds), *The Welsh Veto: The Wales Act 1978 and the Referendum* (Cardiff, 1983).

33. Bogdanor, *Devolution in the United Kingdom*, pp 194–5.

34. Quoted in Devine, *Scottish Nation*, p 610.

35. Bogdanor, *Devolution in the United Kingdom*, pp 199–200.

36. A Labour–Liberal coalition was subsequently formed, similar to that in Scotland.

37. Bogdanor, *Devolution in the United Kingdom*, p 109.

Chapter 8: Britain, Europe, the World

1. For the background to these developments see Paul Kennedy, *The Realities Behind Diplomacy* (London, 1981); David Reynolds, *Britannia Overruled: British Policy and World Power in the 20th Century* (2nd ed, London, 2000); Bernard Porter, *The Lion's Share: A Short History of British Imperialism, 1865–1970* (London, 1975).

2. Canada was similarly reluctant to be drawn into a war by Britain on this issue.

3. Quoted in Judd, *Empire*, p 287.

4. The extensive literature on the topic is surveyed in R.A.C. Parker, *Chamberlain and Appeasement* (London, 1993). See also John Charmley, *Chamberlain and the Lost Peace* (London, 1989).

5. The view finds its clearest expression in the writing of Correlli Barnett, e.g. *The Collapse of British Power* (London, 1972) and *The Audit of War: The Illusion and Reality of Britain as a Great Nation* (London, 1986).

6. Bernard Porter, *Britain, Europe and the World, 1850–1986: Delusions of Grandeur* (London, 1987).

7. For a consideration of the wider questions raised by Suez, see David Carlton, *Britain and the Suez Crisis* (Oxford, 1988).

8. Reynolds, *Britannia Overruled*, pp 197–9; Pugh, *State and Society*, pp 273–5.

9. David Cannadine, 'James Bond and the Decline of England', *Encounter*, September 1979; Andrew Lycett, *Ian Fleming* (London, 1995).

10. Reynolds, *Britannia Overruled*, pp 243–6.

11. Cannadine, 'British Monarchy' in Hobsbawm and Ranger (eds), *The Invention of Tradition*. An alternative perspective is offered in Andrew Marr, *The Day Britain Died* (London, 2000), pp 42–53; Norman Davies, *The Isles, A History* (London, 1999), pp 931–8.

12. On Britain's relations with Europe see Roy Denman, *Missed Chances: Britain and Europe in the Twentieth Century* (London, 1997).

13. *Ibid.*, pp 190–1.

14. The reference is from Churchill's Zurich speech in September 1946. Churchill's attitudes towards Europe are considered in Max Belloff, 'Churchill and Europe' in Robert Blake and Wm Roger Louis (eds), *Churchill* (Oxford, 1993), pp 443–56. See also John W. Young, *Britain, France and the Unity of Europe, 1945–1951* (Leicester, 1984).

15. Sean Greenwood, *Britain and European Cooperation since 1945* (Oxford, 1992) and John W. Young, *Britain and European Unity, 1945–1999* (London, 2000) offer good background accounts.

16. This is the thrust of Denman's book, referred to in note 12 above.

17. Reynolds, *Britannia Overruled*, chapter 8.

18. Phillip M. Williams, *Hugh Gaitskell* (Oxford, 1982), pp 390–414.

19. Alan Sked and Chris Cook, *Post-War Britain: A Political History* (3rd ed, London, 1990), p 305.

20. The deputy prime minister, Sir Geoffrey Howe, whose resignation from the cabinet precipitated Michael Heseltine's leadership challenge to Mrs Thatcher, made it clear in his resignation speech in the Commons that policy over Europe played a large part in his decision.

21. Reynolds, *Britannia Overruled*, p 327.

22. A good introduction to the topic is Colin Holmes, 'Immigration' in Terry Gourvish and Alan O'Day (eds), *Britain since 1945* (London, 1991), pp 209–31.

23. Marwick, *Modern British Isles*, p 372.

24. Harry Goulburn, *Race Relations in Britain since 1945* (London, 1998).

25. The exceptions were Britons with a non-English first language, though this only serves to underline the point about the increasingly non- or inter-national character of English.

APPENDIX 1

PEOPLE AND ORGANIZATIONS

Adams, Gerry (1948–). President of Sinn Fein, MP for West Belfast, 1983–92, 1997–. Active in Irish republican movement since beginning of Northern Irish Troubles in 1960s. Architect of Sinn Fein's political strategy in peace process of 1980s and 1990s through role in Hume–Adams talks and negotiations with Irish, British and American leaders. Member of Northern Ireland Legislative Assembly. Writer.

Anti-Corn Law League. Organization formed by John Bright and Richard Cobden in 1838 to campaign for the repeal of the Corn Laws and for the promotion of free trade. One of the most successful pressure groups of the early Victorian period.

Baldwin, Stanley (1867–1947). Conservative politician and prime minister 1923, 1924–29, 1935–37, on the last occasion as leader of the National Government. Regarded as quintessentially English because of his love of the countryside and the evocation in his speeches of traditional English scenes, he was in fact the principal exponent of a 'one nation' British unionism between the wars and a major factor in the electoral success of the Conservative Party and the National Government.

Balfour, Arthur James (1848–1930). Nephew of Lord Salisbury, Balfour served as Scottish secretary, 1886–87, and chief secretary for Ireland, 1887–92. In the latter post he earned the sobriquet 'Bloody Balfour' for his policies of coercion but also pursued a policy of 'constructive unionism' to combat demands for Home Rule. He was prime minister from 1902 to 1905 and led the Conservative Party from 1902 to 1911. In the inter-war years he helped to provide the definition of 'Commonwealth' that was enshrined in the Statute of Westminster in 1931.

Bevan, Aneurin (1897–1960). Welsh Labour politician who, as Minister of Health in the post-war Attlee government, created the National Health Service. An opponent of devolution who represented the centralizing trend in Labour politics.

British National Party *see* **National Front**

British Union of Fascists (BUF). Founded in 1932 by Sir Oswald Mosley after his New Party failed to win any seats at the 1931 general election. The BUF made little electoral impact (and chose not to contest the 1935 election) but briefly attracted a mass membership in the early and mid-1930s. It lost support after the violent disturbances at its Olympia rally in June 1934 and thereafter became increasingly an anti-Semitic fringe movement. Mosley's fascism nevertheless represented a development of the earlier nationalism of the 'radical right' in Britain as well as an attempt to adapt Italian fascism and German national socialism to British conditions.

Buchan, John (1875–1940). Writer and politician. Born a Scot, and proud of his country's heritage, Buchan was also an ardent supporter of the British Empire and the British state. In addition to thrillers such as *The Thirty-Nine Steps* (1915) and *Greenmantle* (1916) he wrote a number of historical novels, many with Scottish themes. He served as a member of Lord Milner's staff in South Africa, was Conservative MP for the Scottish Universities, 1927–35, and, as Lord Tweedsmuir, was governor general of Canada, 1935–40.

Burke, Edmund (1729–97). An Irishman who became a leading figure in the British state of the late eighteenth century as a politician and political theorist. He supported policies of conciliation towards the American colonies and Irish Catholics. In his *Reflections on the Revolution in France* (1790) he developed the ideological basis of Conservative thinking which became an important component of British patriotic politics during the Revolutionary and Napoleonic Wars.

Burns, Robert (1759–96). Scottish poet who pioneered the use of Scots dialect in popular verse. Often seen as primarily a supporter of radical political and nationalist causes, Burns joined his local Volunteers to defend the country against a possible French invasion. Burns clubs and the commemoration of Burns Night (25 January) became a vehicle for the celebration of Scottishness both in Scotland and among expatriate Scottish communities throughout the world.

Bute, 3rd Earl of (1713–92). Close supporter of George III, prime minister, 1762–63. A leading figure in Scottish politics and 'manager' of Scotland for British governments, Bute was also one of the prominent Scots who attracted anti-Scottish feeling in mid-eighteenth-century England.

Carson, Edward (1854–1935). Born in southern Ireland, Carson became identified with Ulster's pre-war resistance to Irish Home Rule. As leader of the Ulster Unionists he threatened an Ulster rebellion if the Asquith government attempted to impose Home Rule by force. Carson was also, however, a prominent figure in the wider British Unionist Establishment, serving as a minister in the wartime coalition governments.

Casement, Roger (1864–1916). An Irishman who was knighted for his work in the British consular service, especially on behalf of exploited rubber workers in the Congo and Peru, Casement was also an ardent Irish nationalist who, during the First World War, attempted to enlist German support for an Irish rising. In 1916, he was arrested after landing in Ireland from a German submarine, and was subsequently tried and executed for treason.

Catholic Association. A movement of mass protest launched in Ireland in 1823 by Daniel O'Connell to campaign for Catholic emancipation. Its activities were instrumental in securing emancipation in 1829 and its organizational structures provided a prototype for later agitations.

Chamberlain, Joseph (1836–1914). Chamberlain entered politics in the 1870s as a radical Liberal but then split from the Liberal Party in 1886 because of his opposition to Gladstone's plans for Irish Home Rule. As a Liberal Unionist he entered Salisbury's government in 1895 as colonial secretary and became an aggressive promoter of British imperialism at the time of the South African War. In 1903 he left the government to found the Tariff Reform League to campaign for imperial unity and protectionist economic nationalism.

Childers, Erskine (1870–1922). British civil servant and clerk of the House of Commons, Childers was also the author of the novel *The Riddle of the Sands* (1903) which warned of the threat to Britain from Germany's growing navy. He supported the First World War and won a DSC in the British army but was increasingly attracted to the cause of Irish republicanism, having previously been a keen Home Ruler. He became prominent in Sinn Fein and, as a supporter of de Valera's anti-Treaty faction in the civil war, was captured and executed by Free State forces.

Clan na Gael. Irish revolutionary organization founded in New York in 1867, affiliated from 1877 to the Irish Republican Brotherhood. It provided practical help for the revolutionary movement in Ireland and was one of a number of important Irish-American nationalist groups.

Collins, Michael (1890–1922). Irish republican leader. He took part in the 1916 Easter Rising and subsequently became a central figure in the Irish Republican Army during the war of independence as well as a minister in the Irish provisional government. He led the team that negotiated the 1921 Ango-Irish Treaty with the British and, as one of the founders of the Irish Free State, he commanded Free State forces in the civil war before being killed in a roadside ambush.

Cymmrodorian, the Honourable Society of. Founded in 1751 by London Welshmen to promote the study of Welsh literature and culture. One of a number of similar bodies which were part of the Welsh cultural revival during the 'age of revolution' of the late eighteenth and early nineteenth centuries.

Cymru Fydd ('Young Wales'). Initially a cultural movement, Cymru Fydd was re-founded in 1886 as a political organization to campaign for Welsh nationalist objectives, including Welsh Home Rule. It drew most of its support from members of the Liberal Party, although briefly in the 1890s under the influence of Lloyd George it took a more independent position. The movement collapsed in 1896 after its failure to subsume the North and South Wales Liberal Federations in a single body.

Davitt, Michael (1846–1906). A member of the Fenian movement imprisoned by the British for his role in the Irish revolutionary underground, his family background in rural County Mayo gave him an understanding of the post-famine Irish land problems and led him to form the Irish Land League in 1879. In 1882 he became MP for County Meath. He was a supporter of Parnell and a leading figure in radical land reform movements and labour agitation in Britain as well as Ireland.

De Valera, Eamon (1882–1975). American-born Irish nationalist. He played a role in the Easter Rising of 1916, subsequently emerging as the leader of the Sinn Fein provisional government in 1919. He supported the anti-Treaty forces in the civil war but founded the Fiana Fail Party in 1926 to participate in Free State elections. As prime minister in the 1930s and 1940s he completed the work of making the Free State an independent republic and served as president from 1959 to 1973.

Democratic Unionist Party (DUP). Formed in 1971 by the Reverend Ian Paisley as part of a breakaway from the official Unionist Party in Northern Ireland. Opposed to Irish unity and to the involvement of Sinn Fein in the Northern Ireland peace process.

Dilke, Charles (1843–1911). Radical Liberal politician, MP for Chelsea, 1868–86, and for the Forest of Dean, 1892–1911. Supported the republican movement in Britain in the early 1870s but was also author of *Greater Britain* (1868) which expressed pro-imperial ideas.

Disraeli, Benjamin (1804–81). Politician and author; prime minister, 1868, 1874–80; created Earl of Beaconsfield, 1876. In the 1840s Disraeli was identified with the 'Young England' movement and wrote novels such as *Coningsby* (1844) and *Sybil* (1845) which expressed the movement's philosophy of social concern and aristocratic paternalism. As Conservative leader and prime minister he was responsible for making the Conservative Party the party of empire by creating the imperial monarchy and pursuing a jingoistic foreign policy.

Dundas, Henry (1742–1811). Known as the 'uncrowned king of Scotland', under successive governments Dundas controlled the politics of Scotland through patronage networks and electoral management. A close supporter of William Pitt, he also served in

British administrations as home secretary (1791–94) and secretary of state for war (1794–1801).

Elliot, Walter (1885–1958). Scottish Conservative politician. As secretary of state for Scotland from 1936 to 1938 he was instrumental in the administrative relocation of the Scottish Office from London to Edinburgh.

Ellis, Thomas Edward (1859–99) The son of a Merionethshire tenant farmer, Ellis was educated at the University College at Aberystwyth and New College, Oxford, before becoming MP for his native county in 1886. He established himself as a leading light among the Welsh Liberal MPs and as an advocate of Welsh nationalist causes such as Church disestablishment, education, land reform and Welsh Home Rule. He helped found the Cymru Fydd movement in 1886 before becoming Liberal chief whip in 1894. His writings and speeches reflected his strong sense of Celtic identity and history.

Evans, Gwynfor (1912–). Welsh nationalist politician and writer. President of Plaid Cymru, 1945–81. He won the Carmarthen by-election in 1966, lost the seat in 1970 but regained it in October 1974. In the early 1980s he threatened a hunger strike if Wales was not given a Welsh-language television channel. Author of numerous books on Welsh nationalism and history.

Fenians. An Irish revolutionary organization, formed in the late 1850s in Ireland and America, linking the Young Ireland movement of the 1840s to the Irish Republican Brotherhood (which itself overlapped with or grew out of the Fenian Brotherhood). The Fenians attempted an Irish rising in 1867, as well as an invasion of Canada launched from the USA, and carried out a bombing campaign on the British mainland in tactics later emulated by the IRA.

Gaelic Athletic Association (GAA). An organization formed in Thurles, County Tipperary, in 1884 to encourage interest in traditional Irish sports. Its activities had a political dimension and encouraged the Gaelic cultural nationalism that developed in Ireland in the late nineteenth century.

Gaelic League. Formed in 1893 by Eoin MacNeill and Douglas Hyde to counteract the Anglicization of Ireland by stimulating the use of the Irish language. Part of the wider Irish Gaelic revival which also included the GAA.

Gladstone, William Ewart (1809–98). Liberal prime minister of the United Kingdom on four occasions: 1868–74, 1880–85, 1886, 1892–94. In his first two ministries Gladstone attempted to 'pacify' Ireland with policies of educational and land reform and the disestablishment of the Anglican Irish Church. In the mid-1880s he responded to the growth of Irish nationalism by proposing a measure of Irish Home Rule in 1886 and introducing a second Home Rule Bill in 1893. Neither Bill became law, but Gladstone was the first statesman to acknowledge the problems presented by the multi-national character of the British state, being sympathetic to the demands of Welsh and Scottish nationalists within the Liberal Party as well as to those of the Irish.

Grattan, Henry (1746–1820). A member of the Irish Protestant Ascendancy, Grattan nevertheless favoured the legislative independence of the eighteenth-century Irish parliament. He was one of the leaders of the movement that in the early 1780s persuaded the British government to repeal the Declaratory Act to allow the Irish parliament greater freedom. 'Grattan's parliament' remained in existence until abolished by the Act of Union in 1800.

Griffith, Arthur (1871–1922). Irish nationalist and founder of Sinn Fein. He emerged as one of the leaders of the provisional government established by the Dail after the 1918 election and, with Michael Collins, led the delegation that negotiated the Anglo-Irish Treaty. A creative thinker, he had earlier developed a variety of possible constitutional futures for an autonomous Ireland within the framework of the British state.

Griffiths, James (1890–1975). Welsh Labour politician. He supported the granting of greater recognition of the interests of Wales within the British state and served as the first secretary of state for Wales, 1964–66.

Hardie, James Keir (1865–1915). Scottish miners' leader who led the formation of the Scottish Labour Party in 1888 and the Independent Labour Party (ILP) in 1893. After serving as MP for West Ham South from 1892 to 1895 he was elected MP for Merthyr Tydfil in 1900 and held the seat until his death. His prime concern was for the welfare of the working class, but he represented the radical nationalist thinking of the early Labour movement by supporting a variety of Irish, Scottish and Welsh causes, including Home Rule.

Hume, John (1937–). Active in Northern Ireland civil rights movements in the 1960s; co-founder of the Social Democratic and Labour Party (SDLP) with Gerry Fitt in 1970; member of the Westminster parliament since 1983. In the 1980s he initiated talks with Gerry Adams and Sinn Fein which helped to create the conditions for the 'peace process' of the 1990s.

Independent Labour Party (ILP). Working-class socialist party formed in 1893. Joined with the trade unions to found the Labour Representation Committee (forerunner of the Labour Party) in 1900. In the early twentieth century the party developed a strong following on Clydeside. It disaffiliated from the Labour Party in 1932.

Irish Land League. Founded in 1879 by Michael Davitt to campaign for the legal rights of Irish tenant farmers. It was linked to the Home Rule movement through Charles Stewart Parnell, who became the League's president.

Irish Republican Army (IRA). The IRA emerged as the military arm of the Irish revolution after the First World War, although it had its roots in earlier paramilitary/revolutionary organizations such as the IRB and the Irish Volunteers. It fought a guerrilla campaign against British forces in Ireland, 1919–21, which enabled Sinn Fein to negotiate the Anglo-Irish Treaty. The IRA split into pro- and anti-Treaty factions during the civil war. After the end of the civil war the IRA became an underground organization committed to ending partition and carried out bombing campaigns in Northern Ireland and Britain. During the Troubles of the late 1960s and early 1970s the 'Provisional' IRA split from the parent body to become the main purveyor of republican armed struggle until the ceasefires of the 1990s.

Irish Republican Brotherhood (IRB). Irish and Irish-American nationalist organization linked to the Fenian movement. Its members participated in the Dublin Easter Rising of 1916.

Irish Volunteers. Formed in 1913 as the nationalist counterpart of the Ulster Volunteer Force (UVF) at the time of the Home Rule crisis. Initially supportive of John Redmond's constitutional stance, the Volunteer movement was divided by Redmond's support for the First World War. The anti-Redmond Volunteers, despite equivocations on the part of their leaders, supported the 1916 Rising, alongside the IRB and the Irish Citizen Army.

Johnston, Thomas (1881–1965). Scottish Labour politician and secretary of state for Scotland, 1941–45. Responsible for the establishment of the North of Scotland Hydro-Electric Board. An early supporter of Scottish Home Rule, he used the wartime emergency to extend the practical reach of the Scottish Office, especially through intervention in economic affairs.

Kipling, Rudyard (1865–1936). Writer whose poems and novels often have imperial settings and themes, many deriving from his early life in India. Kipling was closely associated with the Unionist Party in Britain and was an active opponent of the third Irish Home Rule Bill. Despite his generally sympathetic imperialism, however, he was also sensitive to the problems of empire and the dangers of hubris, as poems such as 'Recessional' (1897) and his writings on the South African War confirm.

Law, Andrew Bonar (1858–1923). Canadian-born politician of Scots-Ulster ancestry. Elected to Commons in 1900, succeeded Balfour as Unionist leader in 1911 and led parliamentary campaign against the third Irish Home Rule Bill. Served in the wartime and post-war coalitions before retiring because of ill-health in 1921. Returned to active politics to help bring down the Lloyd George coalition and serve as Conservative prime minister, 1922–23.

Lewis, Saunders (1893–1985). Welsh writer and politician. One of the founders of Plaid Genedlaethol Cymru in 1925 and party president, 1925–45. Took part in arson attack on RAF bombing range at Penyberth in 1936, for which he was imprisoned and dismissed from his university teaching post. Received into the Roman Catholic Church in 1932. Leading novelist, poet, literary critic and journalist in Wales from the 1920s onwards. An ardent enthusiast for the Welsh language, he inspired the foundation of Cymdeithas yr Iaith Gymraeg (the Welsh Language Society) in 1962.

Liberal Unionists. Those Liberal MPs and peers, led by Lord Hartington and Joseph Chamberlain, who split from Gladstone's Liberal Party because of their opposition to the first Irish Home Rule Bill in 1886. They allied thereafter with the Conservatives, with whom they formed a coalition in 1895. The two parties merged their organizations into a single Conservative and Unionist Party in 1912.

Liberation Society. Founded in 1844 as the Anti-State Church Association to campaign for Church disestablishment. The Liberation Society (as it became in 1854) became an important vehicle for Nonconformist nationalism in mid-nineteenth-century Wales and contributed to the development of the Liberal Party as a popular political movement.

Lloyd George, David (1863–1945). Liberal politician; prime minister, 1916–22. In his early career Lloyd George was associated with the causes of Welsh radicalism and nationalism and supported campaigns for Church disestablishment and Welsh Home Rule. In the pre-1914 Liberal governments he pioneered taxation and social welfare reform before leading Britain to victory in the First World War. His career illustrates the integration of a specifically Welsh politics in the larger political fabric of the British state.

MacCormick, John (1904–61). A former member of the ILP who was one of the founders of the Scottish National Party (SNP) and a leader of the Scottish Convention movement.

MacDiarmaid, Hugh (1892–1978). Born Christopher Murray Grieve. Scottish nationalist and writer, one of the leaders of the 'Scottish renaissance' between the wars and a founder of the National Party of Scotland. Works include 'A Drunk Man Looks at the Thistle' (1926).

MacDonald, J. Ramsay (1866–1937). Scottish-born politician, one of the founders of the Labour Party and the first Labour prime minister, 1924, 1929–31, as well as prime minister of the National Government, 1931–35. MacDonald was an early supporter of Scottish Home Rule, although he represented English and Welsh constituencies and his career emphasized British themes.

MacNeill, Eoin (1867–1945). Professor of Medieval History at University College Dublin and a vice-president of the Gaelic League, he became chief-of-staff of the Irish Volunteers and later a Sinn Fein MP. However, he did not support the 1916 Rising and his orders countermanding plans for Volunteer manoeuvres may have contributed to its failure.

Major, John (1943–). Conservative politician and prime minister, 1990–97. A staunch unionist, Major opposed Scottish and Welsh devolution and emphasized the integrity of the British state, although he also played an important part in the Northern Ireland peace process and was one of the signatories to the Downing Street Declaration of 1993. As prime minister he was responsible for negotiating the British 'opt-out' from the single European currency.

Milner, Alfred (1854–1925). Imperial official and politician. High Commissioner in South Africa, 1897–1905; active on Unionist right during the political controversies of the Edwardian period; member of Lloyd George's coalition government. Created Viscount Milner, 1901.

Mosley, Oswald (1896–1980). Conservative, Independent and Labour MP, 1918–31. Left the Labour Party following its rejection of his proposals for reducing unemployment. Founded the New Party (1931–32) and the British Union of Fascists (1932). Later launched the Union Movement (1948) on a British nationalist, anti-immigration platform.

Muirhead, Roland (1868–1964). With John MacCormick, one of the founders of the Scottish National Party (SNP).

National Association for the Vindication of Scottish Rights. Formed in 1853 to campaign for greater constitutional and political recognition of Scotland's separate identity within the British state. Its effectiveness was limited, and it became moribund in the late 1850s, but it raised questions which re-emerged in the 1880s with the campaign to establish a Scottish secretaryship.

National Front. Extreme right-wing, neo-Nazi party formed in 1967 through the merger of the British Movement and the League of Empire Loyalists. It capitalized on anti-immigrant feeling in London and the English Midlands but had little electoral success. Its successor, the British National Party (BNP), preserved the main elements of NF ideology in the 1990s.

Northern Ireland Civil Rights Association (NICRA). Founded in 1967 to spearhead the campaign for equality of treatment for Catholics in Northern Ireland in areas such as housing, education, employment and local government. Influenced by the US civil rights movement, its activities provoked a Protestant backlash which was one cause of the modern Troubles.

O'Connell, Daniel (1775–1847). Irish lawyer and politician. Founded the Catholic Association to organize a popular campaign for Catholic emancipation. After emancipation had been granted in 1829, O'Connell became leader of an 'Irish party' of MPs at Westminster which extracted concessions from the Whig governments of the 1830s as a price of support. In 1840 he launched the Repeal Association to mobilize Irish opinion in favour of repeal of the Act of Union, but although a series of 'monster' meetings was held in the early 1840s the movement failed in the face of opposition from Peel's Conservative government.

O'Connor, Feargus (1796–1855). Irish leader of the British Chartist movement, founder of the Chartist newspaper the *Northern Star* and of the National Charter Association. Elected MP for Nottingham in 1847 but died insane.

Orange Order. Protestant Loyalist organization founded in Ulster in 1795 to uphold the Protestant Ascendancy and, subsequently, preserve the Union. Named to commemorate the victories of William of Orange in the battles of the 1690s, Orange lodges were founded in parts of south-west Scotland with strong Ulster connections, and the Orange Order remained a factor in Northern Irish and Scottish politics throughout the nineteenth and twentieth centuries.

Orwell, George (1903–50). Pen name of Eric Arthur Blair, writer and socialist. Best known for his attacks on Stalinism in *Animal Farm* (1945) and *Nineteen Eighty-Four* (1949), Orwell also attacked poverty and injustice in the depression England of the 1930s (*The Road to Wigan Pier*, 1937) and developed insights into aspects of English character, especially in *The Lion and the Unicorn* (1941).

Paisley, Ian (1926–) Founder of Free Presbyterian Church of Ulster (1951) and the Democratic Unionist Party (DUP). MP for North Antrim since 1970 and MEP for Northern Ireland since 1979. Paisley was an organizer of the anti-civil rights protests of the 1960s and opposed the Northern Ireland peace process in the 1990s because of the inclusion of Sinn Fein and the IRA.

Parnell, Charles Stewart (1846–91). Protestant landowner and Irish nationalist politician. Entered parliament in 1875 and took over the leadership of Home Rule MPs from Isaac Butt in 1879, which he combined with the presidency of the Irish Land League. The success of the Nationalists in winning 86 seats at the 1885 general election forced Home Rule on to the British political agenda, but Parnell's involvement in the O'Shea divorce case in 1890 split his party and may have cost Parnell's British Liberal allies electoral support.

Pearse, Patrick (1879–1916). Irish poet, scholar and nationalist. One of the leaders of the 1916 Rising who, as head of the Provisional Government of the Irish Republic, read the Proclamation of the Republic on the steps of the General Post Office in Dublin. After the Rising he was tried and executed by the British.

Peel, Robert (1788–1850). Conservative politician and prime minister, 1834–35, 1841–46. Chief secretary for Ireland, 1812–18; reluctant supporter of Catholic emancipation in 1829. As prime minister he maintained his interest in Irish affairs, supporting the Catholic seminary at Maynooth, appointing the Devon Commission to inquire into Irish land problems and responding to the potato famine by authorizing the purchase of American grain and accelerating plans to repeal the Corn Laws. He was nevertheless a strong unionist and opposed O'Connell's campaign to repeal the Act of Union.

Pitt, William (1759–1806). Prime minister, 1783–1801, 1804–6; architect of the Act of Union that created the United Kingdom of Great Britain and Ireland in 1801. He had hoped to combine this with Catholic emancipation, but his plans were thwarted by George III.

Plaid Cymru ('Party of Wales'). Welsh nationalist party founded (as Plaid Genedlaethol Cymru) in 1925, committed to Welsh independence and the protection of Welsh language and culture. The party won its first parliamentary seat at the Carmarthen by-election in 1966; the return of three Plaid Cymru MPs in October 1974 persuaded the Labour government to press ahead with plans for Welsh devolution. In the first elections to the National Assembly for Wales in 1999 Plaid Cymru won the second largest number of seats behind Labour and became the main opposition to the Labour administration.

Redmond, John (1856–1918). Irish nationalist leader who reunited the Irish parliamentary party after Parnell's death and used the Nationalists' improved bargaining position after 1910 to force the Liberals to introduce the third Irish Home Rule Bill. Redmond's controversial decision to support the First World War divided the nationalist movement and the Irish Volunteers. After the Easter Rising Redmond and the constitutional nationalists became increasingly isolated, although Redmond died before the decimation of his party at the 1918 election.

Reith, John (1889–1971). Scotsman who became director general of the BBC, 1927–38, and exercised a formative influence on the style and content of British broadcasting. He also served as a minister in Churchill's wartime coalition.

Repeal Association. Organization formed by Daniel O'Connell in 1840 to campaign for repeal of the Act of Union between Britain and Ireland. Initially successful in attracting mass support, the movement lost momentum after O'Connell bowed to government demands for the cancellation of the meeting at Clontarf in 1843.

Rhodes, Cecil (1853–1902). British imperialist, entrepreneur and politician. He made his fortune in the South African diamond industry and built up commercial and mining interests throughout Southern Africa which provided a platform for his entry into the politics of Cape Colony, of which he was prime minister from 1890 to 1896. His aim was to establish British predominance in Africa ('from Cairo to the Cape') and he gave his name to the colony of Rhodesia.

Salisbury, Lord (1830–1903). Conservative statesman and prime minister, 1885–86, 1886–92, 1895–1902. Formed the Unionist alliance with the Liberal Unionists which prevented the introduction of Irish

Home Rule. He also presided over the expansion of the British Empire and the growth of popular imperialism.

Scott, Walter (1771–1832). Scottish poet and novelist. He began his literary career as a collector of 'Border ballads' and author of narrative poems on romantic and historical themes before publishing the first of his *Waverley* series of novels in 1814. He became the bestselling author of his generation and was influential in shaping a distinctive Scottish identity within the framework of the Union state.

Scottish Convention. A cross-party movement in the late 1940s and 1950s which publicized the cause of Scottish Home Rule.

Scottish Home Rule Association (SHRA). Liberal-radical organization formed in 1886 to campaign for a Scottish parliament. Its members supported numerous unsuccessful Home Rule Bills before 1914 and the movement revived briefly after the First World War.

Scottish National Party (SNP). Founded in 1934 by a merger between the National Party of Scotland and the Scottish Self-Government Party. Despite the short-lived victory of Dr Robert McIntyre at the Motherwell by-election in 1945, the SNP did not achieve real electoral success until the late 1960s and early 1970s, culminating in the election of 11 MPs in October 1974. After the failure of the Labour government's plans for devolution in 1979 the SNP lost some of its support, but re-emerged as a strong force in the 1990s under the leadership of Alex Salmond, becoming the second largest party in the Scottish parliament elected in 1999. Its ultimate aim remains an independent Scotland.

Sinn Fein. Irish political party originally founded by Arthur Griffith in 1905. Its first real period of growth was after the Easter Rising of 1916, when it became the main political vehicle for Irish republicanism and won a majority of Irish seats at the 1918 election. Sinn Fein split at the beginning of the civil war in 1922 and its abstentionist stance (because of its refusal to recognize the legitimacy of the Free State, or of the Stormont and Westminster parliaments) led to its marginalization. From the 1960s Sinn Fein revived as the political wing of the militant republican movement, especially in Northern Ireland, and, under Gerry Adams and Martin McGuinness, won enough electoral support to play a role in the 1990s peace process.

Social Democratic and Labour Party (SDLP). Constitutional nationalist party formed in Northern Ireland in 1970 by Gerry Fitt and John Hume.

Tone, Theobald Wolfe (1763–98). Protestant Irish lawyer committed to the causes of religious and civil equality and Irish independence. In the 1790s, as one of the leaders of the United Irishmen, he developed his nationalist and republican ideas and took part in planning an armed rebellion, with French support. In 1798 he was captured by the British and sentenced to be hanged, though he committed suicide before the sentence could be carried out. As a martyr and theorist, he provided an inspiration for later generations of Irish republicans.

Ulster Unionists. From the 1880s, the opponents of Home Rule in the north-east of Ireland organized as a Unionist party, represented by the Ulster Unionist Council formed in 1905. Unionists campaigned successfully to preserve the union with Britain, although they accepted the partition of Ireland and the creation of a devolved government in Northern Ireland in 1921. The Ulster Unionist Party (UUP) was the dominant political force in Northern Ireland from the 1920s to the 1960s, when its support began to fragment during the Troubles. However, the Unionists remained the largest party in Ulster and under David Trimble participated in the 1990s peace process and the establishment of a Northern Ireland executive.

Ulster Volunteer Force (UVF). Paramilitary force established by the Ulster Unionists in 1913 to resist the imposition of Home Rule on Ulster.

United Irishmen. Originally a society formed in 1791 in Belfast and Dublin to work for reform of the Irish parliament. In the later 1790s the UI developed into a more revolutionary nationalist organization committed to achieving an Irish republic through force of arms. Despite the arrest of many of its leaders, the UI still attempted to achieve its goal in the failed rebellion of 1798.

Wheatley, John (1869–1930). Irish-born Scottish Labour politician and 'red Clydeside' MP who served as minister of health in the first Labour government of 1924 where his Housing Act was regarded as a substantial achievement.

Wilkes, John (1727–97). English radical politician and opponent of the ministries of George III in the 1760s. As a critic of Bute's ministry and editor of the anti-government paper the *North Briton* he helped to stir up English hostility to the 'Scottification' of politics.

Young England. Conservative reform movement of the 1840s associated with Benjamin Disraeli which responded to the problems of industrial society by advocating a paternalistic alliance between the aristocracy and the working class.

Young Ireland. Irish nationalist society formed in 1841 by Thomas Davis whose aim was to secure independence from Britain, if necessary by force. They attempted an unsuccessful rising in 1848, but the main importance of Young Ireland was to keep alive the intellectual and political traditions of revolutionary republicanism and to introduce some of the ideas of the continental European nationalist movements on to the Irish scene.

Young Scots. A society formed by radical Liberals in Scotland in the Edwardian period to press the Liberal leadership to adopt policies of devolution and social reform.

'Young Wales' *see* **Cymru Fydd**

APPENDIX 2

CHRONOLOGY

1801	Union of Great Britain and Ireland
1814	Publication of Scott's *Waverley*
1815	Battle of Waterloo; end of Napoleonic Wars
1822	George IV's visit to Scotland
1828	Repeal of Test and Corporation Acts
1829	Catholic Emancipation Act
1830	Death of George IV; accession of William IV
	Whig government of Lord Grey takes office
	Abolition of Courts of Great Sessions in Wales
1831	Merthyr riots and demonstrations in favour of parliamentary reform
1832	Great Reform Act
1833	Scottish municipal reform
1835	Municipal Corporations Act (England and Wales)
	Lichfield House Compact between O'Connell's Irish MPs and Whigs
1837	Death of William IV; accession of Queen Victoria
1838–48	Campaigns of Chartist movement for parliamentary reform
1839	South Wales Chartists stage Newport Rising
	Beginning of Rebecca Riots
1840	Formation of O'Connell's Repeal Association
1841	Peel's Conservative Party wins majority in general election; Peel becomes PM
1843	Disruption of Church of Scotland
	Peel bans O'Connell's meeting at Clontarf
1845	Beginning of Irish potato famine
	Poor Law (Scotland) Amendment Act
1846	Repeal of Corn Laws; split in Conservative Party and downfall of Peel's government

1847	Publication of Blue Books on Welsh education critical of quality of provision
1848	Young Ireland rising
1853	National Association for the Vindication of Scottish Rights founded
1857	Indian Mutiny
1865	Foundation of Welsh colony in Patagonia
1866–67	Fenian campaign against British rule in Ireland
1867	Second Reform Act
1868	Liberal victory in general election; Gladstone forms first ministry
1869	Irish Church Act disestablishes Church of Ireland
1870	Irish Home Government Association founded by Isaac Butt
	First Irish Land Act
1872	University College opened at Aberystwyth
1873	Secret ballot introduced for parliamentary elections
1874	General election; Disraeli becomes PM
1876	Victoria declared 'Empress of India'
1879	Irish Land League founded; Parnell becomes leader of Irish party in parliament
	Zulu War in South Africa
1880	First Boer War (1880–81)
	General election; Liberal victory returns Gladstone as PM
1881	Second Irish Land Act
	Welsh Sunday Closing Act
1882	Occupation of Egypt
1884	Third Reform Act
	Formation of Gaelic Athletic Association
1885	Scottish Office and Scottish secretaryship established
	Society for the Utilization of the Welsh Language formed
	General election gives 86 Irish Nationalists balance of power in House of Commons
1886	Gladstone PM for third time; Irish Home Rule Bill defeated and Liberal Party split
	General election results in Liberal defeat and return of Unionist government under Lord Salisbury
	Scottish Home Rule Association and Cymru Fydd founded

1887	Victoria's golden jubilee
	Welsh 'tithe war'
1888	County Councils Act
1889	Welsh Intermediate Education Act
1891	Death of Parnell
	'Newcastle Programme' reaffirms Liberal commitment to Welsh disestablishment
1892	General election; Liberal government formed with Irish support; Gladstone PM
1893	Second Irish Home Rule Bill defeated in Lords
	University of Wales granted royal charter
	Gaelic League founded
1895	General election; Liberals defeated; Salisbury forms Unionist coalition
1897	Victoria's diamond jubilee; Kipling's 'Recessional'
1898	Irish County Councils Act
1899	Outbreak of South African War
1900	Foundation of Labour Representation Committee (LRC)
	'Khaki election' returns Unionists for a second term
1901	Death of Queen Victoria; accession of Edward VII
1902	Peace of Vereeniging ends South African War
	Education Act sparks Nonconformist revolt, especially in Wales
1903	Joseph Chamberlain launches Tariff Reform League
1906	Liberal landslide at general election; Campbell-Bannerman PM; LRC (Labour Party) wins 29 seats
1907	National Library and National Museum of Wales established
1908	Asquith replaces Campbell-Bannerman as PM; Lloyd George becomes Chancellor of the Exchequer
1909	'People's Budget' rejected by House of Lords
1910	Two general elections deprive Liberals of Commons majority
	Death of Edward VII; accession of George V
	Creation of Union of South Africa as new dominion within the empire
1911	Parliament Act removes veto power of House of Lords
1912	Third Irish Home Rule Bill and Welsh Disestablishment Bill introduced

'Ulster Covenant' signals Unionist hostility to Home Rule

1914   Buckingham Palace Conference fails to settle Ulster question

Outbreak of First World War

1915   Formation of coalition government, Asquith remaining PM.

1916   Easter Rising in Dublin

Lloyd George replaces Asquith as PM (December)

1918   Fourth Reform Act introduces universal male and partial female suffrage

End of First World War

'Coupon election' – Lloyd George coalition returned to power with large majority; in Ireland Sinn Fein wins majority of seats and establishes Dail

1919–21   Irish 'Troubles'/War of Independence

Government of Ireland Act (1920)

Anglo-Irish Treaty (1921)

Creation of Northern Ireland and Irish Free State

1920   Disestablishment of Welsh Church

1922   Fall of Lloyd George coalition; return to party politics

1924   First Labour government; Ramsay MacDonald PM

General election; Conservatives return to power under Baldwin

1925   Plaid Cymru founded

1926   General Strike

1927   BBC established as public corporation

1929   General election; second Labour government formed

1931   Statute of Westminster redefines Commonwealth

Collapse of Labour government; formation of National Government

1934   Scottish National Party founded

1937–39   Transfer of Scottish Office from London to Edinburgh

1939–45   Second World War

1945   First SNP MP elected at by-election

Labour landslide at general election; Attlee PM

1947   India and Pakistan given independence

1951   Festival of Britain

General election; Conservative victory begins 13 years of Conservative rule

	Minister for Welsh Affairs appointed
1956	Suez crisis
1962	Cymdeithas yr Iaith Gymraeg (Welsh Language Society) founded
1964	General election won by Labour; Harold Wilson PM
	Welsh Office established; James Griffiths appointed secretary of state
1966	Gwynfor Evans wins Carmarthen by-election to become first Plaid Cymru MP
1967	Welsh Language Act
	Winifred Ewing wins Hamilton by-election for SNP
1969	Civil unrest in Northern Ireland leads to deployment of British troops
1970	General election won by Conservatives; Edward Heath PM
1972	Suspension of Stormont and imposition of Direct Rule in Northern Ireland
1973	Britain joins EEC
	Sunningdale Agreement establishes power-sharing executive in Northern Ireland
1974	Power-sharing executive brought down by Ulster workers' strike
	General elections (February and October) result in gains for SNP and Plaid Cymru; Labour government formed committed to devolution for Scotland and Wales
1975	Referendum confirms British membership of EEC
1979	Devolution proposals for Scotland and Wales fail to secure necessary majorities in referendums
	General election replaces Labour government with Conservative government under Margaret Thatcher
1982	Falklands War
	S4C established as Welsh-language TV channel
1984	IRA bombs Grand Hotel in Brighton during Conservative Party conference
1985	Anglo-Irish Agreement
1988	Beginning of Hume–Adams talks
1990	John Major replaces Margaret Thatcher as Conservative PM
1993	Downing Street Declaration on Northern Ireland
1994	IRA ceasefire (rescinded 1996)

1997   Election of Labour government under Tony Blair
Scotland and Wales vote in favour of devolution in referendums
Renewal of IRA ceasefire

1998   Good Friday Agreement (GFA) on Northern Ireland
GFA approved in referendums in Northern Ireland and Republic; election of Assembly

1999   Election of Scottish Parliament and National Assembly for Wales

2001   Blair government re-elected in second landslide

FURTHER READING

The conceptual approach adopted in the present work owes a great deal to two broad influences: the general theories of nationalism and national identity developed by political scientists and historians, and the so-called 'new' British history pioneered by historians reacting against the Anglocentric tendency of earlier historiography and concerned to treat the history of Britain in a way that gives due prominence to questions of British identity and genuinely British themes. As an introduction to the rationale behind the latter it would be helpful to read the two seminal articles by J.G.A. Pocock, 'British History: A Plea for a New Subject', *Journal of Modern History*, XLVII (1975), pp 601–28, and 'The Limits and Divisions of British History: In Search of the Unknown Subject', *American Historical Review*, LXXXVII (1982), 1, pp 311–36. The work of David Cannadine is equally important, especially his articles 'British History: Past Present and Future?', *Past and Present*, 166 (1987), pp 169–91 and 'British History as "A New Subject": Politics, Perspectives and Prospects', *Welsh History Review*, vol 17, number 3, June 1995, pp 313–31, the second of which is also printed in the valuable collection of essays edited by Alexander Grant and Keith J. Stringer, *Uniting the Kingdom? The Making of British History* (London, 1995). On the more general history of nationalism and national identities the literature is vast, but Peter Alter, *Nationalism* (London, 1989) and E.J. Hobsbawm, *Nations and Nationalism since 1780* (Cambridge, 1990) are useful starting points, while A.D. Smith, *Theories of Nationalism* (London, 1983), J. Breuilly, *Nationalism and the State* (Manchester, 1982) and Benedict Anderson, *Imagined Communities: Reflections on the Origins and Spread of Nationalism* (London, 1986) address some of the principal themes.

There have been a number of attempts to apply these new approaches to works of general British history. Foremost among them, although limited in its chronological scope, is Linda Colley, *Britons: Forging the Nation, 1707–1837* (London, 1996), which not only traced the emergence of a British identity in the eighteenth and early nineteenth centuries but also stimulated a much wider debate about the idea of 'Britishness' and its relevance to British history. Keith Robbins, *Great Britain: Identities, Institutions and the Idea of Britishness* (London, 1998) tackles similar questions in a more general text that ranges from the sixteenth to the twentieth centuries. Both these works deal with the history of a Britain that already had, or achieved, a constitutional and political existence within which British identities could develop. Other writers have taken a wider canvas and based their studies on geographical as much as on historical perspectives, revealing much in the process about the emergence of different nations at different times within the British context. Hugh Kearney, *The British Isles: A History of Four Nations* (Cambridge, 1989) deliberately emphasizes the multi-national character of British history, although he also considers the extent to which at certain times over the centuries internal national divisions were less important than other cultural, geographical and political differences. Norman Davies, *The Isles, A History* (London, 1999) places British history in a broader European setting, while Jeremy Black's *A History of the British Isles* (London, 1996) provides a concise summary of the main features of British history (including the histories of England, Ireland, Scotland and Wales) from Roman times to the 1990s. The multi-authored volume edited by Kenneth O. Morgan as *The Oxford History of Britain* (Oxford, 1983, and various subsequent editions) similarly seeks to integrate the histories of the 'Celtic' nations into genuinely 'British' history, though some of its writers are more successful in this than others.

No existing text covers exactly the same ground as the present volume, but there are some general works that traverse parts of the period from a British perspective. These include Eric J. Evans, *The Forging of the Modern State: Early Industrial Britain, 1783–1870* (2nd ed, London, 1991) and Keith Robbins, *The Eclipse of a Great Power: Modern Britain, 1870–1992* (2nd ed, London, 1994) (both of these in the Longmans *Foundations of Modern Britain* series), Martin Pugh, *State and Society: British Political and Social History, 1870–1992* (London, 1994), Arthur Marwick, *A History of the Modern British Isles, 1914–1999* (Oxford, 2000) and Peter Clarke, *Hope and Glory: Britain 1900–1990* (London, 1996). There are also more thematic treatments that examine particular aspects of British history, such as Michael Hechter, *Internal Colonialism: The Celtic Fringe in British National Development, 1536–1966* (London, 1975), Sidney Checkland, *British Public Policy, 1776–1939* (Cambridge, 1983) and David Hempton, *Religion and Political Culture in Britain and Ireland* (Cambridge, 1996). In addition, each of the 'four nations' has its own historiography, sustained by a range of general texts, specialist monographs and dedicated journals. On Ireland, from among many excellent studies, two established texts stand out: R.F. Foster, *Modern Ireland, 1600–1972* (London, 1988) and F.S.L. Lyons, *Ireland since the Famine* (London, 1973). These can be supplemented by K. Hoppen, *Ireland since 1800* (2nd ed, London, 1999), Alvin Jackson, *Ireland, 1798–1998* (Oxford, 1999) and D.G. Boyce, *Nineteenth Century Ireland: The Search for Stability* (Dublin, 1990).

Scottish and Welsh history are equally well served. T.M. Devine, *The Scottish Nation, 1700–2000* (London, 2000) has been hailed as the definitive contemporary text, though the volumes in the New History of Scotland published by Edward Arnold and Edinburgh University Press – namely Bruce Lenman, *Integration and Enlightenment: Scotland 1748–1832* (Edinburgh, 1981), Olive and Sidney Checkland, *Industry and Ethos: Scotland, 1832–1914* (Edinburgh, 1989) and Christopher Harvie, *No Gods and Precious Few Heroes: Scotland since 1914* (Edinburgh, 1993) – are valuable, while Christopher Harvie, *Scotland and Nationalism since 1707* (3rd ed, London, 1998) offers a stimulating extended essay on Scottish intellectual life, culture and politics, and Michael Fry, *Patronage and Principle: A Political History of Modern Scotland* (Aberdeen, 1991) provides a coherent analysis of party-political trends.

For Wales, John Davies's *A History of Wales* (London, 1993) is a brilliantly comprehensive single-volume account that encompasses all Welsh history, from cave-dwellers to coalminers. Equally brilliant, if more epigrammatic, is Gwyn A. Williams, *When Was Wales?* (London, 1985), which similarly spans the centuries from prehistory to modern times. On the more recent past, the leading authority is Kenneth O. Morgan, whose *Rebirth of a Nation: Wales 1880–1980* (Oxford, 1980) is the final book in a six-volume History of Wales published jointly by the university presses of Wales and Oxford – a venture that is in itself testimony to the strength of national historiography in the principality since the pioneering efforts of J.E. Lloyd, David Williams and others.

By contrast, separate English historiography is more difficult to find. Many of the older texts which purportedly deal with 'English' history (such as the Oxford histories) in fact indiscriminately include material on general British and Irish themes. Just as, constitutionally, England was deprived of a separate political identity within the

British state, so too, it seems, the very pre-eminence of England deprived it of a separate historical identity as well, at least in the modern period. An otherwise excellent text such as E.L. Woodward, *A History of England* (3rd ed, London, 1965) seamlessly merges English history with that of Britain from the eighteenth century onwards. Only more recently, as the debate over 'Britishness' and 'Englishness' has gathered pace, have historians begun to re-establish England's national identity in historical terms, as for example in Jeremy Black's *New History of England* (Stroud, 2000).

Most of the more specialist works on particular topics have been referred to in the chapter notes. It may, however, be helpful to recapitulate the most important titles relating to the main periods and themes, and to add other relevant works which have not so far been mentioned. The earlier dimensions of the 'British problem' and the origins of the British state can be traced from various angles in B.P. Levack, *The Formation of the British State: England, Scotland and the Union, 1603–1707* (Oxford, 1987), Brendan Bradshaw and John Morrill (eds), *The British Problem c1534–1707: State Formation in the Atlantic Archipelago* (London, 1996) and William Ferguson, *Scotland's Relations with England: A Survey to 1707* (Edinburgh, 1977). The eighteenth and early nineteenth century is the preserve of Linda Colley's *Britons*, already mentioned, but there are other works of interest, among them G. Newman, *The Rise of English Nationalism: A Cultural History, 1740–1837* (London, 1987), Paul Langford, *Englishness Identified* (Oxford, 2000) and L. Brockliss and D. Eastwood (eds), *A Union of Multiple Identities: The British Isles, c1750–1850* (Manchester, 1997).

For the nineteenth and early twentieth centuries, Keith Robbins, *Nineteenth-Century Britain: England, Scotland and Wales, the Making of a Nation* (Oxford, 1988, reprinted as *Nineteenth Century Britain: Integration and Diversity*) is a polished analysis of Britishness and its relationship to other national cultures embracing not only politics and economics but religion, music, sport and much else besides in a series of essays based on the author's Ford Lectures. Other writers have tilled narrower fields in greater depth. Kenneth O. Morgan, *Wales in British Politics, 1868–1922* (3rd ed, Cardiff, 1980), originally published in 1963, was a ground-breaking study of the rise and fall of Welsh Nonconformist Liberal nationalism within the British state. There is no direct equivalent for Scotland, although I.C.G. Hutchinson, *A Political History of Scotland, 1832–1924* (Edinburgh, 1986) is a detailed and scrupulously researched account of party and electoral politics, while R.J. Finlay, *A Partnership for Good? Scottish Politics and the Union since 1880* (Edinburgh, 1997), though a slighter work, has useful insights into the Scottish Home Rule movement and its place in the political mainstream. Ian Donachie, Christopher Harvie and Ian S. Wood (eds), *Forward! Labour Politics in Scotland, 1888–1988* (Edinburgh, 1989) is a collection of essays on the movement that became the dominant force in Scottish politics for much of the twentieth century. Irish affairs have been even more extensively covered. The general texts by Foster, Lyons and Boyce have already been mentioned. D.G. Boyce, *The Irish Question and British Politics, 1886–1996* (London, 1998) is a concise survey of the importance of Irish issues in the politics of the British state; Alan O'Day, *Irish Home Rule, 1867–1921* (Manchester, 1998) is a good analysis of the Home Rule question from its emergence in the mid-Victorian period to partition, with a collection of primary sources. Roger Swift, *The Irish in Britain, 1815–1914* (London, 1990) looks at another aspect of Irish–British relations, centred on Irish immigration to Britain and the growth of Irish communities. On other aspects of the history of the British Isles which have a bearing on the themes of nationhood and identity, two books by G.I.T. Machin, *Politics and the Churches in Great Britain, 1832–1868* (Oxford, 1977) and *Politics and the Churches in Great Britain, 1869–1921* (Oxford, 1987) are standard works. Richard Holt, *Sport and the British* (Oxford, 1980) has chapters on the importance of sport in the national identities of the individual nations of Britain and Ireland as well as in relation to Britain's imperial identity. Similar themes are tackled in J.A. Mangan (ed), *The Cultural Bond: Sport, Empire and Society* (London, 1992) and J.M. MacKenzie (ed), *Imperialism and Popular Culture* (Manchester, 1987).

The wider imperial history of the British state can be studied in general surveys such as Denis Judd, *Empire* (London, 1996), Lawrence James, *The Rise and Fall of the British Empire* (London, 1994) and Bernard Porter, *The Lion's Share: A Short History of British Imperialism, 1865–1995* (3rd ed, London, 1996). The nineteenth-century empire is dealt with in R. Hyam, *Britain's Imperial Century, 1815–1914* (London, 1993), C.C. Eldridge, *Victorian Imperialism* (London, 1978) and the same author's edited collection, *British Imperialism in the Nineteenth Century* (London, 1984). The two-volume survey by P.J. Cain and A.G. Hopkins, *British Imperialism, Volume 1, 1688–1914* and *Volume 2, 1914–1990* (London, 1993) is especially informative on economic aspects; there are also interesting essays in the respective volumes of the recently published *Oxford History of the British Empire, Volume III: The Nineteenth Century* (edited by Andrew Porter, Oxford, 1999) and

Volume IV: The Twentieth Century (edited by Judith Brown, Oxford, 1999). In the twentieth century especially, though, the empire needs to be seen in the broader context of Britain's changing world role, summarized in David Reynolds, *Britannia Overruled: British History and World Power in the 20th Century* (2nd ed, London, 2000) and Bernard Porter, *Britain, Europe and the World, 1850–1986: Delusions of Grandeur* (London, 1987). Corelli Barnett has explored the topic of British national decline in a controversial trilogy of studies: *The Collapse of British Power* (London, 1972), *The Audit of War* (London, 1986) and *The Lost Victory* (London, 1995). Relations with Europe and the emerging European Union are the themes of Roy Denman, *Britain and Europe in the Twentieth Century* (London, 1997) and John W. Young, *Britain and European Unity, 1945–1999* (London, 2000). L.J. Butler, *Britain and Empire: Adjusting to a Post-Imperial World* (London, 2001) examines the 'end of empire' in the context of global and European events. There is also a growing literature on the legacy of empire in terms of immigration and multi-culturalism. P.B. Rich, *Race and Empire in British Politics* (Cambridge, 1990), K. Lunn, *Hosts, Immigrants and Minorities: Historical Responses to Newcomers in British Society, 1870–1914* (London, 1980), Colin Holmes, *John Bull's Island: Immigration in British Society, 1871–1971* (London, 1988) and P. Panayi, *Immigration, Ethnicity and Racism in Britain, 1815–1945* (Manchester, 1994) provide over-views, while P. Fryer, *Staying Power: The History of Black People in Britain* (London, 1984), P. Gilroy, *There Ain't No Black in the Union Jack* (London, 1987) and D. Hiro, *Black British, White British* (London, 1971) examine aspects of multi-culturalism.

The debate over the contemporary re-making of the British state began in the 1960s and 1970s. Vernon Bogdanor, *Devolution in the United Kingdom* (Oxford, 1999) is the best introduction to the consti-tutional issues (a comparison with his earlier 1979 volume, *Devolution*, shows how the debate moved on in the next 20 years). Much of the earlier writing on these themes was necessarily ephemeral, but the 1970s discussion did produce some works of more permanent interest, both as sources for contemporary opinion and for their deeper insights, notably Tom Nairn, *The Break-Up of Britain: Crisis and Neo-Nationalism* (London, 1977) and John Osmond, *The Divided Kingdom* (London, 1988). Historians, political scientists and other commentators gradually began to take more seriously the importance of nationalist movements and the constitutional and cultural implica-tions of national diversity. Raphael Samuel (ed), *Patriotism: The Making and Unmaking of British National Identity* (London, 1989) was a product of this reawakened interest, as were Bernard Crick (ed), *National Identities: The Constitution of the United Kingdom* (London, 1991), Neil Evans (ed), *National Identities in the British Isles* (Harlech, 1989) and David McCrone, Stephen Kendrick and Pat Straw (eds), *The Making of Scotland: Nation, Culture and Social Change* (Edinburgh, 1989). Scholarly accounts of the rise of the nationalist parties in Scotland and Wales included Alan Butt Philip, *The Welsh Question: Nationalism in Welsh Politics, 1945–1970* (Cardiff, 1975), R.J. Finlay, *Independent and Free: Scottish Politics and the Origins of the Scottish National Party, 1918–1945* (Edinburgh, 1994) and K. Webb, *The Growth of Nationalism in Scotland* (London, 1977). There were also studies of the devolution process and the referendums of 1979 and 1997, among them David Faulkes, Barry J. Jones and R.A. Wilfrid (eds), *The Welsh Veto: The Wales Act 1978 and the Referendum* (Cardiff, 1983) and Bridget Taylor and Katarina Thomson, *Scotland and Wales: Nations Again?* (Cardiff, 1999).

By far the greatest volume of attention, however, continues to be devoted to the problems of Northern Ireland, with the works produced from the outbreak of the contemporary Troubles in the 1960s to the late 1990s reflecting either optimism or pessimism depending on the state of the 'peace process' and the perspective of their authors. For guidance on the complexities of the source material and objective accounts of the recent history of Northern Ireland and its place in the British state, the following accounts can be recommended: Sabine Wichert, *Northern Ireland since 1945* (2nd ed, London, 1999), Thomas Hennessey, *A History of Northern Ireland, 1920–1996* (Dublin, 1997) and Caroline Kennedy-Pipe, *The Origins of the Present Troubles in Northern Ireland* (London, 1997). Obviously there is much more of a specialist nature that can be consulted, and more detailed recommendations for further reading on this as on the other topics discussed above will be found in the bibliographies of the works cited.

INDEX